DEMOCRACY AND POWER

# DEMOCRACY AND POWER

## Essays in Political Theory 1

BRIAN BARRY

CLARENDON PRESS · OXFORD

1991

Oxford University Press, Walton Street, Oxford OX2 6DP

Oxford New York Toronto
Delhi Bombay Calcutta Madras Karachi
Petaling Jaya Singapore Hong Kong Tokyo
Nairobi Dar es Salaam Cape Town
Melbourne Auckland

and associated companies in
Berlin Ibadan

Oxford is a trade mark of Oxford University Press

Published in the United States
by Oxford University Press, New York

Democracy, Power, and Justice: Essays in Political Theory, first published as a hardback 1989
First issued in Clarendon Paperbacks in 2 volumes with new material 1991

British Library Cataloguing in Publication Data
Barry, Brian
Democracy and power: essays in political theory.
1. Politics. Theories
I. Title
320.01
ISBN 0–19–827297–9

Library of Congress Cataloging in Publication Data
Barry, Brian M.
Essays in political theory/Brian Barry.
p.  cm.
Includes bibliographical references and index.
Contents:  1. Democracy and power — 2. Justice and liberty.
1. Political science.  I. Title.
JA71.B347 1991   321.8—dc20   90–21341
ISBN 0–19–827297–9 (v. 1)
ISBN 0–19–827299–5 (v. 2)

Typeset by Wyvern Typesetting Ltd, Bristol
Printed in Great Britain by
Courier International Ltd, Tiptree, Essex

*For Anni*
*and for Dammy and Julian*
*who brought us together*

# ACKNOWLEDGEMENTS

Most of the pieces reprinted here originally contained expressions of thanks for helpful comments on drafts. Consolidating these, I should like to thank the following for pointing out mistakes or forcing me to think harder about what I was saying: Bruce Ackerman, James Andrews, Chris Archibald, Benjamin Barber, Charles Beitz, Peter Brown, G. A. Cohen, Hans Daalder, David Donaldson, Patrick Dunleavy, Jon Elster, John Ferejohn, James Fishkin, Bruno Frey, Robert Fullinwider, Allan Gibbard, Robert Goodin, Kenneth Goodpaster, John Gray, Russell Hardin, Albert Hirschman, Keith Hope, Samuel Huntington, Aanund Hylland, Peter Jones, Julian Le Grand, Robin Lovin, Douglas MacLean, John Maguire, Jane Mansbridge, Derek Parfit, Carole Pateman, Douglas Rae, Ronald Rogowski, Jim Sharpe, Charles Silver, Robert Simon, Miller Spangler, Arthur Stinchcombe, Albert Weale, and Aristide Zolberg.

I should also like to thank Claire Wilkinson for obtaining the permissions to reprint and helping with revisions for this volume, and Anni Parker for making proof-reading as near to being a pleasure as is humanly possible.

I am grateful for permission to include the following in this collection:

'The Strange Death of Political Philosophy', originally published in *Government and Opposition*, 15 (1980), 276–88.

'Is Democracy Special?', originally published in Peter Laslett and James Fishkin (eds.), *Philosophy, Politics and Society*, Fifth Series (Oxford: Basil Blackwell; New Haven, Conn.: Yale University Press, 1979), 155–96, copyright © by Basil Blackwell.

'Does Democracy Cause Inflation? The Political Ideas of Some Economists', originally published in Leon N. Lindberg and Charles S. Maier (eds.), *The Politics of Inflation and Economic Stagnation* (Washington, DC: The Brookings Institution, 1985), 280–317, copyright © 1985 by The Brookings Institution.

'Political Accommodation and Consociational Democracy', originally published as a review article in *British Journal of Political Science*, 5 (1975), 477–505 (published by Cambridge University Press).

'The Consociational Model and its Dangers', originally published in *European Journal of Political Research*, 3 (1975), 393–412, copyright © 1975 by Martinus Nijhoff Publishers; reprinted by permission of Kluwer Academic Publishers.

'Self-Government Revisited', originally published in David Miller and Larry Siedentop (eds.), *The Nature of Political Theory* (Oxford: Clarendon Press, 1983), 121–54.

'Exit, Voice, and Loyalty', originally published as a review article in *British*

*Journal of Political Science*, 4 (1974), 79–107 (published by Cambridge University Press).

'Power: An Economic Analysis', originally published in Brian Barry (ed.), *Power and Political Theory* (London: Wiley, 1975), 67–101, copyright © 1975 by John Wiley; reprinted by permission of John Wiley and Sons, Ltd.

'Is it Better to be Powerful or Lucky?', originally published in two parts in *Political Studies*, 28 (1980), 183–94 and 338–52.

'The Obscurities of Power', originally published in *Government and Opposition*, 10 (1975), 250–4.

'The Uses of "Power"', originally published as a review article in *Government and Opposition*, 23 (1988), 340–53.

# CONTENTS

# INTRODUCTION

This is the first of two volumes containing articles written in the past fifteen years and originally published in roughly equal proportions in a variety of journals spanning several disciplines and in multi-authored books—a notoriously hit-and-miss way of disseminating one's work. I am therefore pleased to have these pieces appearing in a more accessible form. Volume I contains what might be called analytical political theory, with primary attention paid to questions about the theory and practice of democracy and about the analysis and study of power. Volume II falls within the sphere of normative political philosophy. It focuses especially on justice and its application in a variety of contexts and on some central issues within liberal political theory.

In this volume, the first piece stands out from the others because it is not about either democracy or power. It is designed, rather, to form an introduction to the rest by offering some thoughts about the development of political theory as an academic subject in Britain and America. 'The Strange Death of Political Philosophy' was originally written in 1980 for a special issue of the journal *Government and Opposition* to celebrate its twenty-fifth birthday. Since it was then exactly twenty-five years since I had begun to study Philosophy, Politics, and Economics at Oxford, I indulged myself by giving my contribution an autobiographical turn.

It is natural to ask how things look from the vantage point of a further decade. There seems little doubt that political theory in all the forms I mentioned in my article is flourishing institutionally. It continues to attract good graduate students and has even spawned several new journals—both remarkable in an unpropitious climate for universities. When it comes to substance, I have to confess to a somewhat less buoyant attitude than that of ten years ago.

The post-Rawlsian political philosophy that I talk of on pages 18–21 continues to be pursued in books and in the pages of journals such as *Philosophy & Public Affairs* and *Ethics*. But in recent years I have observed with a certain amount of trepidation an increasing tendency towards broodiness amongst those in the field. The earlier 'death' of political philosophy, which I discuss on pages 14–15, was caused to some extent by the view that the activity was impossible. Its fate was reminiscent of that suffered by Algernon Moncrieff's imaginary friend Bunbury: the doctors found out that he could not live, so he died.[1] The revival of political philosophy depended on a tacit agreement to set such worries aside. Citizens and politicians would go on arguing about political morality and acting on their conclusions, whatever the epistemologists might say, and it was felt that political philosophers could contribute to the process. I am not, of course, opposed to reflecting upon what one is doing, but the possibility has to be faced that the whole subject may implode in coming years.

Turning now to the kind of political analysis discussed on pages 21–2, it seems to me that the picture is mixed. The formal theory of voting (and more generally social choice theory) has run into the sand, at any rate as far as any relevance to politics is concerned. At the same time, game theory has become (by default, one might say) the only generally applicable theoretical apparatus in political science. But the ideal of a rigorous theory of political constitutions is still far off. Has western political science anything to offer the democratizing movements in Eastern Europe except good wishes? I think it has, but it falls far short of an articulated body of knowledge. Coming closer to home, it is easy enough to poke fun at people in Britain who claim that the erosion of civil liberties in the past decade would be reversed by enhancing the power of a judiciary whose leading members seem bent on proving each day their unfitness to carry out even their existing functions. But we do not have a strong theory of institutions on the basis of which to propose alternatives.

In the light of these remarks, it is not too surprising that the four chapters following the first one are concerned to cast doubt on certain general theories about democracy. I wish to say, however, that in political theory it is just as important to discredit false theories as it is to formulate true ones. For nothing is more dangerous than to act with the confidence that comes from having a theory when that confidence is in fact unfounded.

Chapter 2, 'Is Democracy Special?', argues that a common justification for representative government, that it implements the 'will of the people', cannot be sustained. The question from which it starts is as follows. Suppose we take as given the contents of a certain law or public policy. Is the strength of its claims on our obedience to it affected by the procedure which brought it into being? Specifically, what if it has been enacted by some procedure that in some way aggregates citizen preferences, either directly as in a referendum or indirectly as when representatives are elected under universal suf-

[1] Oscar Wilde, *The Importance of Being Earnest*, Act III.

frage? Does the fact that a certain law or policy is the outcome of such a process provide a reason for obeying it that would not exist if the identical outcome had occurred under some different set of decision-making arrangements?

The argument of the chapter is that there is no virtue that can be claimed universally for an outcome simply on the basis of its democratic origins. I do, however, suggest that there is all the same a reason for obeying democratically arrived at laws that does not apply to others. This is that obedience to the laws helps to sustain the political system, and that system is itself valuable. Its value lies in the fact that, at any rate under modern conditions, the only determinate and generally acceptable basis for a right to rule is winning an open election. As a contingent matter, then, but one that is very solidly grounded, democracy is the only system of government compatible with at once political freedom and political stability. The basis for this claim is offered in the text of chapter 2.

It is important to get clear exactly what is the question being asked in this chapter. If this is misunderstood, the whole chapter is liable to be misinterpreted, and I have found that this has in fact happened on occasion. The question is not the very broad one: 'What in general can be said in favour of democracy?' That is a perfectly valid question but it is not the question asked here. Rather, the question I ask is: 'Do democratic procedures endow outcomes with a special claim to respect, holding constant the actual content of those outcomes?'

If we were asking the broader question, it would be very much to the point to argue that, at any rate under favourable conditions, democracy has a tendency to produce better outcomes than any other system of government. I think this is indeed true, and in chapter 2 I offer some account of what those favourable conditions are. But what has to be observed about this line of justification is that it flows not from procedure to outcome but from outcome to procedure. Since, on this view, the value of democracy is purely instrumental—that it tends to produce better laws and policies than alternative decision-making institutions—it follows that, if some other form of political institution offered better prospects, it should be preferred to democracy.

In contrast to this kind of justification by results, what I am concerned with in chapter 2 is justification in abstraction from outcomes, which I am here using quasi-technically to cover laws and policies. The negative part of my case is that there is no a priori argument in favour of outcomes simply in virtue of their democratic provenance. The positive part is that, if we look at the consequences of democratic government over and above outcomes in the sense defined, we can see that it is worth supporting. And since disobeying laws has a tendency to undermine a regime, this provides indirectly a special reason for obedience to democratically arrived at laws and policies.

Chapters 3 to 5 take up the question that was laid on one side in chapter 2. They ask under what conditions democracy has a tendency to produce good outcomes. They also ask whether institutional tinkering holds out hopes of improving the performance of democracies. It must be admitted immediately that there may be disagreement about what constitutes a good outcome. It is, indeed, such disagreement that gives substance to democratic politics. However, in these three chapters I attempt to finesse the difficulty by taking criteria that should be fairly uncontroversial.

In the first of them, 'Does Democracy Cause Inflation?', I assume that, whatever a good macroeconomic policy may be, a bad one is one that runs counter to the long-run interests of the vast majority of the population. The claim to be discussed in this chapter is that democratic government has built into it the feature that it tends to produce bad outcomes in precisely this sense. According to an influential school of 'public choice' theorists (mostly though not exclusively economists), there is a fatal flaw in democracy that results in governments persistently following policies that lead to levels of inflation that are too high, whether our standard be the interests or the policy preferences of their citizens.

The heyday of this school was the mid-1970s, when the chapter was originally written. As far as I am aware, however, none of the members of this school has publicly recanted. And in any case it is I think instructive to trace the shoddy reasoning by which people basically ill-disposed to democratic government for other reasons used the inflation bogey as a way of advancing their proposals for the hobbling of democratic governments. It is worth noting, incidentally, that in the USA the budget deficit has provided an excuse for dusting off what are essentially the same arguments. The hidden agenda remains the same: the entrenching of existing economic privilege against political majorities.

In chapters 4 and 5, the implicit criterion of a good outcome is different but I hope equally uncontroversial. Most people would agree that, whatever a good outcome may be, it does not include the oppression by one community within a country of another community within that country distinguished from the first by race, religion, language, or descent. In these two chapters, then, we are concerned with communally divided societies, where giving the majority what it wants is not the solution but the problem.

Because communal hostility can so easily lead to bloodshed and to the breakdown of constitutional government, the taming of communal conflicts is manifestly a matter of the greatest practical importance. These two chapters are devoted to the critical examination of a school of writers who claimed to have discovered a formula for the peaceful resolution of communal conflicts. The members of this school observed certain ways in which communal conflicts were successfully defused in some of the smaller Western European democracies, generated from these observations a model of 'consociational democracy', and proposed it as a scheme to be applied in other communally divided societies.

The theory of consociational democracy thus has two aspects, explanatory and prescriptive. Each of the chapters devoted to the theory focuses on one of these aspects. 'Political Accommodation and Consociational Democracy' is a critical review of the literature on the conceptualization of consociational democracy and on the operation of consociationalism in divided societies. 'The Consociational Model and Its Dangers' is addressed to the policy proposals deduced from studying consociational practices.

It is perhaps worth setting the second of these chapters in its historical perspective. At the time when it was written, in the mid-1970s, it was scarcely possible to open a newspaper such as the London *Times* without coming across an article recommending 'power sharing' as a solution to communal conflict in Northern Ireland and Cyprus, and pointing to its successes elsewhere. (These were held at that time to include the Lebanon.) The burden of my argument was that such claims for the enforcement of consociational devices were naïve. Provided the leaders of the communities wish for accommodation and can carry their communities with them, there is no question that devices such as a 'grand coalition' and proportional filling of sensitive offices can contribute to the stabilizing of whatever deal they strike. What I should have made more of, perhaps, was that the experience of collaboration can itself contribute to the process of stabilization by encouraging mutual trust among the partners. But what still has to be emphasized is that consociational devices cannot create the conditions for political accommodation where these do not exist. The leaders must want to make a deal to settle the issues in contention, and the followers must be prepared to follow them. That is fundamental, as the subsequent histories of Cyprus, Northern Ireland, and the Lebanon illustrate all too well.

In recent years, the claims of consociationalism have been advanced in another unpromising context, that of South Africa. Within the country, interest in consociational devices comes from Whites who recognize that the present system cannot endure indefinitely but wish to maintain as much as possible of their privileged position as a White minority in a multiracial political regime.[2] Outside the country, there are many figures in politics and business in Britain and the USA who fear that, after the many decades in which their governments have protected the White regime, a government based on a Black majority might not be very well disposed.

We are therefore beginning to hear suggestions for future constitutional development in South Africa that are reminiscent of the 'Bishop Muzorewa' constitution with which the British government sought to saddle an independent Zimbabwe. The essence of any such scheme is that, by some means or other (and there are many possibilities), the representatives of the Whites should have in effect a veto on any large-scale changes that might threaten their social and economic position. The fallacy here is patent. Consociational democracy is a device for freezing the status quo. It must therefore follow the achievement of a settlement that is satisfactory to all parties. But in South Africa the current situation is one of grotesque inequality, with the Whites owning all the best agricultural land, all the land with mineral deposits, and all the firms of any significant size. Whites also monopolize positions of power in the private as well as the public sector. Any kind of scheme that rules out in advance drastic measures to give Blacks their fair share of the society's resources and a dominant position in running its major institutions will inevitably be rejected by the African National Congress—and rightly so. (It is readily apparent that the mere abolition of official apartheid would do virtually nothing to redress these injustices.)

In some cases, a single state experiences conflict between different ethnic communities that occupy distinct territories, or would occupy distinct territories with some manageable transfers of population. A possible solution in such cases is for each community to have a state of its own. Although the principle of national self-determination has profoundly shaped politics in this century, it has received a generally

---

[2] See e.g. Denis Worrall, 'The Real Struggle in South Africa: An Insider's View', *Ethics and International Affairs*, 2 (1988), 115–37.

bad press from political theorists. In the chapter 'Self-Government Revisited', I point out that this hostility to nationalism is quite understandable when one considers the biographies of most of those who have written on the subject. I argue, nevertheless, that nationalism is a defensible criterion for the drawing of state boundaries. I should add that the chapter originally appeared in a memorial volume for John Plamenatz, whose Montenegrin origins may well have accounted for his relatively favourable view of the principle of national self-determination.

Chapter 7, which follows this, forms a bridge between the analysis of democracy and the analysis of power, since it discusses Albert Hirschman's idea that people can respond to the unsatisfactory performance of organizations by two means: exercising 'voice' and engaging in 'exit'. Hirschman's *Exit, Voice, and Loyalty* is deservedly a classic of modern social theory. In my review article on it I took issue with some details of the theory but in the main tried to illustrate the fertility of the basic ideas.

The next four chapters are concerned with the concept and measurement of power. This is something I have wrestled with off and on over my entire career, and the four pieces reprinted here include the oldest and the newest in the collection. The first of these, chapter 8, offers an 'economic' analysis of power, by which I mean an analysis of getting people to do what they would not otherwise choose to do by the appropriate deployment of threats of sanctions and offers of rewards. There are other ways of getting people to do what they would not otherwise choose to do, and I begin with a general discussion of these. But the main focus is on threats and offers. Within the limitation that I consider only two parties to the transaction, the analysis is intended to be comprehensive.

Chapter 9, the next of the chapters devoted to the analysis of power, shifts away from the kind of power that flows from threats and offers to the kind of power that flows from participation in some formally specified system of collective decisionmaking, typically one in which decisions are taken by voting. A considerable literature has been devoted to the construction of 'power indexes', which are supposed to represent the relative power of actors in any given system. The subject has given rise to a good deal of nonsense, and I offer a way of thinking about power in a decisionmaking body that seems to me to avoid the pitfalls that the standard power indexes run into.

Chapter 10 is a fairly brief review of a very short book, Steven Lukes's *Power: A Radical View*. Lukes espouses the fashionable view that power is an 'essentially contested' concept. In my view the notion of essential contestability is not only mistaken but has pernicious effects on the quality of intellectual life. The review, however, does not take such high ground but argues that Lukes's own position is in any case self-contradictory. As far as the larger issue is concerned, rather than add to the heap of stuff already written on essential contestability I would rather try to show that the concept of power can be made clear and that what gives credence to the thesis of essential contestability is the prevailing confusion.

I have tried to make further progress towards this aim in the last of the pieces on power, which is entitled 'The Uses of "Power"'. This takes the form of a review of a recently published book on the analysis of power by Peter Morriss. A great strength of this book is that it brings together within a single framework the analysis of interpersonal power and power within committees or legislatures. I have therefore had the opportunity to show, picking up on themes from Morriss's book, how the topics of chapters 8 and 9 can be brought into relation with one another.

Readers of this volume are entitled to know how far what appears here has been altered from the form in which it originally appeared. A number of cross-references have been added. Spelling and punctuation have been brought into line with British usage wherever the original source was American. Such matters as italicization of words in foreign languages have been made uniform. So have symbolic conventions: actors are always $A$, $B$, and $C$, actions $x$, $y$, and $z$. Minor changes have been made throughout in the interests of euphony and clarity. In some cases new introductory or concluding material has been added in order to head off, as far as possible, misreadings that the pieces attracted in their originally published form. Various bits of academic shorthand acceptable in a learned journal have been expanded so as to make the pieces printed here accessible to non-professionals. I have also deleted a few paragraphs that, on rereading, seemed to me to hold up the argument rather than advance it. I have not, however, made any attempt to update anything, either to take account of later political events or later publications on the subject.[3] Doing this thoroughly would involve creating a quite different kind of book, and doing it sporadically would, I feel, reduce the value of the collection by leaving the reader unsure whether some successful prediction was a lucky shot or the result of an addition made with the

---

[3] I have, however, on occasion substituted more accessible versions or reprints for articles originally published in obscure places or in books that are now out of print.

benefit of hindsight. In place of such updating in the text, I have sought in this Introduction to offer a current view of the topics, taking account of later political developments and contributions to the literature.

# I

# THE STRANGE DEATH OF POLITICAL PHILOSOPHY

All invitations to write something that come with far distant deadlines are a subtle exercise in entrapment (and I speak here from experience as both hunter and quarry), resting on the usual tendency to discount the future. How could anyone resist the temptation to talk about everybody's favourite subject—themselves—when it is enhanced by the flattery implicit in the suggestion that other people might be interested? So easy too: just a few thousand words about changes in the discipline in the last twenty-five years and the way in which one sees it.

It turns out not to be so easy after all. Exactly twenty-five years ago, in July 1955, I left school and in the following October became an Oxford undergraduate. How can I hope to distinguish changes between then and now in me from changes in the intellectual milieu over the same period? And can I hope to avoid reconstructing the past in the light of my current ideas and preoccupations?

In his study of R. G. Collingwood, Alan Donagan demonstrated that the famous *Autobiography* is more usefully viewed as an illustration of his later philosophical theories than as a veridical account of the process by which he came to hold them.[1] Collingwood, of course, made the mistake of having published the evidence on the basis of which his story could be judged. But perhaps that is the only feature that sets his case apart from that of the rest of us.

Thus, to take my own case, it is certainly my firm belief that there has been no substantial change in my basic outlook in the last twenty-five years—or even longer. I cannot remember any time when I was anything other than an atheist with a soft spot for the Church of England, a socialist exasperated with all sections of the Labour Party, and a sympathizer with the tribal vision of England à la Orwell ('a family with the wrong members in control') slightly suffocated by the reality of it. But who knows? It may be that these suspiciously neat ambivalences are just the latest attempt to impose order on chaos.

[1] Alan Donagan, *The Later Philosophy of R. G. Collingwood* (Oxford: Clarendon Press, 1962).

Well, this is all very fine, but it is hardly calculated to keep the printer in employment. What can be done? For an answer, I have resorted to the broom cupboard which passes for a filing system with me, and dug out a paper that I wrote in November 1961. It was called 'Has Political Philosophy a Future?' (How the title itself recalls those dim distant days!) I shall take it as the text for this chapter. First, I will say something about the background. Then I will summarize the argument, with enough extracts to recapture the flavour. Then in conclusion I will offer some comments from my present vantage-point, eighteen years later, in November 1979. As an exercise in multiple realities I must confess that the result is less gripping than *Rashomon*. But I hope at least that it has some of the awkward charm of those old snapshots that enliven books about Bloomsbury. (Was the inability to manage mechanical things like cameras part of the cult?)

To give the background of the paper, I need to say a little about the period between 1955 and 1961 (thus, rather neatly it seems to me, encompassing the required twenty-five-year span). Right from the start, as an undergraduate reading Philosophy, Politics, and Economics, I was drawn by both philosophy and economics and in the end chose between them because I thought I would get better teaching in philosophy. The study of politics, as conceived in Oxford, seemed to me a sad affair. The two required papers were British history from the mid-nineteenth century to 1945 and the politics of several countries since 1945. (Later, when I came back to Oxford, I was on one occasion privileged to be present at an apparently serious discussion among members of the politics subfaculty on the question of the date at which history ended and politics began. The majority view was that by then it had moved on to 1956, though there was also sentiment for 1951 and 1958.) Warmed-over facts with a topping of *Times* editorializing seemed to be the formula. If anybody had any notion that politics could be distinguished analytically rather than chronologically, it was a well-kept secret.

Philosophy, meanwhile, was an enormously exciting business. 'Bliss was it in that dawn to be alive . . .' It is hard to recapture in cold print the atmosphere of a place where people feel they have an approach that is paying off with solid results and is going to continue to do so. Normally it happens only in the natural sciences: Copenhagen in the twenties for physics, or Cambridge in the sixties for molecular biology, are perhaps the right kinds of analogue. Philosophy was visibly advancing—by minute steps perhaps but inexorably. You could see it happening as, say, Miss Anscombe wrestled with the concept of a want week after week.

This collective self-absorption may seem a little ridiculous, or even sinister, in retrospect. When you put together a number of bright people who write little and read less but talk a lot, you may unleash some powerful social dynamics. (I would reverse the usual Oxford view of Ernest Gellner's *Words and Things*:[2] the sociology is in my view better than the philosophy.) Still, there were three things that I got out of philosophy at Oxford in the late 1950s (I stayed on for two postgraduate years) that I still value.

The first was the idea that arguments should be pressed to the point at which the question is settled one way or the other. The second was that arguments must stand on their own feet and that one should avoid cluttering up the discussion with appeals to the authority of the illustrious dead. No faithful attender at Gilbert Ryle's 'informal instructions' could fail to learn that one. (They also taught one the pedagogical uses of silence—another very useful lesson.) The third was that philosophy is defined by its method rather than its subject-matter.

This last was of crucial importance to me because I have an extremely unspeculative turn of mind. I am a sucker for elegant structures of thought like those of physics and economics. (I have always regretted having to choose between 'arts' and 'sciences' at school and I'm glad my son doesn't have to make the same absurd choice.) But speculations that promise neither to explain a phenomenon nor to tell us how we should act leave me cold. Like Rickie in E. M. Forster's novel *The Longest Journey* I could never, even as an undergraduate, maintain more than a polite interest in questions such as where the cow is when nobody's looking at it. Naturally, this left me high and dry when the subject, even at Oxford, turned back to its traditional metaphysical concerns in the 1960s.

Only one more piece of background is needed. To provide it, I must move on to September 1961, when I settled in Cambridge, Mass. (or more precisely in an adjoining slum, since yuppified) for the year. The fellowship that I had allowed me to locate anywhere I liked, and I chose Cambridge because John Rawls was at that time at MIT. We did in fact have a couple of nice chats during the year, but the rest of the time I hung around at Harvard—something I was able to do thanks to

[2] Ernest Gellner, *Words and Things: A Critical Account of Linguistic Philosophy and a Study of Ideology* (London: Gollancz, 1959).

the good offices of C. J. Friedrich in fixing me up with an honorary fellowship for the year.

Since there seemed to be nothing much of interest going on in the philosophy department, I finished up by sitting in on Thomas Schelling's course on game theory and Edward Banfield's course on 'Political Economizing', which was a pioneering introduction to the 'public choice' perspective in political analysis. (I also started attending a course given by Henry Kissinger, but I'm pleased to say that I was thrown out for questioning the premisses: that American national interest was the only criterion of foreign policymaking and that the deployment of military force was the only means worth discussing.) These courses—and, equally, the conversation among graduate students in the lunch room at the top of the Littauer Building—had for me the force of a revelation. Politics didn't have to be the dull stuff we were taught at Oxford—it could actually have intellectual content!

These were, as far as I can now reconstruct them, the main experiences, positive and negative, that entered into the making of 'Has Political Philosophy a Future?' The paper was prepared for presentation to the philosophy department at Princeton, which had expressed some interest in hiring me. It opened as follows:

If a major war is somehow avoided, the next decade or two in English-speaking academic political philosophy could be interesting. This may at first glance appear eccentric to the point of perversity. Political philosophy is dead, we are told; indeed so moribund is it that even this has to be said by people who are not philosophers, because most philosophers are not even sufficiently interested in the subject to talk about it. Thus, in 1958, Robert Dahl wrote (in a review of Bertrand de Jouvenel's *Sovereignty* entitled 'Political Theory, Truth and Consequences', *World Politics* 1958, p. 89): 'In the English-speaking world, where so many of the interesting political problems have been solved (at least superficially), political theory is dead. . . . In the West, this is the age of textual criticism and historical analysis, when the student of political theory makes his way by rediscovering some deservedly obscure text or reinterpreting a familiar one.' And two years earlier, in 1956, Peter Laslett had written (in his introduction to the series of essays entitled *Philosophy, Politics and Society*): 'For the moment, anyway, political philosophy is dead. . . . A survey of our philosophical periodicals for the purposes of this collection gives the impression that their editors have often included articles on political subjects merely out of a sense of their conventional duty. Their contributors, too sometimes give the feeling that they have turned their attention to politics only because the curriculum of their university requires it.' Moreover, the essays reprinted in that series seemed intent on proving the editor's point. Even where they were of some individual quality they were entirely independent of each other and of any other contemporary work, representing the fruit of their authors' own ruminations and reading, rather than arising out of any current dialogue or debate.

If we turn from periodicals and essays to books of so-called 'political philosophy' or 'political theory' we find firstly the historical work mentioned by Dahl—e.g., the general works of Sabine, McIlwain, Strauss, Cobban, Cassirer, Coker and Vereker; and secondly, books of rather loosely-organized reflections of the kind which book reviews in the heavy press are likely to describe as 'mature', 'timely', 'thoughtful', etc. I refer to such authors as Barker, Field, Greaves and de Jouvenel. There is, of course, also Weldon's *Vocabulary of Politics*, but a book about the impossibility of political philosophy can hardly be counted as a portent of future life for it.

Why then do I nevertheless espouse a moderate optimism? For my answer I shall point as briefly as I can to four areas in which work has been produced which already has some achievements to its credit and promises more for the future. Academic philosophers have, however, had little hand in this work so far, and it has not been published or received much attention in their own journals.

What were these four areas? The first was 'work on the formal theory of voting'. I mentioned here first the work of Dahl, Downs, and Tullock as attempts to formalize Madison, James Mill, and Schumpeter; and then 'at a more abstract level' the work of Duncan Black and Kenneth Arrow, and the 'continuing discussion' of the latter's *Social Choice and Individual Values*.[3] I commented here that I hoped that eventually this field would become more transparent rather than more technically complicated, so that 'in ten or twenty years time we shall have a vocabulary in which it will be possible clearly to express our present gropings and see immediately which were right, which were wrong and which were so confused that they must be adjudged to have been meaningless'.

The second area I picked out was game theory.

Does it hold out any immediate prospect of enlightenment to a theoretically-minded student of society or is it merely a fashionable gimmick? Certainly the part which is most fruitful mathematically, the zero–sum part where one man's gain is another man's (equal) loss, has little application. Moreover, of the rest, the part seized on by R. B. Braithwaite, in his *Theory of Games as a Tool for the Moral Philosopher*, i.e. the problem of so-called 'games of fair division', seems to me more a branch of mathematical aesthetics than a more precise explication of ordinary notions of morality. As John Rawls has

---

[3] Kenneth J. Arrow, *Social Choice and Individual Values* (New Haven: Yale University Press, 1951; 2nd edn., 1963).

said '"To each according to his threat advantage" is hardly the principle of morality'. This work on so-called fair division is in fact closely related to the efforts of economists in the last two centuries to give precise mathematical content to the general idea of a 'fair' or 'equitable' tax burden in the theory of fiscal policy, of which Myrdal wrote (*The Political Element in the Development of Economic Theory*, p. 186): 'Bemused by the search for fictitious principles, it has succeeded in little more than in learned expositions and complex proofs of empty catch-phrases.'

The best chance lies in the direction of attempts to present formally ideas about threatening, bargaining, promising, deterring, etc. This study is still in its infancy. But already I think it is realistic to hope that this theory will find a framework within which a number of strands of thought, already worked out in other terms can be integrated. Duncan Black's treatment of conferences in *The Theory of Committees and Elections* and J. R. Hicks's treatment of collective bargaining in the *Theory of Wages* could be restated in game-theory terms. W. J. Baumol's *Welfare Economics and the Theory of the State* could, I think, go into the terminology of game-theory fairly easily. More precisely, it would come out as an extended application of the so-called 'Prisoners' Dilemma', that is, the kind of case where an enforceable agreement between two parties not to choose the most individually advantageous course makes both better off. It might also be instructive to try expressing the thought of, say, Hobbes, Hume and Rousseau in this form.

The third area, to which I devoted more time, was welfare economics which was, I remarked, like political philosophy 'periodically pronounced dead, having reached theoretical perfection and practical futility in the formulations of Bergson and Samuelson'. I argued that, although there was a lot in this, the abstract structure of welfare economics (and particularly the notion of trade-offs) was useful for thinking about policy questions, and that some of the ideas of economists about 'utility' were of philosophical significance.

The fourth and last source of input into political philosophy that I located was 'the attempts which some academic political scientists have made to appraise institutions in terms of stated principles or, if you like, "values"'. Here I took up two ideas: that the concept of the public interest had no content and that democrats must be procedure-fetishists. (Both of these points eventually turned up in *Political Argument*.[4]) I argued that these ideas could be shot down by appropriate theoretical reasoning.

[4] Brian M. Barry, *Political Argument* (London: Routledge and Kegan Paul, 1965; reissued with a new introduction, Hemel Hempstead: Harvester/Wheatsheaf, 1990 and Berkeley and Los Angeles: University of California Press, 1990).

I concluded, rather nervously, as follows:

Even if it is granted that the research in these four areas is significant in itself, two questions still remain to be asked: is this a continuation of political philosophy as traditionally understood? and even if it is, should not philosophers renounce any claims to competence in it?

The answer to the first question clearly turns on one's answer to the question: what was the subject of political philosophy as traditionally understood? I shall offer the answer that it was concerned with the nature and conditions of the good society, and, particularly, with the nature and conditions of good forms of government. If this characterization is accepted, then I think the relevance of my fourth category is immediately established since that is precisely what it is about. And the other three can I think be looked on as technical aids to clear-thinking about this traditional subject matter. We should no more spurn them because they are more technical than the conceptual apparatus used by Plato and Aristotle than we should spurn modern symbolic logic because *it* is technical.

In answer to the second question, I suggested that philosophy had a professional commitment to asking questions about the fundamentals of subjects that practitioners of them were liable to brush aside.

The time is long past when philosophers were the people who supplied society with its quota of lofty speculation. Our contemporary Hegel is Professor Parsons, the two-by-two matrices of the latter replacing the triads of the former. Our contemporary scholastics are the welfare economists, the game theorists, and the voting analysts, drawing out with wonderful ingenuity the implications of axioms which themselves go largely uncriticized. Philosophers can best help, I suggest, by maintaining their characteristic critical posture.

After that, the Princeton philosophy department and I both independently decided against taking the matter any further, and I am sure we were both right. No self-respecting department of philosophy could have been too comfortable with the role of under-labourer's mate (relegated to carrying the tools) to which I had assigned philosophy in that paper. And for me it seemed to make more sense to be a theorist in a department of politics than a political philosopher in a department of philosophy—something which I arranged a year later.

Looking back now on that paper, one thing that seems undeniable is that I at any rate predicted the trend correctly. The description of the actual conditions in 1961 is, as far as I can see, absolutely accurate. Things were just as desperate as I then said they were. You really could turn over whole volumes of the philosophical journals and find nothing about political philosophy—indeed very little substantive moral philosophy except for an occasional piece of utilitarian casuistry.

I would also say that it was quite acute of me to have picked on not merely the paucity of material but the lack of any dialogue between the different contributions, such as they were. Comparing then and now, the biggest difference lies exactly here.

When I was writing my thesis (published in revised form as *Political Argument*) there simply wasn't a 'literature' to which one could relate one's work. There was nothing for it but to make the stuff up as one went along. Now, on just about every topic discussed in *Political Argument* there is an elaborate article literature of assertion, rebuttal, modified assertion, synthesis, and so on. This is, of course, what the professionalization of a field means.

If anything, the problem today is the opposite of the one I diagnosed back in 1961. I occasionally have a nightmarish feeling that 'the literature' has taken off on an independent life and now carries on like the broomsticks bewitched by the sorcerer's apprentice. Let me juxtapose the old snapshot with a recent one. I wrote in the October 1979 issue of *Ethics*, upon assuming the editorship of that venerable journal (founded as *The International Journal of Ethics* in 1890), that I was concerned at the tendency for submissions 'to recapitulate existing controversies or repeat with only slight variations points already made elsewhere'. I continued as follows:

I can think of a number of perfectly understandable reasons why philosophers (who make up the great majority of our contributors) should be reluctant to break new ground. First, there are philosophically OK subjects, whose pedigree is established by their having been written about by OK philosophers, and one incurs a risk of professional oblivion by going outside them. Second, writing on a new topic may require a serious investment in learning the analytic techniques of some discipline and assimilating a mass of empirical material. And, third, it is damned hard work—much harder than reading six articles and pounding out a seventh on the same subject—with no guarantee of success.

These reactionary grumblings were, I hope, salutary in their context; but who would have imagined in 1961 that one would so soon have the luxury of being able to complain about a glut of political philosophy? The only thing wrong with the expression of 'moderate optimism' back then was that, while it was about right for the first decade, it was quite inadequate to the period since then.

In fact, 1971 is the key date. This is the year in which John Rawls's

*A Theory of Justice* was published.[5] And it is also the year in which the first issue of the journal *Philosophy & Public Affairs* appeared.

It is difficult to overemphasize the significance of the Rawls phenomenon. In the end it is of secondary importance whether one thinks his theories are right or wrong. What matters is that the book caught the imagination of scholars not only in philosophy but also in disciplines such as political science, sociology, economics, and law. *Political Theory* published a bibliography in its November 1977 issue which gives an indication in rough quantitative terms of the scale of the phenomenon. For 1972 there are 12 references. This rises sharply to 40 in 1973. 1974 is the peak year, with 52 entries. Then there is a decline to 35 in 1975 and 28 in 1976. This falling-off after 1974 (which would be continued if the list were extended to later years) is in a way misleading, however. For although 'Rawls articles' have become a drug on the market, this really reflects the way in which Rawls has now been thoroughly assimilated. His presence is therefore more ubiquitous than ever, but it is now more diffuse.

Why was this extremely long, poorly organized, and stylistically undistinguished book such a smash hit? It was immensely ambitious in its claims to deduce principles of justice from the construction of an 'original position' and at the same time could be regarded as constituting a massive synthesis of contemporary liberal political thinking. Those two points no doubt take one a long way. But in addition, I think that for many social scientists, reared on simple-minded logical positivism in graduate courses on 'methodology', the most exciting thing about Rawls was that he showed that one could sustain rational argument about questions of 'values' over 600 or so pages. Among philosophers, logical positivism, with its doctrine that all 'value judgements' are merely 'emotive utterances'—boos and hurrahs—had already been discredited. But Rawls was the first person to carry the message to non-philosophers. He thus got personal credit for a more general shift in philosophical ideas. But this was quite well deserved in that he was the first to do it on the grand scale rather than simply argue that in principle one could argue rationally about questions of political philosophy.

If Rawls's *A Theory of Justice* was the internal stimulus to the outpouring of political philosophy that we have witnessed since 1971, the Vietnam War was unquestionably the crucial external stimulus. Individual choices had to be made about draft resistance and other

[5] John Rawls, *A Theory of Justice* (Cambridge, Mass.: Harvard University Press, 1971).

forms of civil disobedience; and those who condemned the war had to develop the categories in which to show what was wrong with the means by which the war was being waged by the USA. Small wonder, therefore, that articles on the morality of civil disobedience, on the 'just war', and on the responsibilities of combatants proliferated.

This was the intellectual background out of which *Philosophy & Public Affairs* (like *The New York Review of Books*, with which it shares a certain common ambience) came into being. Thus, in the first issue, there was an article by Richard Wasserstrom on 'The Relevance of Nuremburg' and an early exposition by Michael Walzer of some of the ideas that were to appear six years later in *Just and Unjust Wars*.[6]

*Philosophy & Public Affairs* immediately settled down as a first-class journal devoted, as its 'statement of purpose' puts it, to 'philosophical discussions of substantive legal, social and political problems, as well as discussions of the more abstract problems to which they give rise'. To be hypercritical, one might say that in practice 'public affairs' have tended to be defined as issues before the US Supreme Court, especially abortion and reverse discrimination. But the range of subjects covered in the last eight years is quite impressive, and so is the consistently high quality of the contributions. *Philosophy & Public Affairs* has been central in creating the dense 'literature' of political philosophy to which I referred earlier.

Going back to my thoughts about the future of the subject in 1961, it is obvious that my big failure lay in missing out on the growth of self-sustaining normative political philosophy done by philosophers. I had, of course, identified Rawls as the most significant figure in contemporary political philosophy, which is why, as I have said, I was in Cambridge, Mass. in 1961 in the first place. But there had been no visible response to his article 'Justice as Fairness', which had been published in 1958. The bibliography of 'Rawls on Justice' already mentioned has no entries before 1963 (except one for 1957—i.e. *before* the article was published). And it records only fourteen items for the period between 1963 and 1970.

At our first meeting, Rawls had been kind enough to give me a copy of the book manuscript in its then existing form. (In those pre-Xerox days, getting hold of one was no easy matter.) But it seemed to me that the whole argument stood or fell by the validity of the derivation of the principles of justice from the original position, and that was, as far

---

[6] Michael Walzer, *Just and Unjust Wars* (New York: Basic Books, 1977).

as I could see, unsalvageable. I still think so, but it turned out that that did not preclude the fantastic reception that *A Theory of Justice* actually received.

The other stimulus to the growth of political philosophy was also on the Harvard campus, and I have already mentioned him, but I missed his true significance completely. I thought that Henry Kissinger was, as an academic, intellectually second-rate and dishonest. This was quite correct. But I did not foresee that, as the architect of the last and least defensible five years of the Vietnam War, he would drive a generation of Americans into a personal concern with the basic problems of political morality.

If one takes these developments as having engulfed my fourth category of incipient political philosophy, 'the attempts which some academic political scientists have made to appraise institutions in terms of principles', where does this leave my first three categories? I would say that here I score pretty well, though my time frame of 'a decade or two' was only just enough. Formal economic-style analysis of democratic institutions has, of course, taken off since 1961; and what I called the 'continuing discussion' of Arrow amounted in 1961 to only a dozen or so papers but is now numbered in the hundreds or even thousands. Yet I would say that it is only quite recently that there has begun to be any displacement of interest from making the applications more complicated to reflecting on the validity of the fundamental premisses and on the real implications of the formal theories for the evaluation of institutions. Similarly, it has taken longer than I expected for the crippling limitations of zero-sum game theory to be seen through and for it to be generally recognized that the central contribution of game theory is to the clarification of the analysis of problems of power and collective action.

Welfare economics, my third category, has developed in two directions since 1961, though both lines of development were already under way by then (and found their way into *Political Argument*). The first is cost-benefit analysis. In 1960 the kind of systems analysis that was to be brought to the Pentagon as PPBS was advocated by Hitch and McKean in *The Economics of Defense in the Nuclear Age*.[7] Since then cost-benefit analysis has, of course, proliferated. Its assumptions have been criticized by economists such as E. J. Mishan and academic lawyers such as Lawrence Tribe. Philosophers, whether because they allowed themselves to be blinded by science or thought it too crass to

[7] C. J. Hitch and R. N. McKean, *The Economics of Defense in the Nuclear Age* (Cambridge, Mass: Harvard University Press, 1960).

be worth attacking, have done little work on it. I think this was a missed opportunity.

The second direction in which welfare economics has moved was also foreshadowed in 1960, this time by the 'Coase theorem' set out in Coase's article 'The Problem of Social Cost'.[8] Since then an entire theology under the name 'economic analysis of law' has been developed, especially at the University of Chicago, based on the rather simple idea that all bargains are Pareto optimal. The Virginia school of constitutional engineering of James Buchanan represents an even more crude and ideological application of the same simple idea. Here lawyers and political scientists have contributed critiques, but philosophers have also been active to some extent.

However, as I emphasized (perhaps a little tactlessly) in my 1961 paper, political philosophy is political philosophy no matter who does it. The crucial difference between 1961 and now is that then it was a slogan—*in principle* it does not matter what department someone is in, so long as he does the right kind of thing. But in practice it almost always made a difference: the mind-sets, the authorities appealed to, and the standards of argument tended very strongly to vary according to departmental affiliation. Since then there has been an enormous change in just this respect, with a rapid growth in the number of interdisciplinary journals and associations and an increasing tendency of people to read and cite articles in journals outside their 'own' field. In the *Ethics* editorial from which I have already quoted my apprehensions about the risk of scholasticism, there followed the more cheerful thought that:

Scholars in a variety of disciplines have started to become frustrated by the sterility of most 'mainstream' work and have begun to look for kindred spirits in other disciplines. I am thinking here, for example, of people interested in the theory of social choice who are not content to see its development either as a pure exercise in technical virtuosity or as the vehicle for a half-baked ideology of Pareto-optimality but who wish to bring its techniques into relation with the rich traditions of democratic theory and the theory of distributive justice. I am also thinking of people in public policy programs, law schools, and elsewhere, who are interested in the evaluation of public policy but are repelled by the arrogant naïveté of the standard works on cost-benefit analysis, public policy analysis, and so on. At the same time, philosophers have increasingly tired of their 'one-sided diet' of desert-island examples and have begun to bring the traditional concerns of social and

---

[8] R. H. Coase, 'The Problem of Social Cost', *Journal of Law and Economics*, 3 (1960), 1–44.

political philosophy into relation with the methods and findings of social science.

Coming from many directions, scholars in different disciplines are finding common ground. Already it is possible in certain contexts (for example at certain sessions of the Public Choice Society) to listen to a discussion without being able to tell from what is said that one speaker is from economics, another from law, another from philosophy, and another from political science. What we are seeing, in other words, is a new kind of interdisciplinary development: not a wary rapprochement across disciplinary boundaries but the creation of autonomous spheres of discourse that draw on existing disciplines but represent a genuine synthesis.

When I read my old paper again for the first time in eighteen years, I couldn't help being struck by how little my hopes for the future of political philosophy seem to have changed between then and now. There are, I suppose, two alternative explanations of that fact. One is that my hopes have continued on their own course oblivious of reality. The other is that reality has already been kind enough to them to make it quite rational to keep the faith. Time will tell. I look forward to having an opportunity to superimpose another snapshot on these in 2005 when we are asked to look back over fifty years.

# 2

# IS DEMOCRACY SPECIAL?

*Martin*  If government, in the sense of coercion, has hitherto been essential to society, that is because no society has yet been founded on equity. The laws have been made by one class for another; and there was no reason, other than fear, why that other class should obey them. But when we come to imagine an ideal society, would government, in this sense, be essential to it?

*Stuart*  I suppose there would always be recalcitrant people.

*Martin*  Why should there be? What makes people recalcitrant, save the fact that they are expected to obey rules of which they do not approve?

*Stuart*  But make your institutions as just as you like, and your people as public-spirited as you like, there must always be differences of opinion as to this or that law or regulation; and if those differences become acute there must be a point at which coercion comes in. . . .

G. Lowes Dickinson, *Justice and Liberty: A Political Dialogue*

I

The question to which this essay is addressed is the following: does the fact that a law was passed by a democratic procedure provide a special reason for obeying it? Let me begin by explaining what I mean by 'a special reason'.

If we look at any law we can say that there are usually reasons for obeying it, such as fear of punishment, anxiety about the general effects of disobedience on social stability, and unwillingness to take advantage of the compliance of others (the essence of the John Rawls's 'duty of fair play'). There are also often reasons for disobeying it, of which personal advantage is the most obvious. In addition it seems plausible that approval of the content of the law makes the case for obeying it stronger than it would otherwise be, while disapproval makes it weaker. 'Approval' and 'disapproval', however, are anodyne generic terms, which conceal a range of relevantly different responses. It seems on the face of it reasonable to say, for example, that equally strong disapproval of two laws, one on the basis of its imprudence or inefficiency, the other on the basis of its injustice or immorality, should have different implications.

Exactly how and why all these factors provide reasons in favour of obedience or reasons telling against it is by no means straightforward. Nor, I am sure, would everyone agree that all of them should be reckoned as reasons at all. For the purpose of this chapter, however, I shall simply assume that at least some of these factors, and perhaps others like them, provide reasons for obeying or disobeying laws. My question then is whether an entirely different sort of consideration, namely, the procedure by which the law was enacted, or, in the case of long-standing laws, the procedure by which it might have been repealed and has not been, should be a reason for obeying a law.

More specifically, the question I wish to raise is whether or not a law's having been enacted (or not repealed) by a democratic procedure adds a reason for obeying it to whatever reasons exist independently of that. By a democratic procedure I mean a method of determining the content of laws (and other legally binding decisions) such that the preferences of the citizens have some formal connection with the outcome in which each counts equally. Let me make four comments on this definition.

First, I follow here those who insist that 'democracy' is to be understood in procedural terms. That is to say, I reject the notion that one should build into 'democracy' any constraints on the content of the outcomes produced, such as substantive equality, respect for human rights, concern for the general welfare, personal liberty, or the rule of law. The only exceptions (and these are significant) are those required by democracy itself as a procedure. Thus, some degree of freedom of communication and organization is a necessary condition of the formation, expression, and aggregation of political preferences. And in a state (as against a small commune, say) the only preferences people can have are preferences for general lines of policy. There are not going to be widely held preferences about whether or not Mr Jones should be fined £10 for speeding or Mrs Smith should get supplementary benefit payments of £3·65 per week. At most there can be preferences for a speeding tariff or for general rules about eligibility for supplementary benefit. If magistrates or civil servants are arbitrary or capricious, therefore, they make democracy impossible.

Second, I require that there should be a formal connection between the preferences of the citizens and the outcomes produced. My intention in specifying a formal connection is to rule out cases where the decisionmaking process is *de facto* affected by the preferences of the citizens but not in virtue of any constitutional rule. Thus, eighteenth-century England has been described as 'oligarchy tempered by riot'.[1] But, however efficacious the rioters might be, I would not say that their ability to coerce the government constituted a democratic procedure. In the concluding words of the judge appointed to enquire into riots in West Pakistan in 1953: 'But if democracy means the subordination of law and order to political ends—then Allah knoweth best and we end the report.'[2]

Third, by 'some formal connection' I intend deliberately to leave open a variety of possible ways in which democratic procedures might be implemented. In particular, I wish to include both voting on laws by the citizens at large and voting for representatives who exercise the law-making function. I shall take either of these to constitute 'some formal connection with the outcome' in the sense required by the definition: in the first case the citizens choose the laws and in the second they choose the law-makers (in both cases, of course, within the limits of the choice presented to them).

Finally, the phrase 'each counts equally' has to be read in conjunction with the preceding phrase 'some formal connection with the outcome'. That is to say, nothing is suggested by the definition of democratic procedure about equality of actual influence on outcomes. The equality is in the formal aspect: each adult citizen is to have a vote (only minor exceptions covering a tiny proportion of those otherwise eligible being allowed) and there are to be no 'fancy franchises' giving extra votes to some.

What about the notion that each vote should have an 'equal value'? This is valid if we construe it as a formal requirement. If there are two constituencies each of which returns one representative, the value of a vote is obviously unequal if one constituency contains more voters than another.[3] To talk about 'equal value' except in this a priori sense is sheer muddle. In recent years, for example, supporters of systems of proportional representation in Britain have succeeded in scoring something of a propaganda victory by pressing the idea that the vote for a candidate who comes third (or lower) in a plurality system is 'wasted' and the people who vote for the candidate are 'effectively

---

[1] W. J. M. Mackenzie, *Power, Violence, Decision* (Harmondsworth: Penguin, 1975), 151.

[2] Quoted in Hugh Tinker, *Ballot Box and Bayonet: People and Government in Emergent Asian Countries* (Chatham House Essays, 5; London: Oxford University Press, 1964), 83.

[3] This is, it may be noted, the line taken by the US Supreme Court in its decision requiring redistricting to secure approximately equal constituencies. (The leading case is *Reynolds* v. *Sims*, 377 US 533 (1964).)

disfranchised'. But then why stop there? The only way of making sense of this argument is by postulating that anyone who voted for a candidate other than the actual winner—even the runner-up—was 'effectively disfranchised'; and it was not long before some academics stumbled on this amazing theoretical breakthrough.[4] I do not think that anyone of ordinary intelligence would be found saying of an election for, say, the post of president of a club: 'I didn't vote for the winning candidate. In other words my vote didn't help elect anybody. And that means I was effectively disfranchised.' It is a little alarming that such palpably fallacious reasoning should have the power to impose on people when the context is a parliamentary election.

## II

There is one simple, and on the face of it attractive, reason for giving special weight to laws arrived at by democratic procedures. This is that, on any given question about which opinion is divided, the decision must, as a matter of logic, accord with either the preferences of the majority or the preferences of the minority. And, by something akin to the rule of insufficient reason, it seems difficult to say why the decision should go in the way wanted by the minority rather than in the way wanted by the majority. Let us call this the majority principle.

Obviously, even if the majority principle were accepted, there would still be a gap between the majority principle and democratic procedures as I have defined them. The implication of the majority principle is, fairly clearly, that the best form of democratic procedure is that which permits a vote on issues by referendum. There is no guarantee that elected representatives will on every issue vote in such a way that the outcome preferred by a majority of citizens will be the one chosen. However much we cry up the effects of electoral competition in keeping representatives in line, there is no theoretical reason for expecting that a party or coalition of parties with a majority will always do what a majority of voters want. (Persistent non-voters will in any case have their preferences disregarded by competitive parties —though it may be noted that this is equally so in a referendum.) Even a purely opportunistic party would not necessarily be well advised to back the side on every issue that the majority supports, as Anthony

---

[4] An analysis with whose general line I concur is Paul E. Meehl's 'The Selfish Voter Paradox and the Thrown-Away Vote Argument', *The American Political Science Review*, 71 (1977), 11–30.

Downs pointed out.[5] And in practice no party is purely opportunistic
—indeed a purely opportunistic party would in most circumstances be
an electoral failure because it would be too unpredictable. The party or
parties with a legislative majority are therefore always liable to have a
package of policies approved of by a majority and policies opposed by
a majority. (On many other issues there may be no single policy with
majority support, but that is a complication in the specification of the
majority principle that I shall discuss below.)

All this, however, is not as damaging for democratic procedures as
might be supposed. For it may surely be said that no method of
selecting law-makers and governments that was *not* democratic (in the
sense defined) could provide a better long-run prospect of producing
outcomes in accord with the majority principle. However disappointed an adherent of the majority principle might be in the actual
working of democratic procedures, it is hard to see what he or she
would stand to gain by helping to secure their overthrow. In principle,
of course, this majoritarian might assist the rise to power of a group of
dedicated majoritarians who would be committed to acting in accord
with majority preferences as ascertained, say, by sophisticated
opinion polling. But, once they were in power, what reason would
there be for confidence in the good faith of these people, or, even more
perhaps, of their successors?

I think, therefore, that an adherent of the majority principle would
be prepared to disobey laws that were enacted (or not repealed) in the
face of clear majority sentiment. But he or she would not take part in
any activity either designed for or having the predictable consequence
of bringing about the collapse of democratic procedures, because in
the long run democratic procedures are more likely to produce
majoritarian outcomes than are alternative procedures. Of course, it
does not follow that a majoritarian who is satisfied that there is a clear
majority against a piece of legislation is thereby committed to disobeying it. All the reasons for not breaking the law that I mentioned at
the beginning of this chapter may still apply. The only thing that the
absence of majority support does for a majoritarian is to remove one
(conclusive) reason for obedience.

Can an adherent of the majority principle break the law in an
attempt to get the majority to change its mind? I think that this may be
done consistently with the principle if it is formulated so that not just
any majority counts but only one based on a serious and informed

    [5]  A. Downs, *An Economic Theory of Democracy* (New York: Harper and Bros., 1957), 55–60.

consideration of the issue. Thus, on the facts as stated by him, Bertrand Russell's campaign against nuclear weapons could be consistent with a majoritarian standpoint.[6] But it is essential to the honesty of such a position that one must be prepared to specify what would constitute a fair test of 'real' majority opinion in a way that does not fall back on the proposition that 'No majority can *really* be in favour of *x*'.

I have suggested, then, that the majority principle provides fairly strong backing for democratic procedures. What now has to be asked, of course, is whether there is any reason for accepting the majority principle. The view that there is something natural and inevitable about it was expressed forcefully by John Locke in paragraphs 95–9 of the *Second Treatise*. The argument is tied up with Locke's consent theory of political authority but can, I think, be detached from it. The nub is that if there is going to be a body capable of making binding decisions then it 'must move one way' and 'it is necessary the Body should move that way whither the greater force carries it, which is the *consent of the majority*'. Locke adds that 'therefore we see that in Assemblies impowered to act by positive Laws where no number is set by that positive Law which impowers them, the *act of the Majority* passes for the act of the whole, and of course determines, as having by the Law of Nature and Reason, the power of the whole'.[7]

In my first book, *Political Argument*, I put forward the example of 'five people in a railway compartment which the railway operator has omitted to label either "smoking" or "no-smoking"', each of whom 'either wants to smoke or objects to others smoking in the vicinity'.[8] (I should have added that the carriage should be understood as one of the sort that does not have a corridor, so the option of changing compartments is not open.) I still think that the example was a good one. Unless all five can reach agreement on some general substantive principle—that in the absence of positive regulation there is a 'natural right' to smoke or a 'natural right' for any one person to veto

---

[6] 'Long and frustrated experience has proved, to those among us who have endeavoured to make unpleasant facts [about nuclear weapons] known, that orthodox methods, alone, are insufficient. By means of civil disobedience a certain kind of publicity becomes possible. . . . Many people are roused into inquiry into questions which they had been willing to ignore. . . . It seems not unlikely that, in the end, an irresistible popular movement of protest will compel governments to allow their subjects to continue to exist.' Bertrand Russell, 'Civil Disobedience and the Threat of Nuclear Warfare', in Hugo Adam Bedau (ed.), *Civil Disobedience: Theory and Practice* (New York: Pegasus, 1969), 153–9, at 157.

[7] John Locke, *Two Treatises of Government*, ed. Peter Laslett (New York: The New American Library, Mentor Books, 1965), 375–6.

[8] B. M. Barry, *Political Argument* (London: Routledge and Kegan Paul, 1965), 312.

smoking—it is difficult to see any plausible alternative to saying that the outcome should correspond to majority preference.

The position of someone who is outvoted but refuses to accept the decision is difficult to maintain. As I have suggested, quite persuasive arguments can be made for saying that the decision should not simply reflect the number of people who want to smoke as against the number who dislike being in the presence of smokers. But, since opposing principles can be advanced, the existence of relevant principles does not seem to offer a sound basis for resistance to a majority decision. Or suppose that one of the travellers happens to be the Archbishop of Canterbury. He might claim the right to decide the smoking question on the basis either of his social position or on the basis of his presumptive expertise in casuistry. If his claim is accepted by all the other passengers, no decisionmaking problem arises because there is agreement. If not all the fellow-passengers accept his claim, however, it again seems difficult to see how the question can be settled except by a vote. And if he finds himself in the minority it must be because he has failed to convince enough of the others of his claim to authority. He may continue to maintain that it should have been accepted, just as a believer in the natural right to smoke may continue to maintain that the others should have accepted that principle. But, in the face of actual non-acceptance, the case for bowing to the majority decision looks strong.

On further analysis, however, we have to recognize that the 'naturalness' of the majority principle as a way of settling the dispute rests on several features of the particular example which are not commonly found together. I am therefore now inclined to say that it was a good example in the sense that it illustrated well the case for the majority principle but that it was in another sense a bad example because of its special features. I shall single out four, the first three of which make the majority principle determinate while the fourth makes it acceptable. First, we implicitly assume that the people in the compartment have to make only this one decision. Second, only two alternatives are envisaged: smoking or non-smoking. Third, the decisionmaking constituency is not open to doubt. And fourth, nothing has been said to suggest that the outcome on the issue is of vital importance for the long-term well-being of any of those involved.

To begin with, then, let us retain the feature from the original case that the decisions to be made are dichotomous (that is to say, there are only two alternatives to choose between) but now say that several different decisions have to be taken. In addition to the question whether to permit smoking, the passengers also have to decide whether to allow the playing of transistor radios. Suppose that a vote is taken on each question and there is a majority against each. It may be that a majority of the passengers would nevertheless prefer permitting both to prohibiting both, if they were given a choice in those terms.

Let us assign the following symbols: $w$ is no smoking, $x$ is smoking allowed; $y$ is no playing of radios, $z$ is playing allowed. The preferences of the five passengers ($A$, $B$, $C$, $D$, and $E$) are in descending order as in Table 2.1.[9]

TABLE 2.1

| Rank order | $A$ | $B$ | $C$ | $D$ | $E$ |
|---|---|---|---|---|---|
| 1 | $wz$ | $wz$ | $xy$ | $wy$ | $wy$ |
| 2 | $xz$ | $xz$ | $xz$ | $wz$ | $xy$ |
| 3 | $wy$ | $wy$ | $wy$ | $xy$ | $wz$ |
| 4 | $xy$ | $xy$ | $wz$ | $xz$ | $xz$ |

In a straight vote $A$, $B$, $D$ and $E$ all prefer $w$ to $x$; and $C$, $D$, and $E$ prefer $y$ to $z$. The outcome would therefore be $w$ and $y$. But the pair $wy$ is less well liked than the opposite pair $xz$ by $A$, $B$, and $C$.

We now ask: what does the majority principle prescribe in a situation like this? Are we committed to the view that neither smoking nor playing radios should be allowed, because there is a majority against each? Or can we take account of the fact that there is a majority in favour of overturning the result of the two separate votes and substituting their opposites?

A sufficient (though not necessary) condition of there being an outcome that is preferred by a majority to any other is that preferences should be what is called 'single-peaked'.[10] All this means is that it should be possible to arrange the alternative outcomes along a single line in such a way that, when we draw for each of the people involved a curve whose height represents their relative preference for each outcome, we get a curve with a single peak for each.

To illustrate this, let us allow for a choice with respect to smoking

[9] Adapted from Example 1 in Nicholas R. Miller, 'Logrolling, Vote Trading, and the Paradox of Voting: A Game-Theoretical Overview', *Public Choice*, 30 (1977), 49–75, at 69.
[10] The *locus classicus* is Duncan Black, *The Theory of Committees and Elections* (Cambridge: Cambridge University Press, 1963).

among three possibilities instead of two: no smoking at all, smoking of cigarettes but not pipes and cigars, and unrestricted smoking. Call the first policy $x$, the second $y$, and the third $z$. We may imagine the preference orderings of our five people to be as in Table 2.2, which corresponds to Figure 2.1. It will be seen that in this case the preferences are capable of being arranged along a single dimension (which can be labelled pro-smoking/anti-smoking) so that each person's preferences are single-peaked.

TABLE 2.2

| Preference ranking | A and B | C | D and E |
|---|---|---|---|
| 1 | x | y | z |
| 2 | y | z | y |
| 3 | z | x | x |

When preferences are single-peaked we know not only that a majority winner exists but we also know how to find it easily. The simple rule is that the outcome that is most preferred by the median person is the outcome that is preferred by a majority to any other. The median person is the one (for an odd number of participants) who has exactly as many others on one side as on the other. If there are $n$ people ($n$ being an odd number) whose preferences are to be taken into account, we should start counting at one end (it doesn't matter which since the answer will be the same) and stop when we get to $\frac{1}{2}(n+1)$. This will be the median person. In our example of five people $\frac{1}{2}(n+1)$

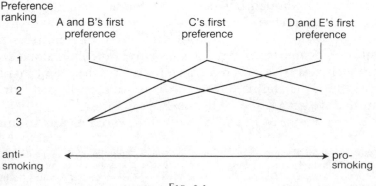

FIG. 2.1

= 3 and it will be seen that we get to $C$'s most preferred position by counting to three from either end. Where there is an even number of people there is no unique median but the people at $\frac{1}{2}n$ and $(\frac{1}{2}n) + 1$ (again counting from either end) occupy positions each of which is capable of gaining a majority against any other position. These two positions have an equal number of supporters when matched against each other so, on the majority principle, they may be regarded as equally good.

The trouble is that there may not be any outcome that is capable of getting majority support against any other (or, in the case of even numbers, two that are equally good in the sense just specified). Thus, suppose now that $D$ and $E$ do not like to smoke cigarettes and, if they cannot smoke their pipes, would prefer a smoke-free environment to one contaminated by $C$'s cigarette smoke. Then the preference matrix becomes as in Table 2.3. We now pit each possible outcome against each other in a series of three pairwise comparisons and get the result that $x$ beats $y$ ($A$, $B$, $D$, and $E$ prefer it), $y$ beats $z$ ($A$, $B$, and $C$ prefer it), and $z$ beats $x$ ($C$, $D$, and $E$ prefer it). Thus, a quite plausible distribution of preferences generates a 'paradox of voting' in which the majorities arising from pairwise comparisons form a cycle.

TABLE 2.3

| Rank order | $A$ and $B$ | $C$ | $D$ and $E$ |
|:---:|:---:|:---:|:---:|
| 1 | $x$ | $y$ | $z$ |
| 2 | $y$ | $z$ | $x$ |
| 3 | $z$ | $x$ | $y$ |

The two sources of indeterminacy in the majority principle that I have so far been pointing out may be considered rather dull and technical, incapable of arousing political passions. This is by no means true. Consider, for example, the importance that both sympathizers of President Allende and apologists for the coup that overthrew him have attached in their polemics to the question whether or not he had majority support for his policies. Given a political set-up with three blocs, Allende was able to come into power as President on a bare plurality; and the Popular Unity Coalition that supported him never achieved a majority of votes cast. It was on the basis of these facts that the junta claimed legitimacy in terms of the majority principle for overthrowing the constitutional government. On the other side, however, it may be argued that 'one cannot infer that those who opposed Allende necessarily supported a military coup, especially the bloody one that ensued following his overthrow. Thus there is little evidence that a majority of Chileans wanted Allende overthrown by the military.'[11]

It is not my intention to join in this debate, merely to point out that, where the majority principle is indeterminate, generals find it worth appealing to it and scholars find it worth rebutting that appeal. However, if we measure the importance of a question by the blood spilt over it (and I find it hard to think of a better criterion) the importance of the third reason for the indeterminacy of the majority principle can hardly be denied. The question is the deceptively innocent one: majority of *what*?

In the railway carriage example this is not a problem. If the decision about permitting or prohibiting smoking is to be made according to majority preference there can be no doubt that the people whose preferences should be taken into account are the five people in the railway carriage who will be affected by the decision. But when the question is the boundaries of political entities—empires, supranational organizations, federations, nation-states, provinces, or other subdivisions—and their respective decisionmaking powers, the question 'who is included?' is an explosive one.

There is no need to labour the point. The briefest survey is enough. In Western Europe, after centuries of wars between states, civil wars, and heavy-handed centralizing government, Northern Ireland is paralysed by conflict, Scottish nationalism is a powerful force, the centralized Belgian state has been virtually partitioned, unfinished business from the nineteenth century still hangs over the Swiss Jura and the Alto Adige, while in Spain Basque and Catalan separatism are stirring again after the long freeze. In Eastern Europe almost every state has claims on the territory of at least one other. Order, of a kind, is maintained by the Soviet Union, which is itself a patchwork of nationalities held together by coercion. And nobody is taking bets on the existence of Yugoslavia in ten years' time. In North America, Quebec has a separatist government, and the unity of the country is in question. In the Middle East three wars have been fought over the boundaries of Israel and no end is in sight. In Africa, the boundaries bequeathed by the colonial powers, after a period of surprising stability (interrupted only by the Biafran and Katagan secessions), are

[11] James Petras and Morris Morley, 'Chilean Destabilisation and Its Aftermath', *Politics*, 11 (1976), 140–8, at 145.

coming under pressure in the Horn of Africa, and the trouble looks as if it may well spread further in coming years. The Indian subcontinent has seen first the convulsion of the creation of Pakistan and then the almost equally bloody process of its splitting into two; while in India the states have had to be reconstituted, amid a good deal of disorder, in an attempt to satisfy the aspirations of linguistic groups. There are few parts of the world where boundaries are not a potential source of serious conflict, and where we do not hear that they are (e.g. China) this is as likely to reflect our ignorance as the absence of potential conflict.

The only thing that has to be established, beyond the existence of conflicts over boundaries, is that the majority principle has no way of solving them, either in practice or in theory. In practice, the majority principle, so far from alleviating conflicts over boundaries, greatly exacerbates them. It may be tolerable to be ruled over by a cosmopolitan autocracy like the Austrian empire, or a more or less even-handed colonial power like the British in India. But to be subject to a majority of a different language, religion, or national identity is far more threatening. In an area where nationalities are intermingled, like the Balkans, every move to satisfy majority aspirations leaves the remaining minorities even more vulnerable.

On a theoretical level, any use of the majority principle in order to establish boundaries must involve begging the question. Locke, to do him credit, saw that the majority principle could come into play only after the constituency has been identified, but he finessed the problem by resorting to the fiction that those who are to form 'one body' all individually agree to do so. This approach obviously fails to provide any guidance in any situation where it is actually needed, that is to say where people are disagreeing about the 'body' they want to be members of.

The so-called 'principle of national self-determination' espoused by the Versailles Treaty of 1919 says, in effect, that if a minority within a state wishes to secede and the majority does not wish them to secede the minority should win—provided the minority is a 'nation'. As it stands, this is both question-begging (since the crucial judgement is packed into the question of whether the would-be secessionists constitute a 'nation') and contrary to the majority principle. But the attempt to reformulate it so as to derive it from the majority principle simply begs the question in a different way.

Suppose we say: the majority in any given territorial area should decide on the political status of that area. Then the question is thrown back one stage further. What is the relevant territorial area within which to count preferences? Consider, for example, the Irish question as it stood between 1918 and 1921. Simplifying somewhat, there was (probably) a majority in the UK as a whole (i.e. the British Isles) for the maintenance of the union; within Ireland (i.e. the whole island) there was a majority in favour of independence for the whole of Ireland; within the six provinces that became Northern Ireland there was a majority for partition as a second-best to union; but within two of those six counties there was a majority for unification with the south as a second best to independence for the whole of Ireland. But why stop at counties? Counties could have been further divided and some areas within them would have had one sort of majority and others other sorts.

A contemporary puzzle of the same sort is offered by Gibraltar: 'London insists that it will respect the wishes of the 25,000 Gibraltarians, a mixture of people who, for the most part, tend to favour retaining their colonial connection with Britain. Madrid insists on regaining sovereignty over what a broad spectrum of Spanish opinion considers a usurped segment of national territory'.[12] Is the majority of Gibraltarians the relevant one, or the majority of people in Spain plus Gibraltar?

It seems clear that the majority principle can offer no guidance. If we feel that (within limits of contiguity and feasibility) the right answer is to try to satisfy the wishes of as many people as possible to form a polity with those they wish to have in it and only those, we are moving beyond the majority principle to another, and in my view more defensible, notion. This is that what matters is not to satisfy the preferences of a majority but to respect the interests of all. I shall argue in the next section that democratic procedures can, under some conditions, be defended in terms of that conception.

Meanwhile, it should be noted that the upshot of the discussion is that any attempt to justify boundaries by appealing to the majority principle must be void. You can have as many referenda as you like, and show every time that over half of the people within the existing boundaries approve of them, but you cannot use that to prove to a minority that wants to secede that they ought to acquiesce in the status quo. If their loyalty is to be awakened, other and better arguments —backed by deeds rather than votes—are needed.

I shall take up the question of boundaries in chapter 6 below. For the

[12] James M. Markham, 'Talks on Gibraltar Due in October', *The New York Times* (25 Sept. 1977), 4.

purpose of the present chapter let us now assume that the composition of the group that is to be subject to a common policy is not at issue, and that the two more technical sources of indeterminacy are absent. Does that make the majority principle unassailable? Of course not. The fourth and last of the special features of the railway carriage case that I singled out was that, as the story had been told, we had no reason to suppose that the question of smoking or not smoking was of vital importance to any of the people involved. (It might be said that smoking is inherently a vital interest in that being smoked at lowers one's expectation of life; but, if we put it as a question of interests, is a few minutes more life a greater interest than the freedom of the addict from withdrawal symptoms?) Suppose, however, that one of the passengers suffers from severe asthma or emphysema, and that being subjected to tobacco smoke is liable to precipitate a dangerous attack. No doubt one would hope that this fact, when explained, would lead the others to agree not to smoke, however many of them would like to. But say that it does not. It seems clear to me that the person at risk would be behaving with an almost insane disregard for his or her interests in accepting a majority decision to allow smoking. The obvious recourse would be, I presume, to pull the communication cord and bring the train to a grinding halt.

It might be argued that nothing said here shows that the majority principle lacks universality. The majority principle, it may be said, always has a certain weight, but in some cases the reason it provides for obedience is overridden by a more pressing consideration, such as self-protection against a risk of substantial harm. This is not a correct representation of the position, however. Where the decision is sufficiently threatening to the vital interests of (some of) those affected by it, its pedigree is neither here nor there.

Take for example a group of youths like those in *A Clockwork Orange* who beat up strangers for fun. Would we be inclined to say 'Well, at least there's one redeeming feature: they choose their victims by majority vote'? I think not. This example of course raises the question of constituency, since the victim is outside the decisionmaking group. But if we modify it so that the members of a group decide by majority vote to beat up one of their own number the chosen victim has no less reason to resist or escape than he would if the decision were taken by a strong-arm leader. I do not see any significant respect in which my modified example of the railway passengers differs from that. Someone might adduce the difference between deliberately causing harm and doing something whose known but unintended consequences are harmful, but that is not in my view a morally relevant distinction. (See chapter 12 section III.)

The political parallels hardly need to be filled in. No minority can be, or should be, expected to acquiesce in the majority's trampling on its vital interests. Unfortunately the parallel to pulling the communication cord—bringing the state, or that part of its policy that is objectionable, to a grinding halt—is a much more messy business and carries the risk of incurring costs much higher than a £25 fine. But the principle is clear enough. Nobody but a moral imbecile would really be prepared to deliver himself over body and soul to the majority principle.

This is not to say that no reason can be found for giving weight to the fact that a law arose from a democratic procedure. But it is to say that the majority principle is a broken reed. The attraction of the majority principle lies in the claim that the majority 'naturally' is entitled to act for the whole. If it turns out that this 'naturalness' is contingent on the presence of a number of highly restrictive conditions, we must press our enquiries further and ask whether we can identify some more fundamental basis for saying that democratic procedures matter.

III

At several points in the preceding section, I gestured towards the lines on which an alternative defence of democratic procedures might be mounted. In arguing that the majority principle is helpless in the face of boundary disputes, I suggested that we might adopt the principle not of satisfying the preferences of the majority but of safeguarding the interests of everyone; and, in making the point that the majority principle cannot be regarded as sacrosanct even where it is perfectly determinate, I suggested that no minority should respect laws that disregard its vital interests. I now want to follow up those ideas and lay out systematically if sketchily the theory from which they can be derived.

It should be emphasized that the framework within which I am operating is not the familiar one of asking what is the 'best' decision-making system. Rather, I am concerned with the question that each person must ask: 'Given the procedure and the outcome, am I to obey this law?' The advantage of focusing on this practical question can be seen by reflecting on the discussion of the majority principle in the previous section. Social choice theorists often write as if all our problems would be over if (*per impossibile*) we could crack the Arrow General Possibility Theorem. Yet, for a single dichotomous choice, the majority principle satisfies all of Arrow's conditions for a satisfactory system of aggregating preferences into a 'social decision' and other stronger conditions as well. For all this, as we have seen, it is perfectly possible for a single dichotomous decision to be one that nobody with any elementary regard for self-preservation would voluntarily submit to. We thus get much deeper into the real problems of politics by asking not what is the best procedure but what one should do about actual decisions, taking account (among other things) of the procedures by which they were reached.

In order to offer any general statements we have to be able to imagine ourselves in all the possible positions that a person might get into, and ask what for someone in this position would be the right thing to do. A dramatic though not essential way of setting up the problem is to say that we are to imagine ourselves behind a Rawlsian veil of ignorance.[13] A person behind a veil of ignorance does not know his or her talents, aspirations, race, sex, etc., but must choose principles that will be binding on whoever he or she turns out to be. Unlike Rawls, I shall posit (and not suggest that I can derive it from the specification of the choice situation and the notion of rationality) that someone who is looking at all the possible positions he or she might turn up in will be particularly concerned with the protection of vital interests.

The first question to be asked is whether to have laws at all, and, if so, what is to be their status. One possibility is that there should be no rules of any kind. Another is that there should be rules but that they should have only the status of suggestions to aid interpersonal co-ordination. Alternatively, there might be a society in which laws carried sanctions but nobody ever considered anything except the sanction in deciding whether or not to obey the law (just as in our society we buy a bottle of Scotch if it is worth it to us after paying a large sum to the government); or there might be one in which the existence of a law was taken as a reason for obeying it but no sanction was attached to disobedience. Finally, the existence of a law might be taken as a reason for doing what it requires but there might be sanctions against disobedience too.

The question has been set up in classical 'social contract' terms, and the classical 'social contract' answer is that the last of these possibilities

---

[13] John Rawls, *A Theory of Justice* (Cambridge, Mass.: Harvard University Press, 1971), 136–42.

is preferable to any of the others: we need stable expectations that
certain rules will be generally followed, we want there to be sanctions
underwriting the rules, but we don't want people to keep the rules
only when the sanctions are sufficiently probable to make obedience
the course of action that pays on a prudential calculation. I think that in
general this is a good answer.

But it is one thing to say that one would wish the standard situation
to be one in which people accept the existence of a law as a reason for
obeying it. That still leaves open the question whether or not something's being a law should always be taken as a decisive reason for
obeying it. And, if the answer to that question is negative, it leaves
open the question of particular concern here, namely, whether or not
the law's origin in a democratic procedure should make a difference.

The first of these questions does not seem too difficult. Looking at
the matter impartially, taking account of all the contingencies to
which he or she could be exposed, it is surely apparent that our person
choosing principles and institutions would not wish to be committed
to unconditional obedience to law. In some cases open disobedience or
rebellion may be right. I shall discuss these later. But I should like to
say a word here for ordinary non-heroic disobedience, in other words
crime, that is to say law-breaking undertaken for private rather than
public ends and with the intention of avoiding detection if possible.

A typical reaction among political philosophers is that 'the ordinary
criminal may be viewed as acting primarily out of motives of self-
interest—motives which render him morally blameworthy and
socially dangerous'.[14] Presumably it is not simply the self-interested
motive that makes for a presumption against the moral acceptability
of ordinary criminal law-breaking. Most market behaviour is
motivated by self-interest but is not normally taken to be *ipso facto*
reprehensible. I think that the basic reasons for condemning ordinary
law-breaking are that breaking the law causes harm to the victim(s)
and that it is unfair to take advantage of the forbearance of others to
secure a private advantage. The criminal is, in Rawlsian terms, a 'free
rider' on the scheme of social co-operation from which he or she
benefits. This rationale, however, fails to apply in two kinds of cases:

---

[14] Jeffrie G. Murphy, in his Intro. to a book of readings on *Civil Disobedience and Violence*
(Belmont, Calif.: Wadsworth, 1971), 2. Similarly, H. B. Acton, in 'Political Justification', repr.
in Bedau (ed.), *Civil Disobedience*, pp. 220–39, having said that 'disobedience . . . may take a
variety of forms', dismissed that of 'not obeying and of endeavouring to escape the legal
consequences' as 'of no interest to us in this paper, since either it is nothing but a sort of
unprincipled subterfuge or else it leads to [rebellion, i.e. the attempt to overthrow the
government by force]' (p. 222).

where nobody is benefited by the actor's forbearance and where the whole scheme of social co-operation is not on balance beneficial to the actor.

We must, as Dr Johnson exhorted, clear the mind of cant. Will anyone seriously maintain that he or she has ever stopped drinking in a pub at exactly 10.40 p.m. (assuming that the landlord is prepared to go on serving) out of respect for the licensing laws rather than out of fear of possible unpleasantness with the police? There are a whole range of laws whose observance benefits nobody—laws against Sunday entertainment, laws prohibiting off-course betting, laws against contraception and abortion, laws regulating the sexual relations of consenting adults, and so on. There can be no unfairness to others in disobeying such laws, and it is surely significant that people break them on a massive scale without guilt feelings. The 'what if everybody did that?' argument against breaking the law has no force in such a case, as long as 'that' is understood as 'breaking the same law'.[15] For, *ex hypothesi*, the case is one where disobedience has no ill-effects whatever the scale. And in as far as mass disobedience has a tendency to bring about the demise of the law as a by-product, that is a plus factor in the reckoning. As Christian Bay has pointed out, the massive evasion of Prohibition in the USA had no high-minded motives 'for the Volstead act was usually evaded in secret, even if Clarence Darrow is said to have referred to bootleggers as fighters for American liberties and predicted the erection of statues to Al Capone in many a public park'.[16] But it still made repeal virtually unavoidable.

These are cases where nobody benefits from forbearance. The other cases are those where there are indeed beneficiaries from forbearance, but there is no mutual benefit. Thus, let us say that the system of apartheid in South Africa benefits (at least in the short run) the White minority. It clearly does not benefit the rest of the population and I can conceive of no reason other than concern for his or her own safety why anyone subject to this apparatus of legal oppression should pay it any respect. Published reports suggest that the hundreds of pass-law violators who are processed by the courts each day regard the inevitable fine as an incident of life in an unjust society rather than as the expiation of personal wrongdoing.[17] Turning T. H. Green on his

---

[15] Compare Richard A. Wasserstrom, 'The Obligation to Obey the Law', repr. in Bedau, *Civil Disobedience*, 256–62.

[16] Christian Bay, 'Civil Disobedience: Prerequisite for Democracy in Mass Society', repr. in Murphy, *Civil Disobedience and Violence*, 73–92, at 85.

[17] See Larry Garbus, 'South Africa: The Death of Justice', *The New York Review of Books* (4 Aug. 1977).

head (the time-honoured treatment for idealists), one may say that force, not will, is the basis of the state, and that this legitimates a purely pragmatic attitude to law on the part of the oppressed majority.

We now need to face the question whether a law's having been passed by a democratic procedure should provide a special reason for obeying it. A common argument for accepting an outcome reached by a democratic procedure even when you dislike it is that you should take the rough with the smooth: you can't win them all, but in the long run you can expect to win more than half the time because on each issue the majority principle ensures that more people win than lose. I want in the rest of this section to take this popular idea, see what it presupposes in order to be persuasive, and then ask what should be done where it breaks down.

As we have already seen, the majority principle cannot be equated with democratic procedures (as I equated it in presenting the view to be discussed), so it will make for clarity to split the analysis into two parts. First, I shall show that the application of the majority principle produces satisfactory results so long as the preferences to be taken into account are distributed in certain ways. Following that I shall try to establish a connection for such cases between the outcome required by the majority principle and the general tendency to be expected of democratic procedures.

Consider, then, a country in which all issues are dichotomous and in which the following characteristics hold: (1) each of those who are in the majority stands on the average to gain as much satisfaction from the passage of any given law as each of those in the minority stands to lose from it; and (2) on each issue there is an independent probability for each person of being in the majority that is equal to the proportion of the total number in the majority on that issue. The first condition says in effect that the stakes of each person are the same on any given issue (though they may not be the same on different issues). The second says in effect that, whatever we know of a person's previous voting record, we cannot do better than predict that he or she has a 0·6 probability of being in the majority if the majority is 60 per cent, a 0·7 probability of being in the majority if the majority is 70 per cent, and so on.

The second condition entails that, over a period sufficient for a number of issues to come up, decisions made in accordance with the majority principle can be expected to yield approximately equal satisfaction to each person. Adding the first condition, we can go further: if we count getting the outcome you want as +1 and getting the outcome you don't want as −1, then each person can expect $(x - 0.5) \times 2$ units of satisfaction, where $x$ is the average majority. (For example, if the average majority is 0.7, each person can expect 0.4 units of satisfaction.) But in addition the first condition alone tells us that the majority principle maximizes average satisfaction, for it can never increase average satisfaction to please fewer people rather than more, given that the average gain of each winner is the same as the average loss of each loser.

If the person choosing from behind the veil of ignorance were seeking to maximize the average of the levels of satisfaction of all the people he or she might turn out to be, the first condition alone indicates that the majority principle would be the one to pick. But suppose instead that the person behind the veil of ignorance were to follow Rawls's recommendation and choose a rule for aggregating preferences with the object of making the lot of the worst off of all those that one might turn out to be as desirable as possible. Then, because in the special case stated in the second condition everyone has the same expectation of satisfaction, it would still be best to pick the majority principle. For any other principle lowers the average and, since everyone's expectations are the same, that means that on any other principle each of the people he or she might turn out to be would be worse-off.

Let us take this idea and cash it out into the choice of sanctions for breaking the law and principles about obedience to the law. Obviously, when we say that people get satisfaction from getting a law they want or lose satisfaction from getting a law they do not want, we are speaking in shorthand. What people gain or lose satisfaction from is not the enactment itself but the operation of the law. If those who are in the minority on any law ignore it with impunity, they do not suffer the loss associated with it; but those in the majority do not experience the gain associated with it either, at any rate if the minority is large enough for its disobedience to undermine the law. But in the case as specified there is a net gain from each law (that is, from the operation of each law) and each person stands in the long run to share equally in these gains. Therefore, from behind the veil of ignorance it is advantageous both to support sanctions and to adopt the principle as binding on all that laws which have majority approval ought to be obeyed even in the absence of prudential motives.

Now, by contrast, suppose that the second condition does not hold, though the first still does. It still maximizes the average satisfaction of all the people one might turn out to be to endorse the majority principle. But if one is concerned to avoid the worst threats to one's interests, the majority principle is no longer so attractive. Take the opposite extreme from the atomistic society in which there is no association between one person's vote and any other's and consider a society permanently divided into two rigid groups. Each group always has monolithic preferences, so the same people are always in the majority and the minority. The average of all the people one might be is still $(x - 0 \cdot 5) \times 2$, though here $x$ is simply the proportion of the whole constituted by the majority group. But the expectation of each member of the minority group is $-1$, since on every issue they lose.

If in addition we give up the first condition, we can no longer even be confident that the average satisfaction will be maximized by adopting the side on every issue that corresponds with the majority preference. Thus, suppose we assume that politics is a zero-sum game, so that on every issue the amount gained by those who are on the winning side is exactly equal to the amount lost by those on the losing side.[18] This entails, of course, under the majority principle, that winners always win less per head than losers lose. Then it would obviously be better to have no procedure for making laws. Anyone who wants gratuitous risks can always gamble privately—there is no point in forcing risks on everyone.

The upshot of this very crude analysis is that, from behind the veil of ignorance, a person of reasonable prudence would accept outcomes produced in accordance with the majority principle for an atomistic society or a pluralistic society, which we may take as the closest real-life approximation: that is to say, a society in which there are many groups and the relations between them are fluid. In such a society the majority principle gives each group a good chance of being in the majority over half the time. This description of the pluralistic society is, of course, recognizable as the picture of the USA drawn by the celebrants of the 1950s. It is probably a fair description of the way the system works for the best-placed 60 or 70 per cent of the adult population. Conversely, the more closely a society approximates to the model of a monolithic majority bloc facing a minority which is always on the losing side, the more would reasonably prudent people refuse to accept that, if they found themselves in such a society and in the minority group, they would be bound to respect the laws that had been passed by the majority over minority opposition.

The assumption that all issues are dichotomous is a very restrictive

[18] This assumption is implicit in William J. Riker, *A Theory of Political Coalitions* (New Haven, Conn.: Yale University Press, 1962).

and unrealistic one. Let me extend the analysis just one step, to the simplest case beyond: that where all preferences lie on one dimension. I have already, in section II, pointed out that in such a case the majority principle picks out one point as the unique one that is capable of gaining a majority in a pairwise comparison with any other. This is the point corresponding to the preference of the median person, in other words the person with exactly as many others on each side. In investigating the properties of the majority principle, then, all we need to do is examine the properties of the median.

Consider first a case in which these three things are true: (1) on any issue, each person experiences the same loss of satisfaction for any given distance between the most preferred outcome and the actual outcome; (2) for each person the loss of satisfaction is linear with distance, in other words it is always true that an outcome twice as far away represents twice as much loss of satisfaction; and (3) on each issue, each person has an independent probability of being in any position that is equal to the proportion of the total number of people in that position.

Here, conditions (1) and (2) correspond to the first stipulation for the dichotomous case. That said that winners always gain and losers always lose equal amounts per head. Conditions (1) and (2) entail that the aggregate loss from any given outcome can be obtained by summing over all the people concerned the distances between their ideal points and the outcome. In the dichotomous case, the first stipulation implied that we maximize gain by making the outcome the one preferred by a majority. In the present case, conditions (1) and (2) have the implication that loss of satisfaction is minimized when we make the outcome the one preferred by the person in the median position. This follows from the fact that the sum total of distances from the median position is the smallest possible, however people may be distributed along the line. The reason for this can be seen by imagining people standing at various points along a real line. Place yourself in front of the person at the median position and then move either to left or right. As you move, you get nearer to some people and further from others. But it must be true that you move away from more people than you move towards. Finally, condition (3) corresponds to the second stipulation for the dichotomous case. It guarantees that everyone in the long run loses the same amount, so that each person receives the average loss.

Analogously with what was said in the dichotomous case, conditions (1) and (2) alone would be sufficient to lead anyone who was

concerned only with the average level of satisfaction to endorse the
majority principle (here implemented by choosing the median position). Adding the third condition, which produces equal expectations
for all, would also make the median position the choice either of a
maximizer or of someone concerned to minimize the losses of the
person losing the most.

At this point, however, the analogy with the dichotomous case
breaks down. In dropping the second stipulation for the dichotomous
case—the atomistic assumption—we went to the opposite extreme
and imagined a society with no changing of places at all, and decided
that a person of reasonable prudence would not endorse the majority
principle for such a society. In the one-dimensional case, however, a
similar total lack of fluidity in relative positions does not necessarily
have such disturbing implications for the majority principle.

Consider the most neutral assumption about the way in which
preferences are distributed: that they are evenly distributed along the
dimension. If we plot the density of preferences on the vertical
dimension, a distribution of this kind looks as in Figure 2.2. Now the
interesting thing about this distribution is that the median position
(marked m) not only minimizes average loss (as does the median with
any distribution, given the first two assumptions) but also minimizes
the maximum loss of any person. For, if we move away from it in
either direction, the people at the far end are made worse off than they
were when the outcome was at the median.

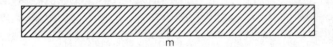

m

FIG. 2.2

As may be apparent, a rectangular distribution is not needed to
generate this result. Any distribution such that the median point lies
half-way between the extremes will do it. Therefore all symmetrical distributions—that is to say distributions such that one half of the
line is a mirror-image of the other half—satisfy the requirement. Examples are Figures 2.3 and 2.4. Of course the average loss of satisfaction differs between the three distributions: it is greatest in Figure 2.4,
least in Figure 2.3, and intermediate in Figure 2.2. The society
depicted in Figure 2.3 has more ability to satisfy its average member

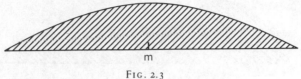

FIG. 2.3

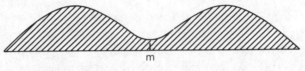

FIG. 2.4

than the society in Figure 2.2, and that in Figure 2.2. more than that in Figure 2.4. Failing some realignment of preferences—the rise of a different issue, perhaps—it might be as well for the two groups in the last society to split off into separate polities, or form a federation allowing each the maximum autonomy; or if they are too geographically mingled for that they might at least try *verzuiling* (functional decentralization). But if there *is* going to be one set of policies binding on all of them, the median is the one that anybody choosing from behind a veil of ignorance will have to go for.

The natural reaction to Figure 2.4 is, I think, to dispute the analysis and suggest that the median position is unlikely to be the outcome. I agree, but mainly because the situation as depicted is so finely balanced. The tension between the two groups would be extreme because so much was at stake: changes in the birth-rates or the migration rates, or a little gerrymandering, could so easily swing the outcome a long way to one side or the other. The reasonably prudent person choosing from behind a veil of ignorance would not, I concede, give unqualified allegiance to the majority principle for a society so evenly balanced between two blocs, with so few people in the region of the median, as in Figure 2.4. The logic of the situation is illustrated by Figure 2.5. This shows how, once we move away from a symmetrical bimodal distribution like that in Figure 2.4, the median position leaves those in the minority group out in the cold. The average loss is still minimized but the maximum loss is great.

Notice in passing that moving the unimodal distribution of Figure

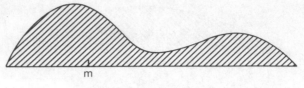

FIG. 2.5

2.3 away from symmetry does not have the same kind of drastic results. Figure 2.6 illustrates the way in which the median shifts a little away from the centre, but not dramatically. A distribution of this kind may be thought of as a rough sketch of a politics of economic interest in an otherwise homogeneous society, where income and status follow a pattern of continuous graduation (as against dichotomous classes) but where the distribution of income and status is in the traditional 'squashed diamond' shape.

How do these results relate to those we obtained for the dichotomous case? We can establish two fairly direct parallels. The atomistic society, in which people distribute themselves randomly on dichotomous issues, is, I suggested, a rose-tinted model of the USA in the 1950s. It might be realistic for other societies with a fluid social structure, perhaps the USA and other settler societies at a certain stage of development. The one-dimensional model with random placement may be thought of as a more complex version of the same thing, with the dichotomous assumption relaxed to allow a range of different positions on each issue. The alternative model of two rigid groups facing one another on successive dichotomous issues approximates the condition of a society with a deep structural cleavage running through it: a division based on ethnicity, language, race, or possibly (where there is a sharp gulf between landlords and peasants or owners and workers) on class. The one-dimensional model with a bimodal

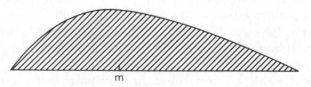

FIG. 2.6

distribution refines on this by allowing for a fixed range of positions within the groups and the possibility of some people holding intermediate positions. But the general implications are much the same as in the dichotomous case: outcomes in accordance with the majority principle may be highly injurious to the interests of the minority group.

Where we get something distinctively new from the one-dimensional analysis is in the case of a fixed unimodal distribution. For we can see here how fixed positions may be compatible with acceptable outcomes. Admittedly the people on the two tails of the distribution will be dissatisfied with the outcomes that the majority principle calls for, that is to say the outcomes preferred by the person in the median position. But what alternative can they seriously propose? Those in the minority group have a good cause for complaint when there is a bimodal distribution and the median person is in the majority group. But with a unimodal distribution any move towards one set of extremists leaves the extremists at the other end even more dissatisfied than they were in the first place. From behind the veil of ignorance it would be inconsistent to say that if one found oneself on one tail of a unimodal distribution one should resist outcomes corresponding to the median position without acknowledging that those at the other extreme should also resist them, for there is no way of distinguishing the two. 'The end I happen to be at' will not do.

Although we started from a defence of the majority principle that was expressed in terms of winning and losing, we have finished up with a case where the majority principle can be defended even though the line-up is the same on each question that comes up for decision. That is to say, on each question the same single dimension defines the positions of each of the actors and they find themselves in the same places. We got here by transforming the winning and losing in the dichotomous case into a value of getting the outcome you want and a (negative) value of getting the outcome other than the one you want. We then made a natural extension of that way of thinking so as to accommodate the analysis in one dimension by assuming that the distance between the preferred outcome and the actual outcome provides a measure of dissatisfaction with that outcome. We are thus able to evaluate the median position as an outcome in terms of the distribution of loss of satisfaction that it produces, without any need to refer to winning and losing.

To see that winning and losing is irrelevant, go back for a moment to the set-up depicted in Figure 2.1, where *A* and *B* take one position,

*C* a middle position, and *D* and *E* the position at the other end of the line. If the final vote on each issue is between *C*'s position and one of the others (which is what we would normally expect), *C* will always be on the winning side, but whether or not *A* and *B* 'win' or *D* and *E* 'win' depends on the way the choice is structured. If the choice is between the outcome preferred by *A* and *B* and the outcome preferred by *C*, then *C*, *D*, and *E* will vote together and *A* and *B* will go down to defeat. If the position preferred by *D* and *E* is set against that preferred by *C*, we will get the result that *A*, *B*, and *C* combine against *D* and *E*. Yet in both cases the outcome is the same: the outcome preferred by *C* is the one that gets a majority. This simple example illustrates the fallacy of counting up 'wins' and 'losses' where there are more than two possible positions. The only sound procedure is to compare the position preferred by each actor with the actual outcome.

The unimodal model of preference-distribution fits reasonably well the Scandinavian countries, New Zealand, Australia and Great Britain (but not Northern Ireland). Other countries are not adequately represented by this unimodal model, in which political differences reflect the socioeconomic stratification of an otherwise relatively homogeneous population. Yet at the same time they do not exhibit the radical pluralism of societies such as Guyana, the Lebanon, Indonesia, Nigeria, Cyprus, or Malaysia, in which different groups live side by side, sharing no common institutions except those of the state. These other societies, of which the Netherlands and Belgium are paradigmatic, have a division between 'spiritual families' (and, in the Belgian case, an ethnic cleavage) but are at the same time sufficiently integrated to have the potential for a politics of socioeconomic interest cutting across these ascriptive lines. An adequate model of preference-distribution in such societies requires two or even three dimensions. However, except for special cases, there is no longer a unique point picked out by the majority principle once we move away from one dimension. There is in general no Condorcet winner, no point capable of gaining a majority over all others. The problem of circularity rears its head once more. I cannot afford the space here to follow up the complexities that arise in analysing spaces of two or more dimensions, since I still have not made the connection, even for the one-dimensional cases, between the majority principle and democratic procedures. Having established that connection, however, I shall be in a position to take some short-cuts in the analysis of the politics of plural societies.

So far, then, I have been operating with the majority principle as the object of analysis. But if this analysis is to tie up with democratic procedures, I have to argue that democratic procedures have a tendency to produce the outcomes called for by the majority principle. This I believe to be true in general, and I think that theoretical arguments can be offered to show why it is not accidental that it happens, but I can do no more than sketch the argument here.

In the dichotomous case, I have already suggested in section II that democratic procedures are more likely to produce the outcomes desired by a majority than any alternative procedure. All that needs to be added here is that the case in which a purely opportunistic party would sometimes support minority policies is ruled out for any case where the per capita gains and losses of majority and minority are equal.

The one-dimensional case requires a little more analysis. With direct voting between all pairs of positions, we know that the median position can obtain a majority over all rivals. But even in a committee cruder devices are used. In a referendum, only two choices are commonly offered: to accept the proposal or reject it. This leaves a good deal of scope for manipulation to whoever is able to set the terms of the referendum. For, if preferences are one-dimensional, the option closer to the median will win; but, if both the options are some way off the median, the result will obviously not have the desirable properties attributed here to the median. This suggests that referenda are dubious unless either (*a*) the topic 'naturally' creates a dichotomy or (*b*) it is open to any group of fair size to place an alternative on the ballot and some form of preferential voting is employed.

Voting for representatives is not subject to the same difficulties because the parties in effect do the work of sifting issues and putting together a majority. Very crudely, let me divide the types of party system to be analysed into two-party and multi-party systems. In two-party systems, the parties will tend to converge towards the median voter's position if they are concerned with winning elections. This is because, if each voter votes for the party whose position is nearer his own, the party nearer the median voter must get the most votes.[19] The argument is, in my view, compelling, and can be extended by observing that even if parties are not trying to win elections (or have other aims as well) it is still true that the party nearer the median voter will win. So the tendency for the party that gets a majority to be somewhere in the neighbourhood of the median voter

[19] Downs, *An Economic Theory of Democracy*, ch. 8.

does not depend on strong assumptions about party motivation, only on the assumption that, for whatever reason, at least one party will usually be fairly near the median voter at an election. (See chapter 7, section VIII for an argument to the effect that even ideologically motivated parties will tend towards the median.)

The multi-party case is more controversial. Downs argues in effect that with multi-party systems no systematic relationship between voter preferences and the policies pursued by governments can be expected.[20] In my view this is false to experience and also contrary to the logic of parliamentary tactics. Downs assumed that if several parties formed a coalition government the policy of the government would be some sort of average of the positions of the parties making it up. But his assumption has no rational foundation. The same logic that leaves the median voter with the whip-hand in a direct vote leaves the party containing the median legislator (call it the median party) with the whip-hand. Give me the minimum assumption that, other things being equal, parties prefer to be in governments that pursue their own programmes to being in governments that pursue other parties' programmes. I can then show that for any majority coalition with a policy other than that of the median party there is another majority coalition (which must contain some overlapping members) with the policy of the median party, and that all the members of this coalition will prefer it to the first one. Qualifications are of course needed, and cannot be given here, to deal with anti-system parties, cartels, and so on. But I believe that the basic tendency of multi-party systems that fall along one dimension is towards implementing the policies desired by the median party.

It still has to be shown that the median party's position can be anticipated to be in the region of the median voter, but this can be done fairly easily. As in the two-party case, we can say immediately that, if each voter votes for the nearest party, the median party will have been voted for by the median voter. But, in a multi-party system, the median party is normally quite closely hemmed in by other parties, so the range within which it is closer to an elector than any other party is likely to be quite small. So there is good reason for expecting the median party and the median voter to be near one another.

The upshot of this analysis is that the earlier discussion of the strengths and weaknesses of the outcomes corresponding to the majority principle can be transferred to the outcomes that we can

---

[20] Ibid., ch. 9.

expect democratic procedures to produce. (To the extent that party competition and coalition formation do not operate in the way I have postulated, our confidence in the reliability of this coincidence must of course be weakened.) Thus, the tendency of democratic procedures in societies with a bimodal distribution of preferences will be to produce outcomes that are highly prejudicial to the interests of the minority group. And in the less extremely fragmented societies of Western Europe we can say that democratic procedures have the same tendency when the political parties draw their support on the basis of ethnic, religious, racial, or other ascriptive criteria rather than competing by offering alternative positions on the dimension of party preferences related to location in the system of socioeconomic stratification.

What would be a sensible attitude to adopt towards obedience to law? Although we do not observe people choosing from behind a veil of ignorance, we do see the way they choose in real life and from that we can infer the relative strength of different motives—information that would be needed before an intelligent choice could be made from behind the veil of ignorance. And if we look at the empirical evidence we find that people do in fact tend to deny the legitimacy of a regime—however much it may bolster itself up by appeals to the majority principle—if they find the group to which they belong systematically discriminated against, treated as second-class citizens, denied cultural expression or communal organization, and generally not dealt with in terms of equal partnership.

It does not follow from that, however, that disobedience should be prescribed from behind the veil of ignorance. We need to examine the evidence. It seems clear that resistance to the majority has in some instances produced a more acceptable outcome, especially where it was backed up by the threat that disunity within the country might result in its loss of independence. If we look at instances where majorities have drawn back from pressing their maximum claims and accepted minorities as equal partners in what has been called 'consociational democracy', we find that they come about when the minority has established (given the background of the international situation) a capacity to cause trouble to the majority. These conditions can be seen in the stock examples of the conciliation of a minority: the Swiss settlement in 1848 following the Sonderbund war, the Dutch 'pacification' of 1917, the complex Lebanese balancing act and the Austrian compromise between 'black' and 'red' in 1945. In two cases (Switzerland and Austria) the minority lost a civil war, and in the Lebanese case the possibility of a civil war was (as recent events have tragically proved) too clear to miss. At the same time, in all of them, the international situation was threatening. Switzerland's integrity was threatened by the growing idea that state boundaries should correspond to 'nationalities', with the prospect that Switzerland might be dismembered and the parts absorbed into national states. The risk to the survival of the Netherlands of harbouring a discontented minority predominantly located on its border with Germany are too clear to need spelling out. The position of the Lebanon has always meant that internal disturbances risked outside intervention—as in the recent civil war. And in Austria the country was under four-power occupation in the post-war period, the withdrawal of the Russians could not be taken for granted, and the country was bordered by states under Russian influence. (These points are extended in chapters 4 and 5 below.)

There are, it need hardly be said, other situations that are far less favourable to the minority, where the only effect of resistance is to increase the degree of injustice and repression. In such cases, the minority has prudential reasons (though no others) for refraining from resistance, and hoping that some new turn of the wheel of international politics will bring about a more propitious situation, in which the ability to create a disturbance will be a stronger bargaining counter.

IV

The premiss of the previous section was ruthlessly instrumental. The assumption made was that people were concerned to get the outcomes they wanted, and were interested in procedures only as a means to that end. The content of the laws, not the way in which they were brought into existence, was all that mattered. The case for democratic procedures was simply that, under favourable circumstances, they were likely to produce acceptable outcomes. But any other procedure that produced the same outcomes would be equally acceptable. I am convinced that there is more to be said for that view, both morally and as a way of predicting how people will actually behave, than there is for the 'majority principle'. And yet—wasn't there *something* in the idea mooted in section II that there is a certain naturalness about majorities as a basis for settling matters that are in dispute? I think there is and in this final section I shall try to say what I think it is.

Come back for a moment to the notion of consociational

democracy. The essence of it is that the élites may be able to prevent democratic procedures from exacerbating conflict if they co-operate (maybe but not necessarily in a formal 'grand coalition') to find an agreed solution to the divisive issues and then sell it to (or impose it on) the electorate. Arendt Lijphart, who was responsible for introducing the term into contemporary political science, remarked that 'consociational democracy violates the principle of majority rule, but it does not deviate much from normative democratic theory'.[21] But the whole idea of consociational democracy is clearly at odds with any notion that the point of democratic procedures is that the parties are forced by the exigencies of competition to articulate the preferences for public policies of their supporters. The defining characteristic of 'consociational democracy' is that the party leaders do *not* press for the interests of their supporters (as those supporters see them), but rather somehow manage to carry their followers along a path of compromise.

Obviously, if peace and stability can be achieved only by preventing the electoral pressure from deflecting the party leaders from compromise, it is natural to ask why they should have to put up with electoral sanctions at all. Why not just have 'consociation' and drop 'democracy'? In practice, it might be said, this is what does happen in some states: where representative institutions produce a clash between ethnic groups, a non-representative system permits controlled 'consociation' from the top in the shape of participation of members of different groups in the government. (Nigeria and Kenya could both be cited as examples.) But if there is in the literature of consociational democracy an implicit value judgement that, other things being (approximately) equal, it is better to have representative institutions, on what is that judgement based? Clearly, not on the majority principle, since the essence of 'consociational democracy' is to avoid finishing up with what the majority wants. The answer would, I think, have to be on the lines that, *if* the trick can be brought off, the combination in divided societies of elections and élite collusion is superior to either elections without collusion or collusion without elections, because it satisfies both the value of peace and stability and the value of freedom of speech and organization.

How would this claim be made out? I think the key is the following

[21] Arend Lijphart, 'Consociational Democracy', repr. in Kenneth McRae (ed.), *Consociational Democracy: Political Accommodation in Segmented Societies* (Toronto: McClelland and Stewart, 1974), 70–89, at 77. See also Arend Lijphart, *Democracy in Plural Societies: A Comparative Exploration* (New Haven, Conn.: Yale University Press, 1977).

assertion: once a society reaches a level of development in which there is widespread education and where the bulk of the population enjoys independence from grinding poverty and continuous toil, the choice can *only* be between repression (including arbitrary action against citizens, making political prisoners out of critics and tight restraints on freedom of publication, assembly, etc.) and a system of representative government. This may appear to be a quite banal generalization and yet if it is true (and it seems to stand up well empirically) it is surely a remarkable fact.

In principle, after all, any kind of regime might be able to establish itself with sufficient acceptance to allow freedom to its critics. One would gather, for example, from Michael Oakeshott's *On Human Conduct* that there is no particularly favoured basis for the legitimacy of regimes. Their authority simply rests on the fact of recognition. He offers as an 'analogue' the case of the Marylebone Cricket Club's having acquired over time recognition as the arbiter of the rules of cricket. Its authority 'has nothing to do with the recognition of the desirability of the rules or with the constitution of the committee'.[22] I am inclined to think that this analogue tells us more about Oakeshott's view of the world than about the world. Who cares, to put it bluntly, what the rules of cricket are? Certain modifications of, say, the lbw rule may provide special opportunities for bowlers with a particular technique to cramp the style of certain batsmen, but on the whole any rule leaves teams as well placed in relation to one another as they were before. It is in the nature of rules of a game (and therefore makes them highly tendentious paradigms of political decisions in general) that any rule, so long as it is simply applied impartially, defines a fair procedure for determining who wins. It is therefore less important what the rules are than that everyone plays by the same ones. I venture to suggest that if the MCC claimed jurisdiction over any matter that has anything in common with the normal stuff of politics—if, for example, it were able to levy a royalty on every game of first-class cricket played in the world and the question arose how the money raised were to be spent—it would not be long before the demand would arise for the body charged with disbursing the funds to be put upon some kind of representative basis.

Why is this? It would be easy to say that 'democratic ideology' is triumphant and therefore provides the only basis for general consent. But it would be so easy as to be worth very little. The use of 'ideology'

---

[22] Michael Oakeshott, *On Human Conduct* (Oxford: Clarendon Press, 1975), 154n.

in this context is an essentially irrationalist one and implies that some other basis of legitimacy with a different content altogether might just as well have become established in the world. Such a view would ignore the very real advantages of competitive election as a rationale for placing the government in one set of hands rather than another.

The point I am driving at was put more effectively than by anyone else I have come across by Sydney Smith in one of his 'Four Speeches on the Reform Bill'. The Reform Bill in question was that of 1832 and it was of course (considered in relation to universal suffrage) a very limited measure. But the logic of his argument shows how difficult it is to find any determinate stopping-place short of universal suffrage.

It is not enough that a political institution works well practically: it must be defensible; it must be such as will bear discussion, and not excite ridicule and contempt. It might work well for aught I know, if, like the savages of Onelashka, we sent out to catch a king: but who could defend a coronation by chase? Who can defend the payment of £40,000, for the three-hundredth part of the power of Parliament, and the resale of this power to Government for places to the Lord Williams and Lord Charles's, and others of the Anglophagi? Teach a million of the common people to read—and such a government (work it ever so well) must perish in twenty years. It is impossible to persuade the mass of mankind that there are not other and better methods of governing a country.[23]

The most important point about a system of election for representatives is that it provides an intelligible and determinate answer to the question why these particular people, rather than others perhaps equally well or better qualified, should run the country. If people can be induced to believe in the divine right of kings or the natural superiority of a hereditary ruling caste, it may be possible to gain general acceptance for rule based on the appropriate ascribed characteristics. But once the idea of the natural equality of all men has got about, claims to rule cannot be based on natural superiority. Winning an election is a basis for rule that does not conflict with natural equality. Indeed, it might be said to flow from it. For if quality is equal (or, as Hobbes more exactly put it, quality must be taken to be equal as a condition of peace) the only differentiating factor left is quantity. Once we supply the premiss of natural equality, we can see why it seemed obvious to Locke that the majority 'necessarily' constitutes the 'greater force'. Justification for rule in terms of the specific achievements of the government lacks this essential feature of determinacy.

---

[23] Sydney Smith, *The Selected Writings of Sydney Smith*, ed. W. H. Auden (London: Faber and Faber, 1957), 346.

Others can always claim that their performance would be superior, and who is to say it would not be?

To express any confidence in the possibility of democratic institutions continuing to rest on a basis of mass acceptance is, of course, highly unfashionable. Theorists of the left and the right agree that the jig is up. There is a 'legitimation crisis' in the advanced capitalist societies: they have become 'ungovernable', governments are 'overloaded' by popular demands, and the 'economic contradictions of democracy' are revealing themselves ever more starkly.[24] Events may indeed prove these Cassandras right, but my own view is that they are grotesquely over-reacting to the disequilibriating effects of a sudden fourfold increase in the price of crude oil.

It seems to me that the only perspective from which things could be said to look sticky now for democratic institutions would be one from which the 1950s and the first half of the 1960s constituted the norm. But that period of prosperity and peace among all the advanced capitalist economies was historically unique. (I am not denying that favourable objective conditions help.) A simple exercise is to run back decade by decade to the beginnings of universal suffrage in each of the major countries and to ask in how many of these periods (except the 1950s) democratic institutions looked more firmly established in popular sentiment than they are today.

It is, of course, true that there is a tension between the formal political equality of one-man-one-vote and the inequalities of wealth, status, and actual power over the lives of others (especially their working lives) generated by the other institutions of these societies. But this is hardly a new thought: it was a commonplace to Victorian conservatives and was elaborated by ideologues of the privileged strata like Maine and Lecky. The tension is still there but I see no sign that the forces that have kept it within bounds until now are losing their efficacy.

I conclude, therefore, that there is a case for democratic procedures over and above the instrumental one developed in section III. It is related to the majority principle in one way: it makes use of the idea

---

[24] As a representative sample see: Jürgen Habermas, *Legitimation Crisis* (Boston, Mass.: Beacon Press, 1975); Alan Wolfe, *The Limits of Legitimacy: Political Contradictions of Contemporary Capitalism* (New York: The Free Press, 1977); Michel Crozier, Samuel P. Huntington, and Joji Watanuki, *The Governability of Democracies* (New York: New York University Press for the Trilateral Commission, 1975); Anthony King, 'Overload: Problems of Government in the 1970s', *Political Studies*, 23 (1975), 290–5; Samuel Brittan, 'The Economic Contradictions of Democracy', *British Journal of Political Science*, 5 (1975), 129–59; James O'Connor, *The Fiscal Crisis of the State* (New York: St Martin's Press, 1973); and Richard Rose and Guy Peters, *Can Government Go Bankrupt?* (New York: Basic Books, 1973).

that decision by majority has a natural attractiveness about it. But it really differs quite fundamentally. The majority principle, as I defined it following a whole body of 'social choice' literature, is that outcomes are legitimate if they correspond to majority preference and illegitimate if they run counter to majority preference. Democratic procedures are justified (to the extent that they can be) in terms of their tendency to bring about outcomes that correspond to majority preference. In contrast, the argument in this section has been that elections are a way of picking out, without reference to inherently arguable claims to superior competence, a unique set of rulers.

The implication is, I think, that a qualification has to be added to the results arrived at in section III. Laws that systematically violate the vital interests of a minority are still devoid of any claims to obedience except prudential ones. But we must expand the sphere of prudential reasons beyond sanctions to encompass long-term consequences. If the price of changing the laws is the collapse of a democratic system, that is a heavy price to pay because it will include the suppression of freedom of publication and political organization. In non-democratic systems, the choice between trying to prevent the government from implementing unjust policies and trying to overthrow the government is a purely tactical one: the only question is which route has the better chance of success and the lower expected cost. In democratic regimes, however, the choice is not purely tactical. There are strong reasons for aiming at a result that leaves the government resting on election but accommodating the interests of the minority as the recognized price of gaining their co-operation.

The course of the argument in this chapter is rather tortuous. I have found, when presenting these ideas in academic gatherings, that many people find difficulty in grasping the distinction between the argument in favour of democratic procedures that I reject and the one that I accept. Let me therefore juxtapose the two in the hope of making the contrast more apparent.

The first argument relates in the first instance to the relation of preferences to policies and only secondarily to institutions such as voting. The notion here criticized is that there is something natural, obvious, or almost inevitable in the principle that the policy put into effect ought to be that corresponding to the majority preference. I accepted the correctness of that claim for the special case of the five people in the railway carriage but went on to suggest that the obviousness of the principle was an artefact of a number of special features either specified or implied in the description of the case. If anything, I was perhaps too lenient with the principle. For we might imagine as alternatives to agreement on a substantive meta-principle (such as the right to breathe uncontaminated air) or some principle of authority (like the one that the Archbishop's decision should be binding) procedural solutions other than the majority principle. For example, the participants might agree in a more 'consociational' spirit to divide up the estimated length of the journey into five equal periods and give each passenger control of one segment.

What I wish to emphasize is, in any case, the difference between the majority principle and the rationale of voting for representatives put forward here in section IV. This argument does, like the first one, invoke the claim that a certain procedure appears natural or obvious. But the assertion in the second case is not that naturalness is in itself a justification for the procedure. Rather it is that, if voting for representatives settles the question of who should rule in a way that claims to superior competence or claims to inherent personal superiority do not, it permits freedom of speech and organization as no other regime does.

# 3

# DOES DEMOCRACY CAUSE INFLATION?

## The Political Ideas of Some Economists

It is not the popular movement, but the travelling of the minds of men who sit in the seat of Adam Smith that is really telling and worthy of all attention.

Lord Acton, letter to Mary Gladstone

Since inflation has ebbed but democratic institutions have not radically changed, some economists may prefer to forget one of their major themes of the 1970s, namely, the view that inflation is the inevitable outcome of the normal functioning of democratic political institutions. But even if the economists who maintained this view are bashful, it is worth recalling their analysis and, at least retrospectively, analysing the premises that might once again be appealed to if high levels of inflation recur. Since none of this group has himself recanted, it seems reasonable to assume that their doctrines and prescriptions still stand. These economists proposed the simple view that political authorities create or permit inflation by their control of fiscal and monetary policy. Applying the standard methodology of economics to the analysis of political phenomena, this new school of 'political economists' (which is represented in this discussion principally by the work of James Buchanan and the Virginia School) went on to propose that central aspects of economic policymaking be removed from the control of elected representatives, such as governments in parliamentary systems.[1]

[1] See William D. Nordhaus, 'The Political Business Cycle', *Review of Economic Studies*, 42 (1975), 169–90; C. Duncan MacRae, 'A Political Model of the Business Cycle', *Journal of Political Economy*, 85 (1977), 239–63; Richard E. Wagner, 'Economic Manipulation for Political Profit', *Kyklos*, 30 (1977), 395–410; Assar Lindbeck, 'Stabilization Policy in Open Economies with Endogenous Politicians', *American Economic Review*, 66 (1976, *Papers and Proceedings*, 1975), 1–19; Michael Parkin, 'The Politics of Inflation', *Government and Opposition*, 10 (1975), 189–202; Larry A. Sjaastad, 'Why Stable Inflations Fail: An Essay in Political Economy', in Michael Parkin and George Zis (eds.), *Inflation in the World Economy* (Manchester: Manchester University Press, 1976), 73–95; James M. Buchanan and Richard E. Wagner, *Democracy in Deficit: The Political Legacy of Lord Keynes* (San Diego: Academic Press, 1977); Samuel Brittan, *The Economic*

Perhaps the remedy would have been worse than the disease; but, to establish that, it must first be determined whether the disease—what has been termed the 'democratic distemper'—was really so serious.

To decide that, three questions have to be asked. First, how important is it to ensure that inflation cannot occur? How bad are its economic, social, and political consequences? (The alternatives also have consequences.)[2] Second, is it true that representative institutions have built into them an inevitable tendency towards inflation? Third, in the light of the answers to these questions, how should the proposals for constitutional change that have been put forward be assessed? Because constitutional changes are relatively irrevocable, prudence demands that the arguments in their favour be subjected to the strictest scrutiny.

The methodological techniques that the expounders of the new political economy bring to the analysis of political phenomena constitute a serious encumbrance. Their adherence to a vulgarized Popperian methodology, particularly as represented in Milton Friedman's paper 'The Methodology of Positive Economics',[3] requires, as a matter of faith, that the assumptions used in theory-building not be subjected to direct test. A theory is taken to be true if its implications fit the facts sufficiently, and no effort is made to check the adequacy of the story it tells about the phenomena. In practice, no serious attempt is ever made to determine whether or not fundamental assumptions should be abandoned.[4] Since it is likely that, with enough ingenuity, *some* theory can be found that will incorporate them and give rise to implications that fit the facts sufficiently, the assumptions are in effect beyond challenge.

---

*Consequences of Democracy* (London: Temple Smith, 1977), 223–89, 'The Economic Contradictions of Democracy', *British Journal of Political Science*, 5 (1975), 129–59, and 'Can Democracy Manage an Economy?' in Robert Skidelsky (ed.), *The End of the Keynesian Era: Essays on the Disintegration of the Keynesian Political Economy* (New York: Holmes and Meier, 1977), 41–9.

[2] 'It may be true that if demand is sufficiently restricted, and unemployment correspondingly increased, collective bargaining will in time no longer operate to force up wages and prices, while other sources of inflation will prove unimportant. But restrictive policies can have other consequences that operate even more powerfully: governments may fall from power and entire societies be torn apart before inflation dies away. It is necessary, therefore, to weigh up the *total* consequences of policies recommended.' Alec Cairncross, *Inflation, Growth and International Finance* (State University of New York Press, 1975), 14.

[3] Milton Friedman, *Essays in Positive Economics* (Chicago: University of Chicago Press, 1953), 3–43 (Friedman does not refer to any philosopher later than John Maynard Keynes's father). See Brian Barry, 'On Analogy', *Political Studies*, 23 (1975), 208–24; Martin Hollis and Edward J. Nell, *Rational Economic Man: A Philosophical Critique of Neo-Classical Economics* (Cambridge: Cambridge University Press, 1975).

[4] Friedman, *Essays*, pp. 22–3, virtually admits this.

If the orthodox methodology of contemporary economics is a cut-down version of a fifty-year-old development in logical positivist doctrine,[5] the official theory of value subscribed to by most economists is an even more antique form of logical positivism. Many economists still treat 'value judgements' (statements, for example, that one form of society is better than another) as 'preferences', and follow Lionel Robbins in believing that the interpersonal comparison of utilities is impossible.[6] Since Kenneth Arrow has shown that the aggregation of ordinal preferences into a 'social welfare function' is impossible,[7] the only criterion left is unanimity of preferences, that is, roughly, Pareto optimality.[8] The consequences of professing an irrationalist theory of value are that economists do not engage in open discussion of questions of value. Rather, they smuggle their values into their analyses, where they are immune to rational criticism.

I   ECONOMISTS' EVALUATION OF INFLATION

The orthodox approach of welfare economics has had great difficulty in identifying a welfare loss from inflation at all commensurate with that often loosely attributed to it. In terms of static allocational inefficiency, the only welfare cost that can be identified is that people keep smaller cash balances than they would choose to do in the absence of inflation, because they are, in effect, losing money by holding cash. Even this is not an unmitigated welfare loss, for taxes have to be raised somehow and a tax on cash holdings (which is one way of looking at inflation) is as good a tax as any other. An economist with impeccably orthodox credentials has therefore suggested that an inflation rate of, say, 5 per cent might be regarded as beneficial, in the 'second-best' world where taxation is a fact of life.[9]

---

[5] See Karl Popper, *Logik der Forschung* (Vienna: Julius Springer, 1935).

[6] Lionel Robbins, *An Essay on the Nature and Significance of Economic Science*, 2nd edn. (London: Macmillan, 1969).

[7] Kenneth Arrow, *Social Choice and Individual Values* (New Haven: Yale University Press, 1951; 2nd edn. 1963).

[8] This of course brings the economists' theory of value into contact with the venerable tradition of social contract theory. The connection has been made explicit by the Virginia School. See James M. Buchanan and Gordon Tullock, *The Calculus of Consent: Logical Foundations of Constitutional Democracy* (Ann Arbor: University of Michigan Press, 1962); James M. Buchanan, *The Limits of Liberty: Between Anarchy and Leviathan* (Chicago: University of Chicago Press, 1975). For a critique, see Brian Barry, 'Review', *Theory and Decision*, 12 (1980), 95–106.

[9] J. S. Flemming, *Inflation* (London: Oxford University Press, 1976), 112. David Laidler and Michael Parkin discuss inflation as a tax on money balances in 'Inflation: A Survey', *Economic Journal*, 85 (1975), 791–4.

Leaving aside the alleged social and political by-products of inflation, it is hard to maintain that the consequences of inflation are
enormously serious, especially when that level of inflation is arrived at
over a number of years so as to allow for some adjustments of
expectations along the way. The difficulties with mortgage repay-
ments, long-term leases, and so on, are not negligible, but there are
expedients available for dealing with them. (There is no reason why
people should not be assured a positive inflation-discounted return on
their savings.) And although these expedients deal with the distributive effects of inflation only in a rough-and-ready way, the residual
distributive effects seem relatively small when set beside problems like
unemployment and the underemployment of resources generally,
pollution, depletion of resources, and so on.[10]

Hyperinflation is another matter, in that a market economy breaks
down if money has to be spent within a few hours before it loses its
value. But experience suggests that there is no inexorable development of hyperinflation from ordinary inflation. In spite of quite severe
inflation in most member countries of the Organization for Economic
Co-operation and Development (OECD) in the 1970s, none let it get
out of control and accelerate in the classic pattern of hyperinflation.

Even if the monetarists are right and there is no trade-off between
unemployment and inflation in long-run equilibrium, there is no
reason for expecting to get into long-run equilibrium. Meanwhile, the
ill-effects of anti-inflationary policies are quite certain. There are clear
losers—those who would be thrown out of employment (or who
would lose overtime or piecework bonuses).[11] The anxieties of being
unemployed may be partially allayed by institutional change (high
unemployment benefits); nevertheless, unemployment has profoundly disrupting social and psychological effects that even full
replacement of income would do nothing to obviate. It is not therefore
necessary to depict governments as composed of cynical manipulators
to explain why they have tended to choose economic policies that have
inflation as one of their consequences. A sincere desire for the public
good and a rational preference for the avoidance of certain evils in the
near future rather than the avoidance of speculative evils in the distant

---

[10] Harold T. Shapiro, 'Inflation in the United States', in Lawrence B. Krause and Walter S.
Salant (eds.), *Worldwide Inflation: Theory and Recent Experience* (Washington, DC: Brookings
Institution, 1977), 290.

[11] The studiously non-controversial Congressional Budget Office suggested that in order to
achieve a reduction of 1 per cent in the rate of inflation by 1980 it would be necessary to cut the
Federal budget, beginning in 1978, by an amount that would decrease GNP by 3 to 4 per cent in
each year (though the loss would decrease after peaking in 1979). US Congressional Budget
Office, *Recovery with Inflation* (Washington, DC: CBO, 1977), 36, and Table 2, p. 37.

future would have led in the same direction. The assumption underlying much of the new political economy—that the economic outcomes of democratic politics diverge sharply from those that would be brought about by a wholly benevolent dictator—is not self-evident.

## Inflation as 'moral rot'

Is there perhaps some evil of inflation so serious that economists might be justified in seeking institutional changes (such as the insulation of the central bank from political pressure) that would ensure a lower inflation rate than that produced by the workings of a competitive political system, responsive in broad terms to popular preferences? Are the citizens of the Western democracies so corrupt that their preferences can legitimately be disregarded in the higher pursuit of saving them from themselves?

To some academic economists, and to many social critics and journalists, inflation is both a reflection of and a major contributor to a general collapse of values. Buchanan and Wagner identified a '*zeitgeist*, a "spirit of the times" . . . at work in the 1960s and 1970s', that they described as 'a generalized erosion in public and private manners, increasingly liberalized attitudes toward sexual activities, a declining vitality of the Puritan work ethic, deterioration in product quality, explosion of the welfare rolls, widespread corruption in both the private and the governmental sector, and, finally, observed increases in the alienation of voters from the political process.' And they contended that inflation 'plays some role in reinforcing several of the observed behavior patterns. Inflation destroys expectations and creates uncertainty; it increases the sense of felt injustice and causes alienation. It prompts behavioral responses that reflect a generalized shortening of time horizons. "Enjoy, enjoy"—the imperative of our time—becomes a rational response in a setting where tomorrow remains insecure and where the plans made yesterday seem to have been made in folly.'[12] They cited in support Wilhelm Röpke's even more apocalyptic view that 'inflation, and the spirit which nourishes it and accepts it, is merely the monetary aspect of the general decay of law and respect for law. . . . Laxity about property and laxity about money are very closely bound up together; in both cases what is firm, durable, earned, secured and designed for continuity gives place to what is fragile, fugitive, fleeting, unsure and ephemeral.'[13]

[12] Buchanan and Wagner, *Democracy in Deficit*, pp. 64–5.
[13] Ibid. 65 n. 16, quoting Wilhelm Röpke, *Welfare, Freedom and Inflation* (Tuscaloosa, Al.: University of Alabama Press, 1964), 70.

Similarly, the editor of *The Times*, William Rees-Mogg, saw inflation as part of a general twentieth-century decay: 'The damage that Dr. Spock did was that he destroyed confidence in discipline for children; the damage that Freud did was that he destroyed belief in the necessity of discipline in sexual conduct; the damage of the explosion of science was that it destroyed discipline in man's dealings with nature.'[14] (The remedy, according to Rees-Mogg, was God and Gold in equal doses.) He was seconded by another conservative journalist, Robert Moss, who argued that 'the recent trends that are pulling us towards strato-inflation are related both to an inflation of expectations in the post-1945 consumer society, and to a loss of broader concepts of patriotism and citizenship. . . . The psychology of inflation is deeply implanted'.[15]

The fact that academic economists accepted this sort of diagnosis so readily just reflects the tendency of the Friedmanite 'methodology of positive economics' to divide the social realm sharply into one area where the deductive method can be put to work and another that is subject to no canons of science and is therefore open to unconstrained speculation.

Fortunately, data as well as assertions exist. A political scientist, Ronald Inglehart, has also studied the question of whether a fundamental shift in values is occurring in Western countries.[16] His findings support the notion of a generational shift in values away from hard work, self-discipline, production, public order, patriotism, and the like, towards such values as self-expression, self-realization, political participation, and concern with the 'quality of life'. His survey of post-materialist attitudes in the European Economic Community and the United States in 1973 produced a close correlation between the first set of values and a high priority on control of inflation. There was a strong relation between the proportion in each category of materialist interests and in ranking by age-group in the EEC countries.[17] In a simpler survey, respondents were asked to choose the two most desirable of four aims. Two pairs (of a possible six pairs) accounted for half the responses: 'maintaining order in the nation' combined with 'fighting rising prices', and 'giving the people

---

[14] William Rees-Mogg, *The Reigning Error: The Crisis in World Inflation* (London: Hamish Hamilton, 1974), 103. (In 1988, Rees-Mogg, now ennobled, was given the job by a grateful government of keeping smut off Britain's television screens.)

[15] Robert Moss, *The Collapse of Democracy* (London: Sphere Books, 1977), 69–70.

[16] Ronald Inglehart, *The Silent Revolution: Changing Values and Political Styles among Western Publics* (Princeton, NJ: Princeton University Press, 1977).

[17] Ibid. 54.

more say in important political decisions' combined with 'protecting freedom of speech'.[18] The first are termed materialist and the second post-materialist; the distribution of responses by age cohort is shown in Table 3.1 on page 68. In the post-materialist columns the growth of this outlook among the younger generation is striking: in West Germany and France it rises from a negligible 1 to 2 per cent among the oldest to 19 to 20 per cent among the youngest age-group.[19]

Suppose that the generational change is sufficiently established to be accepted. The under-thirties show a higher incidence of a complex of attitudes, including attributing a relatively low priority to fighting inflation. To that extent, the thesis of the emergence of a new *Zeitgeist* is confirmed (though even among the most susceptible age-group in only a fifth or less). But there are no good grounds for accepting the assertion that inflation is a significant factor in creating and reinforcing this *Zeitgeist*. It seems to be the experience of affluence rather than the experience of inflation that is responsible for post-materialist values. For example, France since 1948 has been persistently one of the most inflationary countries and West Germany one of the least, but both have undergone economic transformation and the two display remarkably similar profiles of age-related attitudes. It is surely reasonable to suppose that the quest for more control of one's life and for a satisfying rather than a merely lucrative job will be a result of experiencing the diminishing returns of affluence and not of a change in the numeraire. A check in the rate of inflation cannot be expected to reverse the process of change in values—except in so far as the measures taken to reduce the rate of inflation produced such a decline in production and employment as to raise the priority of material goods and economic security again.

What conservatives decry as a 'collapse of values' seems to be more accurately depicted as the result of two forces: a decline in respect for established hierarchies, which has been working itself out for several

---

[18] Ibid. 21.

[19] Inferring a change in values from one generation to another on the basis of cross-sectional data is, of course, always suspect. Inglehart suggests that the difference in distributions of materialist and post-materialist values between generations should be greater the more contrasting their experiences. Thus, intergenerational difference is least in Britain and the United States, neither of which has experienced defeat or change of regime in this century, and both of which were relatively wealthy countries in 1945 and have had a moderate rate of economic growth. Conversely, in Germany the older generation can remember the hyperinflation of the 1920s, the mass unemployment of the 1930s, and the ruin and chaos immediately after the war, while those in the youngest cohort have known only the prosperity of the post-1948 'economic miracle'. The differences between generations in Germany are extreme. For other countries also the degree of difference between generations correlates well with difference in the life experience of the generations.

TABLE 3.1. Materialist attitudes among respondents to surveys in ten countries, 1972–1973[a]

| Country | Percentage point spread across age groups | Percent in age-group | | | | | | | | | | |
|---|---|---|---|---|---|---|---|---|---|---|---|---|
| | | 19–28 | | 29–38 | | 39–48 | | 49–58 | | 59–68 | | Over 68 | |
| | | Materi-alist | Post-ma-terialist | Materi-alist | Post-ma-terialist | Materi-alist | Post-ma-terialist | Materi-alist | Post-ma-terialist | Materi-alist | Post-ma-terialist | Materi-alist | Post-ma-terialist |
| W Germany | 56 | 24 | 19 | 39 | 8 | 46 | 5 | 50 | 5 | 52 | 7 | 62 | 1 |
| France | 51 | 22 | 20 | 28 | 17 | 39 | 9 | 39 | 8 | 50 | 3 | 55 | 2 |
| Italy | 42 | 26 | 16 | 41 | 8 | 42 | 7 | 48 | 6 | 49 | 4 | 57 | 5 |
| Belgium | 39 | 18 | 23 | 20 | 17 | 22 | 10 | 25 | 10 | 39 | 3 | 39 | 5 |
| Ireland | 36 | 24 | 13 | 31 | 9 | 41 | 6 | 37 | 6 | 45 | 3 | 51 | 4 |
| Netherlands | 35 | 27 | 14 | 22 | 17 | 28 | 9 | 40 | 10 | 41 | 12 | 51 | 5 |
| Denmark | 34 | 33 | 11 | 34 | 9 | 47 | 4 | 44 | 5 | 48 | 4 | 58 | 2 |
| Switzerland | 32 | 27 | 15 | 26 | 17 | 30 | 15 | 35 | 9 | 34 | 6 | 50 | 6 |
| USA | 26 | 24 | 17 | 27 | 13 | 34 | 13 | 32 | 10 | 37 | 6 | 40 | 7 |
| UK | 17 | 27 | 11 | 33 | 7 | 29 | 6 | 30 | 7 | 36 | 5 | 37 | 4 |

[a] Countries ranked by spread across age-groups.
Source: Inglehart, The Silent Revolution, Table 2.2, pp. 36–7.

centuries in the West, and an extension to wider sections of the population of aspirations for autonomy and personal fulfilment. There is no reason for supposing that these profound modifications in the expectations that people hold about the conditions of co-operation with others are affected much by the experience of inflation.

It might be argued that there is indeed a causal connection that runs in the opposite direction to that so far considered. Existing industrial and governmental structures that are not going to adapt to new demands may well respond to abnormal discontent by allowing pay increases, thus buying time even at the expense of increased inflation further down the road. The big (and inflationary) pay rises for French workers that the government oversaw following the events of May 1968 constitute a clear example of this. Or inflation may occur as a result of the weakening of group leaders' authority to bind their members to accept deals that have been struck in their names, thus unleashing competition between groups. In the Netherlands, for example, the elaborate system of parcelling out state functions among corporate groups has come under increasing attack and has in some matters begun to crumble. The Swiss almost carried an initiative to restrict drastically the number of foreign workers, in the face of opposition from almost every established organization, including all the political parties. In Norway, the referendum on joining the EEC produced a majority vote against, in spite of support for entry from most major organizations, including the political parties with all but a handful of seats in the parliament. In economic affairs high-level agreements on national wage and salary rates have been increasingly strained—even in Sweden, normally regarded as the country in which comprehensive national bargaining is most highly developed. To the extent that trade union leaders cannot bind their followers to a programme of mutual restraint, one might expect an increase in the rate of inflation, as different groups scramble for relative advantage.

If there is a causal connection running from sociocultural change to inflation, rather than the other way round, the possibility must be seriously entertained that inflation acts as a safety valve, blunting the impact of incompatible demands. Even if that is going too far, it may be that inflation is a by-product of other things that are happening and cannot be held responsible for them.

*Inflation as a cause of regime collapse*

However unreasonable the intense feelings against change may be, they can, under certain conditions, give rise to the overthrow of a democratic system and its replacement by a regime such as that of Franco, the Greek colonels, or the Chilean junta. In this sense, it is true that inflation poses risks to the continuance of democratic institutions. Those who adhere to the idea of a collapse of values tend to conclude that nothing can be hoped for from democracy, since democratic institutions result in public policies that reflect the majority outlook. Support for some kind of authoritarian regime is a natural (if not often acknowledged) implication of their views. The tension between economic freedom (as understood by the proponents of the market) and political freedom (the freedom to publish, to organize, and to vote governments out of office) goes back over a century. (See further on this chapter 20 below.) Milton Friedman was not the first enthusiast for the market to endorse a collection of thugs, with his support for Pinochet. Vilfredo Pareto, an admirer of Mussolini, was a distinguished predecessor.

Some observers who profess to favour the continuation of democratic institutions still express fear that inflation will result in the replacement of a democratic regime by one less benign. The lesson to be drawn, however, is not that inflation and other things that arouse the violent dislike of reactionary army officers are political evils; rather, that it is important not to have an officer caste drawn from a narrow sector perpetuating an ideology in which the military stand as saviours of 'the nation' from the politicians. Where such a state of affairs exists it is difficult to change it: for every Cárdenas there are many Allendes. And where it cannot be changed, or the risk of a counterstroke is too great, an honourable political leader may judge that it is better to run a hobbled democratic government than to provoke a coup. If so, then the things that are liable to result in a coup—whether they be long hair, rock music, strikes, or inflation —become things to be avoided for political reasons.

There is, however, another commonly expressed idea that inflation in a democratic system leads to massive popular discontent and thus to the collapse of the regime. The distinctive feature of the theory is that the overthrow would apparently be met with popular support, or at least acquiescence. Supporters of this hypothesis tend to rely heavily on the German hyperinflation of 1922–4 and the success of the Nazis in 1933 in securing almost half the popular vote. But the Weimar

Republic, despite the fact that it was never accepted by the leaders of most of the powerful institutions and early alienated many of its natural supporters in the working class, survived the trauma of the Great Inflation. And the Nazis failed miserably in their attempts to attract support in the early 1920s. The obvious candidate for an economic explanation for their success is surely the very high level of unemployment in the early 1930s. The lesson to be drawn would thus seem to be that massive unemployment rather than hyperinflation is the serious threat to democratic institutions.[20]

None of this is to deny that hyperinflation is normally followed by the collapse of the regime under which it occurred. In this respect, the Weimar case is an exception. But the explanation is that the hyperinflation is one of the most dramatic signs of the government's failure. Hyperinflation typically occurs when government, because of war, revolution, the antagonism of powerful groups in the society, or the incapacity of its own administrative apparatus, is unable to collect sufficient taxes to finance its expenditures and therefore resorts to the printing press. It thereby buys a year or two of time, but it would be quite misleading to say that the hyperinflation led to its eventual downfall.[21]

The difficulty is one that bedevils much analysis in social science, namely, that of impossible counterfactuals. Roughly speaking, to say that *a* caused *b* is to say that, if everything else had been the same except that *a* had not occurred, *b* would not have happened either.[22] In many instances it makes perfectly good sense to pose questions about politics in those terms—for example, 'Would Nixon have completed his term of office if the Watergate break-in had not been discovered?' The question can properly be posed because the possibility that the 'plumbers' might have been less sloppy or the guards less vigilant is not inconsistent with the way the world works. But questions about the effects of large-scale social phenomena are liable to run into trouble.

John Stuart Mill set this point out in the course of his argument that the methods of agreement and difference are inapplicable to social

---

[20] For recognition that the collapse of Weimar followed on unemployment, but an argument that inflation had already eroded its democratic centre, see Brian Griffiths, *Inflation: The Price of Prosperity* (New York: Holmes and Meier, 1976), 177.

[21] For an analysis on these lines of the Indonesian hyperinflation of 1965–6 (in which President Sukarno lost power), see Dudley Jackson, H. A. Turner, and Frank Wilkinson, *Do Trade Unions Cause Inflation?* (Cambridge: Cambridge University Press, 1972), 52–4.

[22] See J. L. Mackie, *The Cement of the Universe: A Study of Causation* (London: Oxford University Press, 1974), 29–58.

phenomena.[23] His example—the effect of a protective tariff on a country's prosperity—is precisely the kind of association between two macro-level variables that is involved in the question about the relation between inflation and regime collapse. 'Two nations which agreed in everything except their commercial policy would agree also in that. Differences of legislation are . . . effects of pre-existing causes.'[24] Similarly, it does not in general make sense to ask what would have happened if everything else had been the same in a country except the inflation rate.[25]

Especially in Latin America inflation has been widely understood as a way of accommodating conflict by displacing an explicit zero-sum conflict over the distribution of the social product into a more loosely structured scramble for competitive advantage. Of course, at some point (which has been suggested to lie at an inflation rate of about 50 per cent per annum), 'demands develop for drastic government action',[26] and one consequence may well be the fall of the regime and its replacement by a more repressive one, either as a prelude to stabilization or as a reaction to the unpopularity of the government's efforts at stabilization. None of this entails the view—which members of the monetarist school are fond of attributing to others—that inflation is 'caused' by conflict, as if the supply of money had nothing to do with it. To be sure, though, inflation may be a response to conflict—including in this a response by the monetary authorities.

## From interests to preferences

It has so far been proposed that there is no objective basis for the scaremongering of those who would like to use inflation as the occasion for removing economic policymaking from the province of ordinary politics. It might be argued, however, that inflation is so unpopular with the public that the institutions of democracy must

[23] John Stuart Mill, *A System of Logic: Ratiocinative and Inductive* (University of Toronto Press, 1974), bk. 6, ch. 7. Most social scientists whom I have polled informally have the impression that Mill *advocated* the use of these methods in the social sciences! One eminent political scientist has cited 'the influence of J. S. Mill's *Logic*' as one of the main reasons why 'the comparative observation of unmanipulated cases could ever have come to be regarded as any sort of equivalent of experimental method in the physical sciences.' Harry Eckstein, 'Case Study and Theory in Political Science', in Fred I. Greenstein and Nelson W. Polsby (eds.), *Handbook of Political Science*, vol. vii: *Strategies of Inquiry* (Reading, Mass.: Addison-Wesley, 1975), 117.

[24] Mill, *Logic*, bk. 6, ch. 7, p. 882.

[25] For a sophisticated contemporary treatment of counterfactuals, see Jon Elster, *Logic and Society: Contradictions and Possible Worlds* (Chichester: Wiley, 1978), ch. 6. I have criticized some aspects of Elster's treatment in Brian Barry, 'Superfox', *Political Studies*, 28 (1980), 136–43.

[26] Jackson, Turner, and Wilkinson, *Do Trade Unions Cause Inflation?*, p. 35.

therefore have been failing in periods of high inflation. The notion that democratic institutions are justified because they are the most efficient way of ensuring that there is some match between the policy preferences of the citizens and the policy outputs of government naturally appeals to market-oriented economists because it parallels the standard defence of a market economy.[27] The concept of consumer sovereignty—originally imported from the political vocabulary to suggest that consumers, merely by choosing how to spend their money, 'control' producers—has been reimported into politics, to suggest that voters 'control' elected representatives merely by deciding how to dispose their votes. In the process the concept of sovereignty in politics loses its original meaning of the power to give authoritative commands.

On the basis of the theory that political systems are to be judged by the extent to which they produce policy outcomes corresponding to the preferences of voters (ignoring the question of how those preferences are to be aggregated), democratic institutions can be condemned if politicians adopt policies that bring about inflation despite its unpopularity. That opens the way for proposals to limit the fiscal and monetary discretion of elected governments so as to ensure that the citizens get the outcomes that they really want. Requirements of a balanced budget or of a fixed (and small) rate of increase in the money supply can prevent politicians from getting between the people and the outcomes they wish to have brought about. 'Just as an alcoholic might embrace Alcoholics Anonymous, so might a nation drunk on deficits and gorged with government embrace a balanced budget and monetary stability.'[28]

But is inflation so unpopular that its existence can be taken as evidence for the failure of democratic institutions to work as they should? Buchanan and Wagner wonder how the 'ordinary democratic process' can seemingly produce 'a regime of continuous and mounting deficits, with subsequent inflation, along with a bloated public sector [that] can scarcely be judged beneficial to anyone. . . . Where is the institutional breakdown?'[29] This blithely assumes that the size of

---

[27] Arrow, *Social Choice and Individual Values*, p. 5, says that 'voting and the market mechanism' can both be regarded as 'special cases of the more general category of collective social choice'.

[28] Buchanan and Wagner, *Democracy in Deficit*, p. 159. This sample of their rhetoric is by no means atypical.

[29] Ibid. 94. It is a consequence of the antique logical positivist faith that Buchanan is committed officially to the view that no 'value judgement' can be made about any change unless everyone stands to benefit from it, or at any rate some benefit and none lose.

the deficit, of the public sector, and of the rate of inflation are too large by 'social choice' standards. Is this true? It is noteworthy that the bulk of the big increase in government expenditures in the 1970s was accounted for by transfer payments rather than by the government's spending a larger share of the gross national product on collective goods such as defence, roads, and other public services.[30] Since transfer payments simply place spending money in the hands of different people from those who had it before tax (including social security contributions here as a tax), it may be presumed that those who receive such payments do not object, nor do those who would otherwise have to care for them, or those who regard such transfers as just or as socially and politically stabilizing.

Collective expenditures raise more difficult questions. I believe that most people would find it very difficult to estimate the value to them of collective expenditures, still less of alternatives departing widely from the status quo.[31] It is conceivable (as Buchanan and Wagner apparently believe) that, in a fully informed judgement, most people would conclude that they are getting more public provision than they would be willing to pay for. But that could hardly be the case for the United States, where the lack of collective expenditure on the amenities of civilized life is painfully apparent. It would certainly be rash to assert dogmatically that the size of the US budget constitutes evidence for the failure of the democratic process to give people what they want. Of course people dislike paying taxes, but they also (as the tax-cutting enthusiasts often complain) value the services the government provides.

Some people believe that if 'waste' were eliminated from public expenditure, the same services could be provided with less taxation. But by the standards according to which public authorities waste billions, private consumers waste hundreds of billions. If a public authority builds a facility costing 10 million dollars that turns out to be

---

[30] Old age and other insurance plus public welfare payments in the United States rose from $15.3 billion (10 per cent of total government expenditure) in 1960 to $70.5 billion (18 per cent) in 1972; Michel Crozier, Samuel P. Huntington, and Joji Watanuki, *The Crisis of Democracy* (New York: New York University Press for the Trilateral Commission, 1975), Table 2, p. 69. Huntington (ibid., pp. 71–2) notes that these transfer payments are popular with the public, which seems to cast direct doubt on the Buchanan and Wagner conspiracy theory of public expenditure. For the United Kingdom, see James Alt and Alec Chrystal, 'Endogenous Government Behaviour: Overture to a Study of Public Expenditure', Discussion Paper 108 (Colchester: University of Essex, Dept. of Economics, Dec. 1977).

[31] This makes implausible the contention of Albert Breton that political discontent occurs when people are failing to get (in their own estimation) value for money from their taxes: see *The Economic Theory of Representative Government* (London: Macmillan, 1974), 71–3.

unnecessary, or spends 10 million dollars more than the minimum to do the job, that is excoriated as waste; if a million people spend 10 dollars on dud appliances or spend 10 more dollars than they needed to spend to achieve the same end equally effectively, that is regarded as a normal incident of a market society. Of course, it may be possible for either governments or individual consumers to do better, but campaigning against 'waste in government' should be recognized for what it is—campaigning against government.

The assertion that inflation 'can hardly be judged beneficial to anyone' is extraordinarily implausible. To the extent that inflation is purely redistributive, there are (by definition) net gainers as well as net losers. To the extent that it has effects that are not cancelled out in this way, the news is still not all bad. Against the 'welfare loss' arising from people keeping smaller cash balances than they would like and the 'cost' attributable to uncertainty about the future price level must be set the losses of real income and employment created by attempts to reduce inflation by the use of monetary or fiscal policy.

It may nevertheless be said that, whether beneficial or harmful, inflation is provably unpopular and that this is enough to condemn democratic institutions for failing to deliver the outcomes that are desired by citizens. But how exactly are the preferences of ordinary citizens for economic outcomes established? When answers to public opinion poll questions are accepted as evidence that inflation is the country's number one problem, what does that actually mean? It ought to mean that people dislike increases in the price level. But do most people have such a clear grasp of economic concepts as this requires? Such studies of popular understanding of economic terms as have been made suggest that it would be rash to assume so. People often have a hazy idea that, in the absence of inflation, they would have been able to have their latest pay increase and keep its purchasing power through the whole of the subsequent year. Thus, a 10 per cent inflation is looked on as equivalent to a 10 per cent loss of real income. In endorsing the absence (or reduction) of inflation, they are opting for a state of affairs in which nominal incomes would have gone up but prices would not have risen at all, or at any rate as fast as they actually had done.

The deliberate confusion of inflation with a corresponding loss of real income is pervasive. For instance, Michael Blumenthal, less than a week before his dismissal as treasury secretary, was reported to have said that inflation had 'cut sharply into workers' real incomes', and to have warned that 'workers should not try to make up for their loss in income because that would only result in higher prices and worse inflation'.[32] Obviously, if inflation were a gratuitous deduction from an otherwise attainable level of real income, it would be perfectly reasonable to respond by restoring the level of real income. But why should it be assumed that increases in nominal incomes would be wiped out in real terms by price increases if it makes sense to imagine that workers could have had their present money incomes *without* inflation?

Blumenthal's successor, G. William Miller (while he was chairman of the Federal Reserve Board), had similarly beclouded the relation between inflation and real income. '"What is the social benefit for programs that are well meaning but wreck the wealth and incomes of all Americans", Miller asked. "An 8 percent inflation is a $160 billion tax." '[33]

Another, more indirect way of estimating public opinion about inflation is to correlate changes in voting intentions or in support for incumbents with changes in economic indicators. The rates of inflation, unemployment, and change in real income (the usual aggregate indicators used in regression equations) are not, however, brute facts of experience but are mediated by newspaper and television reporting. Even inflation is an abstraction from the movements of all prices. In the absence of standard indexes, people might be aware over time of a trend in prices, but they could no more say whether the inflation rate was 5 per cent or 10 per cent than most people could say whether the outside temperature is 85° or 90° without looking at a thermometer. Until Stanley Jevons constructed the first index,[34] apparently nobody had noticed that the rises in some prices and falls in others between 1845 and 1862 in England had not balanced out, but amounted to an inflationary trend. Aggregate unemployment rates and changes in real income in a society are, obviously, even less plausibly regarded as immediate data of experience.

Scholars who analyse public opinion are well aware that the popularity of incumbents depends on more than the state of the economy. They attempt to remove disturbing factors by introducing dummy variables such as 'Watergate'. But when all the major changes

[32] *New York Times* (14 July 1979).

[33] Patrick R. Oster, *Chicago Sun-Times* (21 Nov. 1978). The notion of the whole loss of purchasing power of a given nominal income as an inflationary 'tax' is, of course, to be distinguished from the more sophisticated idea of inflation as a tax on cash balances.

[34] W. Stanley Jevons, *A Serious Fall in the Value of Gold Ascertained, and Its Social Effects Set Forth* (London: Edward Stanford, 1863), cited in *The Collected Writings of John Maynard Keynes*, vol. x: *Essays in Biography* (London: Macmillan, 1972), 119–22.

in public opinion over a period are 'explained' by political events involving the actions of incumbents or their opponents, one may wonder how much faith to have in assurances that the residual changes should be laid to the account of the economy. And precise claims about the way in which, say, 1 per cent more inflation changes government support, other things being equal, should be viewed cautiously. They never are equal, and that is just what creates the measurement problem in the first place.

Furthermore, there is no reason for expecting that the state of the aggregate economic variables will have a fixed relation to the popularity of incumbents. Even if there is no change in the pleasant-ness or unpleasantness of a particular mix of those variables in people's minds, there may be a change in the degree to which they hold the government responsible for that mix. A government may improve its standing in the polls either by improving the state of the economy or by convincing people that it is doing as well as can be expected. Hence, for example, the (not wholly unreasonable) efforts of successive administrations to attribute much of the responsibility for the stag-flations of 1973–4 and 1979–80 to the Organization of Petroleum Exporting Countries (OPEC). People may (as seems to have hap-pened in Britain) continue to give a fair degree of support to govern-ments that have presided over varying combinations of high inflation, high unemployment, and declining real income that would earlier have been a guarantee of political suicide, not because they like it but because most of the time they despair of any other government doing any better.[35]

This again, however, raises the question of why politicians persist in making inflation more of a bogey than it deserves to be. If the alternative to doing better is to make people feel that what you are doing already is not so bad, why pile on the agony in this gratuitous way? My answer is, admittedly, speculative.

There are three ways in which governments can seek to control inflation in an economy where the key economic decisions remain in private hands. The first is to deflate the economy enough for economic activity to decline to a point at which people will be glad to take jobs at any rate of pay, and prices will begin to fall. A second route is through neocorporatism or, more prosaically, tripartite agreement between business, labour, and government. In the United States particularly there is an obvious problem of ideological incompatibility between

[35] See Alt and Chrystal, 'Endogenous Government Behaviour'.

this kind of high-level fix and the ethos of antitrust, business union-ism, and limited government. But there is also a simple problem of feasibility. The institutions do not exist: no organization can speak for all workers or all employers and deliver on any deal that is struck. The roots of societal collaboration in countries such as Austria and the Netherlands go back centuries; such understandings and practices cannot be wished into existence. Moreover, it may not be an accident that the examples of successful neocorporatism are all countries with only a few million inhabitants. Perhaps the sheer size and diversity of the United States (or even Britain) rule out corporatist solutions.

The only remaining path is exhortation, and it is not therefore surprising that this is the chosen instrument of governments whose concern for popularity (or even governability) leads them to eschew the first course and whose ideological commitments or practical necessities rule out the second. But exhortation requires that the evils of inflation be painted so dramatically that people will voluntarily take less than the market will bear, out of deference to the anti-inflation guidelines. Since inflation is not really evil enough to lead a rational person to pass up the chance of making a buck, creative confusion steps in to fill the gap.

To summarize, I do not believe it is realistic to hope for very exact guidance about public attitudes to inflation. But even if there were agreement that inflation *is* unpopular, does it really follow that the institutions of democracy have been failing to work as they should? I do not believe so. There has, of course, been inflation (at widely differing rates) in all the economically advanced democracies. And governments have taken harsh contractionist measures in the hope of reducing the rate of inflation in their societies—measures that inevit-ably have adverse effects on employment and real income. Assuming that people care about unemployment and loss of real income as well as inflation, have governments in general been too lax about fighting inflation, taking as a criterion the preferences of the public? I can see no reason for thinking that, given the choices, politicians opt for more inflation than their constituents, if they understood the choices, would opt for. My own suspicion is the reverse. I cannot prove it. But I maintain that the whole presumption that underlay the economists' criticism that democracy produces more inflation than the citizens want has rested on extremely shaky foundations.

## II  THE 'NEW POLITICAL ECONOMY'

Economists have attempted to shore up their conclusions with models of electoral behaviour. But the premisses of these also deserve careful scrutiny. In fact, there is not just a single theory of the effects of electoral competition on the rate of inflation, but a family of models that share certain basic features. At the core of their economic component is the idea, whose essentials can be traced back to David Hume's essay 'Of Money', that an increase in the quantity of money has an initial effect of raising the level of economic activity and only later dissipates itself in a general rise in prices. At first the extra money will be used to buy and sell more at the old prices, and only later will the shortfall of supply drive prices up. 'It is easy to trace the money in its progress through the whole commonwealth; where we shall find, that it must first quicken the diligence of every individual, before it increases the price of labour.'[36] In modern terms: people act on expectations about future prices that are doomed to be disappointed, and it is the mismatch that makes for the increase in activity.[37] It follows, then, that the more sluggish the response of inflationary expectations to the actual experience of inflation, the more a government can stimulate the economy in a certain period (for example, in the run-up to an election) without the bulk of the inflationary effects showing until a later period.

The same analysis can be expressed using the device of the Phillips curve—a curve relating the inflation rate (on the vertical axis) and the level of unemployment (on the horizontal axis). The original Phillips curve was plotted from the observed levels of change in money wage rates against unemployment in the United Kingdom from 1861 to 1957.[38] Since the points fell on a single curve, the implication was that to every level of unemployment there corresponded a unique level of increase in money wage rates, and it was hypothesized that this relationship might be accounted for by labour market conditions—the tighter the labour market, the more wages go up.[39] On the view underlying the theory of the politico-economic cycle, however, this

[36] David Hume, *Essays: Moral, Political and Literary* (London: Oxford University Press, 1963), 294.
[37] See the strikingly Humean formulation of the 'new macroeconomics' in D. E. W. Laidler, *Essays on Money and Inflation* (Chicago: University of Chicago Press, 1975), 9–10.
[38] A. W. Phillips, 'The Relation between Unemployment and the Rate of Change of Money Wage Rates in the United Kingdom, 1861–1957', *Economica*, 25 (1958), 283–99.
[39] Richard G. Lipsey, 'The Relation between Unemployment and the Rate of Change of Money Wage Rates in the United Kingdom, 1862–1957: A Further Analysis', *Economica*, 27 (1960), 1–31.

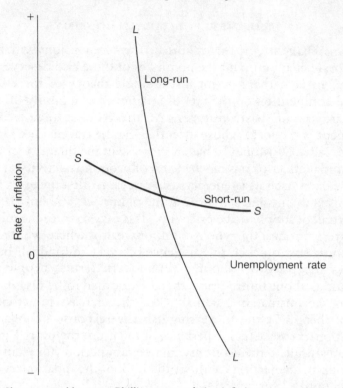

FIG. 3.1. Short-run and long-run Phillips curves relating inflation to unemployment

idea of a single curve must be abandoned for a pair of short-run and long-run Phillips curves. In the short run, a given increase in employment is associated with a smaller increase in wages (or prices) than in the long run, so the short-run Phillips curve has a flatter slope than the long-term one. Thus, in Figure 3.1, if the economy is at the point where the two curves intersect, the shape of the curves implies that the government could reduce unemployment in the short run (by moving the economy leftward along the curve *SS*) at a lower cost in inflation than could be sustained in the long run. Any point below and to the left of the long-run curve *LL* designates a combination of inflation and unemployment that is better than can be achieved in long-run equilibrium, when expectations have had a chance to adjust fully and behaviour is in accord with those expectations.

Conversely, of course, the shapes of the curves also imply that a government wishing to reduce inflation must accept a move to the right along the short-run curve *SS* until expectations have adjusted to the new conditions. Since this means moving to a point above and to the right of the long-run curve, the analysis implies that the economy will in the short term have a worse combination of inflation and unemployment than could be maintained indefinitely once the economy had settled down and expectations had once again adjusted.

Since the long-run curve is a theoretical entity, its shape is subject to theoretical arguments. Modern monetarists suggest that it must be vertical because, at any level of unemployment except one (the 'natural rate' for that economy), the rate of inflation will (in the long run) tend to go up or down. Any stable inflation rate is compatible with the same unemployment rate. The actual rate of inflation itself will be a function of the rate at which the money supply increases in relation to the real national income. While the deduction is logically impeccable, it says nothing about the world. Maybe this 'long run' is never reached; that would mean, for instance, that it is never true that all contracts could be negotiated in such a way as to cancel out the rate of inflation. Even if the long run does exist, it may be measured in decades or even centuries. I therefore follow the convention of making the long-run curve steep but not vertical.

Economists who venture into formal analysis of the political system tend to assume that politicians are conscienceless seekers of power, those in office being prepared to inflict any amount of damage on their countries in order to increase, however fractionally, their share of the vote. At the same time, politicians are assumed (for the purpose of model-building) to be consummately skilful at manipulating the levers of economic policy in pursuit of the end of re-election. Voters, by contrast, are assumed to have barely any cognitive or ratiocinative capacities. They are hardly able to remember the economic record of the current government when election time comes round, and have no ability to anticipate the future (or if they do then somehow this anticipation does not affect their actions). Within the limits set by their defective memories, these zombies react with approval or disapproval to past experience of inflation and unemployment rates and also perhaps to the direction in which those rates are changing; but they do not attempt to make any estimates of the future course of these variables.

If these are the premisses, it is hardly surprising that the conclusion turns out to be that democracy is a flawed form of government. What could anyone hope for from a system characterized by a collection of rogues competing for the favours of a larger collection of dupes? Characteristically, the premisses of politico-economic models developed by economists are baldly stated, with little discussion of their plausibility.[40] And only anecdotal evidence at best is normally adduced in support of the conclusions. Yet, for no democratic country do the economists' assumptions appear to approximate to the truth. Studies of national-level politicians in democratic countries suggest that they are motivated either by policy concerns or by service of a personal kind to their constituents.[41] These 'satisfactions of office' are derived from doing something with the office that is thought to be worthwhile. Moreover, political leaders are very often highly motivated by the thought of their reputations in history and may well be unwilling to pay a price of ignominy for doing something with predictably bad consequences in order to secure some short-run electoral gain. Even Richard Nixon, by risking further obloquy in his subsequent attempts to justify himself, illustrates the importance of reputation to politicians.

Voting studies suggest that voters try to decide which candidates would do better on the issues that they care most about and tend to vote according to the answers they come up with.[42] They also try to form estimates of the competence of alternative candidates, something way beyond the picture of voters merely responding to the 'goodness or badness of the times' by voting for the ins or the outs.[43] If voters sometimes find it hard to make clear judgements about policy differences between candidates, this may reflect the reluctance of politicians to go beyond generalities. When politicians differentiate themselves clearly on an issue, the evidence suggests that voters are usually aware of it.[44]

There is no lack of evidence that voters give extra weight to the

[40] 'Once it is recognized that macroeconomic policy is made by self-interested, not disinterested or other-interested politicians, a new perspective on macroeconomic policy appears, particularly if politicians believe that economic conditions can affect their survival prospects.' Wagner, 'Economic Manipulation', pp. 396–7. (Note: *recognized* rather than *postulated*.)

[41] See Robert D. Putnam, *The Beliefs of Politicians: Ideology, Conflict, and Democracy in Britain and Italy* (New Haven: Yale University Press, 1973).

[42] See V. O. Key, *The Responsible Electorate: Rationality in Presidential Voting, 1936–1960* (Cambridge, Mass.: Harvard University Press, 1966); Samuel Popkin *et al.*, 'Comment: What Have You Done for Me Lately?' *American Political Science Review*, 70 (1976), 779–805.

[43] Popkin *et al.*, 'Comment', show convincingly how much George McGovern was hurt in the 1972 presidential campaign by perceptions of lack of competence following the Eagleton affair.

[44] See Benjamin I. Page, *Choices and Echoes in Presidential Elections: Rational Man and Electoral Democracy* (Chicago: University of Chicago Press, 1978).

more recent performance of the economy, but if they are trying to decide whether to endow the government with another term of office, that does not seem an unreasonable thing to do. After all, for a year or even two, a government can with some legitimacy blame troubles on its predecessor; but the longer it has been in office, the better the case for judging its priorities and capabilities on the current state of the economy. Pessimistic analyses of democratic political economy imply that a government might find it advantageous to stage a massive deflation in its first two years if it could get the unemployment rate down again and combine it with a lower rate of inflation by election day. But I think that kind of gratuitous deflation would be remembered because it would be important information about the way the government worked. The Republicans, to give the most obvious example, were distrusted by many people for a whole generation because of what 1929–32 was taken to have told about their complacency in the face of mass unemployment.

## The political business cycle

The basic idea of the political business cycle can be explained using the apparatus of short-run and long-run Phillips curves. Figure 3.2 illustrates the characteristic clockwise loop that the theory seeks to explain. Starting at $A$, the government brings about a pre-election boom, moving the economy along the short-run curve $S_1S_1$ to $B$. As expectations adapt, this favourable combination of unemployment and inflation cannot be maintained and both deteriorate (presumably after the election) to $C$. But suppose that $C$ is too high in inflation to be popular electorally. The government therefore wishes to bring down the rate of inflation, which it can do only by moving the economy along the short-run curve $S_2S_2$ to $D$. This brings the economy back onto the long-run curve at $A$, but of course if there is time before the next election to stage a boom, it will be possible to get to $B$ for it (assuming the intervening experience has not changed the shape of the short-run curve—an important proviso), and so the cycle is set off again.[45]

In principle the political business cycle thus generated could occur even if the voters based their decisions at election time on the experience of the whole period since the previous election, equally

[45] Compare Nordhaus, 'Political Business Cycle'; Lindbeck, 'Stabilization Policy'; MacRae, 'Political Model'; Bruno S. Frey, *Modern Political Economy* (Chichester: Wiley, 1978).

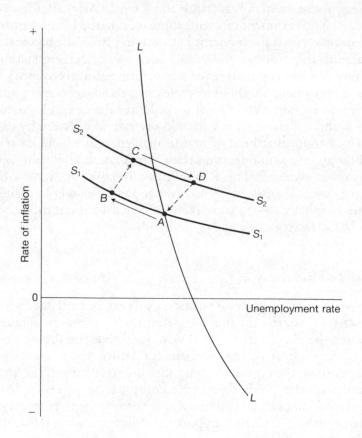

FIG. 3.2. Short-run and long-run Phillips curves and the clockwise loop of the political business cycle

*Note*: Solid arrows represent moves along the short-run Phillips curve brought about by government policy decisions; dashed arrows represent subsequent adjustments in the economy that shift it from one short-run Phillips curve to another.

weighted. The driving mechanism is the possibility of producing an advantageous combination of inflation and unemployment before the election and the assumption that the long-run rate of inflation arising after the election is unpopular. However, it is clear that the motivation for government to engage in the kind of behaviour depicted is enhanced if the voters discount the early years in office when judging the government's economic performance. For then the high unemployment of stage $D$, an 'investment' in getting lower on the long-run curve, carries a reduced electoral penalty.

The simplest test of the notion that a political business cycle is endemic in democracies is to see whether the rates of inflation and unemployment correspond with the predictions of the model. The unemployment rate would be expected to increase as soon after an election as the government could get its policy instruments to work, and then to decline as the next election approached. The course of inflation is more difficult to predict on the basis of the theory. Because the new government inherits inflationary pressures, the rate of inflation should increase to begin with, but then it should decline as the increase in unemployment begins to take effect. However, it is compatible with the theory that inflation should turn upwards again as the government boosts the economy in the run-up to the next election.

Tests of the theory are relatively crude. They focus on the predictions about unemployment, since these are more definite, and make comparisons between a period before the election (one month, one year, two years, or half the inter-election period, for example) and the rest of the time since the preceding election. Bruno Frey has tested the hypothesis that unemployment rates are lower on the average in the two years preceding general elections in Britain and presidential elections in the United States than the rest of the time. Assuming, as Frey[46] and Nordhaus[47] do, that unemployment can be increased quickly after an election and will then decline steadily, the path of unemployment should be saw-toothed, and the average level in the first half of an inter-election period higher than in the second. Frey concludes that for Britain the reverse tended to be true if anything from the mid-1950s to the mid-1970s, while for the United States the evidence points in no particular direction.

Edward Tufte claims better success with trends rather than averages of US unemployment from 1948 to 1976, except in the period of the Eisenhower presidency. He claims that, excluding the 1956 and 1960 elections, unemployment was lower in November of each election year than for most of the preceding twenty-four months—results he describes as 'phenomenal'.[48] But, during the whole of the eight years of the Democratic administrations of Kennedy and Johnson, there is

---

[46] See Frey, *Modern Political Economy*, p. 131.
[47] See Nordhaus, 'Political Business Cycle', p. 185.
[48] Edward R. Tufte, *Political Control of the Economy* (Princeton, NJ: Princeton University Press, 1978), 21.

no sign of any cycle: unemployment fell almost continuously month by month. The Nixon–Ford record Tufte himself describes as 'mixed', which leaves only the Truman administration of 1948–52 and the Nixon 'game plan' of 1968–72, both of which do show the rise and then fall in unemployment. Looking at the unemployment chart armed only with the theory of the political business cycle, it would be very hard to guess where the elections came.

William Nordhaus has tested the proposition that unemployment has a rising trend for the first half of the inter-election period and a falling trend for the second half, against post-war data for nine countries in which 'a cursory examination of macro-economic policies pointed to the possibility that the three conditions for the political business cycle would be met'. His conditions were 'that the government be chosen in periodic competitive elections', that it 'have sufficient economic control and sophistication to move the economy in the desired direction', and that voters should evaluate governments purely on the basis of the performance of the economy since the previous election. But Nordhaus was able to claim only three countries in which 'the coincidence of business and political cycles is very marked', namely, the Federal Republic of Germany, New Zealand, and the United States.[49] (The other countries tested were Australia, Canada, France, Japan, Sweden, and the United Kingdom.)

Even then his conclusions have to be treated with caution, for he misleadingly excludes results that do not negate his theory even if they do not confirm it. Nordhaus gives for each country the number of times the trend was downward in the second half of the inter-election period (confirming the theory) and upward (disconfirming the theory), and the number of times in the first half that the overall trend was upward (confirming the theory) and downward (disconfirming the theory). But the numbers fall far short of the number of post-war elections for some countries. The missing cases are presumably those where the unemployment rate was the same throughout or where it went both up and down in the period. But if the theory of the political business cycle predicts a rising unemployment rate and the unemployment rate does not rise, that is a negative result for the theory.

To see that this makes a difference, take the two countries where Nordhaus claims to have found 'some modest indications of a political cycle', France and Sweden.[50] For France, Nordhaus claims six hits and three misses. But the nine periods add up at the most to eighteen of the

[49] Nordhaus, 'Political Business Cycle', pp. 185, 186.          [50] Ibid. 186.

twenty-six years covered by his study. Thus the confirmatory experiences total at best only twelve of the twenty-six years—hardly a robust demonstration. In the case of Sweden, Nordhaus counts seven hits and five misses, and even this slender margin of success would disappear if the omitted periods were added and counted as failures for the theory.

A deeper problem is the role of caprice in deciding whether to count a set of twenty-four monthly unemployment figures as an upward trend, a downward trend, or neither. Thus, in the 1946–72 period in the United States, Nordhaus counts 1954–6 as a success for the theory, whereas Tufte does not, while Tufte counts 1960–2 and 1966–8 as successes but Nordhaus does not. Both count 1948–52 as a success, but the two-year period following the 1948 election shows a fairly symmetrical rise and fall back to the election-day level, so it hardly represents a rising trend. At any rate, it does not fit Nordhaus's hypothesis of a trend over the two years. Tufte gives unemployment as 'rising' in the two years after the 1960 election, on the basis of an infinitesimal increase in the few months after the election, followed by a substantial drop sustained through the whole of the second year, whereas in 1972 a fall in unemployment extending over almost a year after the election followed by a substantial rise is also described as 'rising'.

In another study Tufte purports to show that, in twenty-seven democracies (some with rather dubious credentials), there were nineteen in which 'short-run accelerations in real disposable income per capita were more likely to occur in election years than in years without elections',[51] between 1961 and 1972. However, a number of the differences appear trivial. For example, in Belgium and also in Ireland real disposable income is shown as having increased in 67 per cent of election years and 63 per cent of non-election years—in both countries, two out of three election years and five out of eight non-election years. Five-eighths represents the closest it is possible to come to two-thirds.

It does look as if there is a political-economic cycle for about half the countries. However, this is a cycle in real disposable income and not necessarily in the overall level of economic activity. It could be consistent with a uniform level of unemployment and economic growth if governments tended to raise taxes early in their term, start building roads, schools, and so forth, in time to have something to

[51] Tufte, *Political Control*, p. 11.

show by the next election, and tried to reduce taxes or give out increased cash benefits in their final year. The cycle would then be one of public as against private consumption.

That the two phenomena are different is suggested by the fact that Nordhaus concluded that 'for the entire period a political cycle seems to be implausible as a description for Australia, Canada, Japan and the U.K.', whereas these four countries are among the most striking examples of the disposable real income cycle, the ratio of percentage increases in election years to those in non-election years being, respectively, 75:29, 100:57, 100:29, and 67:38. Conversely, West Germany, one of Nordhaus's three cases of a 'marked' cycle, does not have a disposable real income cycle: disposable real income is shown as increasing in a slightly smaller proportion of election years than of non-election years.[52] Similarly, Tufte cites a study of the Philippines describing the economy as moving in a 'biennial lurch', with real income rising and falling within the electoral cycle;[53] yet the Philippines are shown in his table as not having increases of real disposable income more frequently in election years.

The Tufte data on changes in real disposable income are, therefore, suggestive in their own right but do not do anything to add to the limited support that the Nordhaus evidence provides for the theory of the political business cycle.

## Politico-economic models of inflation

The theory of the political business cycle leads to the conclusion that inflation and unemployment should both rise immediately after an election, to be followed by a period of high unemployment accompanied by a falling inflation rate, and then a period of falling unemployment extending to the next election accompanied by a rate of inflation that, whether continuing to fall or starting to rise again at the end, is lower than could be combined with that rate of unemployment in the long run. No country shows this complex sequence more than occasionally, which is hardly surprising in view of the exogenous shocks to which an economy is subject. Apparently only a few show even disjointed bits of it.

Even if the theory were better supported than it is, however, it would do nothing to suggest that democracy has any built-in tendency to produce inflation. The rate of inflation, according to the

---

[52] Nordhaus, 'Political Business Cycle', p. 186; Tufte, *Political Control*, p. 12.
[53] Tufte, *Political Control*, pp. 13–14.

theory, will fluctuate within the electoral cycle, but that is not to say either that it will fluctuate around a rising trend or, if around some constant level, whether that level will be high rather than low. The most natural expectation, assuming that vote-maximizing govern-ments manipulate the economy for their own purposes, might seem to be that the rate will fluctuate around the level corresponding to the point on the long-run Phillips curve that is most popular with the electorate. And the clockwise loop described by the economy would cycle around that point.

The combinations of inflation and unemployment that might gain, respectively, 50, 51, and 52 per cent of votes are depicted in Figure 3.3 on p. 90. On the assumption that inflation and unemployment are both disliked, these isopsephic curves slope down to the right;[54] the further they are from the origin, the smaller the share of the popular vote the government will garner if it comes up to an election with the economy in that state. The best point on the long-run Phillips curve for the government to pick is that tangent to the highest attainable isopsephic curve—in Figure 3.3 the point $T$—which gives the govern-ment 51 per cent of the vote. Thus, the rate of inflation will depend on the shapes of the Phillips curve and the isopsephic curve. Other things being equal, the steeper the Phillips curve, the lower the inflation rate that will be chosen by a vote-maximizing government. (If the long-run Phillips curve is vertical, as monetarists claim, the most popular position attainable will be one with stable prices, assuming that isopsephic curves bend back at zero inflation—that is, if voters dislike falling prices as well as rising prices.) And, other things being equal, the steeper the slope of the isopsephic curves the higher the rate of inflation that will maximize votes. For a steep slope would mean that the voters were relatively tolerant of inflation as compared with unemployment.

The conclusion to be drawn is that voters get the rate of inflation that has the most support and that it is not necessarily high or low. And though they might prefer to do without the occasional clockwise loops of the electoral cycle, there is no evidence that the welfare losses from the part of the cycle that lies above and to the right of the long-run Phillips curve outweigh the gains from the part that lies below and to the left of it.[55] In any case, adding the political business cycle would

[54] I call these *isopsephic* curves rather than using the customary but barbarous term, *isovote* curves.

[55] Lindbeck, 'Stabilization Policy', p. 13, says that 'the experiences of recent years have shown how high the economic and social costs are during this deflationary phase of the policy cycle', but he does not mention in the same breath the gains from the good part of the cycle.

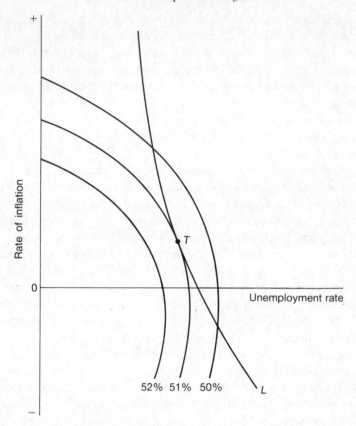

FIG. 3.3. Vote-gathering configurations of inflation and unemployment rates on the long-run Phillips curve

not raise the average level of inflation or cause it to increase over time without limit. Yet economists and journalists and other commentators on current events frequently suggest that the level of inflation produced by electoral competition tends to be higher than most people want, or indeed that there is some inexorable process tending to make the rate of inflation go up over time.

## The Nordhaus model

Critics, it is apparent, are often expressing disapproval for what voters allegedly want (supposedly, higher inflation), rather than solicitude for their failing to get what they want. None the less, William Nordhaus has sought to make a narrower case—namely, that vote-maximizing among a myopic electorate brings about an inflation rate higher than the amount that would get the biggest majority out of all points on the long-run Phillips curve. He has tried, unsuccessfully I believe, to formalize the idea that vote-maximizing by governments produces a level of inflation that is higher than the most popular rate. His model supposes that, if the economy is on the short-run Phillips curve $S_1 S_1$ after an election, the government picks the point $E_1$ on the curve that is at a tangent with the 53 per cent isopsephic curve (Figure 3.4). However, it cannot in fact keep the economy at any point that lies off the long-run Phillips curve, which is by definition the series of points at which any particular mix of unemployment and inflation can remain constant. By the time of the next election, therefore, the position will have deteriorated so that the short-run Phillips curve $S_2 S_2$ applies. The new government will do the best it can electorally, again on the assumption that it cannot shift the short-run curve before the next election, so it will pick the point $E_2$. Since this too is off the long-run Phillips curve, it cannot be maintained for an extended period either, so the economy will slip to the short-run Phillips curve $S_3 S_3$ by the next election. The point of tangency with the highest attainable isopsephic curve, $E_3$, now lies on the long-run Phillips curve. And the story stops there, for no government can do better than pick $E_3$—provided the relations between the macroeconomic variables remain the same. A government, however, can be too pessimistic as well as over-sanguine. If an election is held at a time when the short-run curve $S_5 S_5$ applies, the government will pick $E_5$, and be pleasantly surprised by the move to $S_4 S_4$. It will hence move to $E_4$ and thence to the improved curve $S_3 S_3$ and point $E_3$.

Nordhaus also views the long-run equilibrium point $E_3$ as the solution to a problem in collective choice, the purely myopic point $U_M$ (Figure 3.5). It is the point that would be chosen by the biggest majority if the future were wholly discounted. If the future were not discounted at all, the point that would gain the biggest majority *on average* over an indefinitely long period would be $U_G$, where the isopsephic curve $V_2 V_2$ is at a tangent to the long-run Phillips curve. For, over a long enough period, the cost of getting to that point

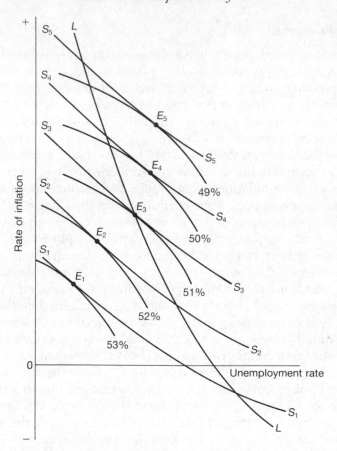

Fig. 3.4. Nordhaus model of vote-maximizing governments' effect on inflation
*Source*: Nordhaus, 'Political Business Cycle', Fig. 4, p. 179.

becomes relatively insignificant. Somewhere between $U_M$ and $U_G$ lies $U_W$, the point that would win by the biggest majority, given the 'appropriate' rate of time discount. This point is taken by Nordhaus to be the 'general welfare optimum'.[56] Its exact location obviously depends on what is taken to be the appropriate discount rate, and

[56] Ibid. 177.

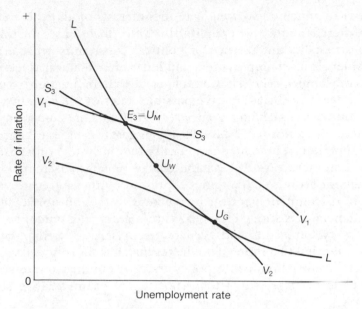

F IG. 3.5. Nordhaus model of the relation of an economy in equilibrium to various rates of time discount
*Source:* Nordhaus, 'Political Business Cycle', Fig. 5, p. 179.

Nordhaus does not discuss that question. I am doubtful of the propriety of discounting future welfare: as Sidgwick said, 'the time at which a man exists cannot affect the value of his happiness from a universal point of view'.[57] Economists often appear to move without adequate justification from the point that $100 now is worth more than $100 in ten years' time (which is true if only because the $100 could be invested now so as to come to more in ten years' time) to the quite different notion that the same amount of welfare has more value now than in ten years' time.

Of course, for an individual it makes sense to discount his own future welfare because the further ahead it lies the more doubtful it must become that he will be around to enjoy it. But in spite of the menace of nuclear holocaust and the possibility that a chance asteroid may destroy the earth, it seems to me that the only morally acceptable

[57] Henry Sidgwick, *The Methods of Ethics* (London: Macmillan, 7th edn., 1907), 414.

course is to attach equal weight to the interests of all generations.[58]

Still, there is a more general difficulty. Nordhaus raises the following question: 'In the absence of political constraints what are the
optimal levels of unemployment and inflation?' In alternative terms,
what is the 'appropriate criterion, or social welfare function' to use in
order to evaluate the alternative possible states of the economy that
might confront 'a planning agency constructing a medium-term plan
for a mixed economy?'[59] Nordhaus suggests using the aggregate
voting function, represented graphically by the system of isopsephic
curves. This means in effect that the ideal planner is to try to maximize
the votes for economic outcomes expressed by the aggregate voting
function, discounted over time by whatever is the appropriate factor.
But in general it is surely clear that vote-maximizing outcomes have
no necessary connection with welfare, in any sense of welfare satisfying the condition that more of it is better than less. In a divided society,
the overall vote-maximizing policy may be one that oppresses the
minority in the interests of the majority, for example. (See below,
chapter 4.)

What can, however, be more plausibly claimed is that vote-
maximization is an appropriate criterion for assessing the operation of
a democratic political system. It can, of course, be questioned whether
'giving people what they want' is something that should be asked of
political leaders; and it may also be questioned whether, when some
want one thing and others something else, the best form of aggregating those conflicting wants is to see what policy would get the biggest
majority. Whatever the answers to these questions, it is important to
know whether the forces of electoral competition can be expected to
operate in some systematic way to give people what they do not want,
or more specifically to give them something that would be defeated by
some alternative in a straight vote. For this would suggest that there is
some kind of internal flaw in democracy, so that it turns out not even
able to do the one thing that might be claimed for it as against other
forms of regime, namely, to give people what they want (in the
majoritarian sense specified).

If a vote-maximizing welfare criterion is used in this way, then it is
apparent that the future should be discounted at whatever rate the

---

[58] Uncertainty may, however, enter into a social welfare calculation in a different and more
acceptable way, namely, as uncertainty about the future course of events. If a government creates
unemployment now in the hope of moderating inflation in the future, the unemployment is
certain, whereas the moderation of inflation is hypothetical. There is therefore some reason for
discounting the future benefits, not because they are future but because they are uncertain.

[59] Nordhaus, 'Political Business Cycle', p. 175.

voters actually discount it. The policy $U_W$ will thus be the one that would get the biggest majority if the voters were (contrary to Nordhaus's assumption) knowledgeable about the macroeconomic structure of the economy and thus able to compare all possible alternative policies over an indefinitely long future. Provided the rate of time discount used by most voters is neither zero nor infinity, the result arrived at by Nordhaus can be reaffirmed: $U_W$ will lie between $U_M$ and $U_G$ on the long-run Phillips curve.

If the rest of his analysis is correct, then, it will have been proved that the tendency of electoral competition is to produce more inflation and less unemployment than the voters want. But is it correct?

The model put forward by Nordhaus to show the inflationary tendencies of democracy is independent of his model of the political business cycle. It is, indeed, incompatible with his or any other model of the political business cycle. It is also internally inconsistent. The key result reached by Nordhaus requires the assumption that, over its term of office, a government is restricted to choosing a point on the short-run Phillips curve.[60] Yet the notion of the political business cycle makes no sense unless a government can, within its term of office, shift the position of the short-run Phillips curve. Moreover, the model purporting to show the inflationary tendency of democracy incorporates a shift in the short-run Phillips curve from one election to the next, so long as the economy is off the long-run Phillips curve. Thus, the model actually requires that the position of the short-run Phillips curve shift between elections but at the same time has the government acting as if it did not.

The conclusion by which Nordhaus sets great store is that in equilibrium the 'democratic outcome' is a rate of inflation that is 'purely myopic . . . where the implicit rate of time preference is infinite'.[61] This conclusion will obviously hold true if a government is seeking to maximize votes at the next election and can choose only points on the short-run Phillips curve. For the vote-maximizing point is the point at which the short-run Phillips curve is at a tangent with the isopsephic curve. But this conclusion is completely dependent on the assumption that the government operates over its whole term of office as if it had a time horizon of zero. This is obviously not consistent with vote-maximizing behaviour on the part

[60] 'In a two-party system the incumbent party chooses economic policies consistent with the current short-run trade-off, but it cannot move the short-run trade-off substantially in its incumbency.' Ibid. 178.
[61] Ibid. 179.

of the government, which requires (if it does not look beyond the next election) that its time horizon begin with the number of years to the next election and decline steadily to zero on the next election day.

The model of the political business cycle depends precisely on the idea that government has foresight. It

predicts that the government will usually cut back aggregate demand after the election in order to bring down the rate of inflation, to squeeze out inflationary expectations and hence to shift down the short-term Phillips curve, as well as to reduce the deficits in the current account, well in time before the next election, so that new expansionary actions can be undertaken again before that election without immediately running into high inflation and a large current account deficit.[62]

Clearly, the government would not take unpopular actions after the election unless it was following a strategy for the whole inter-election period.

Nordhaus has, in effect, produced a theory of the rate of inflation where a vote-maximizing government always expects the next election to take place tomorrow. That the economic outcome will be 'completely myopic' in such conditions is a trivial consequence. Perhaps its only relevance is to cast doubt on the wisdom of Lindbeck's tentative suggestion ('a theoretical possibility') to 'let the exact time of elections be determined by a random process'.[63] The idea underlying this is obviously that if the government does not know when the next election is going to come, it has no incentive to run a political business cycle, because it cannot plan ahead for a non-inflationary boom timed for just before the next election. But if the government reacts to this inability to plan ahead by acting all the time so as to be in the best possible position to fight an election, the result would be like that produced by Nordhaus, at any rate for governments unconstrained by any considerations except vote-maximization. More generally, the greater the time between elections the bigger the cycles would be (especially if voters heavily discount the path of the economy to its election-day position), but the shorter the period between elections the higher the average rate of inflation. Thus, even on its own terms, Nordhaus's model fails because it is incoherent. It presupposes both that positions on the short-run Phillips curves (except where they intersect the long-run curve) cannot be maintained

[62] Lindbeck, 'Stabilization Policy', p. 13.
[63] Ibid. 18 n. 8.

over an inter-election period[64] and that governments nevertheless behave as if they could.

### III   INFLATION AND DEMOCRACY

There is no reason for attributing to inflation of the kind experienced in the advanced industrial societies in recent decades any ill-effects over and above the patent ones: the inconvenience of constant price adjustments, the uncertainty about future changes in the price level, and, to the extent that the inflation is not anticipated or compensated for by deliberate policy, a certain degree of redistribution along lines that have no particular ethical attraction. However, to the extent that the distribution of wealth and income in these societies is ethically unattractive in the absence of inflation anyway, it seems unreasonable to worry very much about a crosscutting and relatively minor form of unjust enrichment.

There is a common argument to the effect that inflation in the United States in the 1970s was particularly hard on the poor, because the highest price rises were in things whose purchase constituted a large proportion of their expenditure and that could not easily be done without. This rests on confusion between inflation and changes in relative prices. If the things the poor buy more of, like heating oil, become more expensive in relation to other things, then the poor will inevitably become worse off, whatever happens to the general price level. Suppose that the overall price level had remained unchanged over a year, with a few prices going up a lot and the rest going down a little to keep the consumer price index level. The poor would be poorer to exactly the same extent as in an inflationary period. The only way of compensating for changes in relative prices is to give the poor relatively more money. Inflation is (as so often) a red herring.

On objective grounds, there is no basis for saying that democratic institutions, by permitting inflation, can be shown to have failed and should be superseded. As for the argument that democratic institutions can be seen to have failed in terms of their own justification, because they produce outcomes that are in conflict with citizens' preferences, there is no factual evidence for the assumption, and the kind of model from which it is to be deduced rests on highly dubious premises and even then does not entail any such conclu-

[64] In fact, the slopes of the short-run curves in Fig. 3.5 are if anything flatter than the slope Nordhaus gives for an empirically derived curve for the US economy that is claimed to be a 'first quarter or impact' short-run Phillips curve. Nordhaus, 'Political Business Cycle', pp. 170, 171.

sion. Once again, therefore, the case against democracy must be dismissed.

I shall close by suggesting that, for most of the economist constitution-mongers discussed in this chapter, inflation was never really the main issue anyway. The economists who make proposals to require balanced budgets, to fix the money supply automatically according to some formula, to go back to the gold standard, to make central banks more autonomous, and so on, are, for the most part, economic liberals in the nineteenth-century sense. That is, they believe that collective action carried out through the state should be kept to a minimum and that the market should determine what gets produced and who receives what income. There is, as both defenders and critics of the market have been forced to recognize over the last hundred years or so, a built-in tension between liberalism (in the nineteenth-century sense) and democracy.[65] Monetarism, and, more generally, market liberalism, is, as Ernest Gellner has written, inevitably betrayed by democratic governments.[66] For the workings of the market are not in fact conducive to the well-being of the majority of the population, and any government concerned with re-election finds itself intervening, whatever its official doctrine, to cushion people from the effects of unconstrained market forces. The demand management, guidelines, statutory controls over wages and prices, and other devices that governments use in order to try to moderate inflation are simply an aspect of this general phenomenon.

Anyone whose primary commitment is to the market must, therefore, look on the democratic state, with its inevitable tendency to regulate, make collective provision, and redistribute, with antipathy. The political problem facing that person is how to get democratic approval for tying the hands of elected governments in perpetuity. Such problems do not of course arise in non-democratic regimes, and it is not therefore surprising that it is territories with authoritarian

[65] Sir Henry Sumner Maine, *Popular Government* (London: John Murray, 1885; Liberty Classics, 1976) made the point a century ago. The quotation from Lord Acton at the opening of this chapter is from his letter of 11 Nov. 1885 to Mary Gladstone, commenting on *Popular Government*. He continued: 'Maine tells me that his book, A Manual of Unacknowledged Conservatism, is selling well. It is no doubt meant to help the enemy's cause, and more hostile to us [liberals] than the author cares to appear. For he requested me not to review it.' Quoted in George Feaver, *From Status to Contract: A Biography of Sir Henry Maine, 1822–1888* (London: Longmans, Green, 1969), 237. William Edward Hartpole Lecky, in *Democracy and Liberty* (London: Longmans, Green, 1896; Indianapolis: Liberty Classics, 1981), carried the argument further and injected a greater note of stridency. The same ideas inform the views of their descendants, the so-called Mont Pelerin group, including von Mises, Hayek, and de Jouvenel.

[66] 'A Social Contract in Search of an Idiom: The Demise of the Danegeld State?', *Political Quarterly*, 46 (1975), 127–52.

regimes such as Hong Kong, Taiwan, and South Korea that are often the apple of the market economist's eye.

The beauty of inflation is that it can be used as a rallying cry to sweep up people who might otherwise be chary of plans to cripple the ability of governments to make economic policy. A perfect example is James Buchanan's decade-long call for a 'constitutional counterrevolution' to undo the work of the New Deal and the Warren Court.[67] Anti-inflationary hysteria is an opportunity to mobilize behind proposals that would, in calmer times, be widely recognized as reactionary twaddle. That is in the end the only reason why inflation is important.

[67] Buchanan, *Limits of Liberty*; James M. Buchanan, *Freedom in Constitutional Contract: Perspectives of a Political Economist* (College Station, Tex.: Texas A & M University Press, 1977); Barry, 'Review'.

# 4

# POLITICAL ACCOMMODATION AND CONSOCIATIONAL DEMOCRACY

SHALLOW. Better accommodated! it is good; yea, indeed, is it.
Good phrases are surely, and ever were, very commendable.
Accommodated! it comes of *accommodo*. Very good; a good
phrase.

BARDOLPH. Pardon, sir; I have heard the word. Phrase call you
it? By this day, I know not the phrase; but I will maintain the
word with my sword to be a soldier-like word, and a word of
exceeding good command, by heaven. Accommodated; that
is, when a man is, as they say, accommodated; or when a man
is, being, whereby he may be thought to be accommodated:
which is an excellent thing.

*Henry IV*, Pt. 2.

I

As my Shakespearian quotation shows, the word 'accommodate'
gradually entered into English usage in the sixteenth century and, if
Bardolph's efforts are any guide, the problems of definition to which I
shall draw attention are not new. 'Accommodation' as a noun came a
little later, the first use found by the *Oxford English Dictionary* (actually
in *Othello*) being recorded in 1604. There it meant lodgings, and this
has remained its most common use. Indeed, I have come across a
number of people who are firmly convinced that Arend Lijphart's
book *The Politics of Accommodation* is a study of Dutch housing policy.
But the meaning relevant here—referring to the process, the outcome,
or the spirit of mutual conciliation—is well established and can be
traced back to the seventeenth century. The *OED* cites this from a
pamphlet on *Liberty of Conscience* published in 1645: 'By accommodation I understand an agreement of dissenters with the rest of the
Church in practical conclusions' (*sub* 'accommodation' 4). This use is,
however, rarely found in popular speech or writing, and, as far as I
know, it has never become common currency in politics by being
attached to a particular issue, like 'appeasement' (of Germany and Italy

in the 1930s) or '*détente*' (with China and the Soviet Union in the 1970s). My own casual observations on contemporary usage suggest that it is employed in order to introduce deliberate vagueness about the form and content of any possible agreement. Thus, the most frequent application I have found is in the context of the Arab–Israeli conflict, when the writer wants to speculate about whether the two sides might reach an 'accommodation', without committing himself on whether this would be a signed treaty or a gradual acceptance of some status quo, or on what the terms (written or unwritten) would be.

'Consociation' is a much rarer word than 'accommodation', though with an equally long pedigree, and indeed I do not believe I have ever seen it used outside the writings of contemporary political scientists. According to the *OED* it can be used as an abstract noun for 'the action or fact of associating together; union in fellowship; combination' or to refer to actual associations, unions, and combinations. In the sense of 'an alliance or confederation' it is now said by the *OED* to be obsolete, but it seems that its main use at any time (and now its sole use) as a concrete noun has been in the context of formal co-operative arrangements among Churches and in particular to refer to confederal ties among Presbyterians and (in the USA) Congregationalists.

The point of this philological excursion is to show that 'accommodation' is a word of extremely general application, referring to any kind of agreement or settlement, while 'consociation' is simply a more or less obsolete word meaning much the same as 'association' and sharing with it the characteristic that it can be used both as an abstract noun (for the fact of association) and a concrete one (for actual associations). So what? It is no part of my intention to play the linguistic conservative and suggest that words should never be redefined for scholarly purposes so as to make them more specific. But it is very easy to run into formidable conceptual difficulties by doing so, and we need to be aware of these.

The problem is particularly great where, as here, an expression ('political accommodation' or 'consociational democracy') encapsulates a theory. The existence of 'theory-laden' terms occurs in all sciences as soon as they get beyond classifying objects according to observable similarities. Thus, to give a simple example, a phylum is defined as a group of organisms descended from a common ancestral form, so the word encapsulates the theory of the differentiation of species through evolution. In the 'hard' sciences, the difficulties are kept at bay during periods of 'normal science' by general acceptance of the underlying theory. If, however, the underlying theory comes to be questioned, the elements that have been yoked together in a single word dependent on that theory come apart. Thus, suppose that the idea of the evolution of species were to be rejected. We would then have two criteria for phyla: the definition in terms of common ancestry and the lists of species arranged under phyla. We could either say there are no phyla or we could drop the definition in terms of ancestry and keep the word 'phyla' for the classification.

In the social sciences, as has often been pointed out (with either relish or distress), we do not enjoy the conditions of 'normal science', and the introduction of 'theory-laden' terms is therefore much more hazardous. Let me try to illustrate the problem in connection with 'political accommodation' and 'consociational democracy'.

In *The Politics of Accommodation* we read:

Dutch politics is a politics of accommodation. That is the secret of its success. The term accommodation is here used in the sense of settlement of divisive issues and conflicts where only a minimal consensus exists. . . . A key element of this conception is the lack of a comprehensive political consensus, but not the complete absence of consensus. . . . The second key requirement is that the *leaders* of the self-contained blocs must be particularly convinced of the desirability of preserving the system. And they must be willing and capable of bridging the gaps between the mutually isolated blocs and of resolving serious disputes in a largely nonconsensual context.[1]

It would be naïve to say that the third sentence in this quotation is a definition and the rest empirical statements. It would be more sensible to say that the use of the deceptively simple assertion 'Dutch politics is a politics of accommodation' commits one to all these ideas:

(*a*)  divisive issues are settled in the Netherlands;
(*b*)  the settlements are between blocs that have a low level of consensus between them;
(*c*)  the settlements are between blocs that are 'self-contained' and 'mutually isolated';
(*d*)  these blocs have leaders, who are responsible for negotiating settlements; and
(*e*)  the bloc leaders are convinced of the need for settlements.

Finally, although it is not made explicit in the quotation, I think we may, in the light of the earlier theoretical discussion in the book, add the 'cross-cutting cleavage' hypothesis in its 'associational' form:

---

[1] Arend Lijphart, *The Politics of Accommodation: Pluralism and Democracy in the Netherlands* (Berkeley and Los Angeles: University of California Press, 1968), 103–4.

(*f*) there is a causal connection between the fact that the blocs are 'self-contained' and the fact that there is a low level of consensus between them.

The term 'political accommodation', as used by Lijphart, encapsulates all these ideas. What I mean by this is that we would no longer be able to speak of the Netherlands (or some other country) as the site of a 'politics of accommodation' if we came to disbelieve any of these propositions. For example, it would not be enough that divisive issues were settled if they were not between isolated blocs, if the blocs did not have low consensus, if the settlement were not by bloc leaders, or if the bloc leaders were not convinced of the need for a settlement.

The same line of analysis can be applied to 'consociational democracy', and Lijphart in his paper with that title is very clear about the fact that he is putting forward a complex theoretical construction encapsulated in the term. An often quoted sentence from this paper runs: 'Consociational democracy means government by élite cartel designed to turn a democracy with a fragmented political culture into a stable democracy.'[2] What is less often noticed is that Lijphart goes on to say that consociational democracy has four requirements (in brief, that the 'élites of rival subcultures' are willing and able to 'accommodate the divergent interests and demands' because they are committed to the maintenance of the system and they see the need for accommodation as a means to this) and that '*these four requirements are logically implied by the concept of consociational democracy as defined in this paper*'.[3]

In addition, Lijphart speaks in the paper of 'consociational devices', which correspond to the 'rules of the game' in *The Politics of Accommodation*. Examples are grand coalition and proportionality or circulation of certain posts over time according to some formula. This expression 'consociational devices' packs further theoretical baggage, since anyone using the phrase is in effect committing himself to the idea that these devices (or variants on them) are essential aspects of the élite accommodation that is a defining characteristic of 'consociational democracy'. An illustration of the problem is provided by Val Lorwin, who, in a postscript written to Kenneth McRae's collection of articles, refers to 'the structures of segmented pluralism or

[2] A. Lijphart, 'Consociational Democracy', *World Politics*, 21 (1969), 207–25. Repr. in Kenneth McRae (ed.), *Consociational Democracy: Political Accommodation in Segmented Societies* (Toronto: McClelland and Stewart, The Carleton Library, 1974), 70–106. I shall give page references for this and other articles in McRae's convenient collection, citing it as 'McRae'. The quotation in the text appears on p. 79.

[3] Lijphart, 'Consociational Democracy', in McRae, p. 79 (my italics).

consociational democracy in Belgium' in a context where the whole point is the *increasing inadequacy* of the structures to contain conflict.[4]

The crucial point that has to be grasped about Lijphart's definition of 'consociational democracy' is that a consociational democracy is necessarily stable and successful in mediating conflicts. This follows from the way in which the term was introduced by him as a modification of Gabriel Almond's typology of political systems, put forward in the well-known 'Comparative Political Systems' article in 1956. In Almond's typology, cultural homogeneity and overlapping memberships are associated with stable and effective government, while separate subcultures and segmentation (reinforcing memberships) are associated with unstable and ineffective (*immobiliste*) government. Lijphart advocates the recognition of a third category of countries, like Switzerland and the Netherlands, which combine the political characteristics (stability and effectiveness) of Almond's first category with the socio-cultural characteristics (separate subcultures and segmentation) of his second. 'These deviant cases of fragmented but stable democracies will be called "consociational democracies." '[5] (The logic of this two-by-two matrix suggests that we should also look for countries which are culturally homogeneous, with overlapping memberships, but whose politics are unstable and ineffective. I suppose some people would put forward Britain and the USA as candidates.)

'Consociational democracy' as conceptualized by Lijphart puts together in a package stability, dissensus, segmentation, élite accommodation, and some mix of the 'consociational devices'. As the genesis of the typology makes clear, there is underlying this concept the implicit theory that under conditions of dissensus and segmentation *only* élite accommodation institutionalized in consociational devices can produce stability. This yoking together can be seen from the way in which 'consociational democracies' are first defined as 'fragmented but stable democracies' and then as countries with 'government by élite cartel'. Obviously, there could in principle be countries which were 'fragmented but stable' and where nevertheless this stability had not been brought about by 'government by élite cartel'. This possibility is ruled out by the typology, just as the

---

[4] Val R. Lorwin, 'Belgium: Conflict and Compromise', printed for first time in McRae, pp. 179–206, at p. 206.

[5] Lijphart, 'Consociational Democracy', in McRae, p. 75. Almond's article 'Comparative Political Systems' appeared in the *Journal of Politics*, 18 (1956), 391–409.

possibility of *any* 'fragmented but stable' democracy was ruled out by
the Almond typology.

In the introduction to his collection of articles *Consociational
Democracy*, Kenneth McRae speaks of 'the four "classic" cases of
consociationalism among developed Western democracies, namely
the Netherlands, Austria, Belgium, and Switzerland'. Although this
is perhaps the most explicit statement we could find of the paradigmatic status of these four countries, Lijphart writes of 'the Low
Countries, Switzerland and Austria' as the 'deviant cases . . . to be
called "consociational democracies"', and Lorwin's 'segmented
pluralist' countries are these plus Luxembourg.[6] I propose to argue in
this chapter for the following propositions: (1) that Switzerland
provides no support for the theory of consociational democracy; (2)
that the Austrian case is less clear-cut than is often assumed; (3) that
Belgium and the Netherlands, although plausible supporting cases,
still fall short of fully bearing out the theory; and (4) that the relevance
of the 'consociational' model for other divided societies is much more
doubtful than is commonly supposed.

It may be asked—and it is a fair question—who am I to cross swords
with the experts on these countries? I do not claim any expertise, but it
is not my intention to produce any facts of my own. My information
will be drawn almost entirely from the writings of those identified
with what Hans Daalder has called the 'incipient school' of adherents
to the theory of consociational democracy, and it will be on this
information that I base my arguments.[7] This seems to me fair enough.
In Anglo-Saxon jurisprudence it is considered to be the job of the
advocate to produce his own supporting facts, and although this may
not be a good way of organizing a legal system it seems to have served
well enough in scholarly debates.

## II

My analysis of the Swiss case will be based mainly on Jürg Steiner's
book *Amicable Agreement versus Majority Rule*.[8] This is an ambitious
and fertile book, with many more interesting ideas in it than can be
discussed here. The point on which I shall focus is this: that, although

---

[6] McRae, p. 13; Lijphart in McRae, pp. 74–5; Lorwin, p. 36 in McRae.

[7] H. Daalder, 'The Consociational Democracy Theme', *World Politics*, 26 (1974), 604–21, at
609.

[8] J. Steiner, *Amicable Agreement versus Majority Rule: Conflict Resolution in Switzerland* (Chapel
Hill: University of North Carolina Press, rev. and enlarged edn. 1974, tr. from German edn. of
1970).

Steiner identifies himself closely with other members of the 'consociational democracy' school, he does not show—or indeed really try to
show—that Switzerland fits the model of 'consociational democracy'
as a theoretical construction. Switzerland does, of course, have
consociational devices and in *that* sense is a consociational democracy
(though even this statement has to be qualified), but these devices do
not function in the way postulated by the theory.

The object of Steiner's study is to explain why 'strong subcultural
segmentation' does not lead to 'intersubcultural hostility' in Switzerland. These terms are defined as follows. Subcultures are defined in
Robert Dahl's words as 'distinctive sets of attitudes, opinions, and
values that persist for relatively long periods of time in the life of a
country and give individuals in a particular subculture a sense of
identity that distinguishes them from individuals in other subcultures'.[9] The strength of subcultural segmentation, Steiner adds,
depends on the intensity of self-identification of the different subcultures. 'Possible indicators are responses to attitudinal survey questions, frequency of interactions among the members of a subculture,
and organizational ties within a subculture.'[10] 'Subcultural hostility'
exists 'if two or more subcultures perceive one another in such
negative terms that they have a desire or at least a readiness to damage
one another.'[11]

What, then, is the explanation? 'Along with Lehmbruch and Lijphart I consider the predominant pattern of decision-making the key
explanatory variable.'[12] In the light of my earlier discussion it is
important to notice that Steiner refers to Lijphart's terms 'consociationalism' and 'accommodation' as referring to a 'peculiar type of
decision-making' and goes on: 'Other concepts to describe roughly
the same decision-making model are *contractarianism* [Bluhm], *amicable
agreement* [Lehmbruch], and *Konkordanzdemokratie* [Lehmbruch and
Reich].'[13] Thus, for Steiner, a 'consociational democracy' would be
identifiable by the presence of 'consociational devices', whether or not
these were carrying out the role of conflict-prevention ascribed by
Lijphart. What we have to ask, however, is whether the 'consociational devices' function in the way postulated by the theory encapsulated in the term 'consociational democracy'.

First, though, it is worth making sure that Switzerland really is

---

[9] R. A. Dahl (ed.), *Political Oppositions in Western Democracies* (New Haven, Conn.: Yale
University Press, 1966), 371.
[10] Steiner, *Amicable Agreement*, p. 3.
[11] Ibid. 4.                    [12] Ibid. 6.                    [13] Ibid. 4–5.

'consociational' in the descriptive sense as against the theory-laden sense. Is decisionmaking predominantly by the model of 'amicable agreements' rather than by the model of 'majority rule', to use the terms preferred by Steiner? There is the convention that the major parties are represented (since 1959 on a roughly proportional basis) in the seven-man executive, the Federal Council. But these men are thought of as individuals administering departments rather than as party oligarchs reaching concordats binding on their followers. The representatives of a party elected to the Federal Council may not always be those nominated by the party and the fact that a party is represented does not inhibit it (or some section of it) from voting against a proposal put forward in the name of the Federal Council. As Steiner says, 'It is even doubtful that it makes sense to talk about the Federal Council as a coalition government.'[14] What is much more to the point is the tendency, which Steiner emphasizes and illustrates with several case studies of policymaking, for new legislation or policy initiatives to be hammered out among the 'interests' involved (probably in secret) and a single unanimous proposal presented. This is the core of 'amicable agreement': there is indeed 'élite accommodation', in which representatives of the parties play a part, though it is only very partially mediated through the Federal Council.

This, however, does not entail that the method of political decision-making in Switzerland is one of 'amicable agreement', because of the existence of the referendum and the popular initiative. Thus, one of Steiner's case studies is of the decision to create a university in the Aargau canton, in which he was closely involved himself. In thirty-five pages he describes in detail the way in which the proposal was developed to the point at which all the party spokesmen were favourable (only two members of parliament voted against it) and every conceivable pressure group had been squared. As he rather naïvely says, 'since there was no organized opposition to the university project, the estimates of public opinion were diffuse and hard to make'.[15] But in spite of all this the proposal was carried in the referendum by only 31,460 votes to 28,945. Thus, although one way of describing the outcome would be to say that it was one of 'amicable agreement' among the élite, another would be to say that it was one in which 52 per cent of those voting imposed their will on 48 per cent. Or, more pointedly, one in which 52 per cent of the people plus the whole of the carefully solidified élite imposed their will on 48 per cent of the people.

[14] Ibid. 37.     [15] Ibid. 199.

This is of course a cantonal example, but an important federal case with much the same characteristics was the constitutional amendment promoted by James Schwarzenbach ('Over-foreignization Initiative II'), designed to 'limit the number of foreigners in any given canton (except Geneva) to 10 per cent of the population'.[16] This came too late to be mentioned by Steiner, whose book appeared in German in 1970, but is discussed by Benjamin Barber in his admirable work on the canton of Graubünden (Grisons). The Aargau university case was one with the 'establishment' solidly in favour; the Schwarzenbach initiative showed it equally solidly against.

> The Federal Council . . . was implacably opposed to the measure; the National Council, presumably representative of popular opinion, voted 136 to 1 against it (prior to the referendum); the Council of States (*Standerat*, representing the cantons) rejected it 39 to 0. Manufacturing, trade, and industrial interests were unanimously critical and funded a record-breaking publicity campaign urging defeat of the proposal and defaming its supporters [as Nazis and racists]. . . . Not a single major political party, not one significant pressure group or voluntary association could be found that was favourable to the amendment. . . . Yet on June 7 [1970], no less than 46 per cent of a postwar record turnout (over 74 per cent of the electorate) voted yes on the amendment, while in seven of the twenty-two cantons the proposal actually carried.[17]

The picture that emerges is one of 'amicable agreement' among the élite (either painfully cobbled together as in the Aargau university case or spontaneous as in the Schwarzenbach case) but at the same time a pattern in which binding collective decisions may be taken on very small popular majorities. Indeed, although this is speculative, is it not possible that some of the élite practices described in such detail by Steiner (and in some of which he was an active participant) are responses to the existence of the referendum and the initiative? I am thinking here particularly of the attempts to co-opt all the relevant experts and to 'homogenize' the statistics and estimates produced by different sources, so that only one set of figures ever becomes publicly available. Surely this kind of conspiratorial behaviour is typical of those who wish to maximize their influence over an outcome while knowing that they do not have the final say. Thus, Royal Commissions in Britain always attach great importance to making a unanimous report. Those who insist on rocking the boat and produ-

---

[16] Benjamin R. Barber, *The Death of Communal Liberty: A History of Freedom in a Swiss Mountain Canton* (Princeton, NJ: Princeton University Press, 1974), 252.
[17] Barber, *Death of Communal Liberty*, pp. 253–4.

cing a minority report seem almost invariably to run into the hostility of their fellows. Recent examples may be drawn from the Royal Commission on Local Government (Maud) and the Royal Commission on the Constitution (Kilbrandon).

In other countries with 'consociational' devices we also find co-optation and suppression of information, in order to minimize the chance that people outside the élite will have enough ammunition to be able to stir up trouble against negotiated agreements. But in these other countries there is not the same possibility of a challenge through constitutional channels, and the emphasis on these features is perhaps less. The leaders can afford to let it be known that there are differences of view so long as they can hold their own supporters in line behind them organizationally. They do not have to fear repudiation in the privacy of the polling booth.

To the extent, however, that consociational democracy (in the purely descriptive sense) entails restriction of information, this may help to explain why it has so far existed only in small countries. The reason usually assigned, that consociationalism requires a 'low foreign affairs load', has recently, and rightly, come under fire. There seems to be no reason why 'consociationalism' should make the conduct of foreign affairs especially difficult and it is significant that most non-consociational countries have all-party coalitions in wartime, presumably the better to deal with external threats. Nor is it obvious that a small country in general needs less agility than a large in adapting to its environment if it is to survive. But what must be true is that a small country will have a relatively small élite and only a small number of experts on any given subject, and this must make much more feasible the project of co-opting all those with expertise on a subject and thus pre-empting their right to oppose the agreed line.

Perhaps, also, the presence of representatives of all the major parties in the Federal Council might be looked on as partially a response to the initiative and referendum. According to Steiner, because of the cost of obtaining the necessary signatures and carrying out a propaganda campaign, 'although it is technically possible for a small party to make use of the right to initiative and referendum, it is improbable on a practical level'.[18] A 'large party' might therefore be defined as one that could upset the apple-cart by demanding a referendum. To put it another way, the existence of such a further decisionmaking stage invalidates the usual parliamentary formula for a 'minimum winning

[18] Steiner, *Amicable Agreement*, p. 19.

coalition'. If we define a 'minimum winning coalition' as one that can with high probability ensure that what its members support will stick, it will have to be one including all those parties capable of routinely financing referenda and, as we have seen, that would (on Steiner's evidence) correspond exactly to the four-party coalition that Switzerland has had. (Incidentally, I think it ought to be emphasized that highly inclusive governments of the Swiss sort are not necessary for consociational democracy in the descriptive sense. Belgium, which, with the Netherlands, is one of the two indisputable cases, has since 1944 almost always had minimum winning coalitions of two parties, and—when the Catholic party won an absolute majority—of one party.)

As I have said, Steiner does not explicitly try to relate the institutions of the popular initiative and the referendum to the model of 'amicable agreement' into which he claims the Swiss system fits. He seems to regard 'amicable agreement' as defined by élite behaviour and the initiative and referendum as something else: a safety-valve (page 236) or a counterbalance (page 283). No doubt it is quite correct to say that in practice these popular votes operate primarily negatively and as ways of registering more or less diffuse protest. But this is not inherent in the procedures themselves. It simply reflects the particular political situation: a highly-unified élite committed to modernization, rationalization, economic growth, and so on facing a people large sections of which are acutely uneasy at such developments.[19]

The crucial point is that the institution of collective decisionmaking by a simple majority of the popular vote is in itself the antithesis of 'amicable agreement'. 'Amicable agreements' must be negotiated among people who either trust one another or do not need to because they can apply sanctions against defaulters. This entails that only a small number of people can be involved in the decisionmaking process. Even more important, 'amicable agreement' requires that the same people should be involved in a number of different decisions and that they should be able to make deals with one another. This makes it possible for a decision favourable to one group to be taken today on the understanding that a decision favourable to another group will be taken tomorrow. This is the process called 'log-rolling' in the USA and in Austria *Junktim*. As Lehmbruch says: 'this procedure means that one of the actors offers a concession he detests in exchange for a concession by his opponent that the latter detests equally strongly'.[20]

---

[19] For this interpretation, see Barber, *Death of Communal Liberty*, pp. 258–74.
[20] Gerhard Lehmbruch, 'A Non-Competitive Pattern of Conflict Management in Liberal

Popular voting strikes at the roots of log-rolling. One issue is decided at a time and there is no way in which a mass electorate voting by secret ballot could set up an enforceable or even plausible agreement whereby one set of people would vote for something they didn't want on one occasion in return for a promise from another set to vote for something *they* didn't want on a future occasion (or even on another item at the same time). Of course, even in a legislature promises are not strictly enforceable, so that if the items of a package are voted on sequentially it would be possible for those due to make the last concession to renege. But the actors in a legislature know they may have to continue to deal with one another into the indefinite future, so the sanction of exclusion from future deals is a potent one.

If, then, the institutions of the referendum and popular initiative are not the instrument whereby those in the majority on some line of cleavage oppress those in the minority, this is not because the institutions themselves would not lend themselves to it but, presumably, because the Swiss do not choose to employ them for such a purpose. This means, though, that we must reject Steiner's central thesis: that the 'predominant pattern of decision-making' is the 'key explanatory variable' in explaining the low 'level of intersubcultural hostility'.[21] The alternative explanation of the low level of intersubcultural hostility is that (except for the Jura question) the members of these subcultures do not have any cause for hostility. They do not have incompatible aspirations such that the fulfilment of one section's aims would spell a threat to the material well-being, cultural survival, or social honour of another. As William Keech observed succinctly in his shrewd research note on 'Linguistic Diversity and Political Conflict', 'an absence of sharp conflict [between linguistic or religious groups] may not necessarily be the result of patterns of conflict resolution, but possibly stem from the absence of sources of conflict, or perhaps a mixture of both'.[22] Steiner cites this note but fails to draw the relevant conclusion: that before the pattern of decisionmaking can be made the explanation for a lack of hostility, it is necessary to rule out the alternative hypothesis that there are no sources of serious conflict anyway.

In fact, if we go back again to the model of 'consociational

Democracies: the Case of Switzerland, Austria and Lebanon', printed for the first time in McRae, pp. 90–106, at p. 92.
[21] Steiner, *Amicable Agreement*, p. 4.
[22] William R. Keech, 'Linguistic Diversity and Political Conflict: Some Observations Based on Four Swiss Cantons', *Comparative Politics*, 4 (1972), 387–404, at p. 388.

democracy' spelt out at the beginning of this chapter, it seems to me that Switzerland fails to fit it at every point. In a 'consociational democracy' there are groups with a low level of consensus between them and that are mutually isolated. The sharply incompatible aspirations of these groups are articulated by different political parties, which fight elections by appealing to the loyalty of their own client group through whipping up group sentiment and making play with the group ideology. The leaders of these parties, having disciplined their supporters into following them by emphasizing the need to unite to fight the others, then use the free hand this gives them to settle the issues dividing the groups in a pragmatic way.

Steiner's own analysis demolishes any notion that Switzerland corresponds to this model. He mentions with approval Girod's statement 'that there is a strong consensus among the Swiss parties on all important questions—even on the question of the relation between church and state and problems related to economic and social policy'.[23] The parties do not therefore articulate dissensual ideologies, as in the 'consociational democracy' model. Nor do the parties appeal exclusively to different subcultural groups in the society. Steiner goes on to 'suggest that the demands of the Swiss parties coincide to such an extent partly because the party cleavages crosscut other important cleavages—in particular, the cleavages of occupational groups, linguistic groups, religious groups, regional groups, cantons, economic interest groups, and voluntary associations'.[24] He then states the classic argument for the moderating effect on party extremism of cross-cutting between party support and membership of ascriptive groups.

A party that draws its supporters from different social groups cannot afford to cater to the interests of one group only. . . . If, for example, party and language lines crosscut, a party cannot afford to represent one-sidedly the interests of a specific language group. On the contrary, every party attempts to articulate demands that pay heed to the needs of all linguistic groups.[25]

I think that the general 'cross-cutting cleavage hypothesis', that all cross-cutting cleavages moderate conflict, is unproven, as Eric Nordlinger argues.[26] But the thesis that cross-cutting between political parties and socio-cultural cleavage lines moderates conflict seems to me much more plausible and better supported. It may well be, even

---

[23] Steiner, *Amicable Agreement*, p. 49.
[24] Ibid.    [25] Ibid.
[26] In *Conflict Regulation in Divided Societies* (Cambridge, Mass: Center for International Affairs, Harvard University, Occasional Papers in International Affairs, No. 29, 1972).

so, that the causal link is mainly in the reverse direction, so that the fact of parties drawing support across cleavage lines is evidence for the relatively low salience of issues related to ascriptive group member-ship rather than the cause of it. (Thus, the institution of the ethnically balanced ticket in US local politics is, in effect, a sign that politicians do not see any advantage in fighting on ethnically related issues. If the parties did want to fight on such issues they would, obviously, clear the decks by choosing ethnically homogeneous tickets.) But if the link runs mainly in this direction, the cross-cutting between party support and ascriptive groups simply provides evidence that there are no crucial issues dividing these groups.

The picture could not be more different from the 'consociational democracy' model. In that model, the parties articulate the divergent demands of different groups, and the possibilities of immobilism or conflict opened up are deliberately averted by overarching élite co-operation. In Switzerland, the process of stifling conflict between groups (if there is really any potential for it) is carried out by the parties right at the stage of electoral competition when they aggregate support across the lines of cleavage. There is therefore nothing left to be done after the election: there are no parties elected on a solidary group basis facing one another.

I queried in parentheses whether there is a basis at the mass level for conflict between the ascriptive groups in Switzerland. Steiner does not give any survey evidence about mass attitudes to possible inter-group issues, but it is certainly hard to imagine that Switzerland is a country where the groups are itching to oppress one another and kept from it only by the manipulations of the political élite. We must, I think, reject the applicability of the item in the 'consociational democracy' model that says there is a low level of consensus between members of the ascriptive groups. The almost perfect consensus among the parties on intercommunal issues probably reflects a high (though less perfect) consensus in the population at large.

Finally, on Steiner's evidence, the linguistic and religious groups are not 'isolated' or 'self-contained' as in Lijphart's model of 'consoci-ational democracy'. As a matter of strict logic, it does not seem to me that this feature is necessary to the model. Surely the politically important aspect of relations between the groups is a low level of consensus. If this were to coincide with the absence of isolation between them it would still pose a problem of reconciliation for the élites. It is for this reason that I suggested adding to the model as set out earlier the sixth item (*f*), the cross-cutting cleavage hypothesis in its 'associational' form, to the effect that there is a causal connection between the fact that the blocs are 'self-contained' and the fact that there is a low level of consensus between them. Adding this makes the factor of isolation relevant to the rest of the model by making it a cause (or perhaps more plausibly a sustaining condition) of dissensus.

As I have already mentioned, I do not think the hypothesis is well substantiated. Inasfar as there is an empirical connection, it may reflect the tendency for conflict to lead to segregation rather than for segregation to lead to conflict. But if so it is further indirect evidence for the relatively low level of division between the subcultures in Switzerland. Thus, for example, in sharp contrast with Belgium or with Austria, sporting activities are carried on primarily in organizations that do not follow subcultural cleavage lines. (Nor do they follow lines of party support.) The organizations are, rather, inclusive.[27]

In short, then, we may say: (1) if we give full weight to the potentialities of the referendum and the popular initiative, it is highly doubtful whether the decisionmaking system in Switzerland can be said to be preponderantly one of 'amicable agreement' or 'élite accommodation'; and (2) there is no evidence that there is a low level of consensus between members of the subcultural groups, so even if we allowed that the system were one of 'amicable agreement' this would not be necessary to explain the low level of intersubcultural hostility. These two points show clearly that Swiss politics do not fit the model of 'consociational democracy'. They do not, however, entirely refute Steiner's Hypothesis I, which reads: 'In a system with strong subcultural segmentation, the more often political decisions are made by amicable agreement, the more probable is a low level of intersubcultural hostility.'[28] This kind of probabilistic statement is extremely difficult to test since it requires a large number of cases before we can begin to say whether one thing makes another more probable. By contrast, Lijphart's theory of consociational democracy would be disproved by one case of a society characterized by isolated and dissensual blocs plus stable and effective democracy minus the practices of élite accommodation constituting 'consociational democracy' as a description of a pattern of decisionmaking.

Steiner's hypothesis is so weak that it may be true without being important. That is to say, other things being equal, it may be that the more 'amicable agreement' there is, the less intersubcultural hostility.

---

[27] Steiner, *Amicable Agreement*, p. 257.          [28] Ibid. 252.

But where, as in Switzerland, the parties cross-cut the subcultures, the effect of 'amicable agreement' among the party leaders (compared with parliamentary majoritarianism) is likely to be slight. To put it concretely, if Swiss parties were to drop the 'magic formula' and instead the Federal Council were to be made up of representatives of parties with a majority of seats only, it may be that intersubcultural hostility would go up a little (since the parties are not exact micro-cosms of the electorate), but surely not much. Of course, this speculation is flawed by the fact that it does not really make sense to say 'other things being equal', since we have to suppose some prior upheaval to lead to that change. (See above, chapter 3 section I.) But we may at least say that we are assuming that the change, whatever its cause, is not a reaction to some increase in hostility or polarization of opinion between the subcultures.

To conclude this section I should like to take up one argument that is not made by Steiner himself but is parallel to one that has been made in relation to the Netherlands and Belgium. It has been suggested (by Lijphart and Lorwin, for example) that in these countries the 'consoci-ational' mode of decisionmaking is no longer required to mediate conflicts between the 'spiritual families' because these conflicts have died down anyway. Consociational devices are now a sort of institu-tional hangover. But they were needed in the past. Could the same argument be made for Switzerland?

The strongest counter-argument is that, during the period when the institutions of 'amicable agreement' were presumably needed, they did not exist. 'From the founding of the federal state in 1849 until 1891 the Federal Council consisted entirely of Free Democrats who had won a military victory over the Christian Democrats (then called Conservatives).'[29] For forty-two years after the Sonderbund war, then, the stability of the state was maintained while the victors monopolized the executive. Only in 1891 was a Christian Democrat elected to the Federal Council. The same story applies to the Socialists, who qualified on a proportional basis for a seat in the Federal Council in 1919 but did not receive one until 1943 or their proportional share of two until 1959.[30] Although Steiner does not draw attention to the coincidence in dates, he later quotes Girod as saying: 'the present program of the Social Democratic Party (adopted in 1959) is frankly reformist and pragmatic. It does not refer at all to the principle of class struggle, and there is no allusion to marxism.'[31]

[29] Ibid. 33.    [30] Ibid.    [31] Ibid. 54–5.

Thus, 'amicable agreement', at the level of the Federal Council, has never operated as an instrument for reconciling differences between parties. Rather, parties are included in the system of 'amicable agreement' only when, and to the extent that, they have shed their distinguishing features. Indeed, I would suggest that there are good a priori reasons for thinking that the relation in Switzerland between the executive and the legislature (especially the fact that the members of the Federal Council are elected individually and do not agree on a common programme in advance) makes multi-party governments much *less* possible if the parties disagree fundamentally than does the usual kind of cabinet/parliament relationship. Perhaps the very survival of the system in Switzerland is a further sign of the high level of consensus among parties participating in government, since it could not function without it.

### III

Austria is the jewel in the 'consociational' crown because it 'presents virtually the only example of a European state in which an initially unsuccessful parliamentary system turned into a successful one, and in which constitutional and party-structural factors can be held constant over half a century (1919–1969)'.[32] What made the difference between the collapse of democratic government in the post-1918 First Republic and its stabilization in the post-1945 Second Republic? The special ingredient, according to the 'consociational democracy' school, was the practice of 'élite cartel', institutionalized in the grand coalition of the two major parties between 1945 and 1966. According to Lijphart, it is one of the two 'clearest examples', the other being the first years of the Belgian state.[33]

There can, I think, be no question that what happened in Austria during those years completely satisfied the conditions for 'government by élite cartel'. As William Bluhm summarizes the position:

For the whole period from 1945 to 1966 the two great parties renewed their agreement to cooperate following each parliamentary election by signing a pact of coalition (*Koalitionspakt*), by which they divided between them the offices of state at the ministerial level and by which they established a rubric for the day-to-day conduct of policy making during the subsequent legis-

[32] P. G. J. Pulzer, 'The Legitimizing Role of Political Parties: The Second Austrian Republic', *Government and Opposition*, 4 (1969), 324–44, repr. in McRae under title 'Austria: the Legitimizing Role of Political Parties', 157–78, at 158.
[33] Lijphart, 'Consociational Democracy', in McRae, p. 75.

lative period. Included in this was a unanimity rule and an agreement on a system of proportionalism (*Proporz*) for staffing government corporations and nationalized industries whereby each party received positions for its members in proportion to its strength in the electorate.[34]

The significance of the Austrian 'grand coalition' was quite different from that of the Swiss one. In Switzerland, as we saw, a member of the Federal Council is elected as an individual, not as a party leader who thereby commits his party to a common programme. Indeed, some of the parties do not *have* a definite structure of leadership at the federal level. But in Austria the 'grand coalition' was a deal between the leaders of highly-disciplined political parties.

The pacts provided for a coalition commission (*Koalitionsausschuss*) with power to decide any matters of interpretation. Except for the two party leaders (who would be the Chancellor and Vice-Chancellor of the government) the delegates to the commission were whips and party functionaries, not cabinet members. It is evident that in terms of policy-making power the cabinet was subordinate to the commission, as parliament was subordinate to both, since it was the duty of the parliamentary whips to ensure compliance with the decisions of the commission.[35]

The contrast in the method of decisionmaking with that in force during the lifetime of the First Republic is also clear, since the Christian Social Party monopolized the government between the first election in 1920 and the promulgation of a new, authoritarian, constitution in 1934. Equally, there can be no doubt that the tensions between the *Lager* during the existence of the First Republic form a genuine contrast to the relatively harmonious development of the Second Republic. At the same time, 'constitutional and party-structural factors' were, as Pulzer stated, similar in the two Republics. Both were, in formal terms, parliamentary democracies; and the stability of support for the two major political groupings over the periods 1918–34 and 1945–66 was extraordinary when one considers the turnover of the electorate in almost fifty years and the political upheaval in the middle.[36]

We have, it may appear, all the requisites for a 'natural experiment': we hold constant the background conditions (constitutional and party-structural), we vary the élite behaviour (élite conflict in the First Republic, élite cartel in the Second), and we observe a difference in the

[34] William T. Bluhm, *Building an Austrian Nation: the Political Integration of a Western State* (New Haven and London: Yale University Press, 1973), 71.

[35] Pulzer, 'Austria', in McRae, pp. 173–4.

[36] See ibid. 168–9.

result (collapse of the First Republic, stability of the Second). Is there any room, then, for doubting Lijphart's categorical assertion that 'The fragmented and unstable Austrian First Republic of the interwar years was transformed into the still fragmented but stable Second Republic after the Second World War by means of a consociational solution'?[37]

It would be a bold man who would undertake to show that the 'consociational solution' was *not* the explanation of the difference between the experience of the First and Second Republics. I do not propose to be that man. But I do want to argue that there is room for doubt. There were other potentially relevant differences between the First and Second Republics than the behaviour of the political élite; and even if élite behaviour is accepted as a crucially important difference, it may be that a smaller shift than that from a '*Lager* mentality' to a 'consociational solution' would have been sufficient to bring about stability within the same constitutional and party-structural framework.

Expressed formally in terms of the logic of 'natural experiments', the main point is that the *ceteris paribus* condition for ascribing the change in outcome to the 'experimental' change in treatment is not met. Therefore we cannot assert with confidence that the change in treatment (consociational democracy) was either (*a*) a necessary or (*b*) a sufficient condition of the change in outcome (stable democracy). It may be helpful to set out in detail the implications of this for the Austrian case.

(*a*) *Necessary condition.* Given the other changes between the two periods, it may be that the Second Republic would have survived where the First Republic collapsed without the 'consociational solution'. This does not entail the extreme proposition that the Second Republic could have survived if élite behaviour had been exactly the same as it was under the First Republic. Indeed, since the formal end of the First Republic was constituted by a piece of élite behaviour—Dollfuss's coup in 1934—this alternative scarcely makes sense. But what we are saying is that it may be that some less formally institutionalized change from the extremely conflictual attitude of the inter-war period (perhaps no more than a degree of self-restraint) would have been enough, combined with other favourable conditions, to give the Second Republic the same lease of life as it has actually enjoyed.

(*b*) *Sufficient condition.* Given the other changes between the two

---

[37] Lijphart, 'Consociational Democracy', in McRae, p. 75.

periods, the survival of the Second Republic does not show that the First Republic would have survived if the 'consociational solution' had been adopted by the political élite. It is possible that conditions were too unfavourable between the wars for any pattern of élite behaviour to have ensured the survival of the First Republic.

Notice that it is logically possible to take a mixed position. Thus, one might say that the 'consociational solution' was necessary *plus* the other favourable factors to create a stable democracy in 1945, whereas the 'consociational solution' *without* these other favourable factors would not have been enough to create a stable democracy in 1918. Although he does not explicitly commit himself on the second half, this would appear to be Bluhm's position. But it should be made clear that it falls far short of the proposition that the 'consociational solution' was sufficient to transform the First Republic into the Second.

A subsidiary logical point to which I should like to draw attention is this. Even if we allowed that such changes as there were between the inter-war and post-war periods were of no relevance in determining the a priori prospects for the survival of a democratic regime, we could still assert no more than that the change in treatment (consociational democracy) was a sufficient condition of the change in outcome. We could not say that it was a necessary condition because it is possible that alternative treatments to the one actually applied would have produced the same outcome. The Duke of Clarence was drowned in a butt of Malmsey, but we should be unwise to deduce from that that water would not have been just as effective. For many purposes a sufficient condition is adequate. If we are interested in the cause of the Duke of Clarence's death, it is enough to know that he was drowned in a butt of Malmsey. But if we are interested in finding out how to drown people it is highly relevant to know whether the cheaper and generally more readily available substitute of water would have done as well. Similarly, if we wish to extract lessons from the 'consociational democracies' for application to other deeply divided societies, we need to know not only that a 'consociational solution' has caused stability in certain cases but also whether any alternative patterns of élite behaviour (maybe more attainable) would have done so.

Of course, even if we believe the answer to be that no alternative pattern of élite behaviour would have been effective, this is not enough to enable us to recommend a 'consociational solution' to another society. Here my main point comes in again: there may be differences between divided societies that enable a 'consociational solution'—or perhaps other 'solutions' too—to bring about stability in one and not another. I shall enlarge on these problems of extrapolation in the next section of this chapter and in chapter 5.

So far I have merely stated logically possible objections to the thesis that the 'consociational solution' explains the success of the Second Republic in contrast to the failure of the First. What I have to do now is to argue that these objections are not only possible but plausible. What, then, are the alternative explanations of the success of the Second Republic that involve factors other than élite behaviour? I make no claim for originality in adducing two relevant differences between the inter-war and post-war periods: the altered international setting and the contrast between the economic dislocation after the First World War and the growing prosperity of Western Europe (in which Austria fully shared) after the Second.

I have already mentioned William T. Bluhm's *Building an Austrian Nation*. Bluhm places great explanatory emphasis on élite behaviour, and mentions with approval the ideas of Lijphart, Lorwin, and Nordlinger.[38] And he commits himself to a strong claim for the 'consociational solution': that it was a necessary condition of stability. 'If the existence of opposing armies [the great political parties] was not to result in catastrophic conflict, if they *had* to be brought to agreement, this could only be by a procedure resembling a continuous treaty or contract negotiation, a constant conclave of their chiefs, resolving issues through compromise and unanimous decision—a "Grand Coalition".' The words 'could only' entail that if the People's party, after winning an absolute majority of seats in the elections of 1945, had not invited the Socialist party to join them in forming a government, or if the Socialists had refused, the result would have been 'catastrophic conflict'.

At the same time, however, Bluhm presents the evidence on the basis of which this claim can be doubted. The First Republic was born in defeat, as a by-product of the dismemberment of the Austro-Hungarian Empire. It was 'the state that nobody wanted'. 'On November 12, 1918, the Provisional National Assembly unanimously voted a constitutional law declaring that "German Austria is a part of the German Reich".'[39] Refused *Anschluss* by the Allies, the inhabitants of the newly-created Austria had to live together, but without any commitment to doing so.

Compare the situation in 1945. The experience of *Anschluss* had

---

[38] Bluhm, *Building an Austrian Nation*, p. 68 n. 37.     [39] Ibid. 25.

hardly been encouraging, and, by dissociating itself from Germany, Austria had the opportunity of being treated, if not as an honorary victor, at least as a liberated victim. Nor did it make much sense now to regret the loss of the eastern territories. In spite of partial Russian occupation, one might just dare to hope for a unified Austria, but a unified 'Danubian confederation' (the ideal of some after the First World War) was obviously out of the question. Although, as Bluhm shows, there would still be widespread doubts about the existence of an 'Austrian nation', there was little room for disagreement about the necessity for an Austria state.

The contrast in economic performance is just as clear. Indeed, one of the main forces behind the demand for *Anschluss* was the belief that the Austria created in 1918 was economically non-viable.

Everything seemed to point to a need for integration into some kind of a larger political unit. Heavy industry . . . was virtually non-existent. The centers of the empire had been in Bohemia and Moravia, which now were foreign territory. . . . The empire had not formed or accumulated capital to anything like the degree typical of western European industrial states during the second part of the nineteenth century. . . . The Austrian republic, fifteen years after its inception, found itself with a structural unemployment problem; there was a labor force of two million but only 1·4 million jobs.[40]

In 1945 the Second Republic inherited the fruits of an industrial build-up, partly thanks to Hitler, and was further helped by the Marshall Plan. 'During 1948–52 one-third of the net investment was financed by ERP counterpart funds.'[41] The 'soaring productivity and consumer affluence' have 'disproven once and for all the myth of economic nonviability'.[42]

It should be recognized at once that those who wish to assert the unique causal efficacy of élite behaviour in explaining the collapse of the First Republic and the stability of the Second are not thereby committed to denying the relevance of these international or economic factors. But if they are to be consistent they can allow them only as a cause of the cause, not as an independent cause. In other words, they can say that the changed conditions of 1945 provided an incentive to the party leaders to make a go of the Second Republic that was lacking after 1918 when neither side saw the First Republic as more than an unsatisfactory and unviable stopgap.

Even this, however, is dangerous ground. For, if we were to say that the party leaders in 1918 and in 1945 could not have behaved

[40] Ibid. 24.     [41] Ibid. 86.     [42] Ibid. 85.

differently from the way they did, the whole 'consociational democracy' thesis collapses. As Lijphart makes very clear (and he is here followed by Nordlinger), the essence of the theory is to assert that political leaders have an autonomous influence on events and to deny that they are merely the passive instruments of 'social forces' or 'political cleavages'. In a broader setting, the 'consociational democracy' thesis can be seen as part of the movement among political scientists in recent years towards a reassertion of politics as the 'master science', in reaction to the socio-economic reductionism implicit in the explanatory claims of political sociology.

If, therefore, anything significant is to be left of the 'consociational democracy' theory, we have to believe that it makes sense to ask what would have happened if the party leaders had behaved co-operatively in the First Republic or competitively in the Second. Even if the behaviour of the actual leaders was determined by circumstances, we have to be prepared to believe that other leaders (similar in all other respects, perhaps) might have chosen to behave differently. The question to be asked is: what difference would this difference of behaviour have made to the stability and survival of the two Austrian Republics?

The answer can be no more than a matter for speculation, and this must be so where we have only one case from which to draw conclusions. But it can be informed speculation. The information may be about Austria or about other countries. Although it is a truism that every country is unique, this does not entail that there are no valid generalizations in politics, nor does it prevent us from making particular comparisons that are at least highly suggestive.

One of the best-established generalizations in political science is, surely, that a prosperous country is more likely to be stable than one with high unemployment and stagnant or falling production. This is true whatever the regime but, because of the peculiar dependence of representative democracy on widespread consent among the population, it is especially true of that form of regime. On the strength of this generalization and the facts already mentioned concerning Austria's economic performance in the inter-war and post-war periods, we would predict, without any further information, that the First Republic would be less healthy than the Second.

Of course, it could be argued that the contrasting economic performance was itself the result of the difference between one-party and two-party governments. Even if this were so, it would not, strictly speaking, support the thesis that consociational democracy is a way of overcoming otherwise unfavourable conditions. At most, it would suggest that consociational democracy helps create favourable conditions. But in any case the overriding fact is that every Western European country suffered economic dislocation in the inter-war period and every Western European country shared in a sustained boom after the Second World War. In the face of this it seems out of place to look for an explanation of the general features of Austria's economic performance in the two periods by looking for specifically Austrian causes.

If we turn from economic to political conditions, we are again led to wonder how much is left to be explained by the presence or absence of consociational devices. In having its own brand of authoritarian clerical corporatist state (established on 1 May 1934), Austria was in phase with the rest of Western Europe in the 1930s, just as it was after the Second World War in remaining a functioning parliamentary democracy.

More specifically, the Nazi momentum in Germany would have posed a threat to Austrian democracy however its institutions had been operated by the politicians of the Christian Social and Socialist parties. Bluhm speaks of 'the identification of German nationalism with Nazi ideology' and notes that in the local elections of 1932 the National Socialists polled over 200,000 votes in Vienna, winning fifteen seats (fourteen of them Christian Social), while 'Christian Social majorities in Lower Austria and Salzburg had been destroyed by the Nazis'.[43] The end of the First Republic was a Christian Social coup, not against the threat of the Socialists, but against the further erosion of the Christian Social Party's position by the Nazis.

Obviously, we can play the game of 'might have been' in greater elaboration, and suggest that the two major parliamentary parties might have co-operated to check the growth of Nazism. But the essence of consociational *democracy* is that the parties taking part in the collaborative enterprise should be able to hold the support of their followers in free elections. Manifestly, the Christian Social party was failing to hold its support in 1932, and (extrapolating from German experience, which seems reasonable here) one would expect the Nazi surge to have continued if further elections had been held. I can see no reason for supposing that a Christian Social/Socialist 'grand coalition' would have reduced the growth in Nazi support. And it might have increased it: as has often been pointed out, a 'grand coalition' of the

[43] Ibid. 34.

pro-system parties may be counterproductive in driving discontent into anti-system channels.

The threat to the Christian Social electoral position could have been avoided by a bilateral 'red-black' authoritarian regime instead of the unilateral 'black' one. But this would not be consociational *democracy*, nor would it really be *consociation* since it would be co-operation by two political forces to suppress the rise of a third one. For the same reasons, incidentally, I am unwilling to accept the alleged South American examples of consociational democracy that are sometimes put forward. To say, for example, of the agreement in 1958 between the *Blancos* and the *Colorados* in Colombia that it was a 'consociational arrangement', although 'the efficacy of the right to vote is severely restricted', might at best be regarded as heavy irony, since the agreement had the effect that, regardless of the distribution of political sentiment in the population, the two parties would share power in predetermined ways.[44]

As far as the inter-war period is concerned, then, the basic facts are as follows. The First Republic lasted from 1918 until 1934 (or 1933 if we count the dissolution of the National Assembly *sine die* by the President as the effective end of the regime), with a competitive rather than consociational system of parliamentary government. In 1938 Hitler invaded Austria and brought Austrian independence to an end. Since I take it that no previous history of co-operation between the Christian Social and Socialist parties would have enabled Austria to resist this invasion for long, we can say that the only question at issue is whether consociational democracy could have saved the First Republic for an extra four or five years. And this, as we have seen, is quite problematic given the strength of the Nazi challenge within the country. When we reflect on the disadvantages under which the First Republic laboured, we should perhaps be more impressed with the fact that it survived as long as it did than with the fact that it eventually fell.

The relevant question for the inter-war period is: given the economic and political conditions, could the First Republic have survived longer than it did if the two major parties had acted in a 'consociational' fashion? The relevant question for the post-war period is: given the economic and political conditions, could the Second Republic have lasted until now if the two major parties had not acted in a 'consociational' fashion from 1945 until 1966? As I have already

---

[44] See Lijphart, 'Consociational Democracy', in McRae, p. 77.

mentioned, the general economic conditions were more benign, and so were the general political conditions. Democratic institutions in Western Europe were faced in the 1930s with the challenge of Fascism, and it was predictable that the Nazi success in Germany would be reflected within Austria. After the Second World War the parallel threat to democratic institutions was the Communist surge, but indigenous support for Communism in Austria was vanishingly small as a result of the experience of Russian occupation.

The comparison with West Germany seems to me very suggestive, and it is rather surprising that more has not been made of West Germany as a 'control'. The contrast between the precarious existence and ignominious downfall of the Weimar Republic on the one hand and the stability and widespread acceptance of the Federal Republic on the other is surely at least as striking as the contrast between the First and Second Republics in Austria. Yet the West German regime has not been claimed by anyone for the ranks of the consociational democracies.

Perhaps this in itself ought to be a little surprising, since the expression 'cartel of élites', used by Lijphart as one characterization of consociational democracy, was itself borrowed from Ralf Dahrendorf's book *Society and Democracy in Germany*.[45] But Dahrendorf did not mean by this 'universal participation', as Lijphart glosses it. Rather, he intended the expression to refer to the unwillingness of the members of the German élite to take individual responsibility for sweeping policy initiatives.

By the cartel of elites I do not mean any explicit, much less written agreement between generals, entrepreneurs, bishops and party chairmen; the idea would be absurd as the social contract certified by a notary public. [Yet this is exactly what the Austrian *Koalitionspakt* was—B.B.] What I mean is that the elites behave as if they had agreed to cease from all initiative, to distribute social power according to a certain rule and not to dispute this rule. The 'cartel' in this social-political sense is a conceptual implication, not a real institution. . . .[46]

We should not allow ourselves to get sidetracked here by Dahrendorf's belief in the virtues of conflict and his consequently negative evaluation of the respect shown for vested interests in the Federal Republic. We may wish to say that both in Germany and in Austria a certain caution and forbearance among the members of the

[45] See ibid. 76.
[46] Ralf Dahrendorf, *Society and Democracy in Germany* (London: Weidenfeld & Nicolson, 1968), 269.

political élite was a prudent reaction to the excesses of the inter-war period. But the significance for our purpose of the West German case is that it shows us a country establishing a stable and widely accepted regime of parliamentary democracy without the use of consociational devices. The Austrian People's party invited the Socialists to join the government in 1945 although they had won a majority of seats, and the 'grand coalition' continued until 1966. In West Germany, by contrast, the same formative years (until the 'grand coalition' of 1966) were years in which Christian Democrats ruled either alone or in coalition with the small Free Democrat party.

Obviously, the relevance of the West German case can be disputed. Since no two countries are exactly alike, it is always possible to deny that what happened in one is a valid guide to what would have happened in another. And it is certainly true that a sceptic can point to two changes between Weimar and Bonn that do not have parallels in Austria: first a reconstitution of the boundaries of the state and second a change from a fragmented party system to a two-and-a-half party system. But, at the same time, it must be observed that both of these changes make the analogy between post-war Germany and post-war Austria more convincing. The party systems of the two countries have been remarkably similar: a large Social Democratic party, a large Conservative/Christian party, and a small middle-class liberal party sometimes holding the balance of seats in parliament. And, although I would not want to make too much of the point, the loss of Prussia surely left the truncated West Germany more culturally similar to Austria than the whole of Germany had been.

The conclusion towards which I am driving is this. When we set the post-war experience of Austria in a comparative context, we must doubt whether the 'consociational solution'—the combination of a 'grand coalition' and a very strict *Proporz* principle for all sorts of appointments—was really a necessary condition of stable democracy. To put it concretely, suppose that in November 1945, after the Austrian People's party had won a narrow overall majority in elections to the National Assembly, their leader had *not* approached the Socialists with the offer of a coalition but had instead installed himself as Chancellor of a one-party government. Would the result, within a few years, have been either a civil war or a potential civil war averted at the cost of the suppression of free institutions?

Bluhm commits himself firmly to this proposition. 'Parliamentary elections . . . tallied . . . the strength of opposing armies. If the existence of opposing armies was not to result in catastrophic conflict, if they *had* to be brought to agreement, this could only be by a procedure resembling a continuous treaty or contract negotiation, a constant conclave of their chiefs, resolving issues through compromise and unanimous decision—a "Grand Coalition".[47] But is this apocalyptic vision of the inevitable alternative plausible?

We might concede to those who emphasize the importance of leadership behaviour that, if the leaders of the two major parties had been determined to maximize conflict and had organized their followers to carry on an extra-parliamentary struggle, they could probably have made the Second Republic collapse. Even this much, however, may be doubted if we are prepared to draw any general conclusions from G. Bingham Powell's study of a small town near Salzburg (Hallein).[48] Town council politics are quite rancorous in Hallein (though Powell does seem to be rather easily shocked), and the leaders of the two main parties view one another with a great deal of hostility. In spite of this, and the extent to which party supporters are segregated in economic, cultural, and sporting organizations, the level of hostility among the population at large is not high. Of the whole sample in Powell's survey, about 7 per cent would be displeased at the prospect of a child marrying across party lines, and about 14 per cent thought that if the other party came to power nationally it would 'endanger the nation'.[49]

This suggests that the mass is a restraining influence on the élites and not (as in the classic 'consociational' vision) that the élites have to collaborate to keep their supporters away from one another's throats. Strong support for this impression is provided by Powell himself, who reports 'the attitude expressed by the overwhelming majority of survey respondents (more than 75% in both major parties) who thought the political parties should cooperate more at the local level'.[50]

However, let us concede that, with sufficiently determined efforts to produce chronic confrontation at the national level, the party leaders could probably have made the Second Republic unworkable. What follows from this? Not much that is to the point. For there is obviously a wide range of possible élite behaviour between all-out conflict and the peculiarly comprehensive suppression of conflict that was actually instituted in post-war Austria.

It is here, surely, that the West German example is relevant. For it

---

[47] Bluhm, *Building an Austrian Nation*, p. 70.

[48] G. Bingham Powell, jun., *Social Fragmentation and Political Hostility: An Austrian Case Study* (Stanford, Calif.: Stanford University Press, 1970).

[49] Calculated from Table 19, p. 61, of Powell, *Social Fragmentation*.     [50] Ibid. 71.

provides a model of an alternative line of development based on mutual forbearance among the leaders of the main parties rather than on the consociational devices employed in Austria. We should qualify this a little to allow for the use of a kind of *Proporz* in West Germany for manning certain especially sensitive posts, as Lehmbruch has pointed out in an interesting article.

Judges of the Federal Constitutional Court are elected by a parliamentary majority of two-thirds. This rule guarantees a quasi-proportional share of 'black' and 'red' on the bench. Public institutions of political education . . . are placed under all-party supervisory boards, and the supervisory boards of radio and television are formed by representatives of the political parties, large interest groups and churches in order to establish the political neutrality of these media.'[51]

This fairly modest degree of *Proporz* was little increased during the period of the 'grand coalition'; according to Lehmbruch (p. 561), only one ministry was staffed on a proportional basis and that was the Federal Press and Information Office.

As always, we cannot assert, simply on the strength of the fact that they existed, that these modest concessions to consociational management were necessary to the creation of a stable state. But it is easy to see why in these particular areas control by a single party might cause anxiety. If we wish, therefore, we can transfer the West German practice in these matters to our alternative scenario for post-war Austria. We are still left with a quite sharp contrast with what actually happened in Austria.

This discussion raises two points that bear on the consociational theorists' emphasis on the explanatory significance of élite behaviour. The first point arises from the contrast drawn by de Tocqueville between the 'men of letters who are always inclined to find general causes' and the 'politicians' who 'are prone to imagine that everything is attributable to particular incidents, and that the wires they pull are the same as move the world'.[52] Tocqueville added: 'It is to be presumed that both are equally deceived.' But we could more reasonably say that both may be equally correct.

The consociational theorists—Nordlinger is especially explicit about this—are concerned to reverse what they see as the excessive

---

[51] Gerhard Lehmbruch, 'The Ambiguous Coalition in West Germany', *Government and Opposition*, 3 (1968), 181–204, repr. in abridged form in Mattei Dogan and Richard Rose (eds.), *European Politics: A Reader* (London: Macmillan, 1971), 549–63, at 553.

[52] Quoted by Graham T. Allison in the front of *Essence of Decision* (Boston: Little, Brown, 1971), no ref. supplied.

weight given to 'general causes' by orthodox political science, as when the 'political culture' or the 'cleavage structure' are taken as the key explanatory variables. Orthodoxy—as represented for example by Gabriel Almond—is changing too, for in Almond's most recently published project the emphasis is placed on the creative role of politicians in shaping events.[53]

It seems to me, though, that there is a danger of underplaying the 'general causes' and that the consociational theorists fall into this danger. Of course, we can describe in detail how things happen by focusing on the behaviour of politicians, and there is no substitute for this. But we must step back from this level of detail to appreciate the constraints on these actors and the opportunities open to them. The constraints are particularly severe in a democratic system. Rival politicians may get together to suppress dissent and we may if we wish call the result 'consociation'; but if it is to be consociational *democracy*, they must carry their supporters with them voluntarily. Lijphart and Nordlinger both mention this point but treat it as subsidiary. Yet it seems to me crucial. We know that in post-war Austria the two major parties were able to keep their supporters in line while they co-operated. We do not know whether they could have done so in the inter-war period, but we do know that the Nazis were making big inroads into the Christian Social vote in the 1930s. More generally, the 1950s and 1960s have been uniquely favourable for parliamentary democracy in Western Europe. It is hardly a parsimonious explanation to attribute this to the simultaneous decisions of political élites in over a dozen countries.

The second point about the explanatory significance of élite behaviour is that, even if we allow that something about élite behaviour is critically significant, we have to be careful in specifying what it is. Thus, in the post-war Austrian case, perhaps the important thing was the willingness of the party leaders to co-operate rather than the institutionalization of that co-operation through consociational machinery. In other words, it may be that what mattered was the attitude manifested in the offer and acceptance of a 'grand coalition', and that the same attitude without any consociational institutions could also have produced a stable democratic system.

---

[53] G. A. Almond, S. C. Flanagan, and R. J. Mundt (eds.), *Crisis, Choice and Change: Historical Studies of Political Development* (Boston: Little, Brown, 1973). I have reviewed this work in *The British Journal of Political Science* as follows: Part I, 'Plus ça change?', 7 (1977), 99–113; Part II, 'Games theorists play', 7 (1977), 217–53.

IV

We may summarize the upshot of the previous two sections as follows. (1) We eliminated Switzerland as an exemplar of the consociational democracy thesis. Because of the referendum, we argued that it does not even provide a pure case of consociational institutions. But in any case it does not fit the model of deep divisions articulated by different political parties. The political parties cross-cut cleavages in the society and provide a picture of remarkable consensus rather than a highly structured conflict of goals. (2) We accepted without demur that Austria was from 1945 until 1966 a fully-fledged consociational democracy, in the purely descriptive or non-theoretical sense that it had a panoply of consociational devices. But we questioned whether it satisfied the consociational democracy thesis in that the consociational devices may not have been necessary to keep conflict down to a manageable level.

The result is to halve the number of 'classic cases' of consociational democracy from four to two, the remaining members of the class being the Netherlands and Belgium. Both of the Low Countries have been indubitably consociational in their method of conflict-management. This is not exhibited primarily in a tendency to 'grand coalition': the Netherlands often has 'oversized', though far from all-inclusive, coalitions, while Belgium conforms as much as most Western European countries to the 'minimum winning coalition' model. Rather, what makes them consociational is the way in which the composition of the government is not the determinant of major changes in public policy, as it is in Britain, for example.

The government manages the day-to-day affairs of the country, of course. But major developments—especially when they involve relations between the socio-religious blocs—are drawn up by the representatives of the interested parties (parliamentary and extra-parliamentary) in private negotiation and then presented to parliament for ratification. Examples of this process are the Dutch 'pacification' of 1917 and the Belgian school pact of 1958.

How far the Netherlands and Belgium support the theory of consociational democracy cannot be decided simply by a description of what happens in them. As we have seen, we are inevitably involved in a counterfactual conditional when we attempt to answer the question. Nordlinger expresses some qualms about the Dutch 'pacification' on this score: was the degree of conflict sufficient for it to provide a case of 'conflict regulation in divided societies'?

For the present purpose, however, let us accept that the pattern of consociational settlements in the Netherlands and Belgium has contributed to the stability and general acceptability of the system in a way that a more majoritarian pattern of conflict-management would not. There is still a problem. The diminution in the range of 'classic cases' has serious implications for the wider applicability of the model of consociational democracy to other divided societies. Our two surviving cases are contiguous countries and the divisions that have been subjected to consociational management are of the same kind: the Church–State question and the challenge posed by the rise of the working-class movement. The potentially explosive quality of these issues is not to be belittled: even within twentieth-century Western Europe they underlay the tragedy of the Spanish civil war, for example. But we should be cautious in extending the formula to other divisions and in particular to those involving ethnic identity.

In chapter 5 below, I argue for this claim in detail, taking as examples Canada and Northern Ireland. Here I want to offer four general reasons why divisions based on ethnic identity are more likely than others to be resistant to consociational management. First, it simply does seem to be the case that acts of gross inhumanity are more readily engaged in or supported when the victims are members of an ethnically defined out-group than when the basis of differentiation is class or religion, especially when sympathetic identification with the out-group is reduced by large physical or cultural differences.

Second, religious and class conflict is a conflict of organizations. Ethnic conflict is a conflict of solidary groups. Whether these groups have an organizational embodiment is a contingent matter, but in any case they do not need organization to work up a riot or a pogrom so long as they have some way of recognizing who belongs to which group. The importance of this factor for the viability of consociational democracy is clear when we recall the point that the leaders of the blocs must be able to hold the support of their followers for any deal that they agree to.

Ethnic groups may of course have leaders, but an ethnic group is not defined by the fact that it follows certain leaders. If the present leaders agree to something on behalf of their followers it is always open to some rival to denounce the terms as a sell-out and to seek to gather support for repudiating them. By contrast, a Roman Catholic is, by definition, someone who accepts the authority of the Church. Although the Bishops may therefore have trouble with lay organizations that want to be 'more Catholic than the Pope'—more intransigent than the official line—these can usually be brought to heel by an instruction being issued to the faithful. Protestant Churches and working-class organizations obviously differ among themselves in the degree of control that the leaders can exert over the followers. Leaders may be more or less easily replaced, followers may find it more or less difficult or costly to leave. But, to the extent that the leaders do have control, they can, again, take part in consociational arrangements with confidence that they can 'deliver' their supporters.

Third, and related to this, someone can feel confidently that he knows what the advancement of the collective interest of an ethnic group calls for in a certain situation, without the benefit of any complex scheme for interpreting the world. No elaborate theoretical argument is needed to establish that some policy would provide material and symbolic gratifications for the members of one group while inflicting deprivation and degradation on the members of the other. By contrast, the question of whether or not some policy is or is not in the interests of some religion clearly depends on the answer to the prior question of what the religion itself requires. In some religions there is an authoritative source for determining the answer to that question. Although laymen may wish to be 'more Catholic than the Pope', for example, they are in a difficult position to make an effective challenge because the distinguishing characteristic of Roman Catholics *is* precisely that they accept the authority of the Pope, and more generally of the hierarchy. Even where there is no final authority in the hands of the leaders, the fact that the 'right answer' depends on a process of more or less subtle reasoning clearly gives a built-in advantage to the leaders as experts.

Similarly, it is by no means self-evident what constitutes the collective interest of the 'working class' in any given situation, and the same analysis applies as to religion. Either (as in the Communist party) it is a question to be decided authoritatively by the hierarchy, and anyone who dissents is by definition a bad Communist (and if he persists may find himself not a Communist at all), or it is a matter of argument, in which experts presumably have an advantage. Because of this contrast between the apparent clarity of ethnic issues on the one hand and religious or class issues on the other, we should expect that it will be easier for deals to be made by leaders in connection with religious or class issues with some confidence that they will be able to carry their followers with them.

Fourth and last, the question in dispute in class or religious issues is how the country is to be run. The question is thus: how are *we* to get along together? Naturally, a question so posed lends itself to consociational methods of resolution. But where the basis of division is ethnic the question may not be how the country is to be run but whether it should be a country at all. Should one group secede and become an independent state? Should it merge with an ethnically cognate neighbour state? Or should the whole of the existing state absorb or be absorbed by another? These are questions which allow little room for negotiation because at least one party may not want a solution within the existing framework.

The relative potency of ethnic identification as a basis for conflict is brought out well by William Keech in his research note on 'Linguistic Diversity and Political Conflict'. Keech himself uses 'ethnic differences' as a synonym for 'linguistic and religious differences'[54] but I shall not follow him in this, reserving the concept of 'ethnic identification' for the sense of being a 'people' or a 'race' (in the old-fashioned sense in which people used to talk about the 'English race'). The central question raised in Keech's note is why relations between French and German speakers have been so much worse in the Bern canton of Switzerland than in the Fribourg canton, in spite of the objectively worse discrimination suffered by the German minority in Fribourg than by the French minority in Bern. And the answer that he gives is in terms of what I am calling ethnic identification.

A strong case can be made that it is the Jura per se rather than language which is the main basis of separatism, and that language complicates the problem by being more or less congruent with the boundaries of the Jura, rather than vice versa. . . . The attitude seems to be 'It is not because we happen to speak French, but because we are not Bernese and can never become Bernese that we want to be separate from Berne'. . . . Although the German Freiburger has grievances, he does not see them as inconsistent with loyal citizenship in the multilinguistic canton. . . . They think of themselves as Freiburgers and they do not want separatism but, rather, complete equality in the canton. . . . Instead of having no real traditional alternative to membership in the canton, as in Fribourg, the Jura had an 800-year history as a separate political unit, the memory of which emphatically competed with Bern for the loyalty of the Jurassian citizens.[55]

It may well have occurred to the reader that I should already have mentioned the Walloons and the Flemings in Belgium. They are indeed relevant, but mainly in the context of my argument that consociational methods are better adapted to moderating religious or

---

[54] See Keech, 'Linguistic Diversity', p. 387.
[55] Ibid. 400, 401, 402.

class conflicts than ethnic ones. The claim of Belgium to rank as a 'classic consociational' case rests on its handling of the divisions between its 'spiritual families', not on its handling of relations between its two constituent ethnic groups.

The demands of the ethnic groups have not been articulated by the party system, as required by the consociational model. The major parties have continued to be based on 'spiritual' cleavages, and the rise of parties standing explicitly on ethnic platforms—representing Flemings, Walloons, and Francophone Bruxellois—has been seen by the other parties not as an encouraging sign that the problems are on their way to being solved but as a deadly threat to the system. The action that has been taken to defuse the ethnic conflict has not been based on negotiating between the ethnic parties but has been taken by the other parties in pursuit of a common interest in preventing the growth of these parties by stealing their clothes. And, finally, it has taken the form of unscrambling the unitary state set up in 1830 and giving much more autonomy to the ethnically defined regions of the country. To the extent therefore that there is inter-ethnic agreement it is an agreement to go separate ways: a friendly divorce rather than a more complete marriage.

The implications of the Flemish–Walloon conflict for the theory of consociational democracy are obscure because the method has not on the whole been used. It may be argued that that is the problem. Val Lorwin in effect took this line in a paper first presented in 1965. In asking why 'by the mid-1960s the linguistic-regional tensions appeared more intractable than those of ideological difference or social class' his first answer was as follows.

The sentimental and practical interests of the linguistic communities were not effectively organized, and the geographical regions had no administrative or formal political existence as yet. There were no recognized representatives qualified to formulate demands, to negotiate, and to fulfil commitments. The 1962–1963 language laws were negotiated within and between the PSC and the PSB [Catholics and Socialists], the two governing parties. This aggregation of linguistic and regional claims by the governing parties was challenged, not only by the leading opposition party and by the regional and linguistic parties, but also by self-designated linguistic and regional spokesmen within the governing parties.[56]

As I have already pointed out, it is the nature of the case that rival leaders are more likely to spring up when the issue is an ethnic one than

[56] Lorwin, 'Belgium: Conflict and Compromise', in McRae, p. 197.

when it is a religious or class one. But would it be a contribution to social harmony if each ethnic group were represented by a single monolithic organization? If it were so in Belgium, then Belgium would be, as far as I know, unique in the annals of human history. Except where it is the prelude to peaceful fission of the state, a situation in which conflicting ethnic groups are mobilized behind monolithic organizations is a situation of potential civil war or of civil war averted by effective oppression by one group of the other. The clearest contemporary examples of political systems with elections dominated by ethnically based political parties are probably Guyana, Sri Lanka, and Northern Ireland. Nigeria, during its career as a parliamentary system, was another example. None of these is exactly an advertisement for such a system.

It is possible to explain why this should be so if we recall the earlier discussion of the way in which religious and class issues allow more scope for the leaders to impose their interpretation of the collective interests of their followers than do ethnic issues. Because of this we can predict that, if there is to be a leadership of an ethnic group that is not in constant danger of being undercut by challengers, it must inevitably be seen to be taking up an extreme position in defence of the group's interests. And, having done this to gain and then maintain its position, it is not likely to be able to afford to counsel moderation later. Once ethnic feeling has been whipped up, it has a terrifying life of its own, as communal massacres on the Indian subcontinent and in Indonesia since the Second World War illustrate. Cyprus and Northern Ireland provide examples on a far smaller but still depressing scale.

# 5

# THE CONSOCIATIONAL MODEL AND ITS DANGERS

'What curious attitudes he goes into!' 'Not at all,' said the King. 'He's an Anglo-Saxon Messenger—and those are Anglo-Saxon attitudes.'

Lewis Carroll, *Alice Through the Looking Glass*

## I THE CONSOCIATIONAL VOGUE

In a review article on 'The Consociational Democracy Theme', Hans Daalder wrote that the model of 'consociational democracy' challenged 'prevailing normative views, based mainly on American or British perspectives' about 'the conditions of effective and stable democratic rule'.[1] I should like to make two remarks about this claim. First, I question whether the attitudes to which Daalder refers are really 'prevalent', at any rate in America or Britain themselves. And, second, I should like to suggest that the battle has not only been won but is in some danger of turning into a rout. Less metaphorically, the 'consociational democracies' are no longer likely to be written off as being 'isolated phenomena, mainly of folkloristic interest',[2] but their relevance to other societies may now be exaggerated.

In the past few years in Britain the aspects of the political system which have come under fire most frequently are precisely those where it deviates most clearly from the 'consociational' model: the artificial opposition of parties whose members (it is said) largely agree on what should be done (and even more on the limits of what anyone could do), and the tendency for alternating party governments to spend much of the time undoing the work of their predecessors and the rest preparing legislation, much of which does not even reach the statute book before the next election puts it back at square one. It is also worth noting that at any time in the last few years anything from a quarter to a half of the electorate with an opinion has been shown by public

[1] Hans Daalder, 'The Consociational Democracy Theme', *World Politics*, 26 (1974), 604–21, at 605.
[2] Ibid. 604.

opinion polls to agree with statements on the lines of 'Politicians should co-operate together to solve the nation's problems', or specifically to say that they would welcome coalition government. So far, then, from the prevailing mood in Britain being one in which the 'consociational democracies' are regarded as aberrations, it might be nearer the truth to say that there is a great deal of doubt about what had been thought of as the distinctive merits of the system: the electoral system that usually creates a majority party out of only a plurality of votes, and the winner-take-all allocation of political power to the party with a majority of seats in the House of Commons.

It is, in the nature of the case, difficult to prove that this chastened mood about our long-established political habits and political institutions is widespread. But the clearest sign was probably an active correspondence in *The Times* which took place between the February and October elections in 1974, when the unsettled parliamentary situation (the two major parties holding almost equal numbers of seats, the balance being held by minor parties) made reform appear a practical possibility. I pick one as an example, almost at random.

The first paragraph of the letter runs as follows:

Electoral reform seems nowadays to meet with general approval by the public if not by professional MPs. It would, presumably, generally lead to minority or coalition governments and this might be no bad thing. It will, however, be quite ineffective in imposing upon the politicians the necessity for genuine consensus government unless it is accompanied by a major change in the constitutional arrangements of the United Kingdom. This is the removal from the Prime Minister of the day of the power to require a dissolution of parliament.[3]

The significant part of this letter for the present purpose is the idea that minority or coalition government is desirable as a means to genuine consensus government. The writer's own piece of constitutional *bricolage* is significant only as a symptom of the tendency to cast around for foreign devices to import that people usually engage in when they are dissatisfied with their own institutions. But it is a nice irony that the device imported into France—dissolution of parliament before its full term expires—with the object of making the system function more like the British one should now have its abolition proposed in Britain with the avowed object of making the system more 'continental'.

The situation in the USA is, of course, in all kinds of ways different.

[3] Letter from Mr Anthony Sumption, *The Times* (21 Sept. 1974), p. 15, col. 7.

This is clearly illustrated by the fact that the Anglophile supporters of 'a more responsible two-party system' such as Schattschneider and Beer have, correctly, seen themselves as going against the American grain. The norm in Congressional committees is one of businesslike co-operation, with unanimity highly valued and very little overt partisanship except on organizational matters. And the rule requiring a two-thirds majority for *clôture* in the Senate (combined with the reluctance of Senators to invoke it) is an embodiment of Calhoun's notion of the 'concurrent majority', an essentially 'consociational' idea. The only 'majoritarian' feature of the federal system is the Presidency itself, and those who have in the past decried the 'deadlock of democracy' in the USA have tended to pin their hopes on a reconstruction of the parties behind the leadership of the President and (more difficult to institutionalize) a Presidential candidate-designate for the other side. But, under the impact of the abuses of Johnson and Nixon, the emphasis has recently been on cutting the Presidency down to size rather than building it up further. Restraining the Presidency inevitably means building up Congress: that is to say, trying to find ways in which Congress, through its committees, can gain some greater control over what is done by or in the name of the President.

In the intellectual climate I have described, I do not think that any further Anglo-Saxon breast-beating over past hubris in relation to our political institutions is called for. What worries me at present is that attempts to apply the 'consociational model' outside its original areas (especially in ethnically divided societies such as Northern Ireland or Canada) may make things worse. There is always a risk that proposals for institutional transfer from one country to another will partake more of sympathetic magic than of sober science. Maurice O'Sullivan, in his delightful autobiographical book *Twenty Years a'Growing*, quotes an apposite Irish saying: 'Live horse and you'll get grass'.[4] 'Have proportional representation and a grand coalition and you'll become Swiss or Dutch' is not perhaps so different as a mode of reasoning. Let me hasten at once to acquit the exponents of 'consociational democracy' of peddling it as a panacea. But I do think that someone who does not read the small print may go away with the impression that, in order to turn a conflict-ridden democracy into a harmonious one, all that is required is an effort of will by political leaders. Insufficient attention may be paid to the fact that, if the

---

[4] Maurice O'Sullivan, *Twenty Years a'Growing* (London: Oxford University Press. The World's Classics, 1953), 17.

country is a democracy, the leaders can continue to be leaders only so long as they have followers.

I should like to explore briefly the cases of two divided Western societies: Canada and Northern Ireland. It is clearly of considerable practical importance to know whether an attempt to introduce consociational democracy into these societies would be likely to make for more harmonious inter-communal relationships or exacerbate a situation that is already uneasy in Canada and really grave in Northern Ireland. And, although one can have only limited confidence in these matters, I think the balance of probability is on the latter.

## II THE CANADIAN CASE

For Canada, I refer to Kenneth D. McRae's collection entitled *Consociational Democracy*.[5] This book is a useful source of articles on the idea of consociational democracy in general and on the four 'classic cases' of Belgium, the Netherlands, Switzerland, and Austria. But the last quarter of the book is taken up with a section entitled 'Applications and Illustrations: Canada'. The editor, like many Anglophone academics in Canada, is deeply committed to the cause of maintaining the territorial integrity of Canada. In practical terms what this comes to is that he is committed to trying to prevent Quebec from seceding.

The political implications that follow have been set out very clearly by John Meisel in his *Working Papers on Canadian Politics*. He states an 'axiom' as follows: 'when two or more groups of people have it in their power to survive within independent political entities, the only workable basis on which they can arrange the political relations between them is compromise'.[6] And he then fills out the axiom in a way that makes it clearly tautological. (This is not a criticism: tautologies may be illuminating.) The choice, he says, is separation, force, or accommodation. If force is ruled out and separation is to be avoided then 'the sole basis on which accommodation between the two communities can rest is an agreement acceptable to both'.[7] But what form should this 'accommodation' take? 'Accommodation' is a word of very non-specific meaning in this kind of context. If the parties to a dispute 'reach an accommodation' this means that *some* terms of agreement have been reached, but it does not entail that they should take any particular form.

[5] Kenneth McRae, *Consociational Democracy: Political Accommodation in Segmented Societies* (Toronto: McClelland and Stewart. The Carleton Library, 1974).
[6] John Meisel, *Working Papers on Canadian Politics* (Montreal and London: McGill—Queen's University Press. Enlarged edn. 1973), 184–5. [7] Ibid. 185.

There are two possible directions in which accommodation may be pursued that are compatible with the existing party system and are indeed on the political agenda. The first is the attempt to make the Federal government truly 'bilingual' and 'bicultural' by selective recruitment, use of scrupulously bilingual forms and notices, and so on. The second is to allow Quebec more autonomy so that French Canadians can feel that they are in charge of its economic and cultural destiny wthout concluding that they need complete independence to achieve their goals. I mention these because it seems clear that McRae's object is to advocate something different—though not necessarily incompatible with either of them. He takes 'accommodation' to entail the reconstruction of Canadian politics to make it fit the consociational model.

McRae puts his case in the Epilogue to the book with quite a rhetorical fervour. He describes a 'majoritarian attitude' as the 'Achilles heel of the Canadian political system' and 'the *damnosa hereditas* of Anglo–American democracy and Lockean political theory and liberal society'.[8] His argument is that the only alternative to 'a more explicitly consociational political system' is 'the separation or quasi-separation of Quebec', which 'would still leave substantial minorities in Quebec and the rest of Canada'.[9]

McRae never makes it clear quite what he means by 'modifying [Canada's] formal institutions along more consociational lines'. But in the article by himself that he prints on 'Consociationalism and the Canadian Political System'[10] he states the objections to the existing system from the 'consociational' point of view by saying that the two 'weaknesses of the Canadian political system may be summarized by borrowing the terminology of Lijphart: *adequate articulation of the interests of the subcultures* is not guaranteed at cabinet level because of uncertainty and distortion in the electoral system, and *internal political cohesion of the subcultures* is not strong enough to assure that agreements reached in cabinet will be accepted by the electorate'.[11] I want to argue that both general theoretical considerations and the experience of other countries, properly interpreted, combine to suggest that the kind of political realignments that McRae is looking for could only be the consequence of and at the same time an accelerating factor in producing exactly the kind of breakdown in Anglo-French relationships that he is seeking to prevent. And the intellectual origin of this

---

[8] McRae, *Consociational Democracy*, p. 301.
[9] Ibid.          [10] Ibid. 238–61.
[11] Ibid. 252–3, italics in original.

error is the mechanical transfer of supposed lessons from the experience of consociational democracy in Europe.

'Adequate articulation of the interests of the subcultures' and their stronger 'internal political cohesion' (so that whatever the leaders agreed to could be counted on as acceptable to the followers) could, I suggest, occur only as a concomitant of increased polarization between the English-speaking and French-speaking communities, with each community lining up solidly behind extremist leaders. Unity and an absence of challenge to leaders can come about when the issues involve communal conflict, as I pointed out in chapter 4. To wish deliberately to create such conditions so as to create the possibility of resolving the conflict by 'consociational' means is, to say the least, reckless.

The existing Canadian party system is, as everyone agrees, one of 'catch-all' or 'brokerage' parties. Each party's support is, to an unusual degree even by the standards of other members of the 'Anglo-American' political systems—in Almond's famous (or infamous) typology—spread across regional, occupational, religious and linguistic lines. In particular, the Liberal party, which must be regarded as the dominant party for more than a generation past, depends for its position on its ability to attract heavy support in Quebec without forfeiting it in the rest of Canada. The primary site of inter-ethnic accommodation may thus be said to be the Liberal party.

I suggest that the politicians of the major national parties are right to regard this kind of set-up as the best hope for the continuation of the existing federation. As in Belgium, they see the rise of exclusively ethnic parties not as the prelude to smoother co-operation but as the beginning of the end of the existing state. I think they are right. It is *not* necessarily an advantage for the most salient (or potentially salient) line of cleavage to be reproduced by the structure of political division. Communal cleavages are so potentially explosive that they can probably only be accommodated in the interstices of politics, while the politicians ostensibly fight one another over quite different issues.

I have not referred to the way in which McRae ties up his preference for better 'articulation of the subcultures' with a reform of the electoral system designed to replace the first-past-the-post single-member constituency system by some other more proportional system. It seems to me that the desirability or undesirability of the kind of realignment McRae advocates is independent of any question about the way in which such a realignment might be brought about. I have no wish to get drawn deeply into that question unnecessarily, but for what it is worth I offer the comment that there does not seem to be any *general* reason for expecting a more proportional electoral system to bring about an alignment into monolithic blocs along the most salient line of cleavage in the society.

It is surely excessively simple-minded to say that, because the 'Anglo-American' countries tend to have single-member constituencies and broadly-aggregating parties, the first is the cause of the second. The structure of cleavages must also be taken into account. Where there are cross-cutting cleavages, but one is more salient than the other, the logic of a single-member system is to suppress the less salient line of cleavage and create monolithic communal blocs of the kind McRae apparently wants to see.

Northern Ireland provides a perfect test of this proposition, and it is worth noticing that practical politicians have been quite well aware of the way in which the political articulation of potential bases of division may be affected by the manipulation of the electoral system. Northern Ireland came into being with a system of elections in multi-member constituencies (by single transferable vote) to its own parliament. In the first general election, held in 1921 under conditions of great inter-communal tension, the established Unionist party was able to monopolize the Protestant representation. But at the next election, in 1925, 'in Belfast there were four four-member constituencies. Eight candidates appealed for a Protestant anti-Unionist vote. Only one failed to get elected. There were three Labour and four Independent Unionist MPs in the new Parliament. Unionist representation went down from 40 to 32.'[12]

The response of the Unionist government was to introduce legislation providing for elections to be held in single-member constituencies. It is important to recognize that this was not necessary to ensure a comfortable majority of Protestant representatives. With proportional representation, Protestants were assured of two-thirds of the seats in accordance with their two-to-one ratio in the population. And although the eventual outcome of the change was indeed to increase the proportion of Protestant representatives, the condition for this to occur was that the Protestant vote should not be split between rival candidates in any constituency where the Catholic minority exceeded a third of the electorate. The Unionist leaders thus accepted a change from a system that made a Protestant majority certain to one that made a Catholic majority a theoretical possibility,

[12] Eamonn McCann, *War and an Irish Town* (Harmondsworth: Penguin, 1974), 192.

in the hope (which was fully justified in the event) that the risk of letting in a Catholic on a split Protestant vote would force Protestant voters to unify behind the Unionist party.

Every general election would thus be simply a plebiscite on the issue of the border: there would be no way in which a voter could simultaneously vote for or against partition and for or against alternative socioeconomic policies that might cut across the Protestant–Catholic division. The Prime Minister, Sir James Craig, was quite explicit about the objective of suppressing any cleavages cross-cutting the Protestant–Catholic one. Introducing the bill to abolish proportional representation early in 1929, he said: 'What I have been afraid of under the proportional representation system was that certain members might be returned to the house who in a crisis on the one point of vital importance to Ulster might not stand on whichever side it was intended they should stand when they were elected to this house. Therefore, I personally will welcome this opportunity to get down to simple issues instead of the complicated ones that are inevitably brought before us under the old plan'.[13] McCann's comment seems apt in the light of the forty years of political ossification that followed: 'The "simple issues" were the border, whether Catholics should be allowed to sweep the floor in the City Hall, and so on. The "complicated ones" were unemployment, houses, rents, wages and such things, irritatingly being "brought before us under the old plan".'[14] In the election held in 1929 the Unionist representation went up to 37, the Independent Unionists lost one seat, and the Labour party two seats.[15]

The experiment was given a further work-out in 1973 when elections were held for the new Northern Ireland Assembly that came into being at the beginning of 1974. For this purpose the British government reverted to the pre-1929 system of election by the single transferable vote in multi-member constituencies. The objective was explicit: to reduce the pressures towards a monolithic Protestant vote and give a chance to parties (the Northern Ireland Labour party and the newly formed Alliance party) that attempted to play down the Protestant–Catholic line of division.

The strategy succeeded to the extent that the Protestant vote was split between extremists and supporters of the 'power-sharing' constitution, while the Alliance party, although it polled poorly, managed to obtain a few seats—something it could not have achieved

[13] Hansard (N.I.) (1929), vol. 10, p. 29.
[14] McCann, *War and an Irish Town*, pp. 192–3.
[15] Ibid. 193.

in a single-member constituency system. Then, as if to allay any remaining doubts about the mechanics of the process, the British government called a general election for February 1974. This was held in Northern Ireland under the usual UK rules, and the single-member constituency system produced its usual effect of solidifying the Protestant vote, though this time behind a loose alliance of Protestant parties opposed to the pro-power-sharing Unionists.

In Canada, it seems to be a safe bet that the main effect of introducing a more proportional electoral system would be simply to spread the elected representatives of the existing parties more evenly round the country. As Cairns has pointed out,[16] the single-member system greatly exaggerates regional differences of support between parties, so that in terms of parliamentary representation the parties are much more regionally concentrated than is their distribution of the popular vote. Thus, except in a good year, the New Democratic party is almost entirely a highly geographically concentrated party in parliamentary terms, though it has minority support spread widely through the country, in just the same way as in Britain the Liberal party is, except in a good year, almost entirely a party of the 'Celtic fringe', even though there are few constituencies in which it cannot now obtain over a fifth of the votes cast.

The change to a more even geographical spread of party representation might be regarded as desirable from various points of view, but McRae is not interested in minor changes in the representation at the Federal level of parties aligned on the existing 'catch-all' basis. I suggest that there is no reason to suppose that a change in the electoral system would have any tendency to further the kind of realignment that McRae is looking for. On the contrary, the example of Northern Ireland seems to imply that, once parties are aligned on the basis of communal cleavage, the single-member system is highly conducive to maintaining the kind of monolithic ethnic party that McRae apparently wishes to see in Canada.


### III   THE NORTHERN IRELAND CASE

The question posed for the theory of consociational democracy by Northern Ireland is quite different from that posed by Canada. In the case of Canada the question is whether it would be desirable for the party system to articulate the communal cleavage as a precondition to

[16] Alan C. Cairns, 'The Electoral System and the Party System in Canada, 1921–1965', *Canadian Journal of Political Science*, 1 (1968), 55–80.

applying 'consociational' techniques of conflict-management. In Northern Ireland the main line of party division has articulated the Protestant–Catholic cleavage ever since the Province was set up with its present boundaries and a quasi-autonomous status in 1921. Writing in 1971, Richard Rose observed that 'The two major parties are exclusive on religious grounds—95 percent of Unionist supporters are Protestants, and 99 percent of Nationalist supporters are Catholics'.[17] Although the Unionist party has splintered since then and the Catholics have unified behind a new party, the incidence of voting across religious lines is probably if anything even lower now. It is possible to imagine, if we could run the time machine back to the mid-1920s and cancel the change in the electoral system, that there might have been an alternative line of development. One could imagine a situation in which the pro-partition MPs (and perhaps also anti-partition MPs) were divided on internal socioeconomic issues, and in which there were tactical voting alliances across communal lines. One could even imagine that this could lead to inter-communal governments within a framework of pragmatic acceptance of the border.

This would not necessarily, of course, have eliminated 'nationalist' aspirations among the Catholics, even over many years. But it is interesting to note that, even after forty years—with the border as the main issue dividing the parties in Northern Ireland—Richard Rose's 'loyalty survey' in 1968 showed that only 14 per cent of the Catholic sample definitely disapproved of the existing constitutional arrangements because they wanted a united Ireland. It may be added that, although a total of a third (34 per cent) of the Catholics expressed disapproval of the constitutional arrangements, the majority of them either expressed a preference for some new political deal within the boundaries of Northern Ireland or were pretty vague about what they wanted. Perhaps even more striking is the fact that another third (34 per cent) expressed themselves satisfied with the existing constitutional arrangements and the remaining third (33 per cent) said they didn't know. If these figures mean anything, they do not suggest that the Catholics formed a unified nationalistic bloc in 1968.

However, there is no practical profit now in speculating about what might have happened in the past if the Unionist party had not succeeded in structuring the politics of Northern Ireland along a single dimension of cleavage. The current situation is obviously one of great inter-communal discord, and it is unrealistic to expect any electoral

[17] Richard Rose, *Governing Without Consensus: An Irish Perspective* (London: Faber and Faber, 1971), 235.

system to do anything except mirror it (proportional system), as against exaggerating it (single-member system).

We might offer this as a tentative generalization. It is sometimes possible to maintain a system of party alignments cutting across a line of communal cleavage. It is usually possible to shift from this to a system where parties articulate the communal cleavage. But it is extremely difficult if not impossible to move in the reverse direction, because of the primitive psychological strength of communal identification and the effects of social reinforcement on maintaining the political salience of communal identification. Sri Lanka in 1956 provides an instructive example of a case where politicians exploited the ethnic issue (Sinhalese hostility to the Tamil minority) in order to win an electoral advantage and then found that the powerful communal sentiments they had aroused could not be contained.[18]

There is, then, no realistic alternative in Northern Ireland to a system in which the interests and aspirations of the two communities are articulated directly by political parties. This being so, the choice is between repression and accommodation. The first of these was, on the whole, the chosen instrument from 1921 until 1963. The Prime Minister from 1921 until his death in 1940, Sir James Craig (Lord Craigavon), 'himself spoke of the regime as "a Protestant government" and called it "a Protestant Parliament for a Protestant People"'.[19] No attempt was made to cater for the sentiments or the interests of Catholics, and the government relied for its maintenance on the ability and willingness to coerce the minority, notably through the paramilitary Protestant force, the 'B Specials'.

In 1963 Captain Terence O'Neill acceded to the post of Prime Minister and attempted to win the allegiance rather than the coerced compliance of the Catholic minority. Unfortunately, his efforts were largely symbolic (allowing himself to be photographed with nuns, etc.), and the result was that he lost support among Protestants without gaining it among Catholics. Apart from this he pinned his hopes heavily on economic development as a solvent of traditional hostilities, but did nothing to meet the real political grievances of the Catholics: the unequal franchise and gerrymandered constituencies for elections to local authorities and the lack of any statutory protection against job and housing discrimination. At the same time the new atmosphere (reinforced perhaps by the *Zeitgeist* of the 1960s) led to a

[18] Alvin Rabushka and Kenneth A. Shepsle, *Politics in Plural Societies: A Theory of Democratic Instability* (Columbus, Ohio: Charles E. Merrill Publishing Co., 1972), 135–6.

[19] Rose, *Governing Without Consensus*, p. 92.

systematic and determined Catholic demand for improvement, in the shape of the Civil Rights movement. Illegal 'civil rights' marches, and the undisciplined reaction of the regular police (the RUC) and the B Specials, led to a deterioration in relations between the communities. After O'Neill resigned in 1969, the British government became more and more heavily involved in the affairs of the Province, and in March 1972 took direct control of it.

The lesson that has been drawn from this experience by the British political élite is that political accommodation in Northern Ireland is inseparable from the institutions of consociational democracy. Specifically, the official position of both Conservative and Labour parties, in government and in opposition, has been and remains one of exclusive attachment to the notion of a 'power-sharing executive' as the key to the salvation of Northern Ireland. The White Paper of March 1973[20] declared that the British government would devolve power on to a new Northern Ireland Assembly only on condition that there was an 'agreed understanding' to the effect that 'executive powers will not be concentrated in elected representatives from one community only'.[21] A 'power-sharing' executive was set up under the provisions of the White Paper and took office at the beginning of 1974, but it collapsed at the end of May under the impact of a general strike by Protestant workers that paralysed the Province. In spite of this, both parties remain committed to the power-sharing formula, and the constitutional convention elected in May 1975 was told in advance that its proposals must incorporate a power-sharing executive. Since the elections to the convention produced a majority firmly committed to the rejection of power-sharing the prospect is one of deadlock.

It is not my intention to suggest that I have any alternative panacea to offer. In fact my own view of the prospects is extremely bleak. The experiment in accommodation launched by O'Neill has ended in disaster. At the same time a return to the pre-1963 formula of coercion by armed and ill-disciplined Protestant forces would, after all that has happened since 1969, be the signal for a massacre of Catholics (especially in Belfast), rather than a mere return to the status quo ante.

These are the logically exhaustive possibilities for self-government in the existing Province. It is therefore hardly surprising that people should be casting around for alternatives to self-government in the existing Province. One alternative is to keep the existing boundaries

[20] Cmnd. 5259.
[21] *The Times* (21 Mar. 1973), p. 5, col. 1.

of Northern Ireland but to try to lower the stakes of inter-communal politics by integrating it completely into the United Kingdom. It would then retain local government authorities but these would have only the relatively weak powers of local authorities elsewhere in the UK—and even these might be further reduced by legally enforceable guarantees of non-discrimination in the allocation of jobs and houses by local councils. But would this save the British Army from being shot at by men of violence on both sides, and in any case is it really feasible in the long run to go in that direction in Northern Ireland, at the same time as Scotland and Wales achieve partial self-government under elected national assemblies?

Alternatively, self-government might be retained, but the area of the existing Province changed.[22] There are of course many precedents for partition and transfer of populations as ways of alleviating conflict between different communal groups in a single polity. In the case of Northern Ireland this would entail re-drawing the boundary between North and South so as to transfer to the South those tracts of the present Northern Ireland that are predominantly occupied by Catholics, and some arrangement for the evacuation of the Catholic enclave in Belfast to the South or to the mainland of Britain. The truncated Northern Ireland could then either be semi-autonomous within the UK or could form a small independent state. Although this may now be the best hope of restoring stability in Ireland, it is certainly not an easy solution. The human cost of uprooting people must never be underestimated, and in any case an attempt to implement any proposal to transfer territory from Northern Ireland to the Republic might itself occasion bloody resistance from the Protestants.

It is not necessary to pursue these possibilities further here. I mention them only to make the point that there is no easy alternative to accommodation between the two communities. It is therefore important to decide whether the British political élite is right to insist on a power-sharing Constitution as a guarantee that the Catholic minority will be accommodated. I believe that they are probably mistaken, and that this insistence makes some sort of accommodation less likely rather than more likely.

It is always tempting to seize on the visible institutional embodiments of accommodation and to attribute to them an exaggerated influence. The willingness of the leaders of the Austrian People's party

---

[22] See Arend Lijphart, 'Review Article: The Northern Ireland Problem; Cases, Theories, and Solutions', *British Journal of Political Science*, 5 (1975), 83–106, at 105–6.

in 1945 to offer a 'grand coalition' and the willingness of the leaders of the Socialist party to accept the offer was deeply significant because it showed that they were prepared to act in an accommodating way. But the same attitudes might well have served to create a stable polity if the People's party had formed a moderate government and the Socialist party a moderate opposition. Before 1966, when the People's Party did form a government by itself, some writers in Austria had predicted disaster if the 'grand coalition' came to an end: they had made the mistake of taking as essential the formal framework of accommodation. What really mattered was that both sides behaved with restraint: the government did not threaten the position of the opposition, nor the opposition the position of the government. (According to Bluhm,[23] the People's party sent a deputation to London to find out from the Conservative party how to conduct a one-party government!)

In an exactly similar way there can be no question that it would be enormously encouraging for the future of Northern Ireland if a party representing a substantial proportion of the Protestant vote in Northern Ireland were voluntarily to offer a coalition to a party representing a substantial proportion of the Catholic vote and if this party were to accept. For it would show in the clearest possible way that representatives of both sides recognized the necessity for reaching an accommodation.

But the same real desire to reach an accommodation might be shown by a Protestant government trying seriously to remove the grievances of the Catholics and a Catholic party acknowledging the genuineness of the government's attempt and accepting the role of 'loyal opposition'. The beginning of just such a process of normalization did in fact occur in the early years of the O'Neill period. 'The Nationalist Party . . . took half a step toward co-operation within Ulster in 1965 by accepting the title of official opposition'.[24] All this was swept away (and so was the Nationalist party) with the rise of violence, but it illustrates the way in which co-operation can develop without co-optation.

More specifically, there are two reasons why the experience of, say, the Netherlands does not support the constitutional requirement of power-sharing in Northern Ireland. The first is the difference in the basis of cleavage. This is a tricky point in the case of Northern Ireland

[23] William T. Bluhm, *Building an Austrian Nation: The Political Integration of a Western State* (New Haven and London: Yale University Press, 1973).
[24] Rose, *Governing Without Consensus*, p. 99.

because the contending groups are defined in religious terms as Protestants and Catholics. Does this not mean that we can assimilate it to the religious cleavage in the Netherlands? Richard Rose, in the interesting last chapter of *Governing without Consensus*, which briefly pursues a number of comparisons between Northern Ireland and other countries, appears to take just this line:

Among fully legitimate European regimes, the Netherlands, superficially at least, appears to have much in common with Northern Ireland. Within Dutch society religious differences are of major political and social import- ance: in addition to a Catholic party there are two Protestant parties—one fundamentalist and one middle-of-the-road—and two secular parties—one liberal and one Socialist. Each of these three major *zuilen* (literally, pillars) —the Catholic, Protestant and secular—has its own schools, newspapers, television stations and other institutions. These are meant to segregate each group from their fellow subjects.[25]

In spite of this, Rose continues, 'modern Dutch politics is a record of peaceful, if sometimes incessant, bargaining about political dif- ferences among politicians who give full allegiance to the regime'.[26]

In seeking to show why, although both have 'distinctive and multiple differences', Dutch experience does not offer much comfort for Northern Ireland, Rose picks on what I suggest is a mere epiphenomenon: the number of blocs, and in particular the fact that none of them can hope to form a majority by itself:

In consequence of the necessity of coalition government, even that most controversial of issues—the relationship of church and state in education- —was capable of compromise in the Netherlands. The two Christian groups combined to assure state subsidies to separate denominational schools. Either group, in combination with the secular *zuil*, could prevent the monopoly of the other sectarian groups. In a complementary fashion, the secular *zuil* secured the creation of a secular school system, paralleling the sectarian ones. By contrast, the division of Northern Ireland people into two groups, with one permanently in the majority, removes the need or possibility of coalition government with an alternation of groups in power.[27]

This explanation, in terms of formal structural facts (fragmentation of groups, cross-cutting cleavages, etc.), is of a kind that had a general vogue in social science in the 1960s. A typical example was the reduction of a belief that one is a victim of injustice to a feeling of

[25] Ibid. 448.                                                                              [26] Ibid.
[27] Ibid. 449. See also Richard Rose and Derek Urwin, *Regional Differentiation and Political Unity in Western Nations* (London and Beverly Hills, Calif.: Sage Publications, 1975), 49.

'relative deprivation' and the explanation of that in terms of the frequency of interaction with those better-off than oneself. This kind of mechanical approach has not been generally very successful and it would be surprising if it were. Contact with someone better-off than oneself is not a simple stimulus clocking up the relative deprivation count: its impact depends entirely on the framework of beliefs into which it is fitted. Similarly, the place to start in analysing the effects of social cleavage is not its formal characteristics but its content.

By this criterion, the most important thing to notice about the Dutch blocs referred to by Rose is that they are divided on religious, or more generally cultural, questions. The only reason why there is ever any occasion for dispute between blocs differentiated in this way is that at least one is seeking to use political means to expand its membership while the rest are at least committed to maintaining their existing position. In the Netherlands, the secular liberals were seeking a hegemonic position in the nineteenth century, while in Belgium, where evenly-matched Catholic and secular blocs faced one another, both were in an expansionist mood.[28] The Dutch 'pacification' of 1917 was made possible by the willingness of all parties to dig in behind their existing lines and forswear the possible gains of a *Kulturkampf*. Given this willingness to settle for a neutralization of the conflict, the obvious principle on which to do so was that of the caucus race in *Alice in Wonderland*: 'All have won and all must have prizes'. It has indeed been pointed out that the lush development of *verzuiling* in the Netherlands is the consequence rather than the cause of the settlement of 1917. There is nothing more conducive to the growth of organizations than the existence of patronage to be distributed.

The crucial point to notice is that the whole cause of the disagreement was the feeling of some Dutchmen or (until the linguistic/regional issue displaced the 'spiritual' issue) Belgians that it mattered what *all* the inhabitants of the country believed. Demands for policies aimed at producing religious or secular uniformity presuppose a concern (even if a misguided one) for the state of grace of one's fellow citizens. By contrast, the inhabitants of Northern Ireland have never shown much concern for the prospects of the adherents of the other religion going to hell. There has been no attempt at proselytizing, and the question of schools has not been a serious source of division between the communities. The Protestants use the state system, while the Catholics patronize privately run but heavily state-aided schools,

---

[28] See the respective contributions by Daalder and Lorwin in Robert A. Dahl, *Political Oppositions in Western Democracies* (New Haven and London: Yale University Press, 1966).

and the official representatives of both sides are apparently happy to keep it that way.[29] As far as I am aware, even in the current state of extreme hostility between the communities, the school question has not been reopened by either side. Perhaps it would even be an encouraging sign if it were.

Since Rose is surely correct in describing 'the relationship of church and state in education' as the 'most controversial issue' where religious values are at stake, we should have to be puzzled by the lack of conflict on this score in Northern Ireland if we saw the dispute there as religious in origin. But it is not. 'Protestant' and 'Catholic' are ways of designating two distinct peoples, whose divergent histories are constantly kept before each succeeding generation: the descendants of the settlers, mainly from Scotland, planted in the seventeenth century as an act of British policy, and the descendants of the indigenous inhabitants.

The two sides are communal groups identified by religious affiliation, rather than religious groups. There are two issues between them. One is the national issue: Catholics tend to be attached to the idea of a united Ireland politically separate from the rest of the British Isles; Protestants are attached to union with the UK or, failing that, an independent Ulster. It is, of course, a little too simple to say that this is a national issue rather than a religious one. One of the standing objections of the Ulster Protestants to the idea of incorporation in the Republic is the very reasonable one that the Constitution of the Republic of Ireland which was introduced by the de Valera government in 1937 (specifically claiming validity for all thirty-two counties) is avowedly a Catholic constitution. The *Derry Journal* hailed it as 'a magnificent confession of Faith',[30] which is accurate but displays a frightening lack of understanding of the kind of constitution that would really be needed to enable a thirty-two-county Ireland to live in peace.

However, I believe that it is still correct to place the emphasis on the factor of national identity for this reason. Suppose that the offending parts of the existing constitution were repealed and in addition that the right to divorce and birth control and to non-Catholic schooling were constitutionally entrenched in their place, would the Ulster Protestants drop their objections to joining the Republic? I find it very difficult to believe that they would. And if we ask why, we come back to the matter of a separate identity. This is manifested in a lack of

[29]  Rose, *Governing Without Consensus*, p. 336.
[30]  McCann, *War and an Irish Town*, p. 179.

sympathy for other aspects of public policy in the Republic, such as the attempt to build up the status of Gaelic, but it is not reducible to that.

The other issue dividing the two sides is that of relations between the communities in Northern Ireland, not in cultal terms but in terms of power and material advantage or disadvantage. It is incidental to the second issue that the differentiation between the communities is religious: it could just as well be in terms of language or skin colour. In principle, the basis of differentiation might be no more than descent alone, though I believe it would be very unusual for a politically salient characteristic not to be marked in some way in addition to bare descent. That Roman Catholics were discriminated against under the Stormont regime (for example in relation to jobs and houses controlled by public authorities) is not in question. But the point is that the *content* of the discrimination was in no way intrinsically connected with their religious status, as would be a ban or tax on the observance of Roman Catholic worship or some other kind of action peculiarly enjoined by the Roman Catholic religion. By contrast, a job (as distinct from being out of work) and a place to live (as distinct from no place to live) may be said to be extremely widespread objects of human desire, and in the particular context of Northern Ireland their desirability was certainly not a matter on which members of the two communities disagreed. The disagreement was about who should have them.

There is also a political implication of this kind of communal conflict as against one between religious denominations that should be noted: the greater chance of recognized leaders being in a position to 'deliver' the consent of their followers to any deal they may make where the content of the issue is bound up with organizations. If the Catholic hierarchy approves of a settlement of the school question it is hardly open to lay activists to denounce it. But the relation between the Catholic Church and Irish nationalism has been much more equivocal. Nationalist aspirations are not defined by the Church and extreme nationalists have not been deterred by denunciation or even excommunication. 'Loyalism' among Protestant clergy reflects rather than leads 'loyalism' among their congregations and in any case there is more room for Protestants to transfer from one sect to another if they find their current one distasteful politically. The Revd Ian Paisley, for example, is not a member of any established sect.

The second problem in applying the experience of 'consociational' countries to Northern Ireland is that the consociational democracies of

Western Europe are not countries in which the constitutional rules prescribe that governments should have more than a simple majority in parliament. It is one thing for the leaders of a number of parties to decide that stability requires them to join in an 'oversized' government. It is another thing altogether if the constitution requires them to join in an 'oversized' government or have no government at all. The second is a recipe for instability because it means that any group of people (whether represented in parliament or not) who want to bring down the regime know that all they have to do to achieve their end is to make an 'oversized' government unworkable.

This point seems to me to have escaped one political scientist, Cornelius O'Leary of the Queen's University, Belfast, who has explicitly defended the mandatory power-sharing provisions of the 1973 Constitution by invoking '"the politics of accommodation" or "consociational democracy" as practised in these [Switzerland, Canada, and Holland] and other segmented societies (about which there is a rapidly growing literature)'.[31] The confusion emerges plainly when he says that in these 'segmented' societies 'the political arrangements ensure that minorities do share in power'. To the extent that minorities share in power this is because the structure of electoral competition encourages it, given the existing alignments, or because the politicians choose to do things that way, either out of a sense of collective self-preservation (where the collectivity in question may be politicians versus other actors or the state versus other states) or because they believe that that is the way things *ought* to be done.[32]

Apart from the short-lived experiment in Ulster, there are two other examples of *compulsory* power-sharing that can be studied. One, which O'Leary draws attention to (while admitting that it was a failure), is the Cyprus constitution of 1959; the other is some experiments at provincial and national level during the closing years of British rule on the Indian subcontinent. These were likewise not encouraging. An analysis of these two cases concluded that:

the most important lesson of all from experience . . . is this: power-sharing must stem from the will of the communities involved; it cannot be durably imposed upon them. . . . Should we not recognize now that *mandatory* power-sharing and democratic majority rule are incompatible aims, and that no exercise in squaring constitutional circles can replace a painfully-won desire

---

[31] Letter to *The Times* (4 Oct. 1974), p. 17, cols. 6 and 7.
[32] Daalder has emphasized the importance of historical traditions in this matter. See his article 'On Building Consociational Nations', repr. in McRae, *Consociational Democracy*, pp. 107–24.

by both Protestants and Catholics to work together? Consensus, not pre-scriptive power-sharing, is the right objective.[33]

If I am right, then, the lessons of consociational democracy have to be applied with great care in Northern Ireland. Since the parties do articulate the most salient cleavage in the society, that between Protestants and Catholics, there is, I suggest, no question that the future would be relatively bright if the leaders of the two communities saw the desirability of consociational devices (say a 'grand coalition' plus a *Proporz* for various appointive positions) and were able to carry their followers with them in instituting them. But if it were possible in the near future for leaders of both communities to carry their followers with them on such a programme, and not be displaced by more extreme rivals, the situation in Northern Ireland would not be half as bad as it is anyway. Assuming that these relatively benign conditions are not met in the current Northern Ireland, the attempt to create power-sharing by fiat is attractive but, I suggest, ultimately mis-guided. If, however, there is a recognition by both sides that some sort of accommodation has to be reached so as to avoid an indefinite continuation (probably of steadily increasing intensity) in the present communal violence and the disruption of ordinary life, this could be done without any special political arrangements, simply by the Protestant majority making conciliatory moves and the Catholic minority responding. Unfortunately, however, many Protestants probably believe that total victory can be achieved at an acceptable cost. So long as they continue to believe this (and it is not obviously an irrational belief) there can be no very bright prospect of accommoda-tion in Northern Ireland.

[33] H. V. Hodson, 'Cyprus: The lesson is that people cannot be forced into power-sharing', *The Times* (31 July 1974), 16.

# 6

# SELF-GOVERNMENT REVISITED

The least-known of any of John Plamenatz's books is, it seems safe to say, *On Alien Rule and Self-Government*.[1] This may, indeed, be its first citation in a scholarly article. There are, I suspect, two reasons for this lack of influence or (probably) readers. The first is that it must have jarred the expectations of any of its three natural audiences. Those who came to it from Plamenatz's mature work hoping for more of the same must have found that it contained little, at any rate explicitly, on the history of political thought. Devotees of 'conceptual analysis', looking for something on the lines of *Consent, Freedom and Political Obligation*,[2] must have been disappointed by its relative lack of concern for definitions and distinctions. And political scientists, who would in other respects have found its substantive concerns with such topics as nationality congenial, must have been put off by its total indifference to any modern empirical literature and its substitution of 'conversations with Margery Perham' for more conventional source citations. The second reason is that it was overtaken by events. The argument was primarily focused on the case for self-government among peoples who were still under colonial rule, and within a few years of publication the argument had been settled, as far as Britain was concerned (and to a large extent altogether), by history.

In spite of these disadvantages, I would like to suggest that *On Alien Rule and Self-Government* is worth resuscitating. Indeed, I would go so far as to say that the present intellectual climate ought to be more propitious than the one existing when the book was originally published. Nobody can now read the political science of the period without squirming, so Plamenatz's disregard of it means that the book is free of what would otherwise have turned out to be an incubus. Nobody now thinks that conceptual analysis pursued in the absence of some definite theoretical problem is worth doing. And the rise of the contextualists, such as John Pocock and Quentin Skinner, has cast into a (perhaps temporary) eclipse the approach typified by John

---

[1] John Plamenatz, *On Alien Rule and Self-Government* (London: Longman, 1960).

[2] John Plamenatz, *Consent, Freedom and Political Obligation* (London: Oxford University Press, 2nd edn. 1968).

Plamenatz, which was essentially that of a very intelligent and serious man sitting down with a text and trying to make sense of it. But for an intelligent and serious man to sit down with a substantive problem can never be anything but a good thing, however fashions may change. As far as subject-matter is concerned, the question of topicality has by now entirely faded away and what is left is a contribution to an enduring question: that of the basis of the claims that are persistently made by the people in some area to be associated together in an independent state.

Plamenatz took the view, which one might think on the face of it rather commonplace, that there was quite a lot to be said for the principle of self-determination, and that national feeling was a force that should as far as possible be accommodated. In fact, however, such a line was rather heretical for a political theorist in Plamenatz's age-group. Native Englishmen tended not to regard the problem as salient. From the supposed end of the Irish Question in 1921 until its revival in the 1960s, problems of boundary-making and nationalism had little personal significance. This is not, of course, to say that the English are not chock-full of nationalism, but it takes the form of that unconscious assumption of superiority that so infuriates foreigners: Shakespeare is not easily mistaken for Fichte. So, Michael Oakeshott, the leading native English theorist of that generation, takes the existence of a 'society'—with all that that entails—for granted and focuses on the question of the appropriate 'arrangements' for managing such a society.

It becomes more and more striking, as the main outlines of our century begin to emerge, that an extraordinary amount of what makes it intellectually distinctive is the achievement of members of two groups: assimilated German-speaking Jews and Viennese—and, indeed, that an amazingly high proportion is owed to those in the intersection of the two sets. This is true in social and political theory as in other basic subjects. And it is hardly to be wondered at if, in the circumstances, the doctrines of nationalism and self-determination have been treated as inimical to civilized values. Self-determination reduced Vienna from the status of the cosmopolitan capital of an empire to something closer to that of a provincial town. And for assimilated Jews the rise of nationalism obviously threatened at best remarginalization after the emergence from the ghetto and at worst, under Hitler, physical destruction.

One way of meeting the situation was indeed to embrace Zionism. The rise of nationalism in others is then countered by Jewish nationalism. (This is another twentieth-century theme that can be chalked up to Vienna.) Michael Walzer, in the next generation, illustrates the way in which dedication to the cause of Israel can give rise to a general protectiveness towards the claims of the nation-state to autonomous development. This, however, was not the route followed by the distinguished Central European refugees who dominated English-speaking political theory during the quarter century following the Second World War. Karl Popper's attack on what he tendentiously called 'tribalism' (actually nationalism) in *The Open Society and Its Enemies*[3] is the most comprehensive example, but I think that one could find the same basic antipathy to the use of political means for any collective ends—the same repugnance to the idea of a society as anything except the result of individual actions in pursuit of individually defined ends—in Hayek, Talmon, Kohn, and (with more shading) Berlin.

Cold war liberalism was a response not only to the post-war situation but also to the pre-war one. The popularity of the dubious concept of 'totalitarianism' to cover not only Stalinism, Nazism, and Fascism but also (in terms such as 'totalitarian tendencies') any kind of collectivistic thinking is perhaps the best indicator. In the lexicon of, say, *Encounter* in its heyday, charges of 'totalitarian tendencies' could be deployed against a wide variety of targets with remarkable rhetorical effectiveness.

As far as I can tell, Plamenatz adhered to the tenets of what I have here called cold war liberalism except in one respect: he did not share the antipathy to nationalism or more generally to the idea that people might properly use political means to determine the conditions of their common life. As he wrote in *On Alien Rule and Self-Government*, he 'belong[ed] by birth and affection to a "backward" nation',[4] and his sympathy with the aspirations of colonial peoples in the rest of the world is evident. In this chapter I want to undertake an enquiry of a rather abstract kind that I think relates to the concerns that separated Plamenatz from his contemporaries. I want to ask how far, starting from individualist premisses, we can hope to say anything definite about the appropriate criteria for political boundaries. In particular, I want to ask if there is any way of fitting in the characteristic doctrines of nationalism that can be reconciled with individualist ideas.

For the purpose of this chapter, I understand the individualist principle to be that the only way of justifying any social practice is by

<hr />

[3] K. R. Popper, *The Open Society and Its Enemies* (London: Routledge and Kegan Paul, 1962).
[4] Plamenatz, *On Alien Rule and Self-Government*, p. viii.

reference to the interests of those people who are affected by it. By a 'social practice' I mean to include social institutions such as marriage, organizations such as schools or businesses, or methods of reaching collectively binding decisions such as elections and rules of legislative assemblies. The concept of interests is notoriously controversial and the individualist principle takes on a rather different coloration depending on the interpretation adopted. Conceptions of interest fall into three categories: those that identify it with the satisfaction of preferences (perhaps only of certain kinds, e.g. for states of oneself, or only under certain conditions, e.g. perfect information about alternatives); those that identify interest with pleasure, happiness, etc., as in Bentham's statement that 'a thing is said to promote the interest, or to be *for* the interest, of an individual, when it tends to add to the total sum of his pleasures: or, what comes to the same thing, to diminish the sum total of his pains';[5] and, finally, those that identify interests with opportunities to act and with access to material advantages (Rawlsian primary goods are this kind of thing). I intend my definition of individualism to cover all three ways of understanding 'interest'. (Indeed, it is apparent that there are potentially close connections, conceptual and/or empirical, between them.) The individualist principle, understood in this way, may seem so hospitable as to exclude very little, but that appearance simply illustrates its contemporary predominance. It rules out appeals on behalf of God, Nature, History, Culture, the Glorious Dead, the Spirit of the Nation, or any other entity—unless that claim can somehow be reduced to terms in which only individual human interests appear.

From the present broad perspective, all three of the doctrines which are currently regarded in mainstream Anglo-American philosophy as the primary contenders—utilitarianism, rights theories, and contractarian theories—are to be seen as variants on the principle of individualism, as set out above. Utilitarianism in its classical Benthamite form is the most straightforward. It starts from the basic idea of individualism—that interests are what matter—and, indeed, Bentham's most general statement of the principle of utility is simply what I am callng the individualist principle: 'By the principle of utility is meant that principle which approves or disapproves of every action whatsoever, according to the tendency which it appears to have to augment or diminish the happiness of the party whose interest is in question. . . .'[6]

---

[5] Jeremy Bentham, *An Introduction to the Principles of Morals and Legislation* (New York: Hafner Publishing Co., 1948), 3.
[6] Ibid. 2.

Bentham then provides the simplest possible rule for bringing the interests of different people into relation with one another, namely that we sum the total interest-satisfaction over all the people concerned and adopt the criterion that one arrangement is better than another if it produces a larger total.

On the surface, rights theories stand in opposition to utilitarianism; for rights, whatever their foundation (or lack thereof), are supposed to trump claims that might be made on behalf of the general welfare. The point here, however, is that the whole notion of rights is simply a variation on utilitarianism in that it accepts the definition of the ethical problem as conterminous with the problem of conflicting interests, and replaces the felicific calculus (in which the interests are simply added) with one which does not permit certain interests to be traded off against others.

Contractarian thinking is a further twist on the basic individualist principle. We arrive at it by starting again from the general formulation and stipulating that a social arrangement may be justified only by showing that it operates in the interests of each and every participant in it. This contractarian version of individualism may take a variety of forms, depending on the way in which certain key questions are answered. Is the contract taken to be actual or hypothetical? Is weight attached to the contract itself or is the contract significant only as an indication of mutual gain? Must the mutual gain be realized or is it enough for it to be anticipated? If anticipated, what are the circumstances in which the *ex ante* estimation is to be made? And, either way, what is the standard against which 'mutual gain' is to be counted? My object in mentioning these puzzles within contractarian thinking is not to pose them as subjects for present discussion but once again to observe that common to all strands of contractarian thought is the individualist principle that interests are what matter, and that the content of political theorizing is exhausted by the question of how potential or actual conflicts of interest are to be resolved.

Each of the three varieties of individualism—utilitarian, rights, and contract—may be (and has been) advanced as an all-embracing theory. Alternatively, a contract framework may be used to derive one (or some mix) of the other two; or it may be claimed that one can derive (some version of) rights from (some version of) utilitarianism. It is beside my present purpose to follow up these possible lines of analysis. But I think it is worth pointing out that the enduring appeal of the three versions of the individualist principle can readily be explained if we appreciate that each of them speaks to a moral consideraton of undeniable power. However we want to put them together, it seems awfully hard to deny that (in some circumstances at least) the greater aggregate gain should be preferred to the less, that the pursuit of that aggregate gain should be qualified by certain limitations on the way in which people can permissibly be treated, and that one test for the legitimacy of an arrangement is reciprocity of benefit from it.

I myself find it implausible that, even taking all three together, we exhaust the sphere of morally relevant considerations. But it is important to notice that those who share my scepticism are certainly not committed to the rejection of the individualist principle. It is perfectly reasonable to take the position that moral issues should always be conceived of in terms of individual interests, while at the same time denying that the relevant criteria for adjudicating between interests are adequately reflected in any one of the three theories just discussed or in any combination of them.

Having said something about the meaning to be attached, for the purpose of this chapter, to the term 'individualist', let me now ask what illumination theorists within the individualist tradition have provided in their treatment of one question: the criteria appropriate for determining membership within a common state. I think that we can pick out three standard responses, all of which are, I must confess, so weak as to be a serious embarrassment to anyone sympathetic to the general individualist enterprise.

The first, which is simply a refusal to take the question seriously, is Locke's contract of association: people somehow got together to form a political society and this society then set up a particular form of government. There was, indeed, a certain truth obscurely embodied in this idea of a contract to set up a society, namely, that in some circumstances there may be general agreement on the boundaries of the polity, so that disagreement about the form it should take does not always have to entail reopening the question of boundaries. The notion of a contract of association thus functioned in Locke's theory to legitimate the assumption that any change of regime in England would leave the same boundaries. But, as a theory about the way to set about determining on the basis of some principle the boundaries of a state where there is in fact disagreement, some wanting one boundary and others some other, Locke's piece of fiction is obviously quite useless.

A second approach is to assert a right to self-determination. However, if this is put forward as a right of each individual, it hardly makes any sense, except as an alternative way of expressing the

Lockean consent theory; and it breaks down in just the same way wherever there is a lack of agreement because some people want one boundary and others want another—which is, of course, the only context in which there is any problem in the first place.

It is tempting, and the temptation has not always been resisted, to reformulate the individual right as a right to take part in a plebiscite to determine the boundaries of the state that is to include one's current place of residence. But what moral significance could such a right have? Suppose that a majority of the people in an area want the boundaries of that area to be the boundaries of a state, and a minority do not—whether they want to carve a separate state out of that area, attach the whole area or some part of it to another state, or whatever—the question is what claim the majority has in that case. The issue is in effect decided by the choice of the area of the plebiscite, and the minority would presumably begin by dissenting from that. Locke's contract of association, however absurd, did at least correspond to the logic of constructing states out of individual rights. What we have here is in effect an attempt to bypass the step from individuals to a collectivity.[7] We can avoid the impasse by saying that the right is to be attributed not to individuals but to nations. Thus, Article 1 and Article 55 of the United Nations Charter make reference to 'the principle of equal rights and self-determination of peoples'.[8] And the Draft Covenant on Civil and Political Rights shares with the Draft Covenant on Economic, Social, and Cultural Rights a common Article 1, whose first clause runs: 'All peoples have the right of self-determination. By virtue of this right they freely determine their political status and freely pursue their economic, social and cultural development.'[9] But attributing rights to collectivities is incompatible with the individualist principle. As Cobban wrote:

it is one thing to recognize rights, and another to attribute them to a collective body such as a nation. Before allowing that there is a right of national self-determination, we should have to admit that the nation is a self, capable of determining itself. . . . Further, even if we accept the idea of a nation as a single self with a single will, can it have rights as such?[10]

The third position is that it is possible to specify in universal terms

---

[7] See Henry Sidgwick, *The Elements of Politics* (London: Macmillan and Co., 1891), 621–2.

[8] Robert E. Asher *et al.*, *The United Nations and the Promotion of the General Welfare* (Washington, DC: Brookings, 1957), 1084, 1092. The term 'nations' is already pre-empted as an equivalent to 'states'.                                                                [9] Ibid. 1112, 1123.

[10] Alfred Cobban, *The Nation State and National Self-Determination* (London: Collins, Fontana Library, 1969, first pub. 1945), 106.

the interests that states exist to protect, and that we can deduce their appropriate boundaries from that. There are several variants. One is that, since all states ought to do the same things, it should not matter what the boundaries are. Thus, from a Lockean perspective we can say that states exist to maintain property rights (which are not created by the state—hence the prohibition on conquerors appropriating the property of their new subjects), so the laws should be the same everywhere and it ought not to matter to anyone what state his property happens to be in. Naturally, if you happen to live in a country whose government is violating the laws of nature and (say) taxing your property without your consent, you may wish that you lived in some other state; and I suppose that, if you despaired of any improvement from within, you might wish for your state to be absorbed by a better-run state. But the point is that you would be concerned with boundaries purely as a means to getting the same laws honestly administered, not because you cared who else was in the same state or because you expected differently composed states to have different policies.

Elie Kedourie's *Nationalism* argues this kind of case. He claims that, until the French Revolution declared that 'the principle of sovereignty resides essentially in the Nation', nobody believed in nationality as a basis for statehood.

The philosophy of the Enlightenment prevalent in Europe in the eighteenth century held that the universe was governed by a uniform, unvarying law of Nature. With reason man could discover and comprehend this law, and if society were ordered according to its provisions, it would attain ease and happiness. The law was universal, but this did not mean that there were no differences between men; it meant rather that there was something common to them all which was more important than any differences. It might be said that all men are born equal, that they have a right to life, liberty, and the pursuit of happiness, or, alternatively, that men are under two sovereign masters, Pain and Pleasure, and that the best social arrangements are those which maximize pleasure and minimize pain: whichever way the doctrine is phrased, certain consequences can be drawn from it. The state, on this philosophical view, is a collection of individuals who live together the better to secure their own welfare, and it is the duty of rulers so to rule as to bring about—by means which can be ascertained by reason—the greatest welfare for the inhabitants of their territory. This is the social pact which unites men together, and defines the rights and duties of rulers and subjects. Such is not only the view of the *philosophes*, for which they claimed universal validity, but also the official doctrine of Enlightened Absolutism.[11]

[11] Elie Kedourie, *Nationalism* (London: Frederick A. Praeger, 1960), 10.

Kedourie affirms (without offering any supporting arguments) these ideas, and thus finds it incomprehensible that 'a young man of good family' like Mazzini should conspire against 'a government which, as governments go, was not really intolerable: it did not levy ruinous taxation, it did not conscript soldiers, it did not maintain concentration camps, and it left its subjects pretty much to their own devices'.[12] The only explanation he can offer is a psychological one: 'restlessness'. This kind of psychological reduction is indeed inevitable if there is no rational basis for favouring one set of boundaries over another. 'Frontiers are established by power, and maintained by the constant and known readiness to defend them by arms. It is absurd to think that professors of linguistics and collectors of folklore can do the work of statesmen and soldiers.'[13]

   If we say that the task of the state is not only to enforce property rights but also to cope with externalities (or what are sometimes called spillovers), we can come up with a criterion for boundaries, namely that a state should cover an area such that (*a*) most of the externalities generated within that area impinge on the area, and (*b*) most of the externalities impinging on the area are generated within it. Thus, if a lake is potentially subject to pollution, there is, by this criterion, an a priori case in favour of the whole shore of the lake being contained within a single jurisdiction. The basic idea is still that states are in the business of protecting a standard set of interests. Boundaries, on this view, are to be determined on a technical basis, and not with any reference to the desires of the inhabitants to be associated politically with some people and not others. Such ideas are characteristic of market-oriented economists, whose only use for the state is as a remedy for 'market failure', but we can find their influence in political science too, as in this passage:

If, because of its boundaries, a political system lacks authority to secure compliance from certain actors whose behavior results in significant costs (or loss of potential benefits) to members of the system, then the boundaries of the system are smaller than the boundaries of the problem.[14]

The central image in the book, by Robert Dahl and Edward Tufte, from which this quotation is drawn, is of an individual with a set of fixed desires for his personal security and prosperity looking around for political units that will deliver them and favouring boundaries on

---

[12] Ibid. 97.                                                                    [13] Ibid. 125.
[14] Robert A. Dahl and Edward R. Tufte, *Size and Democracy* (Stanford, Calif.: Stanford University Press, 1974), 129.

the basis of the 'capacities' of alternative units to do so. There is a glancing reference to the 'problem of loyalty in a complex polity that begins to transcend the nation-state',[15] but this is presented as a complication in the creation of political units based on technical criteria, although in other works Dahl has shown a good deal of understanding of the importance of communal identifications in politics.[16]

Starting from the same idea, that states should administer a common set of basic services and no more, Lord Acton, in his famous essay on 'Nationality',[17] drew the singular conclusion that it did not matter how states were composed—so long as they were heterogeneous.

Private rights, which are sacrificed to the unity, are preserved by the union of nations. . . . Liberty provoked diversity, and diversity preserves liberty by supplying the means of organization. . . . This diversity in the same State is a firm barrier against the intrusion of the government beyond the political sphere which is common to all into the social department which escapes regulation and is ruled by spontaneous laws.[18]

Hence,

If we take the establishment of liberty for the realisation of moral duties to be the end of civil society, we must conclude that those states are substantially the most perfect which, like the British and Austrian Empires, include various distinct nationalities without oppressing them.[19]

This 'if' is, it need hardly be said, crucial: what Acton is pointing out here is that the best way of confining a state to the pursuit of negative liberty is to ensure that its citizens cannot put together a majority for anything more positive. As Madison said in the tenth *Federalist*, the greater the area and diversity of a political authority, the more difficult it is for it to pursue 'an improper or wicked project' such as redistribution of wealth.[20] This principle has clearly worked pretty

[15] Ibid. 'Epilogue', 141.
[16] e.g. Robert A. Dahl (ed.), *Political Oppositions in Western Democracies* (New Haven and London: Yale University Press, 1966); and *Polyarchy: Participation and Opposition* (New Haven and London: Yale University Press, 1971).
[17] Lord Acton (John E. E. Dalberg-Acton), *The History of Freedom and Other Essays* (London: Macmillan, 1909), 270–300.
[18] Ibid. 289, 290.　　　　　　　　　　　　　　　　　　　　　　　　　　[19] Ibid. 298.
[20] 'The smaller the society, the fewer probably will be the distinct parties and interests composing it; the fewer the distinct parties and interests, the more frequently will a majority be found of the same party. . . . Extend the sphere, and you take in a greater variety of parties and interests; you make it less probable that a majority of the whole will have a common motive to invade the rights of other citizens; or if such a common motive exists, it will be more difficult for who feel it to discover their own strength, and to act in unison with each other. . . . A rage for

effectively in the USA and, indeed, Acton's principle came to the support of Madison's in that the ethnic diversity of later immigrants frustrated class-based organization. Today it has potential applications in Western Europe. The attraction of the EEC to some of the more clear-sighted supporters of British entry was that it would hamper the attempts of British governments to manage the economy by using selective import controls or subsidies to industries while at the same time being too divided for there to be any risk of positive community-level intervention. If you are opposed to positive state action, accept that legitimacy must in contemporary societies rest ultimately on universal suffrage, and fear that majorities cannot be persuaded to share your anti-statism, the best bet is to go for a weak and heterogeneous confederation.

Unlike the contract and rights theories, this third attempt as an individualist theory of citizenship cannot simply be dismissed out of hand. Admittedly, there are objections to each formulation of it: the Lockean theory of property (recently warmed over by Nozick) is palpable nonsense; Kedourie's idea that until the French Revolution everybody believed in Enlightened Despotism is grotesque;[21] it is a fallacy to suppose, as Dahl does, that the only way of assuming that externalities can be taken care of is to have a single authoritative body covering all the producers and all the consumers of the externality;[22]

---

paper money, for an abolition of debts, for an equal division of property, or for any improper or wicked project, will be less likely to pervade the whole body of the Union than a particular member of it. . . .' Alexander Hamilton, James Madison, and John Jay, *The Federalist* (London: J. M. Dent [Everyman], 1911), 46–7. See also Robert A. Dahl, *A Preface to Democratic Theory* (Chicago: University of Chicago Press, 1956), esp. 29–30.

[21] 'Mayor Bilandic showed us a new and surprising side of his personality last week—he is a keen student of world history.

'In an emotional lecture to a gathering of precinct captains, he demonstrated his scholarship by comparing criticism of his administration [much criticized for its inactivity in the face of a record snowfall] with the crucifixion of Christ, the Jewish Holocaust, the enslavement of American blacks, the frequent occupation of Poland, the oppression of Latin Americans and the revolution in Iran. . . . The fact is, history bears out what Bilandic has said. The parallels between history's most famous persecutions and the attacks on his leadership are amazingly appropriate. . . .

'As for Poland, Bilandic was incredibly perceptive when he compared criticism of himself with the foreign oppression of Poland, which has been going on for more than 300 years.

'As most historians have pointed out, when Russia seized part of Poland in 1772, the Russian czar said: "Now we will plow your alleys."

'In 1914, when the Russians were driven out of Poland, Gen. Pilsudski proclaimed: "Now we will plow our own alleys."

'But in 1947, when the Russians took over again, they said: "We have come here because you have not plowed your alleys. We will plow them. We will also clear the cross walks. Rock salt for everyone!"' Mike Royko, 'Plowing into history', *Chicago Sun-Times* (18 Feb. 1979), p. 2. If Kedourie were correct, it would be impossible to explain why this is funny.

[22] If there are, say, two or three states around the lake, and pollution of the lake is bad for all of them, they have a common interest in agreeing to control pollution, and there is a built-in

and Acton's idea that the Austrian and British empires were not oppressive is pretty quaint. But, leaving all that on one side, there is nothing demonstrably wrong with the claim that the role of states should be confined to protecting the property and physical security of their citizens against invasions by one another or by others outside.

It may be objected, of course, that many important human desires that require the state for their fulfilment are going to be frustrated by such a narrow conception of the state's mission. But that does not make it incompatible with the individualist principle, which, it may be worth recalling, I defined as the principle 'that the only way of justifying any social practice is by reference to the interests of those people who are affected by it'. For the interpretation of interests that identifies them with all desires is only one conception. (Note, incidentally, that 'Nothing is to count except desires' does not entail 'All desires are to count'. A strong and widespread wish to (say) burn heretics at the stake does not have to be accepted as an interest by someone who endorses the individualist principle.)

Anyone who is content with the view of the state that flows from conceiving of interests as being confined to protection against loss and harm may stop here. It is no part of the present project to consider what kinds of moves might be made in arguing for or against alternative conceptions of interest. For those who are still with me, however, what I propose to do in the remainder of the chapter is to ask how more full-bodied conceptions of the state articulate with individualist premises. I shall divide up the additional criteria for common citizenship that are to be considered into three kinds: first, those that are so totally at variance with the spirit of the individualist principle as to be clearly ruled out of court by it; second, those that are equally clearly compatible with the individualist principle (given an appropriate conception of interest); and, third, those that present an

---

sanction (assuming compliance can be monitored) in that any state violating the agreement can expect the others to abandon it too. (For a sophisticated treatment, see Michael Taylor, *Anarchy and Cooperation* (London: John Wiley & Sons, 1976), revised as *The Possibility of Cooperation* (Cambridge: Cambridge University Press, 1987).) The solution will not work where the states are not symmetrically situated, as when several states border a great international river such as the Rhine or the Danube. Here an upstream state that pollutes cannot be threatened in kind by a downstream state. However, if we are concerned only with efficiency, the well-known 'Coase theorem' reminds us that the downstream state can always pay the upstream state not to pollute the water. This is objectionable from the point of view of equity, but the downstream state may instead be able to threaten to withold some benefit from the upstream state in some other matter unless it refrains from polluting the river. In any case, the question is whether considerations such as these, even where they have a certain substance, should determine the boundaries of a state.

interesting problem and challenge us to think again about the principle of individualism itself.

First, then, what I shall call ethnicity seems to me clearly excluded by individualist premisses as a basis for political association in a state. In the several years in which I have been reading around in this area I have reached the conclusion that many apparent disagreements of substance actually reflect differences in the meaning given to words such as 'ethnicity' and 'nationality'. Let me therefore try to say as precisely as possible here what I intend to have understood by the term 'ethnicity'.

The narrowest (and etymologically primitive) definition of an ethnic group would make it equivalent to a tribe, in the sense of 'the largest social group defined primarily in terms of kinship'.[23] I shall extend it to include (as the Greeks came to do) a group defined by descent without requiring (even the myth of) common descent from a single ancestor. Ethnicity is thus to be understood as a sort of extended analogue of kinship (e.g. the references in the British Press to Rhodesian Whites as 'our kith and kin' at the time of UDI). The essence is the conception of oneself as belonging to a common 'stock' or 'race' (either in the contemporary sense or the older sense in which people spoke of French and English 'races' in Canada). Needless to say, conceptions of ethnicity have usually been tied up with phoney biology, sociology, and history, but (unless one wants to load the dice—which it appears many scholars do) there is no need to include any of these notions in the specification.

The significant point about ethnicity is negative: that it is not (generally speaking) possible to join an ethnic group by an act of will. 'Men may change their clothes, their politics, their wives, their religions, their philosophies, they cannot change their grandfathers. Jews or Poles or Anglo-Saxons, in order to cease being Jews or Poles or Anglo-Saxons, would have to cease to be.'[24] This definition of ethnicity in terms of descent is quite compatible with the emphasis of much recent scholarship on the mutability of ethnicity: that ethnic identities can be created, can merge into more inclusive ones, or can be differentiated. The plasticity of ethnic identities that we find in Eastern Europe in the nineteenth century and in post-Second World War Africa is not a chance for *individuals* to choose their ethnicity (or only very exceptionally).[25] Nor am I intending to deny that ethnic groups

---

[23] Anthony D. Smith, *Theories of Nationalism* (London: Duckworth, 1971), 180.
[24] Quoted by Carlton J. H. Hayes, *Essays on Nationalism* (New York: The Macmillan Company, 1933), 249–50.
[25] For nineteenth-century Europe, see Eugene Kamenka (ed.), *Nationalism* (New York: St

are often identified by traits such as language; but the point is that the language in question is not the one the person actually speaks, but (as it is revealingly called) the 'mother tongue'.[26]

The reason why ethnicity cannot in itself be a basis for the composition of a state on individualist premises is quite simply that there is no necessary connection between descent, which is a matter of biology, and interest, which is a matter of the fulfilment of human needs and purposes. To this extent Acton was correct: 'our connection with the race is merely natural and physical, whilst our duties to the political nation are ethical'.[27] Saying 'You're a member of the X ethnic group' cannot in itself constitute a ground for saying you should be in a state with (all of and/or nothing but) other members of the X ethnic group if, as the individualist principle holds, an arrangement can be justified only in terms of the interests of those affected by it. We can invoke God, Nature, or History if we choose but that clearly takes us outside the realm of individualism. Thus, Herder (although there is more to his ideas than this, and I shall return to him later) wrote that 'a nationality is as much of a plant of nature as a family, only with more branches' and that 'a kingdom consisting of a single nationality is a family, a well-regulated household; it reposes on itself, for it is founded by nature, and stands and falls by time alone'.[28] This appeal to what is 'natural' and the tell-tale analogy to the family are clearly in contradiction to the idea that any form of association must be referred to the test of human interests. 'Individualism, political conventionalism, and rational justification were the counterpart to the family/state distinction', Gordon Schochet wrote in his study of patriarchalism.[29] All that has to be added is that, as individualism (which in my sense includes conventionalism and rational justification) has strengthened its grip, the family has been assimilated to a voluntary association.[30] James I, in *The Trew Law of Free Monarchies*, 'insisted that, as children

Martin's Press, 1976), 13–14. For the post-Second World War phenomenon of ethnic transformation, especially in sub-Saharan Africa, see Crawford Young, *The Politics of Cultural Pluralism* (Madison, Wisc.: University of Wisconsin Press, 1976).

[26] Cf. Kedourie, *Nationalism*, pp. 71–2: 'a nation's language was peculiar to that nation only because such a nation constituted a racial stock distinct from other nations'. (Kedourie rather characteristically equates the 'racial' theory with Nazism.)

[27] Acton, *History of Freedom*, p. 292.

[28] R. R. Ergang, *Herder and German Nationalism* (New York: Columbia University Press, 1931), 243, 244–5.

[29] Gordon J. Schochet, *Patriarchalism in Political Thought* (New York: Basic Books, 1975), 76.

[30] See David Gauthier, 'The Social Contract as Ideology', *Philosophy & Public Affairs*, 6 (1977), 130–64. Although contractarian thinking is only one form of individualism, much of Gauthier's analysis applies to individualism in general rather than the contractarian variant in particular.

could not rise up against their fathers even when their acts were wicked or foolish, so subjects could not resist their rulers'.[31] Clearly, the antecedent no longer holds, and the Swedes have, quite consistently, begun to think of giving children the right to shop around for alternative parents if they don't get on with their biological parents.

I went to some trouble to give a precise definition of ethnicity because I wanted to ensure that in my usage ethnicity would be distinguished from nationality. For the next stage in my argument is that nationality is a basis for the composition of states that is unambiguously compatible with the individualist principle. However, to anticipate the third stage of the argument for a moment, I shall go on to qualify this by drawing attention to some manifestations of nationalism that pose problems for the individualist principle.

The question is, then: 'What is a nation?', and the answer I wish to employ is the subjective one that Renan gave in his famous lecture with that title.

A nation is a grand solidarity constituted by the sentiment of sacrifices which one has made and those one is disposed to make again. It supposes a past, it renews itself especially in the present by a tangible deed: the approval, the desire, clearly expressed, to continue the communal life. The existence of a nation (pardon this metaphor!) is an everyday plebiscite; it is, like the very existence of the individual, a perpetual affirmation of life.[32]

More austerely, we may take Max Weber's definition of nationalism as 'a common bond of sentiment whose adequate expression would be a state of its own, and which therefore normally tends to give birth to such a state'.[33] My only reservation about calling this subjective is that subjectivity is often confused with arbitrariness. But a sentiment of common nationality is not something people just happen to have. Loyalty to a nation—a wish for it to have a state if it does not have one, a wish for it to continue to have one if it does have one, and a willingness to make sacrifices to those ends—tends to grow out of a habit of co-operation between different groups within the nation. For this gives rise to stable expectations about future group behaviour, and especially to some degree of trust that a concession made today without a precise quid pro quo being specified will be reciprocated at some future time, when the occasion arises.

[31] Schochet, *Patriarchalism*, p. 87.

[32] Ernest Renan, 'Qu'est-ce qu'une nation?' in Louis L. Snyder, *The Dynamics of Nationalism* (New York: Van Nostrand, 1964), 9–10.

[33] Hans Kohn, *The Idea of Nationalism* (New York: Macmillan, 1946), 583 n. 16.

Scholars who have packed into the concept of the 'nation-state' such things as an integrated economy, common social institutions, and a single status of citizen have often been motivated by suspect ideas about 'political development', but I think we can say simply that the lack of such factors—feudal relations, an estates system, or a Furnivall-type 'plural society', for example[34]—must inhibit the development of habits of co-operation, mutual trust, or fellow-feeling. The same goes for such matters as common language or common culture: they are predisposing conditions but not necessary conditions. It is a commonplace that trust and co-operation are facilitated by communication—which is not only a question of language but of shared outlook. (Thus, it has been found that letting people talk together—about anything—before playing an *n*-person prisoners' dilemma game increases co-operation.[35]) We can also understand how it is that the sheer survival of a state over a long period tends to bring about a sense of common nationality among those within its territory. The experience of co-operation tends to create a preparedness to co-operate in the future. As Weber observed, nations without states often formed political units—or more precisely were formed by political units—at some time in the past.

There is a tendency in the literature, I find, to assimilate the nation to either the state or the ethnic group.[36] Reducing the number of elements to two in either way leads to strange consequences. Thus, Reinhard Bendix, in *Nation-Building and Citizenship*, appears (although I can find no explicit definitions) to regard a nation-state as a state that successfully claims sovereignty in the Bodin/Hobbes sense (see especially chapter 4). A nation-state is, it seems, one with 'a minimum of long-run stability, that is, minimal agreement concerning the rules that are to govern the resolution of conflicts'; but it should be noted that this 'agreement' is hardly equivalent to what I am calling a sense of nationality, for Bendix also writes just before that:

Only the total disloyalty or ostracism of a section of the population is a genuine hazard to the underlying agreement of such a community, though

[34] For Furnivall, see Leo Kuper and M. G. Smith (eds.), *Pluralism in Africa* (Berkeley: University of California Press, 1971); and M. G. Smith, *The Plural Society in the British West Indies* (Berkeley: University of California Press, 1974).

[35] Robyn Dawes, 'Experimental Analysis of Commitment to Group Benefit in a Commons Dilemma Situation' (Paper presented to The American Political Science Association meetings, Sept. 1976, at Chicago). See also Anatol Rapoport, 'Prisoner's Dilemma: Recollections and Observations' in Anatol Rapoport (ed.), *Game Theory as a Theory of Conflict Resolution* (Dordrecht: D. Reidel, 1974), 17–34, esp. 22–3.

[36] Smith, *Theories of Nationalism*, p. 176.

coercion can make a nation–state endure even in the presence of that hazard to its foundations, as South Africa demonstrates.[37]

If South Africa constitutes a 'nation–state' then indeed the idea of a 'nation' has no independent content. A nation–state is simply a state in which the government is able to make its writ run within its territory. (This identification of 'nation' with 'state' is quite common, as in the name of the United Nations Organization, which is neither united nor made up of nations.)

Going in the other direction, Karl Popper's hysterical attacks on nationalism in *The Open Society and Its Enemies* (especially chapters 9 and 12) presuppose that the only basis of nationality is some kind of bogus claim that nations are natural:

The attempt to find some 'natural' boundaries for states, and accordingly, to look upon the state as a 'natural' unit, leads to the *principle of the national state* and to the romantic fictions of nationalism, racialism, and tribalism. But this principle is not 'natural', and the idea that there exist natural units like nations, or linguistic or racial groups, is entirely fictitious.[38]

The assimilation of nationality to ethnicity is also illustrated by Orlando Patterson's book, *Ethnic Chauvinism*, though he confuses the issue even further by treating ethnicity as a matter of descent-group but then identifying it with common cultural characteristics, thus finishing up with the assertion that 'the idea of the nation–state is the view that a state ought to consist of a group of people who consciously share a common culture'. Therefore, in terms of this definition, 'Britain, the United States, Canada, and Switzerland are not nation-states. Ireland, France, and most of the other European states are nation–states; so is Japan.'[39] Assuredly, 'Britain was never a unified tribal or cultural entity';[40] but this is not equivalent to denying that Britain has been a nation, except on the basis of Patterson's peculiar conception of nationality. Similarly, if America and Switzerland are not nations, what are they? They are, of course, states, and that would apparently be Patterson's answer; but surely that is not all we can say about them. To share a state with someone is after all merely to recognize a legal fact. Surely Swiss or Americans share more than that: what they share is precisely nationality.

---

[37] Reinhard Bendix, *Nation-Building and Citizenship: Studies of our Changing Social Order* (London: John Wiley & Sons, 1964), 22.

[38] Popper, *Open Society*, i. p. 288 n. 7.

[39] Orlando Patterson, *Ethnic Chauvinism: The Reactionary Impulse* (New York: Stein and Day, 1977), 80.

[40] Ibid. 75.

Patterson's list of 'nation-states' is also dubious. Presumably even he could not face the paradox of denying that France is a nation; but it is hardly a state inhabited by a single (even mythical) descent-group, and even on the criterion of common culture it was a nation before it could seriously be described as culturally unified:

In 1876, a student at a Teacher's College in Limoges couldn't say more than two words about Joan of Arc; as late as 1906, only one military conscript in four could explain why July 14 was a national holiday. When the Marseillaise was written, most Marseillais barely spoke French. At the time of the Third Republic's founding, French was a foreign language for over one-quarter of the population.[41]

For the reasons already set out, one would indeed expect an increase in cultural unity to bring about a higher level of identification with all one's fellow countrymen, and a tendency to weaken loyalties to smaller units. The only point to make is that cultural unity is not *identical* with nationhood. As far as Ireland is concerned it is important to recall that Irish nationalism in the eighteenth and nineteenth centuries was focused on all the people of Ireland: there were Protestant as well as Catholic Irish nationalists (including Parnell and Yeats) though the mass of votes came from Catholics.[42] The effort to create an Irish nationality failed, and politics in Ireland developed along ethnic lines, producing the Ulster problem. But it is too easy to say that it was bound to fail. Again, we need, in order to talk about the phenomena, to be able to distinguish between nationality and ethnicity.

We can see how both the statist and the ethnic definition of nationality bedevil analysis by thinking about the new states in sub-Saharan Africa that inherited the boundaries originally created by the European colonial powers. These boundaries were either drawn as straight lines on a map or followed the lines of rivers. Since in Africa rivers act as a means of bringing communities together rather than separating them, both methods of boundary-creation had the same effects. They split ethnic groups between different territories and brought together in a single territory members of different ethnic groups.

What, then, would be involved in making such territorial entities into nations? According to the statist conception, all that is needed is

---

[41] Peter Gourevitch, review of Eugene Weber, *Peasants into Frenchmen: The Modernization of Rural France, 1870–1914, The American Political Science Review*, 72 (1978), 1140.

[42] See Kohn, *Idea of Nationalism*, pp. 467–74, for the United Irishmen.

that the successor regime should succeed in filling the shoes of the colonial administrators by maintaining 'law and order' and suppressing separatist movements. According to the ethnic conception, on the other hand, creating a nation, so far from being relatively easy, is impossible: the whole idea is an absurdity. According to Patterson, 'the idea of the nation-state was . . . an astonishingly stupid one in these states'.[43] Obviously, if nationality is the same as ethnicity, this is undeniable. But, rather than lunge around in this way, I suggest that it would have been better to ask whether the stupidity does not lie in Patterson's interpretation.

Patterson's alternative to the nation-state is what he calls the juridical state. This is rather ironic in someone who regards 'reactionary' as a term of abuse, since he is in effect calling for a return to the *ancien régime*, under which 'the state was a juristic and territorial concept', defined in terms of a ruler and the land over which he ruled, rather than as the embodiment of a political community.[44] Patterson claims that such a state could have 'referential symbols': 'A state's flag is such a symbol. So are symbols such as a monarch, or titular head of state, or such ritual symbols as independence day celebrations.'[45] But a symbol presumably must be a symbol *of* something. Why should anybody form an attachment to an administrative apparatus with a monopoly of legitimate force within a certain territory? Symbols like this would be infused with life only if they became symbols of the nation rather than symbols of the state: what is important is not the machinery of government but that the people should have a sense of shared political destiny with others, a preference for being united with them politically in an independent state, and preparedness to be committed to common political action.[46]

I hope that, once nationality has been distinguished from ethnicity and statehood, it is not necessary to take a lot of time to belabour the advantages, from an individualist perspective, of nation-states over states that do not satisfy the principle of nationality. First, given the definition of nationality with which I am working, it is a necessary truth that a nation-state fulfils the aspirations of those who belong to the nation embodied in the state. Second, the presence of fellow-feeling obviously facilitates co-operation on common projects and

---

[43] Patterson, *Ethnic Chauvinism*, p. 82.
[44] Cobban, *Nation State*, p. 35.
[45] Patterson, *Ethnic Chauvinism*, pp. 83–4.
[46] See, for a sensitive discussion of what is really entailed in 'nation-building' (as distinct from state-building), W. T. Bluhm, *Building an Austrian Nation: The Political Integration of a Western State* (New Haven and London: Yale University Press, 1973).

makes redistribution within the polity more acceptable. (This is in effect the obverse of the Acton/Madison case in favour of hetero-geneity.) Both of these points were taken account of by Bentham, who defined national patriotism as 'sympathy for the feelings of a country's inhabitants, present, future, or both, taken in the aggre-gate', and insisted that 'as devotion to the commonweal, and especi-ally, to its improvement and reform, national patriotism can be of great service in promoting the greatest good of the greatest number'.[47]

Moreover, as I have already remarked, if trust and understandir͜g have developed between the members of a state, this makes it more possible to carry out policies that apply universalistic criteria and have the result of helping certain regions or groups more than others, because there is some expectation that other policies another time will have the effect of benefiting other groups. Trust might be defined as the willingness to wait: hence the impossibility, according to Hobbes, of covenants in a state of nature. In all kinds of different cultures, paying back gifts or services too quickly is regarded as a refusal of social relations, and in traditional Irish peasant society, where loans among neighbours were common, the first thing one did upon falling out with somebody was to pay off any outstanding loan.

If we put together the lack of sympathetic attachment to the interests of all those within the polity and the lack of trust in the willingness of others to reciprocate benefits when the need arises, we can see why policies such as those designed to help big cities get diluted in the US Congress until they are so non-selective as to be virtually useless. We can also understand how rational decision-making in countries such as Belgium or (pre-civil war) Lebanon is bedevilled by the political necessity of matching each benefit for one group by an exactly equal one for the other(s)—whether it makes sense as an efficient use of resources or not.

What can be said on the other side, from a similarly broad utilitarian standpoint? Sidgwick, who laboured under the moral and intellectual handicap of being a Liberal Unionist, offered several considerations in *The Elements of Politics* in favour of the 'forcible suppression' of any attempt of a national group to secede 'merely on the ground that the interests of the seceders would be promoted or their sentiments of nationality gratified by the change'. There would have to be 'some serious oppression or misgovernment of the seceders by the rest of the community,—i.e. some unjust sacrifice or grossly incompetent

[47] Carlton J. H. Hayes, *The Historical Evolution of Modern Nationalism* (New York: Macmillan, 1950), 128.

management of their interests, or some persistent and harsh opposition to their legitimate desires' (where presumably suppressing their national aspirations does not count).[48]

Sidgwick's arguments boil down to four. First, the state may be concerned for its security 'either through increased danger of war from the addition of the seceding community to the number of possible foes, or from the mere loss of strength and prestige'.[49] Second, there may be a minority within the territory that is opposed to the secession. Third, the loss of the seceding district might be specially serious, from its containing mines or other natural resources, in which the rest of the state's territory was deficient.[50] Finally, 'over and above these calculations of expediency, justifying resistance to disruption, we must recognise as a powerful motive the dislike of the community from which the secession is opposed to lose territory that has once belonged to it, and to which it has a claim recognised by foreigners'.[51]

The last of these points raises in an acute form the question of whether we wish to employ a version of the individualist principle that counts all desires equally if they are of equal strength—the desire to speak and the desire to suppress another's speech, the desire to be free and the desire to oppress, and so on. In any version of the individualist principle that I should be prepared to take seriously, there would have to be some discrimination according to the worth of different desires, and I should therefore regard the desire to hold territory for no reason other than that one has a strong desire to do so as morally irrelevant.

The other three arguments have some force but would presumably be just as strong in defending the annexing of territories against the wishes of a majority of their inhabitants so long as it would increase military security, accord with the wishes of a minority, or make available raw materials. Just about every international atrocity of the past two centuries could be justified on one or other of those grounds —and usually was. Rather than accept Sidgwick's arguments, therefore, I think that we should advocate changes in the international regime that would reduce the importance of ownership of territory for military security and access to natural resources. The problem of minorities is, of course, an intractable one; but if one accepts Sidgwick's claim that a minority loyal to the larger state should have its wishes respected even if this entails overriding the wishes of the local majority, how is one to condemn Mussolini's claims on Dalmatia or

[48]  Sidgwick, *Elements of Politics*, p. 217.       [49]  Ibid. 218.
[50]  Ibid. 218–19.                                    [51]  Ibid. 219.

Hitler's on Czechoslovakia? Only, it would seem, by sanctifying the status quo; but I can see no reason why, if every other relevant factor is the same, force used to defend the status quo is more morally legitimate than force used to change it.

Manifestly, these questions cry out for more careful treatment, but I hope that I have established what I set out to, namely, that there is a strong prima facie case on individualist premises for drawing state boundaries so that they correspond with nationality, as I have defined it. I now want, in conclusion, to take up the aspect of nationalism that seems to me to pose some problems for the individualist principle. This is cultural nationalism, the core of the romantic nationalism of the late eighteenth and early nineteenth centuries.

By no means all the claims that might be associated with cultural nationalism appear to me to create difficulties for individualism, and I shall begin by disposing of two that do not. First, there is nothing contrary to the individualist principle in saying that cultural similarity is a good basis for association. Anne Cohler, in her book *Rousseau and Nationalism*, treats similarity as a 'non-political' factor and draws all kinds of horrendous implications from such a factor's being the basis of political association.[52] Yet there are two quite straightforward advantages in cultural similarity. First, there is a strong causal link between cultural similarity and trust. Hans Kohn quotes Rudyard Kipling's poem 'The Stranger' as an illustration of a 'primitive feeling'.[53] But there is nothing primitive in the idea that the ability to interpret the behaviour of other people depends on a mass of shared understandings.

A second reason for having political units that are as culturally homogeneous as possible is that the provision of public goods is more feasible and their funding from tax revenues more equitable the more similar the tastes of the public. Again, this is simply the same analysis as Acton's, with the opposite conclusion: Acton favoured heterogeneity to avoid any collective action beyond the bare minimum of 'law and order'; but if one takes the view that it is appropriate for states to provide collective benefits, especially where they are 'non-excludable' so that it would otherwise be difficult to raise the money for them, then it clearly follows that the more homogeneous the taxing unit the more scope there is for collective provision. It should, however, be said that this point bears on tax and service-provision units rather than on states, and could be met by making subordinate

---

[52] Anne Cohler, *Rousseau and Nationalism* (New York: Basic Books, 1970).
[53] Kohn, *Idea of Nationalism*, p. 5.

units correspond to areas with different cultures. Even where cultural differences do not cut along convenient geographical boundaries, it is possible to go some way towards public provision for each cultural group by having each person pay a tax (thus avoiding the 'free rider' problem), but permitting each to designate whether the money is to go (say) to a Catholic or Protestant school system or television system, as in the Netherlands. Thus, the public goods argument for a culturally homogeneous state is not very strong in itself.

As far as linguistic homogeneity is concerned, we can again emphasize the relation between communication and trust, and press the view that, for democratic politics to work, the citizens must be able to communicate with one another, and must have access to the same forums of political debate. This was one of the bases of J. S. Mill's endorsement of linguistically defined frontiers, in *Considerations on Representative Government*; but Mill did not make it sufficiently clear that the rationale of linguistic homogeneity here has nothing to do with the usage of language (in the form of 'mother tongue') to establish ethnic group membership, that is to say, nationality in the 'objective' sense in which the sentiments of the people concerned do not count. The California Supreme Court has dealt a blow to this conception of the requirement of intercommunication by permitting the registration to vote of citizens lacking the ability to speak English, and it is quite likely that the requirement of competence in English for naturalization will come under attack in the courts in coming years. The basis for the California decision was that there were (in the Los Angeles area, where the case was brought) a sufficient number of Spanish newspapers, magazines, and television channels to enable monoglot Spanish speakers to collect enough information to be in a position to cast an informed vote. The model underlying this decision is clearly that of the voter having fixed interests which he looks around for a means of satisfying through the political system. The idea that there is an overriding collective interest in the maintenance of a single political community among those formally entitled to take part in political affairs is lacking in such reasoning. One can hardly avoid asking oneself what is the expected longevity of a political system in which the norm of politics as a means for the pursuit of individual interests (rather than as a process in which the conception of one's interests is constantly open to modification through societal communication) has penetrated so deeply that one of the most respected courts acts on it.

The aspect of cultural nationalism that seems to me to create some problems within the individualist paradigm is the claim that the state should be used to preserve the culture of the nation as it has come down and transmit it to the next generation. There are two variants on this which, whatever their merits, do not run into conflict with the individualist principle as I define it. The first is the one that Rousseau advanced in the *Considerations on the Government of Poland*. As Judith Shklar has emphasized, 'quite unlike the later nationalists Rousseau did not believe that the national self had any basis in nature'.[54] But he regarded it as essential for a country like Poland to have a national identity distinct from all others, and insisted that the educational system should stress national peculiarities, even if they were quite devoid of intrinsic value.

Rousseau's advice has begun to be taken in recent years by the governments of some Third World countries, which

have discovered that independence must be taken a stage further [than that of formal political independence] into the cultural fold and pressure must be placed on the radio and television companies (which are normally state-owned) and on the newspapers (which are state-influenced and sometimes state-owned) to indigenize their output, to play down the imported entertainment material and emphasize local news, local and regional culture, indigenous entertainment.[55]

This may be regarded as the obverse of the notion that cultural uniformity within the country makes for the kind of solidarity necessary for politics to work smoothly: the idea here is that difference from other countries also helps. It may be said that this other side is a good deal more sinister in that it seems inescapably bound up with the view that states are to be defined as being in (actual or potential) conflict with others. The situation of Poland in the eighteenth century was perhaps desperate enough to warrant extraordinary measures to play up national peculiarities. The conflict with neighbours was only too apparently present. But it seems hard to justify the fomenting of national peculiarities for purely political reasons as anything but a response to a dire threat of national extinction. The point for our present purpose is, however, that there is no difficulty in seeing how, if the appropriate factual assumptions are supplied, cultural national-ism can be derived from individualistic rather than holistic premises, since it can be argued to be conducive to individual interests.

The other notion of cultural nationalism that is consistent with the

---

[54] Judith N. Shklar, *Men and Citizens* (London: Cambridge University Press, 1969), 161.
[55] Anthony Smith, *The Geopolitics of Information: How Western Culture Dominates the World* (New York: Oxford University Press, 1980), 38.

individualist principle is that of cultural imperialism. If you believe that German culture is better than Slav or that European culture is better than that of the 'natives' of India or Africa, in the sense that it is better *for people*, then you could deduce a 'civilizing mission' for the bearers of the superior culture from individualist premises. This should perhaps count as another variant on the theory that it does not matter what the boundaries are so long as those within them are culturally heterogeneous: that it is a positively good thing for the culturally 'more advanced' to dominate the more 'backward races'. Acton, indeed, believed this too, and much of the essay 'Nationality' is devoted to that theme.[56] It is a common idea among Victorian liberals: we can also find it in Mill and Sidgwick, for example. Clearly, in order to make this go, from an individualist standpoint, one must have a conception of interest that detaches it from preference, since 'natives' have usually had the poor taste to resist colonization. Most of us lack the certainties of the Victorians that we know what is best for alien peoples, though Americans seem to have continued to struggle with the White Man's Burden long after the European powers gave it up. Anyway, there is no need here to evaluate the theory of cultural imperialism. All we have to do is to note that, again with suitable adjuncts, it can be fitted into the individualist framework.

The version that does cause trouble is, ironically, one that is neither manipulative for ulterior political ends like Rousseau's nor arrogant like that of the cultural imperialists. This is the idea that each culturally distinct group has a legitimate interest in maintaining the integrity of that culture and passing it on intact to the next generation. Notice that this is different in a basic respect from either of the views just canvassed because it posits that people attach an intrinsic value to their own culture. On Rousseau's theory, it would be perfectly all right to assimilate to a different culture if this were politically necessary. Separate cultures are important only as the underpinnings of separate polities. And on the cultural imperialist theory it would be positively desirable if the culture to which one was assimilating had a language capable of handling more complex discriminations and a richer

---

[56] As well as the cultural imperialist strand, one also has to take account of the Roman Catholic strand in Acton's thought. This comes out more clearly in another essay, where he wrote: 'Thus the theory of nationality, unknown to Catholic ages, is inconsistent both with political reason and with Christianity, which requires the dominion of race over race, and whose path was made straight by two universal empires. The missionary may outstrip, in his devoted zeal, the progress of trade or of arms; but the seed that he plants will not take root, unprotected by these ideas of right and duty which first came into the world with the tribes who destroyed the civilisation of antiquity, and whose descendants are in our day carrying those ideas to every quarter of the world.' Acton, *History of Freedom*, p. 247.

literature. The view in question is, however, distinct from both of these. According to it, my culture is best for me and yours is best for you. Each of us should preserve and transmit our own culture and respect the culture of others.

Now, it is quite clear that much resistance to assimilation can be related to (whether 'accounted for by' is another question) economic advantage. Cultural nationalism produces 'jobs for the boys', because the criteria for becoming a schoolteacher or a civil servant change so that, instead of competing at a disadvantage in a second language, the members of the newly enfranchised language are at a comparative advantage. But it is impossible to explain the whole phenomenon in this way. Assimilation over a generation or so can be perfect, so that the disadvantage would be transitional: in Belgium, for example, part of the tension in linguistic politics arose from Dutch-speaking parents in the Brussels area choosing to send their children to schools in which French was the language of instruction so that they could obtain better jobs in a French-speaking environment. The Fleming concerns taken up collectively through political action were not for the well-being of individual Flemings, many of whom were happy to have their children assimilate to French, but for the maintenance of the Fleming identity and culture. Similarly, in Quebec, one may explain in terms of self-interest the explosion of pressure on firms to create promotion opportunities for French speakers in the 1960s and 1970s. However, the same self-interest would dictate discouragement of assimilation to French among the rest of the population, yet the current education policies are designed to produce assimilation. Thus, there is (I almost apologize for having to say it) a desire for a French-speaking province over and above the economic considerations.

The school of German nationalism stemming from Herder is the obvious place to look for the arguments. I have already cited Herder's notion of nations as natural growths, but his primary concern, as I understand it, was with the idea that 'the individual can attain his highest self-development only in the life of the group as a whole'.[57] Clearly, if it were true that Germans (say) were naturally (in the sense of biologically) suited to German language and German culture, it would be easy to see why it was important to stick to them. It may be that some people (perhaps including Herder) said things like this, though I suspect that we tend to read into them more differentiated ideas than they had, but anyway such an idea is too stupid to be worth

[57] Ergang, *Herder*, p. 248.

attention. Even if we drop any such notion of the biological basis of particular cultures, we can of course agree that as a matter of biological necessity an individual, to flourish, must grow up and live in *some* culture.[58] But that still leaves us with the question of why it is worth trying to protect one's own culture from being swamped by outside influences—as many people believe it is—and worth trying to ensure that subsequent generations grow up sharing its ideas, reading its literature, and so on.

One possible answer would be that in practice cultural mixing is almost always for the worse. Rousseau's attacks on 'cosmopolitan' culture would obviously align him with this claim. In a contemporary version, it might be argued that what will tend to be picked up are the quickly gratifying, non-demanding, effort-saving, bland, and taste-less aspects of other cultures, at the expense of the more physically, intellectually, and morally strenuous features of the indigenous culture. This is the root of the widespread antipathy around the world to 'Americanization'. And the key to the invasive success of American culture is, perhaps, that it is itself the product of generations of assimilation and has thus selected out for exactly the features mentioned above: American food is notoriously lacking in sharp flavour or distinctive texture; American entertainment tends to require little cultural context to appreciate it; and even American language is designed to minimize the need for a grasp on grammar, so that its sentences are typically assembled out of pre-formed phrases.[59]

I find this argument broadly persuasive, and thus sympathize strongly with the efforts of weaker countries to control the flow of communications across their borders—especially restricting the import of American television programmes.[60] The standard American criticisms of this seem to me to miss the point that, because tastes are changed by exposure, individual 'freedom to consume' cultural artefacts gives rise over time to a pervasive cultural drift within the society, which is a collective phenomenon and a legitimate subject of collective concern and regulation. Of course, to say that something is

---

[58] See Mary Midgley, *Beast and Man: The Roots of Human Nature* (Ithaca, NY: Cornell University Press, 1978), 285–305. 'A culture is a way of awakening our faculties. Any culture does this to some extent. People proficent in one culture can usually make sense of another. There is no prison. We can always walk on if we want to enough. What we cannot do is something which is no loss—namely be nobody and nowhere. I do not mean that some people may not be very unlucky in their culture, either because it is generally bad, or because it suits them badly. But this is still nothing to the misfortune of having no culture at all' (p. 291).

[59] See Tibor Scitovsky, *The Joyless Economy* (New York: Oxford University Press, 1967).

[60] 'The free flow of one section of the globe merely swamps the culture of others.' Smith, *Geopolitics of Information*, p. 37.

a legitimate matter for political intervention is not to underwrite any and every form of intervention, and most actual ones are open to criticism. But the point is simply that, on a broad conception of interest, individual interests are certainly at stake here.

The argument up to this point is that, whatever the existing culture is, it is probably better, not than alternative cultures, but than what would most likely result from the (inevitably partial) assimilation of this one to another. As Sir Arthur Evans said of the culture of the inhabitants of Knossos, the Palace of which he had excavated, 'A poor thing but Minoan'.

Surely, however, this cannot be the whole story. Many people care a lot about the preservation and transmission of their culture as an end in itself. They see themselves as standing in a position of trust between past and future generations. This notion of a culture as something continuous through time, with those currently alive as trustees, recalls to English-speaking readers Edmund Burke. But the idea is more fully developed by the German Romantic nationalists. We can find it in Herder, but it is much more fully expressed in Fichte's *Addresses to the German Nation*, especially the eighth where he asks if the 'man of noble mind' does not 'wish to snatch from the jaws of death the spirit, the mind, and the moral sense' that he displayed in his own life? He invokes the German resistance to assimilation to Rome: 'All those blessings which the Romans offered them meant slavery to them —they assumed as a matter of course that every man would rather die than become half a Roman, and that a true German could only live in order to be, and to remain, just a German and to bring up his children as Germans.'[61] If we steer clear of the references to laws of nature and laws of divine development with which Fichte's text is strewn, we may ask whether we can make any sense of what is left from within the individualist framework.

Here again, everything has to be referred back to the crucial concept of interest. If my interest is identified with my happiness or pleasure (or any other state of myself), it must be the case that I can have no interest in what happens on earth after my death—assuming that death is the termination of consciousness. By the same token, those who are no longer alive can have no interest in what happens now. However, it seems perfectly natural to say that our interests are for states of the world rather than only for states of ourselves. If I want something to happen, I do not merely want the satisfaction of believing that it

[61] Johann Gottlieb Fichte, *Addresses to the German Nation*, tr. R. F. Jones and G. H. Turnbull (Chicago: Open Court, 1922), 132, 144.

happens; and if it happens, I have got what I want even if I never have the satisfaction of hearing about it. If it is reasonable to include in interests having certain things happen (whether one knows about them or not) while one is alive, it seems strange to draw the line at one's death.[62] If interests can include states of the world after one is dead, we have a possible way of justifying, on individualistic premises, a collective decision to try to pass on our own culture intact, even if we believe that it could be transformed without being damaged. (It may be questioned whether such a judgement could be made, since the criteria for damage have to come from somewhere and the obvious candidate is the existing culture, in which case all change will be bad automatically. However, I assume that it is possible to gain some degree of detachment from one's culture and to conclude that some changes impoverish it and others enrich it.)

Obviously, the move to bring cultural nationalism within the individualist fold depends on the actual desire on the part of past and present people to pass on their culture. If that desire exists (or existed), we can talk about an interest and thus get to the answer that cultural transmission satisfies individual interests. What we cannot do, however, is say that people ought to have an interest in passing on their culture even if they do not in fact have any such interest. We could try to persuade them that their lives would take on greater significance if they were to care about the texture of their descendants' lives. But if they still do not care, we have, I take it, reached the outer bounds of individualistic political philosophy. If we want to say that they are *wrong* not to care, then we have to be prepared to say that cultures have a value of their own and that human beings are, as it were, their biological instruments. At a pinch, I could perhaps bring myself to believe this, but on the whole I am gratified to find how far one can get without having to resort to this kind of move.

What I have been saying in these last pages presupposes that it does make sense to talk about people having interests that survive them, and this is, in some people's view, an odd and paradoxical notion. Let me break it down, however, into two parts. The first is the assertion that people have interests in what happens after their deaths. For example, they may want their children to be well provided for, rather than simply wanting the pleasure of believing now that their children

---

[62] See Joel Feinberg, 'Harm and Self-Interest' in P. M. S. Hacker and J. Raz (eds.), *Law, Morality, and Society: Essays in Honour of H. L. A. Hart* (Oxford: Clarendon Press, 1977), 285–308; repr. in Joel Feinberg, *Rights, Justice and the Bounds of Liberty: Essays in Social Philosophy* (Princeton, NJ: Princeton University Press, 1980), 45–68.

will be well provided for. This seems to me fairly incontrovertible. If it were not true, large parts of human behaviour would be simply unintelligible. The second assertion, which is what some people gag on,[63] is that when a person is dead he still has an interest in what happens. I think that Feinberg is right in supposing that, when one really thinks about it, it is actually quite hard to accept the first without accepting the second—or, to put it the other way round, the premisses required to reject the second will jeopardize the first as well.

Both are required if we wish to say that the interests of past as well as present generations are involved in cultural transmission. But only the first is required if we confine ourselves to saying that the members of the present generation have an interest in what happens to their culture in the future, including the time after they are dead. Moreover, it may be argued that we can still bring in the previous generations indirectly. For we can say that the present generation has more chance of having its own current interests with respect to what happens in the future served by future generations if it itself makes a point of carrying out the wishes that previous generations had for the future while they were alive.[64]

However, I am bound to say that for me this proposal brings out the difficulty of accepting the first assertion without the second. Suppose that those now alive (the *A*s) really care about what happens after they are dead and would like their descendants (the *D*s) to regard the *A*s' present concerns for the future as a basis for the *D*s' actions then. Why in that case should the *A*s not accept the past concerns for the present of earlier generations as a basis for the *A*s' actions now?[65] Thus, I do

---

[63] See e.g. Ernest Partridge, 'Posthumous Interests and Posthumous Respect', *Ethics*, 91 (1981), 243–64.  [64] This is Partridge's own answer.

[65] An illustration of this point is provided by the case of Roger Lapham, a keen golfer who wanted to be cremated and have his ashes buried on his favourite golf course—Cypress Point, on the Monterey Peninsula. 'He died in 1966, at the age of eighty-three, and Lewis, on receiving the news of his father's death, hurried out to the family home in San Francisco. Shortly after his arrival, he was informed by his brother that there had been a hitch in the plans: their mother had stated forcefully that she would not permit her husband's body to be cremated or to be buried at Cypress Point. "Under California law at that time, a person did not control the disposition of his remains," Lewis Lapham has recalled. "His executors could disregard his stipulations if they wished to. When I got together with my mother, I suggested that we have a shot of sherry—that seemed a good idea. Then we began discussing things, and I said to her, 'I don't think your position is reasonable. For example, I'm your heir and executor. What would you think if I were to disregard the instructions set down in your will?' 'You wouldn't dare,' she said. 'But consider this,' I went on. 'That is exactly what you are going to do with someone you lived with for fifty-nine years.' I suggested we have another sherry. The upshot was that my mother came round, and my father was cremated and buried on that little ridge overlooking Cypress Point, in sight of the tide rolling in on a small beach."' Herbert Warren Wind, 'The Sporting Scene: From Linksland to Augusta', *The New Yorker* (22 June 1981), 96–111, at 104.

This *could* be interpreted in 'intergenerational social contract' terms, so that the widow

not myself see that the halfway house is a satisfactory resting-point. But I offer it in case it can be shown by some further argument to be internally consistent to accept the first assertion and deny the second.

I have in this chapter traversed a large area, and I shall not attempt to summarize. Let me conclude, then, with the observation that the individualist moral theory, in its general form, is capable of generating a wide variety of alternative conclusions about the rights and wrongs of nationalism in various forms. Ultimately, the disagreements turn on the conception of interest that one plugs into the basic doctrine and on the ways of life that one believes conduce to human interests so understood. Although my main intent here has been to explore the ways in which the argument can go, my not-so-hidden agenda has been to suggest that nationalism has been given a bum rap in recent political theory, and to try to show that the efforts of the Viennese liberals to conflate ethical individualism and anti-nationalism will not withstand scrutiny.

complied with her late husband's wishes *in order to* get the son to comply with hers. But surely the way the story runs makes it clear that the crucial move is an argument from equity: that if you really care about what happens after your own death there is no valid reason for refusing to pay the same attention to the wishes that others had for what would happen after their deaths. And this is exactly the point advanced in the text.

# 7

# EXIT, VOICE, AND LOYALTY

I

My primary purpose in this chapter is to provide a detailed critique of
the internal logic of Albert Hirschman's *Exit, Voice, and Loyalty*.[1]
Before doing this, however, I should like to consider briefly the
phenomenon of which it is an exemplar: the 'in' book, for this raises
some general questions of interest.

One important manifestation of the self-conscious professionalism
of American academics is the way in which a corpus of ideas—often in
severely stripped-down form—is at any given time common property. Indeed, the possession of the current stock of ideas, at least in
rudimentary form, sufficient to enable references to be identified,
might be said to be the badge that distinguishes the professionals and
would-be professionals (advanced graduate students) from the dilet-
tantes, the drop-outs, and the inside-dopesters.[2] The way in which the
corpus is built up would repay investigation by a sociologist of
knowledge, but I shall hazard a few guesses. First, the idea itself must
have the dual characteristic that its essence can be expressed very
simply while at the same time its ramifications are great. Second, the
process of dissemination is almost certainly by word of mouth rather
than by formal channels such as book reviews or footnote citations. So
long as the channels of communication across and within departments
exist in any case, all that is then required is a fairly widespread desire
(whether normatively or prudentially motivated) to 'keep up with the
field'.

The reception of *Exit, Voice, and Loyalty* points up with peculiar
sharpness the difference in the workings of academic political science

---

[1] Albert O. Hirschman, *Exit, Voice, and Loyalty: Responses to Decline in Firms, Organizations,
and States* (Cambridge, Mass.: Harvard University Press, 1970).

[2] One result of the lack of this common professional range of reference in Britain is that
practising politicians, in their relations with professional political scientists, are able to regard
themselves not as the raw materials but as the experts. The same phenomenon can, of course, be
looked at the other way round and one can say that the unquestioned acceptance by many
political scientists of the validity of the actor's point of view (which thus makes the politician's
claim to expertise indefeasible) is one of the main inhibitions on the development of a distinctive
discipline.

between the USA and Britain. In the USA the book became a talking-point upon publication and by now its basic ideas have entered the article literature, while at least one Ph.D. thesis is based upon their application. My impression, which is of course based on only a limited sample, is that relatively few political scientists in Britain have heard of the book and that this is not because there is some *other* book that everyone is talking about but rather reflects the fact that the phenomenon of the 'in' book does not exist.

But the absence of 'in' books is itself only one manifestation of the whole style of British political science, which is characterized by the absence in almost all areas of the subject of 'invisible colleges' composed of those actively engaged on research in this area keeping in touch by exchanging papers as well as through formal and informal meetings and visits;[3] by the lack of common reference points either in the form of a shared conception of a discipline or a shared body of ideas; and (a natural consequence of these) by a tendency to define research as 'about' some place or event or person and not in relation to problems arising from some area of the discipline.

One rather mechanical explanation which must, I think, be rejected as too simple is the 'critical mass' theory, according to which the answer lies in the small total number of academics in the subject and in particular the average size of the departments. This theory would entail that the position should have improved dramatically with the expansion of the past decade, and—to take a *reductio ad absurdum* —would predict that Oxford's sixty or more full-time politics teachers should be far and away the most active and discipline-orientated group in the country. More fundamentally, what has to be explained is why there is so little need felt for regular contact with colleagues who have similar interests. After all, a large proportion of political scientists in Britain can get to a meeting in London and back in a day, and most departments are within travelling distance of several others. Why are departments so isolated from one another, and why has the Political Studies Association failed to develop viable sections?[4] How could we explain why, if the smallness of departments or of the aggregate size of the profession were perceived as a problem, British universities should have been so behindhand in joining the

---

[3] D. de Sola Price, *Little Science, Big Science* (New York: Columbia University Press, 1963).

[4] One simple quantitative comparison is that the American Political Science Association, with twenty times the membership of the Political Studies Association of the UK, has about forty times the number of papers at its annual convention, and this leaves out of account the annual meetings of the regional associations, each of which regularly has more papers presented than are given at the PSA conference.

European Consortium for Political Research, which is designed precisely to get round these problems?

The general lines of the answer must, I think, be those laid down by Halsey and Trow:[5] the continuing strength of the ideal of the academic as one devoted primarily to teaching undergraduates by labour-intensive methods and spending much of the remainder of his time on academic administration of a kind that elsewhere would be in the hands of full-time administrators. This still has to be supplemented, however, by observing that the grip of such a conception of the academic role varies from one subject to another. Physical scientists are much more closely attuned to international norms of professional postgraduate training, research, and intensive communication. And even within the social sciences there appear to be variations, with political science showing a significantly more marked degree of parochialism and inertia than economics. Exactly why this should be I am not sure, but I would suggest that one relevant fact is the one referred to by Edward Shils in his essay on 'British Intellectuals in the Mid-Twentieth Century' when he wrote that 'Outside the China of the Mandarins, no great society has ever had a body of intellectuals so integrated with, and so congenial to, its ruling class, and so combining civility and refinement.'[6] This assimilation is, as Shils points out, a major contributing factor to the stability of British society. The effect on the study of politics is, however, debilitating in that a close identification with the outlook of decisionmakers is inimical to the detachment which is the necessary condition of abstraction and generalization.

To the extent that the differences in intellectual style between the countries have deep-seated cultural causes, they are not amenable to deliberate change. But it seems reasonable to suppose that something could be done to increase the level of intellectual interdependence in Britain if resources were devoted to it. The work of the American Social Science Research Council (especially perhaps its Committee on Comparative Politics) would well repay study in this context. It is, therefore, a real question whether this is a direction in which it would be desirable to move.

The pros and cons are easy enough to set out; the difficulty is to decide on their relative weight. Thus, it would seem that in principle a rapid and intensive circulation of ideas should speed up the development of the subject by allowing everyone to make use of a new idea in

[5] A. H. Halsey and M. A. Trow, *The British Academics* (London: Faber and Faber, 1971).

[6] Edward Shils, *The Intellectuals and the Powers and Other Essays* (Chicago: University of Chicago Press, 1972), 152.

his own work instead of leaving each person to struggle along on his own for many years working on some monograph until eventually the relevant work of others (also in monograph form) comes to his attention.[7] Conversely, the obvious potential disadvantage of an effective communication network is the danger of faddism: the risk that the energies of the profession may be dissipated in scrambling aboard successive intellectual bandwagons, thus crippling the organic growth processes inherent in sound scholarship.[8]

Which of these forces one regards as more significant depends, I think, on two things. The first is whether one believes that the process by which some ideas are selected and others fall by the wayside has an element of rationality in it or whether the rise and fall of ideas is to be explained either in terms of chance or in terms of power. The second is how one evaluates the actual record so far. My own inclination is to believe that, at least in the context of academic discourse, Milton was right in proclaiming the superior survival value of good ideas over bad ones, and also to believe that—if only by exciting a reaction in some cases—ideas such as cross-cutting cleavages, veto groups, the paradox of voting, the prisoner's dilemma, interest articulation and aggregation, Downsian competition, non-decisionmaking, the Olson problem, and Allison's 'three models' have served the discipline well.

My object in this chapter is to ask whether the concepts of exit, voice, and loyalty (and the framework in which they are embedded) form a worthy addition to the list. My answer will be that, in spite of shortcomings in the detail of the book, Hirschman has identified and given shape to an important phenomenon.

---

[7] A helpful way to think about the relative effectiveness of different modes of communication in fostering the transmission of ideas might be in terms of 'reaction time'. This we may define as the average amount of time that elapses from the time when *A* has a new idea until *B* has had an opportunity to react to *A*'s idea and allow it to modify or inspire work which becomes available to *A* or some further person *C*. Consider first a system in which the prevailing mode of communication is the book. If it takes *A* an average of five years from conception to completion and another year to publication, and then an average of a couple of years before *B* hears about the book, we have a reaction time of fourteen years. In these circumstances slow theoretical development will hardly be surprising. A move to article publishing, as is now gradually taking place in Britain, cuts down the reaction time greatly, to perhaps four years—two years from inception to publication for *A* and *B*, and no intervening time, provided that *B* reads the journal *A* publishes in. But clearly the existence of a dense network of personal communications, face to face and by circulation of manuscripts, makes reaction times of a matter of months quite easy, while the attainable minimum from *A* to *B* to *C* is a matter of a few seconds.

[8] I am not here intending to echo F. M. Cornford's remark that ' "Sound scholar" is a term of praise applied to one another by learned men who have no reputation outside the University, and a rather queer one inside it.' *Microcosmographia Academica*, 6th edn (London: Bowes and Bowes, 1964), 19.

II

There is no doubt that *Exit, Voice, and Loyalty* has the features necessary for an 'in' book mentioned earlier: the theory can be stated in a few words, but at the same time has an unlimited range of application. The theory can indeed be stated almost out of the words in the title, as follows. There are two alternative responses to decline in firms, organizations, and states, namely exit and voice. ('Exit' simply means leaving; 'voice' means trying to get the managers to reverse the decline by complaining, protesting, or organizing internal opposition.) Loyalty affects the individual calculus by making voice, as against exit, more probable than it would otherwise have been, all else remaining the same.

'Big deal!' may well be the initial reaction to this piece of intelligence. But such a reaction would, I think, be out of place for two reasons. First, Hirschman succeeds by the use of this simple framework in drawing together a number of apparently disparate phenomena. The second reason is that the book represents a development of the 'economic' approach to political analysis. This point highlights the enormous long-run advantage to a discipline in having a core of common intellectual possessions: once a certain body of analytical material has been acquired it is possible to add to it at low cost. I shall take up these two points in turn, in the present section and the next one.

As I said earlier, the 'in' book exists, for most political scientists, not in its full complexity but in a stripped-down form. Hirschman's book, in this form, simply consists of the idea that exit and voice are alternatives. This is one of those ideas that are obvious once they are stated, but which need to be set out explicitly before they can be used to organize the unlimited body of relevant observations. Indeed, the idea that exit and voice are alternatives, and in particular that ease of exit makes voice less likely, is one that has often been put forward in particular contexts, and once one has been sensitized to the notion one finds examples of it all over the place.

Thus, to give a couple of examples that I came across: Eric Wolf, speaking of seventeenth- and eighteenth-century Russia, says that 'peasants in Cossack-dominated areas became Cossacks, thus escaping from the peasantry rather than solving the problem of peasant oppression', and Samuel Huntington has pointed out that it has been to the advantage of newly established Communist regimes in North Vietnam, East Germany, and Cuba to allow dissidents to leave, since they might otherwise cause trouble.[9] Similarly, it has often been pointed out that the internal peace of the new American republic was helped by the exodus of the supporters of the British connection to Canada, and Hirschman himself suggests that the ease with which defeated opposition leaders in Latin America can slip across the border to a culturally similar state has weakened the development of a coherent opposition.[10]

Again, Huntington has argued that 'outside opportunities for horizontal mobility (urbanization) contribute to the relative stability of the countryside in most modernizing countries',[11] and specific support for this idea is provided by a study which showed an inverse correlation between militancy and emigration from rural Italian provinces before the First World War.[12] It would be interesting to know whether there would be a similar inverse correlation between Black emigration from Southern counties in the USA and political participation by Blacks, but this would seem likely. Indeed, it is worth noticing that Matthews and Prothro, in their discussion of emigration, emphasize the point which is also Hirschman's main concern: that exit may operate as a dampener of voice and thus leave those who are left behind worse-off than they could otherwise have been. They observe that 'those who have paid some attention to this matter generally have concluded that the South is better off without these millions of Negroes', but then add that

the allegedly benign effects of Negro emigration for the South are cast in an entirely new light when we consider its effects on the region's Negro leadership. The South will probably lose from a third to a half of its most highly trained potential leaders as a result of emigration. . . . Without leadership in adequate quantity and quality, the Negro masses will not participate in politics as frequently or as effectively as they otherwise would. The flight from the South by educated Negro youths may prove to be a major—perhaps *the* major—deterrent to the southern Negroes' full and expeditious realization of racial and political equality.[13]

The same inverse relation between geographical mobility (exit) and political participation (voice), this time in an urban setting, is sug-

---

[9] Eric R. Wolf, *Peasant Wars of the Twentieth Century* (New York: Harper and Row, 1969), 52; Samuel P. Huntington, *Political Order in Changing Societies* (New Haven, Conn: Yale University Press, 1968), 310–11.     [10] Hirschman, *Exit, Voice, and Loyalty*, pp. 60–1.

[11] Huntington, *Political Order*, p. 54.

[12] J. S. MacDonald, 'Agricultural Organization, Migration and Labour Militancy in Rural Italy', *Economic History Review*, 2nd ser., 16 (1963–4), 61–75.

[13] Donald R. Matthews and James W. Prothro, *Negroes and the New Southern Politics* (New York: Harcourt, Brace and World, 1966), 449, 450.

gested by one study which explicitly relates itself to Hirschman's terminology. The authors found that Blacks in Columbus, Ohio, were 'more likely to voice in response to problems than are whites of similar status who live in similar urban areas'.[14] And this can, of course, be plausibly related to the much lower chances for Blacks of moving away if they do not like the place where they live.

The sentence following that quoted from Huntington above brings in another important aspect of the exit/voice relationship. In contrast to the high rate of horizontal mobility (migration to the towns) in the rural areas, he suggests that 'there are few opportunities for vertical mobility (occupational and income) within the cities', and that this lack of mobility 'contributes to their greater instability'.[15] This, of course, immediately relates to the parallel idea, put forward for industrial societies, that the belief in the possibility of social mobility depresses support for radical political movements which offer to recast the system so as to improve the lot of the worse-off collectively.

In fact, the statement of the case in what is generally thought of as the *locus classicus* for this kind of idea is a bit more subtle than this. It still, however, falls within the exit/voice framework and thus illustrates the kind of intellectual joy-ride one can get led into by following up Hirschman's idea. For what Lipset and Bendix actually suggest is that the *supposed* possibility of exit from a poor position in the society has the effect of stultifying voice even if the individual does not himself think he will ever exit by upward social mobility; instead he exits either by vicarious social mobility (the belief that his children will do better) or by withdrawal into religion, with its promise of posthumous upward mobility, both literal and metaphorical.[16] Thus,

---

[14] John M. Orbell and Toro Uno, 'A Theory of Neighborhood Problem Solving: Political Actions *vs.* Residential Mobility', *American Political Science Review*, 66 (1972), 471–89, at 484.

[15] Huntington, *Political Order*, p. 54.

[16] Seymour Martin Lipset and Reinhard Bendix, *Social Mobility in Industrial Society* (London: Heinemann, 1959). The key passage runs as follows:

Cultures which emphasize egalitarian values and the possibility of success for all, such as those of the United States and the Soviet Union, presumably expose 'failures' to greater problems of adjustment. . . . Both ['transvaluational religion' and 'high aspirations for children'] may be reviewed as a means of safeguarding society against instability. In America, for example, the depressed strata seem to have turned to evangelical religion rather than to radical politics; in Russia, where political protest is forbidden, there is also some evidence of a 'return to religion' among the poorer strata: and both societies—each in its own way—seem to place an extraordinarily high emphasis on a better life for children. It is in the societies of Europe and Asia where less emphasis is placed on equality of opportunity that left-wing political movements are strong among the lower strata—presumably because they teach that traditional inequalities can be done away with by changing the social system (pp. 262–3).

a sort of choice between voice and exit is presented by Lipset and Bendix as practically invariable: 'In general, it seems to be true that the depressed and the failures who have little hope of individual success have a strong faith either in radical politics or in an emotional religiosity, so that almost nowhere are the lower classes both moderate in their politics *and* indifferent to religion.'[17] This of course leads us on to the debate among historians as to whether Methodism operated as an alternative to political agitation in England and Wales in the first half of the nineteenth century. But I think I have already presented enough examples to illustrate the versatility and fecundity of the basic idea of exit and voice as alternative options.

Since this has been my aim in the present section, I have been content simply to show how the idea has cropped up in a number of widely differing contexts. No doubt readers will doubt some of the alleged correlations and, perhaps even more, wonder whether in some cases the same factors make for exit *and* for lack of voice among those remaining. However, such doubts (which I share) do not seriously detract from the effectiveness of the demonstration, since the fact remains that an inverse relation between exit and voice has been asserted often enough to make the phenomenon worth examination at a general level.

What is more serious is the question of the unity of the phenomenon itself. Although I have set out the cases as neutrally as possible, I hope that readers will have been becoming uneasy and asking themselves whether there is really a common process underlying all these cases, even if they are all accepted as instances of a non-spurious connection between exit and lack of voice. Unlike the other two kinds of scepticism, this one goes directly to the usefulness of the framework for analysis set out in *Exit, Voice, and Loyalty*. It is to that framework that I now turn.

### III

I want to begin by asking what *kind* of analysis Hirschman offers of the relation between exit, voice, and loyalty and the effects of their interaction on the performance of firms, organizations, and states. The answer is, I think, that it falls broadly within the sphere of the 'economic approach' to the study of society.

In a book that was published in the same year as Hirschman's, I said that *The Logic of Collective Action* was 'the only book fit to rank with

---

[17] Lipset and Bendix, *Social Mobility*, p. 263.

Downs's *Economic Theory of Democracy*, as an exemplar of the virtues of the '"economic" approach' outside the conventional subject-matter of economics, and added: 'Both books, as may be expected in pioneering works, suffer from obscurities and ambiguities which become apparent on close examination. But it is greatly to their advantage that, unlike so many books on political and sociological theory, they stimulate and repay this degree of careful attention.'[18] If I venture to quote myself now it is because what I said there about both the strengths and weaknesses of Downs and Olson seems to me so exactly to fit Hirschman as well.

It is interesting, however, to notice that this interpretation of the significance of his work—as a contribution to the 'economic' analysis of politics—is not the one that Hirschman himself offers. On the contrary, he professes an ecumenical spirit which—fortunately for the coherence of the book—he at no point allows to get in the way of a straight 'economic' approach to the phenomena under consideration. In his Preface he says that 'this book does not use the tools of one discipline for the purpose of annexing another. As is shown particularly in the appendixes, the concepts I develop can be translated into the language of traditional economic analysis, and may possibly enrich it; but by no means do they uniquely belong there' (p. vii).[19] Leaving aside the emotive word 'annexing', the state of affairs described in the second sentence is precisely what one would expect where economic modes of analysis are being applied to political phenomena.

A little later Hirschman says that he hopes 'to demonstrate to political scientists the usefulness of economic concepts *and to economists the usefulness of political concepts*' (p. 19, italics in original). There seems to be an equivocation here on the words 'political concepts' and 'economic concepts', between on the one hand political and economic *mechanisms* and on the other hand political and economic *methods of analysis*. The sentence before that quoted clearly rests on the first interpretation: here Hirschman says that 'exit and voice, that is, market and non-market forces, that is, economic and political mechanisms, have been introduced as two principal actors of strictly equal rank and importance' (p. 19). All this says is that economists (not

---

[18] Brian Barry, *Sociologists, Economists and Democracy* (London: Collier-Macmillan, 1970; repr. Chicago: Chicago University Press, 1978), 24, referring to Anthony Downs, *An Economic Theory of Democracy* (New York: Harper and Bros., 1957) and Mancur Olson, Jr., *The Logic of Collective Action: Public Goods and the Theory of Groups* (Cambridge, Mass.: Harvard University Press, 1965).

[19] All quotations with page references in this form are from *Exit, Voice, and Loyalty*.

defined but presumably conventionally understood as people concerned with goods and services) need to look at non-market mechanisms such as protest; and political scientists (again not defined but
presumably understood as people concerned with parties, pressure
groups, states, and all that) need to look at the possibility of leaving
organizations. Left open entirely by this is the question of whether
both the market and non-market phenomena can be studied by using a
characteristically 'economic' approach, in the second sense that I
distinguished. The 'public choice' school (which started life, be it
recalled, by publishing 'Papers in Non-market Decision-Making') is
of course dedicated to the presupposition that 'economic' methods can
cover the whole lot. And, as I have noted, Hirschman in practice
proceeds on exactly the same assumption, never explicitly using any
assumption about motivation that would take him outside an
individualistic maximizing framework of analysis.

In its more or less formal aspects, then, the book offers two things.
The first is an analysis from an 'economic' viewpoint of non-market
mechanisms ('voice') affecting the quality of goods and services
offered by a firm in a market situation. The second is an analysis, again
from an 'economic' viewpoint, of both voice and exit in organizations
other than those supplying goods and services in a market situation. I
shall consider the book as an exemplification of both the virtues and
the deficiencies of the 'economic' approach when it is applied outside
the analysis of market forces. My general conclusion will be that, as in
the case of Downs and Olson, Hirschman's 'economic' approach is as
useful for what it fails to explain as for what it explains successfully,
since such failures point to phenomena which require explanations of a
different kind.


IV

To illustrate this let us begin (as Hirschman does) with firms producing in a market—not necessarily a competitive market but simply a
situation in which its revenues come from sales to customers rather
than (to take the obvious alternative) being raised by taxation.
Hirschman's main point here is that the 'discipline of the market' may
fail to work very effectively, so 'voice' is needed as an antidote to
declining quality and may in some circumstances be a rational
response by consumers. The idea of the 'discipline of the market' is
supposed to be that, when a firm's products or services deteriorate in
quality, enough dissatisfied customers switch to the competing firms

or give up the product or service altogether to make a dent in the delinquent firm's sales and thus profits, and that this leads to an improvement in performance so as to restore the status quo ante.

As Hirschman points out, this scenario can go wrong at a number of points. Thus, there can be a stable situation in which a small number of firms simply take in one another's dissatisfied clients (Hirschman cites General Motors and Ford) so that, although individual customers switch, the net effect is nil since the switches simply cancel one another out. This is reminiscent of the reply attributed to Keynes on being asked why, if businessmen were as stupid as he maintained, they succeeded in making profits: 'Because they only have to compete with other businessmen.' An alternative point of slippage in the 'market discipline' model is what Hirschman calls 'organizational slack'. At the level of the state this corresponds to Adam Smith's remark that there is a lot of ruin in a nation. In relation to firms we can put it by saying that there is a great distance between maximizing profits and going bankrupt, and a firm whose managers prize a quiet life may be able to steer a course between the two for an indefinitely long period of time.

All this leads to the conclusion that voice—direct attempts to modify the policies of firms—may be necessary in order to reverse a deterioration in products or services supplied on a market. And from this conclusion Hirschman deduces other conclusions of a less obvious kind. Thus, in a chapter entitled 'How Monopoly Can be Comforted by Competition', he points out that the mediocre management of a firm with a monopoly in the supply of some good or service may actually welcome the arrival of a competing firm offering better quality at a higher price, thus drawing off exigent customers who would otherwise make life miserable for them by their constant complaints about poor quality. Competition—of the right sort—thus provides the 'lazy monopolist' with the 'freedom to deteriorate'.

From the point of view of public policy, Hirschman suggests that this may make it desirable, where competition has the effect only of leaving the predominant supplier free of his most demanding customers, to enforce a total monopoly. Although Hirschman does not put it in quite this way, what the proposal amounts to is that the more quality-conscious consumers should be required to provide the 'public good' of agitation against poor quality for all consumers of the product or service. This same line of recommendation can be extended beyond firms to other organizations, on the basis of a similar analysis, and this Hirschman in fact does.

Suppose at some point, for whatever reason, the public schools deteriorate. Thereupon, increasing numbers of quality-education-conscious parents will send their children to private schools. This exit may occasion some impulse toward an improvement of the public schools; but here again this impulse is far less significant than the loss to the public schools of those member-customers who would be the most motivated and determined to put up a fight against the deterioration if they did not have the alternative of the private schools (pp. 45–6).

A similar argument might be made against allowing a private sector of medicine to coexist with a state-provided health service.

I shall take up later the value premises which are required in order to generate the judgements expressed in the book that one outcome is desirable and another undesirable, and the recommendations (addressed to various actors) which are made. These value premises are at no time stated, still less defended, but it is possible to infer them. The question that I want to raise now, however, concerns the logic of the argument just set forth. Let us accept the possibility that 'market discipline' may fail to keep firms at full stretch and that public services provided out of tax revenues may feel even less pressure from the withdrawal of quality-conscious consumers. It then follows (since 'voice' comprises everything except 'exit' that might be done by consumers) that if anything is done it will have to be done by means of voice. But how likely is voice to appear in sufficient volume to make it worth the while of managers to improve their performance? The fact that something is 'needed' if some postulated desirable end-state is to be achieved does not, on the face of it, provide any reason for expecting it to happen.

Of course, it would be possible to adopt some sort of functionalist assumption, according to which 'society' is conceived of as a homeostatic mechanism—as having, in some mysterious way, built-in recuperative properties. Hirschman dabbles in this kind of thing to the extent of quoting Arrow as follows: 'I propose the view that, when the market fails to achieve an optimal state, society will, to some extent at least, recognize the gap, and nonmarket social institutions will arise attempting to bridge it . . . this process is not necessarily conscious' (pp. 18–19). However, as the author of *Social Choice and Individual Values* is presumably as aware as anyone, 'society' is an abstraction and any recognizing and acting that is to be done has to be done by people.

The 'plain man', uncorrupted by acquaintance with micro-economics, would probably take this in his stride and say that all we have to do to make things logically watertight is to add a missing link connecting social needs to individual action in the form of an assertion that individuals will recognize the existence of social needs and will strive to see that something is done to satisfy these social needs. But, in spite of his brief unconsummated flirtation with teleological function- alism, Hirschman does not follow this logically respectable reformu- lation. For it introduces a kind of motivation—direct concern for the social good—that lies outside the scope of ordinary economic analysis.

Thus, although he never explicitly raises the matter, Hirschman's formal discussion of the circumstances in which the voice option will be chosen rests on the assumption that each individual is concerned only with the quality of goods or services that he himself buys or receives. The fact that any general improvement in quality which his exercise of 'voice' may bring about will presumably benefit many others besides himself is not treated as a possible motivating factor.

The calculation facing the individual consumer or citizen when deciding whether or not to exercise 'voice' takes a form familiar from Downs and Olson, complicated only by the assumed alternative of exit. (See for a formal statement Appendix B, pp. 132–7.) Suppose that a consumer is faced with a decline in the quality of the goods provided by his usual supplier, and that by exercising voice he has a 0·6 probability of reversing 30 per cent of the decline. Leaving out the alternative of exit, we can say that it will pay him to exercise voice if the certain cost of exercising voice is less than the value to him of a 0·6 chance of improving quality by 30 per cent of the amount it has declined. To take account of the possibility of exit all we have to do is to add to the cost of voice the opportunity cost of forgoing the best available alternative product. We thus say it will pay to exercise voice only if the value of a given probability of a given improvement is higher than the value of the best alternative *plus* the cost of exercising voice.

This analysis can be complicated in three ways. First, a point which Hirschman mentions only in passing, though it is obviously crucial: the choice is not normally merely between voice and no voice but between larger and smaller amounts of voice (including zero), each associated with a given cost. Thus, the question may be whether the extra cost of making a bigger effort to get a change is warranted by, say, an increase in the probability of a given improvement in quality from 0·6 to 0·7.

Second, a given level of voice may be thought of as having not just a 0·6 probability of producing a 30 per cent recovery but of having a 0·8 probability of at least a 10 per cent recovery, a 0·5 probability of at least a 35 per cent improvement, and so on. This is in fact the way Hirschman presents the analysis, and he allows it to make the results indeterminate by suggesting that whether or not voice is chosen may depend on whether the actor is more interested in low probabilities, medium probabilities, or high probabilities. All this complication can be disposed of, however, as Hirschman mentions in a footnote (p. 135 n.), by boiling down the various combinations of probabilities and pay-offs into a single 'expected value' for that level of voice.

The third complicating point is one that applies to the whole book, namely that there is not in general anything logically distinctive about deterioration from a previously superior quality as against a consistently low (or at any rate improvable) quality. The only distinctive feature of deterioration is that, if the quality has been low all along, a member or customer would not have a motive for exit (all else remaining the same) unless he simply discovered that he had made the wrong choice from the available alternatives earlier on.

The *ceteris paribus* proviso is important. Thus, suppose that the product you usually buy stays the same in quality but a new higher-quality contender becomes available, either in the form of a new entrant or an improvement in an old-established rival. You may simply decide to exit, but you might reason that the superiority of another firm's product is prima facie evidence that your usual supplier could do better than he is doing. If there is any reason for thinking that he might be able to do even better than the new opposition, there would be a potential motive for exercising voice, so one would have the choice between exit and voice in a way exactly parallel to that which arises when the usual supplier declines and the rivals stay as good as they were before.

It is also worth spelling out a little more fully the way in which exit is an option even if all else remains the same if you believe not that the product has deteriorated but that you made a mistake about its quality in the first place. For this is, I think, the real logic of the Ford *vs*. General Motors example: the man who buys a lemon from Ford and switches to General Motors for his new car (and vice versa) does not believe that Fords were better than General Motors but have deteriorated; rather, he believes that he overestimated the quality of Ford cars when he bought one.

The most useful way of thinking about the book is to say that it is about situations in which quality can be improved. No doubt one good piece of evidence that quality might be better than it is now is that it was better in the past. But this is not the only form of evidence: there may be other indications of 'organizational slack', such as a situation (as sometimes arises) where the value of the physical assets of a firm is higher than the value placed by the stock market on the company as a going concern. Again, there may be deficiencies in the design or the manufacture of a product which are obviously in principle remediable even if they have never actually been remedied. Or it may simply be possible to *see* by direct examination that a firm or organization is badly run.

Thus, voice should be conceived of not only as a possible 'response to decline' but as a possible response to the belief that a firm or other organization could do better. It is this belief which is a necessary condition (though not, of course, a sufficient condition) for the exercise of voice to be rational—in *any* means–end conception of rationality—since there is no point (though there may be some expressive satisfaction) in exercising voice where it is not believed possible that any improvement could occur. The connection between the belief that improvement could conceivably be brought about and the experience of deterioration is purely contingent.

I have just argued that constant quality may be associated with the belief that improvement is possible; equally, deteriorating quality need not produce a belief that the decline can be reversed, or perhaps even arrested. Thus, Alessandro Pizzorno has suggested that the weakness in Edward Banfield's attribution of collective inaction in Montegrano to 'amoral familism' is that it presupposes that there is something to explain, namely that the inhabitants of this southern Italian village fail to co-operate to improve conditions. But, he points out, Banfield himself admits that 'even if the Montegranians did everything suggested, and the prefects, the government etc., did many others, the conditions in Montegrano would not improve. Consequently, the Montegranians are right in not doing anything, because no one is silly enough to do things that serve no purpose!'[20]

[20] Allesandro Pizzorno, 'Amoral Familism and Historical Marginality', *International Review of Community Development*, 15 (1966), 55–66, repr. in Mattei Dogan and Richard Rose (eds.), *European Politics: a Reader* (London: Macmillan, 1971), 87–98, at 92. This point is of course relevant to the study of rural Italy mentioned earlier, and illustrates my remark that the connection between exit and absence of voice may not be that they are alternatives. It is surely plausible that the apparent impossibility of achieving much of an improvement in conditions even if voice were wildly successful in getting action would itself be a strong incentive to exit.

It is of fundamental importance to consider the fact that the whole world does not appear equally hopeless to the peasant. In fact, he applies this concept of inability solely to himself and to the environment in which he is living at the moment. . . . He feels that he could improve his situation if he could find work in a northern factory or could emigrate to America.

Quoted by Pizzorno, in Dogan and Rose, *European Politics*, from Cancian, 'Il contadino

Let us go back to the most basic formulation of Hirschman's idea. This can be expressed most comprehensively as follows: voice will occur when the expected value of the quality resulting from the exercise of the optimal amount of voice minus the cost of exercising it is higher than the value of the best that can be obtained without using voice. Where the best that can be obtained without using voice is the present product the question reduces to the simple one of whether the expected value of any improvement is greater or smaller than the cost of exercising the corresponding amount of voice. Where there is another currently available alternative it is necessary to make the more complex calculation comparing the value of the present product, the expected value of the present product after exercising voice minus the cost of exercising it, and the value of the alternative product.

This way of putting the criterion for rational action makes it clear that to speak of a choice between exit and voice is in fact to collapse two separate choices into one another. One choice is between exit (leaving) and non-exit (staying), the other is between voice (activity, participation) and silence (inactivity, non-participation). In any situation, one choice has to be made out of each pair of options, even if only by default. Thus, as well as silent exit and non-exiting voice, there is also silent non-exit, and this may well be the rational course to follow if exit is unattractive, even if it is believed that things could be done better by the firm, organization, or state concerned. The fourth combination is exit plus voice and would correspond to a case where someone campaigns for improvements after leaving. An example —though not a very good one—which Hirschman discusses is that of public officials freeing themselves to attack government policy by resigning. I deal with this below, in Section VII.

V

In this section I want to back up the idea just put forward that, in the absence of exit, silence will often be more rational (on 'economic'

---

meridionale: comportamento politico e visione del mondo', *Bollettino delle richerche sociali* (Oct. 1961), 269. An earlier exit available to peasants in some areas such as Lucania was to become brigands: this might be compared with the case mentioned earlier of Russian peasants becoming Cossacks. (See e.g. Carlo Levi, *Christ Stopped at Eboli* (London: Cassell, 1948).) Becoming a bandit, as Hobsbawm points out, is almost always initially an exit phenomenon, though the role may acquire secondary 'voice' aspects, of the 'Robin Hood' variety: 'The State shows an interest in a peasant because of some minor infraction of the law, and the man takes to the hills because how does he know what a system which does not know or understand peasants, and which peasants do not understand, will do to him?' E. J. Hobsbawm, *Primitive Rebels* (Manchester: Manchester University Press, 1959), 16.

premisses) than voice. I also want to suggest that the type of analysis offered by Hirschman fails to explain most actual occurrences of voice, both in the positive sense of failing to predict them and in the *verstehen* sense of failing to capture the nature of the actors' intentions. The first argument provides a foundation for the second so I shall begin with it.

The essence of the first argument is that only in very small groups—of less than a dozen, say—is the expected benefit *to oneself* from the exercise of voice in pursuit of the 'public good' of an improvement in general quality likely to outweigh the costs of exercising it. This is, of course, the theme of Olson's *The Logic of Collective Action*, but although Hirschman mentions it in a footnote he does not seem to me to have appreciated its force in relation to his own work. For, if it is true that voice is rarely an option that a rational person would choose, the idea that the potentialities of voice have been neglected by economists falls to the ground. Similarly, this undermines the notion that it might be advantageous from the point of view of public policy to 'lock in' the customers of a 'lazy monopolist' so that the most quality-conscious customers are forced to deal with him. Although voice may be 'needed' socially in such cases, the logic of collective action suggests that it will not be forthcoming on the basis of any calculations of rational self-interest and that the quality-conscious consumers, denied exit, will simply suffer in silence.

How does Hirschman manage to overlook this apparently serious gap in his theory? The answer is, I think, that he is helped in not facing up to the problem by an equivocation on the concept of 'voice'. He lumps together under 'voice' two phenomena which are quite different both in their attractions to individuals and in their effects on organizations. One form of voice—and the form relevant to Hirschman's argument that quality-conscious consumers who complain perform a service for all consumers—is protest or mobilization in order to secure a collective good in the form of a change of policy or an improvement in administration: the shareholders revolt, the parents press for better schools, the customers join a 'crusade' against lethal or polluting cars, non-returnable bottles, the failure of Distillers' to offer enough compensation to thalidomide children, or what have you. This is the case where the prospect of individual benefits is not likely to provide an adequate motive, but where, if for some reason voice *does* occur in sufficient volume, there will be an effect on overall quality.

The other phenomenon covered by Hirschman's use of the concept of 'voice' is that where the individual consumer pursues an individual benefit, that is to say a benefit private to himself rather than the public good of a change in the running of the organization as a whole. Thus, Hirschman includes as an example of voice the case in which 'dissatisfied consumers are able to turn in defective merchandise' (p. 35) and analyses in Appendix A a hypothetical situation in which 'half of the nonexiting customers complain and . . . the average complaint results in a cost that amounts to one-half of the article's sales price' (p. 131).

I think it is pushing the concept of 'voice' too far to include under it having a defect fixed while the item is under guarantee, but the terminological point is not the main issue. The crucial thing is that this kind of case can perfectly easily be accommodated within the calculus of individual costs and benefits but it is not of a kind that helps where the public good of a general improvement is at stake. It may encourage manufacturers to make their products more reliable (anyway while under guarantee) but does nothing for improvement in design to make the product safer, more convenient, less annoying to others besides the user, more aesthetically appealing, and so on.

Moreover, there may be many cases where only a minority of consumers are both quality-conscious and equipped with enough knowledge or self-confidence to make demands, and where the only effect on the system as a whole is to redistribute resources towards these articulate consumers at the expense of the rest, the net effect being virtually nil. Thus, I suspect that the demands for better individual service made by middle-class parents on the state school system or middle-class patients on the National Health Service have little effect on the average quality of the services but a great deal to do with the way in which the benefits provided are distributed between social classes.

The first part of my argument was that 'voice' in pursuit of a general increase in quality can rarely be expected to occur on Hirschman's premisses. The second part is that much exercise of 'voice' that does occur cannot be explained within Hirschman's theory. A good example is the 'consumer revolution' in the USA, which Hirschman claims to fit in by saying that 'recent experience even raises some doubts whether the structural constraints (availability of close substitutes, number of buyers, durability and standardization of the article, and so forth) deserve to be called "basic" when they can suddenly be overcome by a single individual such as Ralph Nader' (p. 43). But Nader himself can hardly be explained on the assumption that he is motivated by the increase in quality he might experience in the goods he himself buys. This would surely be burning down the house so as to have roast pig. And if Nader is explained quite differently, as a 'political entrepreneur' who draws (in Olson's terms) 'selective benefits' from running a crusade, there is still the problem that it would almost certainly not pay anybody else to contribute time or money to the crusade simply as a way of improving the quality of his own purchases. The answer, surely, is much more likely to be found by reflecting on the words—'revolution', 'crusade', or even the more neutral 'movement'—which are used to refer to the phenomenon. Such things are not, after all, usually characterized by a careful balancing of private costs and benefits.

The general point that has to be made here is that the purely instrumental attitude to voice—as a means to the improvement of one's own consumption—is itself not a constant but a variable. This variability of the instrumental orientation from one context to another is of course one of the great themes of sociology, from Tönnies' *Gemeinschaft* and *Gesellschaft* (community and association) to Talcott Parsons's pattern variables. In the rigorous, unified social science which is waiting to be born the relative strength of instrumental and non-instrumental orientations towards different kinds of groups will itself have to be explained and the appropriate forms of analysis for both developed. In the meantime, if Hirschman were really going to show economists what they have been missing, he would surely draw on the literature of non-instrumental voice, or in other words participation in a group for reasons other than the desire to modify its policy so as to secure a personal benefit. But his mode of analysis remains 'economic' throughout.

It is, of course, always possible to make an 'economic' analysis come out with the 'right answer' by manipulating the value of some cost or benefit so that the result of the postulated individual calculation corresponds to what has actually been observed to happen. But this merely shows that any phenomenon can be redescribed in 'economic' terminology: the 'economic' analysis has no bite unless at the least there is some way of saying before the fact when costs will be high and when they will be low, etc.[21]

Thus, we could always account for the exercise of voice in a given instance by adjusting the cost of voice *ex post* to make it pay, if necessary attributing a negative cost to the exercise of voice. This is, however, only a clumsy, and indeed misleading way of saying that

---

[21] These points are treated more fully in the context of Downs's and Olson's 'economic' explanations of political participation in my *Sociologists, Economists and Democracy*, ch. 2.

people sometimes *want* to exercise voice, irrespective of any calculation (explicit or implicit) that the expected value of the change in policy produced will outweigh the time and effort expended. I think it is reasonable to suggest that this is likely to happen in two very different kinds of social situation. The first is typified by the 'consumer crusade': it is a situation in which individuals are mobilized by some cause and may be prepared to incur considerable costs in pursuing it while the enthusiasm lasts. It is characteristic of mass societies and usually successive movements show a sharp rise and decline in support. It is probably best represented in 'economic' terms as a situation in which the benefits of the success of the cause are greatly inflated, though this is rather artificial and in any case leaves the phenomenon itself—the rise and fall of 'causes'—unexplained.

The second kind of situation is one in which voice in the form of participation in the affairs of some collectivity is simply a part of the form of life consisting of living as a member of that collectivity. An example might be provided by the traditional Swiss commune and many less formal collectivities. This kind of situation is not comparable with voice at the level of a mass society and is characteristically stable rather than fluctuating. Since it is not (as an ideal type) instrumental participation, it can continue even if the policy of the collectivity is considered completely satisfactory; and there is no reason to expect that participation will be increased by discontent with the 'quality of the product'. Indeed, the converse might be more correct, in as far as participation is an expression of membership. Thus, it will not do to say that the 'economic' calculus will still work provided we give the exercise of voice a negative cost. For we would then still be predicting variations above the baseline set by the fixed negative cost of voice, and there is no reason to expect these to occur in a situation where voice is not used simply with the object of securing an improvement in outcomes.

VI

If I have up till now kept the third member of the trio, loyalty, out of the way, it is because the attempt to treat it in economic terms seems to me much more fundamentally problematic than is the case with exit or voice. 'Loyalty' is regarded within the theory as a factor which operates so as to lower the benefit provided by the best competing alternative organization below that which it (as it were) intrinsically offers. As a way of explaining the absence of exit when it would be predicted by the calculus set out in the previous section, the manipulation of the benefit derived from the competing organization suffers from the same faults as does the manipulation of the cost of exercising voice in order to explain the presence of voice when its absence would be predicted by the calculus. Formally, the objection is that it is an *ad hoc* equation-filler. But this is important only because of the material objection that it does not capture a real social phenomenon.

The point here is that any equation can be made to 'work' if it has in it a constant which does not really function as a constant but rather as an error term. It is always possible to 'save the phenomena', as the pre-Copernican astronomers did by adding epicycles to the supposed circular motion of the sun and planets round the earth. Thus, to take a deliberately absurd example, suppose that someone were to put forward the hypothesis that the number of votes cast for candidates in parliamentary elections is proportional to the cube of the candidates' heights, plus or minus a factor of 'personal popularity/unpopularity' which could be different for each candidate. This hypothesis could be made always to fit the facts perfectly, provided its upholder were careful to wait until the election results were declared and then simply fill in whatever value for the personal popularity/unpopularity of each candidate could be calculated to make the answer come out right.

This is a grotesque example simply because the redundancy of the term relating electoral success to height would be apparent in advance from general experience and would also become clear by noticing the inverse correlation between the error term and the height term whenever some plausible factors were substituted for the 'personal popularity/unpopularity' term. The situation is less clear-cut in Hirschman's case, but the logic is exactly the same.

The probability of exit, in Hirschman's theory, is predicted by a two-term equation. The first is a cost-benefit calculation concerning the value of the best alternative and the probability of securing improvement in the existing product or organization at a given cost of voice. The second term is loyalty, conceived of as an imputed internalized tax on the competing product(s) or organization(s). Since loyalty is recognized only by its effects, the equation can always be made to fit the facts *ex post*, by imputing loyalty in sufficient quantity to a person who, on the basis of the first term (the cost-benefit calculation), should have switched but in fact has not done so.

There is, however, a difference between this case and my electoral example, since there is every reason to suppose that Hirschman's first term does correspond to a factor which really operates in at least a large proportion of all relevant situations. But since (as we have already suggested) the cost-benefit framework does not work at all in some kinds of organization, it will still be true that no consistent theory of the determinants of loyalty can be produced, where 'loyalty' is simply the name of the term which has to take up the slack left by the first term in order to get the 'right answer'. Instead of seeking to plug the gap left by cost-benefit calculations with an arbitrary imputed internalized tax, the only solution is to try to develop a more realistic understanding of the reasons why people leave organizations and why they stay in them.

Hirschman's interest in loyalty stems from his evaluative concerns. The starting-place of the whole book, as he tells us in the Preface (p. vii), was the observation that in some circumstances the possibility of exit actually makes things worse rather than better.

In Nigeria, then, I had encountered a situation where the combination of exit and voice was particularly noxious for any recovery [in the performance of the railways]: exit did not have its usual attention-focusing effect because the loss of revenue was not a matter of the utmost gravity for management, while voice did not work as long as the most aroused and therefore the potentially most vocal customers were the first ones to abandon the railroads for the trucks (p. 45).

Since, therefore, exit hampers the operation of voice, it would seem to follow that a mechanism which would reduce the incidence of exit when it is institutionally available ought to increase the incidence of voice.

'Loyalty', as conceived by Hirschman, does tend to have this effect, but the effect is more conditional than Hirschman allows for. In saying that 'as a rule . . . loyalty holds exit at bay and activates voice' (p. 78), he falls into the trap of treating exit and voice as alternatives, whereas, as we have seen, each is one side of a dichotomy (the other side being doing nothing), so there is always the option of silent non-exit.[22] It will

---

[22] The exception which Hirschman goes on to allow to this 'rule' in the passage quoted is not in fact an exception at all, because it does not require loyalty, defined as a reduction in the benefit derived from the best competing organization. He says 'It is true that, in the face of discontent with the way things are going in an organization, an individual member can remain loyal without being influential himself, but hardly without the expectation that *someone* will act or *something* will happen to improve matters' (p. 78). This is quite consistent with the ordinary calculus set out in the previous section, since the person in question expects the present product to improve so that it is once again the best buy. All we need is some once-for-all cost of changing suppliers to prevent the person in question from exiting now and returning when things do get better again. (It is important to distinguish a cost of exit from a tax on the competing product, which is 'loyalty'.) Conversely, if loyalty *is* a tax on the competing product then it is perfectly

be recalled that the calculation facing the consumer is whether the expected value of the product after he has exercised voice is above or below the best available option not involving voice. If the best available option not involving voice is exit, then exit will be chosen; if it is the existing product (because it is still better than the rival or because it is expected to become better owing to the efforts of others) then the choice will be to stay and be silent, in other words to exercise neither 'exit' nor 'voice' options. The effect of loyalty on this calculation is simply to put a tax on the competing product. As Hirschman suggests (p. 136), we can conceptualize the position by subtracting the 'cost of disloyalty' from the value of the competing product. Thus, the value of the competing product may fall after the loyalty tax has been levied on it so that defecting to it is no longer superior to either staying and exercising voice or staying and doing nothing. It should be noticed that we cannot predict which of the remaining alternatives he will choose from the information that in a certain case loyalty has had the effect of inhibiting someone from choosing exit. All we can say is that whether he will stay and exercise voice or stay and suffer in silence will depend on which of these options would have been *second* on his list in the absence of any considerations of loyalty. But since one or other of these choices must be made if exit is abandoned, we can say a priori that the existence of loyalty must raise the probability of voice occurring.

The great problem, however, is not so much that loyalty, as conceptualized by Hirschman, has only limited efficacy in activating voice, but that it is not a significant phenomenon. And I retain enough confidence in the circumspect use of that ordinary-language philosopher's ultimate weapon, the Paradigm Case Argument, to suggest that there is more likely to be a real phenomenon corresponding to the ordinary meaning of 'loyalty' than to a construct which has little relation to this meaning.

To put it concretely, loyalty does not normally mean a mere reluctance to leave a collectivity, but rather a positive commitment to further its welfare by working for it, fighting for it and—where one thinks it has gone astray—seeking to change it. Thus, voice (as well as other forms of activity) is already built into the concept of loyalty. Reluctance to leave is not central, but is in many cases a logical implication of the requirements of loyalty since it is often only

consistent with the model that someone should stay indefinitely with a firm or organization he believes to be inferior, so long as the degree of inferiority is less than the 'tariff barrier' (an analogy Hirschman himself uses) represented by loyalty.

possible to further the welfare of a collectivity while belonging to it.[23] We can check this by noticing that typically disloyalty is predicated of someone who acts contrary to the interests of a collectivity (in the opinion of the speaker) while remaining a member of it. Someone who leaves is usually described as disloyal only if there is some special factor, for example that he has defected to another country, carrying military secrets with him.[24]

We can thus conclude that Hirschman puts things in the wrong logical relationship when he defines 'loyalty' so that it causes non-exit and it is then non-exit in turn which stimulates voice. Rather, loyalty is manifested, in certain circumstances, by voice, and may also require non-exit as a means to the exercise of voice or some other activity aimed at the welfare of the collectivity. It is interesting to notice that the only use of 'loyalty' which does fit Hirschman's definition is that occurring in the expression 'brand loyalty'. For brand loyalty, as I understand it, is precisely the unwillingness of a customer to switch from one brand to another even when the other brand is either objectively better or objectively identical but cheaper, more easily available, and so on. There is a certain irony in this since I suspect that Hirschman would agree that this is a debased form of 'loyalty' (indeed the application of a word like 'loyalty' to soap powder invites Marcusian invective), and in any case it is not loyalty to products on which he bases his hopes for the 'consumer voice'. The 'consumer crusade' à la Nader is a *general* onslaught on the suppliers of goods of a particular kind. It is not the reaction of an outraged 'brand loyalist' who would rather go to great trouble to improve his usual product than switch to a rival product he acknowledges to be perfectly satisfactory.

It would appear that Hirschman is uneasily aware that the move from loyalty to voice via non-exit has something fishy about it. But his efforts at remedying the defect lead him into literal nonsense. He suggests that the belief in one's influence (in the efficacy of one's voice) within an organization may itself result in loyalty. But the attempt to fit this idea into his framework comes to grief, as the following passage shows.

In terms of figure 3 of Appendix B, a person whose influence (that is, the

---

[23] In some cases, however, the welfare of a collectivity can be advanced only by leaving it. Thus, Irish or Pakistani emigrants are loyal to their family or village if they send back money from England or the USA.

[24] Consider the bumper-sticker of a few years ago: 'America—Love It or Leave It'. Presumably, those who professed this sentiment regarded active opposition to the Vietnam war from within the USA as more 'disloyal' than mere exit.

likelihood that he will be able to achieve full quality recuperation) is correctly expressed by a point as high as $V_3$ will be willing to trade off the certainty of the competing product against even a little hope of recuperation for the traditional product. Thus he will choose voice. He who has little influence and knows it, on the other hand, is not likely to take kindly to such a trade-off. If he is to opt for voice rather than exit [N.B. the false dichotomy] he will normally require the certain availability of the competing product to be matched by the near-certainty of recuperation for the traditional variety (p. 78 n.).

The point $V_3$ in Figure 3 shows that the actor in question has about an almost fifty-fifty chance of securing a total recovery to the original quality if he chooses to exercise voice. As far as I can make out, Hirschman says that someone who has an almost fifty-fifty chance of securing 'full quality recuperation' 'will be willing to trade off the certainty of the competing product against even a little hope of recuperation for the traditional product'. This flat contradiction —which requires someone to believe simultaneously that he has a good chance and a very small chance of securing recovery—is merely the dramatic expression of the incompatibility of the whole notion with Hirschman's premisses.

What I think he wants to say here is that the experience of having had influence in a collectivity and the expectation of having influence in the future tend to increase a person's commitment to that collectivity, in other words his loyalty to it in the ordinary meaning of 'loyalty'. And since, as we have suggested, participation to try to put the collectivity back on the right track is a manifestation of loyalty, the more influential, tending to be more loyal, will also tend to be more active in exercising voice even if in a given case they do not expect it to be effective. But all this falls outside the framework set up by Hirschman.

## VII

Before drawing this discussion to a close, I should like to look at the two chapters of Hirschman's book which are devoted specifically to applications of the basic ideas to political phenomena. One is a critique, using the model, of some central notions about party competition put forward in Downs's *An Economic Theory of Democracy*. The other uses the concepts to discuss the excessive 'loyalty' of President Johnson's 'official family', which led to a lack of 'exit' in the face of a deteriorating governmental product—the Vietnam war. Although I happen to be politically sympathetic to the conclusions reached, I regard these chapters as the weakest in the book. They do, however, raise some interesting analytical and evaluative points which will have to be met in any future attempt to use Hirschman's ideas in the development of political theory.

One important analytical point which has significant evaluative implications is that Hirschman introduces his two-party discussion by saying that, up to this point a deterioration in quality has been assumed to be something that all consumers would sooner not have (though some are more sensitive to it than others), but 'this assumption can and will now be dropped' (p. 62). This is to extend the analysis of changes in quality to an area where the whole conception of 'quality' is logically out of place. The concept of 'quality' presupposes a unidirectional standard of judgement, and this presupposition cannot blandly be withdrawn merely by saying one intends to do so. If we want to talk about left and right, or hawks and doves, we should cast our analysis in explicitly dimensional terms. Attempting to carry over into this context a form of analysis worked out in terms of distinctions between high and low quality is simply to invite trouble.

One form which this trouble takes is evaluative. Hirschman, as I mentioned earlier, makes or implies many judgements about the desirability of one thing or another, but never sets out his value premisses. Up to the point where the concept of quality is expanded so that a change in quality can be good or bad, it is fairly clear that the value premiss is that the quality of goods supplied in a market should be as high as possible, at any given price. This is certainly not uncontroversial, but it is the sort of value premiss economists have been using ever since Adam Smith: it assumes that consumption is the object of all economic activity. Thus, Hirschman does not ask whether the gain to consumers from the elimination of 'organizational slack' might be outweighed by the benefits to the managers of a quiet life, or (more seriously) whether it might not be more important for 'organizational slack' to be taken up by pressure within the firm for improvements in the conditions of the employees than in quality improvements to the product.[25]

The evaluative problem becomes much stickier, however, when we are talking not about quality at all but in fact about whether one lot of customers, members, etc. should get the outcome they want or

---

[25] One reader of an earlier draft has shrewdly observed that my opening remarks depend on the unstated assumption that the object of academic life is to maximize the advancement of the discipline and that most academics may prefer to use 'organizational slack' to grow roses, drink port, etc. I must plead guilty.

whether some other lot should do so, for an evaluation now involves a choice between incompatible preferences. This can be seen especially starkly in relation to Hirschman's criticism of the failure of the dissident members of the Johnson administration to resign and denounce the Vietnam war publicly. An obvious difficulty raised by this example is that one may accept Hirschman's arguments because one likes his conclusion. But it is of course possible to say that everyone who could have helped should have done all he could to stop the war, without accepting Hirschman's analysis, which applies to Presidents and their appointees generally. The best way to avoid this trap is to observe that if you buy Hirschman's argument you are committed to saying that, if there were Nixon appointees who were unhappy with the cease-fire terms in Vietnam, it is a pity that their loyalty prevented them from resigning with maximum publicity and trying to whip up feeling against the terms as a sell-out.

There are, actually, at least two separate points at which the analogy with consumers suffering from a decline in quality fails to hold for Presidential appointees suffering from qualms about government policy. First—the point already adumbrated—the talk of 'quality' conceals the fact that what we have in this case is simply a difference of opinion. 'Decline', in the analysis here, means 'decline from the point of view of the dissidents', and the fact that Hirschman (and probably most of his readers by now) agrees with them is neither here nor there since we may disagree with the dissidents equally strongly next time round. Second, the President's appointees are hardly to be assimilated to the consumers of a firm's product—these are surely the citizens at large—but are more similar to the board of directors. So what we would be saying if we bought Hirschman's recommendation is that the chairman should have less loyalty from the other directors. Even then, however, the analogy breaks down because the President is elected and the 'official family' is appointed by him. Democratic accountability rests entirely on the responsibility of the President for major policy decisions. To want, in general, more influence for the appointed at the expense of the elected is to undermine that principle.[26]

---

[26] One might, however, still in general (that is, without regard to the pros and cons of the particular President's policies) be in favour of more disloyalty, on condition that the main effect of disloyalty was not so much to make the President more responsive to his appointees as to make him more responsive to the Congress and the public at large. Watergate provides one example where loyalty to the President meant engaging in subversion of the democratic process itself. In the long run, however, the more important question (raised above all by the Pentagon Papers) is whether the Presidency has broken free of the checks envisaged by the constitution—whether, by a systematic policy of concealment and lies about its actions and its intentions, it can operate without any effective scrutiny, debate, or control by Congress and the public. To the

Analytically, too, Hirschman's discussion of what he calls 'the failure of "unhappy" top officials to resign over Vietnam' (p. vii) does not fit very happily into the framework of the book. It is introduced in partial fulfilment of his declared programme, that of encouraging 'neglected options': voice in economics and exit in politics. I have already suggested that voice is liable to be a weak reed in economic affairs.[27] And the case of the 'unhappy' officials hardly seems a good example of a situation in which exit might have been more efficacious than voice. Exit is supposed to operate on a firm by reducing its sales and profits, but what equivalent effect would more exit have had on President Johnson?

In fact, the question is not one of 'exit' as such at all. Hirschman, in a rather curious way, suddenly notices this in the last two pages of the chapter devoted to the subject. Here he points out that exit from a 'public good' is different from exit in the market. (And he might have added that exiting from the *production* of a 'public good' is different from exiting from the *consumption* of a 'private good'.) 'To exit now will mean to resign under protest and, in general, to denounce and fight the organization from without instead of working for change from within. In other words, the alternative is now not so much between voice and exit as between voice from within and voice from without (after exit)' (p. 105). Just so. But this effectively destroys the exit/voice symmetry between economics and politics. It looks, for all that Hirschman says to the contrary, as if there is no substitute for voice in politics, and that the only question is the choice of voice from inside or outside.[28] In fact, much more relevant to the idea of making

extent that this is so—and the process seems to me far advanced, to say no more—the maximum disloyalty is to be welcomed, especially in the form of leaks about what is really going on. Evaluatively this differs from the Hirschman case in that the desired result is accountability to the consumers (or their representatives in Congress) rather than accountability to the producers (the Presidential appointees). It also differs in that it does not require the disloyalty to be motivated by disapproval of the President's policies themselves. It could in principle be motivated simply by a dislike of concealment and lies or a belief that they are incompatible with free or democratic institutions.

[27] 'Organizational slack' in firms seems more likely to be deterred or corrected by (*a*) takeover bids by other firms; (*b*) state control, forced merger, or nationalization; or (*c*) more effective channels for employees to exert pressure on managers. None of these is considered by Hirschman.

[28] From this perspective it is clear that Hirschman's own description of the theme in the Preface—'the failure to resign'—is misleading. In the last few lines of the chapter he implicitly accepts that there were enough people who *resigned* over Vietnam and that the problem was rather their failure to *denounce* it, when he refers to 'the relief that *would* have been experienced if at least one of the public officials who "dropped out" of the Johnson administration over the Vietnam war had thereupon publicly fought official war policies' (p. 105). Compare the following from Louis Heren, reflecting on the same period: 'The responsibility [for the war] of course rested first with Kennedy and then with Johnson, but few of their advisers could see the

more use of exit in politics would have been a consideration of the possible scope for extending exit in relation to public goods, on Friedmanite lines, and also by giving different areas of a country the maximum chance of adopting radically different policies in relation to the use of cars, land use planning, etc.

VIII

Hirschman's chapter on party competition does not suffer to the same extent from confusions arising from the inappropriate retention of the terminology of 'quality', though it would read much more clearly if all occurrences of the word were struck out. There are still, however, both analytical and evaluative weaknesses.

The evaluative problem is very simple. Hirschman starts from the old Hotelling story about the two shops in the road inhabited along its length at uniform density by consumers who will take their custom to whichever shop is nearer. The 'social optimum'—the location which minimizes average travelling distance from the nearest shop—is for one shop to locate one-quarter of the way along the road and the other three-quarters of the way along, in other words for each to locate itself in the middle of half the customers. But if each shop seeks to maximize its number of customers they will converge towards the halfway point along the road and finish up next door to one another, one taking as customers all those to the left of the centre and the other all those to the right. When the story is carried over to parties (as by Hotelling in passing and by Downs at length) the implication is, of course, that in a two-party system where voters can be arrayed on a single dimension (e.g. left to right) and each voter votes for the party whose position is nearest his own, the parties will converge on the position of the median voter (the mid-point of the line if voters are uniformly distributed along its length).

Hirschman objects to this on a variety of grounds, but one is that Downsians are too complacent about such an outcome. Having set out the case of the location of shops he goes on: 'in a similar way it can be argued that it is probable, but socially undesirable, for parties in a two-party system to move ever closer together' (p. 67). He then confronts in a footnote the obvious objection that, whereas consumers only want a *shop* nearby, voters want not so much a *party* near

madness of it. Fewer were prepared to tell their master, preferring instead to slink back to Harvard and other academic and foundation boltholes.' Louis Heren, 'Pied Pipers at the White House', *The Times* (24 May 1973), 13.

themselves as as *government* near themselves. His reply is: 'it can be argued, however, that a two-party system implies a preference for a risky but meaningful over a meaningless choice' (p. 67n.). I do not, however, see why a two-party system implies any such preference, or indeed quite what is meant by saying that it implies anything. If the statement entails that the citizens of a country with a two-party system are on the average more supportive of the system when the parties are far apart than when they are close together, it is not, I think, in line with the historical record. And it does seem to be something like this that Hirschman intends since he glosses the sentence just quoted as follows: 'the average citizen may well prefer a situation in which a party with which he identifies closely has an even chance of beating one he sharply disagrees with, over a situation in which power is always held by a middle-of-the-road party which he neither likes nor dislikes strongly' (p. 67n.).[29]

Hirschman's objections to the Downsian model of two-party competition have some weight but are vitiated by a failure to relate them in the correct way to the model and also by incorrect analysis at a crucial point. The main objection is that Downs's theory predicts the convergence of parties on the middle of the spectrum and that 'hardly ever was a hypothesis so cruelly contradicted by the facts as were the predictions of the Hotelling–Downs theory by the Goldwater nomination' (p. 71). Presumably the McGovern candidature eight years later would have been adduced by Hirschman as an analogue on the Democratic side, had the book appeared in time to include it. What Hirschman makes much less of is that Goldwater was crushed in 1964—just as McGovern was in 1972. Yet this is crucial if we are to make a correct assessment of the Downsian analysis.

Downs's model is simply an axiomatic system, or more precisely a family of them, one being the one-dimensional two-party case discussed by Hirschman. It does not *predict*, as Hirschman seems to believe, except in the sense of predicting that when the axioms are satisfied the outcomes deduced from them will occur. The political system which Downs sets up in his axioms is unlike the USA in

---

[29] The preference for risk would have to be high if we accept an assumption put forward a little earlier in the chapter. Hirschman states this in words as: 'discontent rises more than proportionately with deviation of the actual from the preferred quality' (pp. 63–4n.). As the accompanying figure shows, what he intends by this is that discontent is not linear with distance but an increasing function of it. This entails that a person with a neutral attitude to risk, given a choice between an outcome a certain distance $X$ from his most preferred outcome and a lottery of (say) a $0.5$ chance of his preferred outcome and a $0.5$ chance of one at a distance of $2X$, would always choose the first alternative.

a number of ways since it involves monolithic parties which by winning an election completely control the country's legislation and administration until the next election. As he himself observes, it comes closest to a tidied-up version of British politics. The separation of powers, party fragmentation, and the Federal Constitution of the USA depart so far from the conditions of the model that it ought to be regarded as a bonus if it works there at all.

Now, in addition to these structural axioms, Downs has an axiom to the effect that politicians seek to maximize votes, because they want to get into office for some reason or other. To the extent that parties are controlled by professional politicians this appears to me a remarkably powerful axiom. Thus, given the rest of Downs's analysis, it follows that in two-party systems the parties will converge in the middle—as the post-war experience of Britain, Australia, or New Zealand illustrates. The point about the USA is that the system of nominating conventions makes it possible for control to be wrested by zealots from the hands of the professional politicians. It still remains true that what the professionals want is a winner who will carry in as many lesser candidates as possible on his coat-tails and provide federal patronage. Where the professional politicians—the men in charge of the state machines, which are the only organizational reality American parties have—do control the nomination they have a pretty good record of going for the candidate they believe (rightly or wrongly) has the best chance of winning, whether they like him or not. (Thus, in 1960 they finally swallowed Kennedy on the basis of his record in primary elections and surveys commissioned and analysed by Kennedy staffers purporting to show him as having the best chance against Nixon.) The process by which right-wing enthusiasts took over state conventions in 1964 simply by turning up at normally routine meetings is described in detail by Theodore White, while in 1972 the new rules for selection of delegates opened the whole process up in the Democratic party.

Thus, what we can say is that American nominating conventions may be controlled by people who are not trying to maximize the number of votes garnered by the party standard-bearer. But the Downsian model still applies at the next stage in as far as voters satisfy the axiom stating that they vote for the ideologically closest candidate. And, as I have pointed out, this stage of the model stands up pretty well in that the two deviant candidates were defeated by spectacular margins.

It is here that Hirschman's argument seems to me to lack coherence.

Having suggested that the extremists will be mobilized by discontent with 'wishy-washy' policies to exercise voice and will thus be able to push their party away from the centre, he says that

> there can be no guarantee that the voice mechanism will bring the party exactly back to the somewhat problematical 'social optimum' which, in analogy to Hotelling's treatment of the location problem, can be defined as the point at which the sum of the ideological distances between the party and its clients is minimized. The influence of those who have nowhere else to go may well make the party overshoot that point, with disastrous consequences for its vote-gathering objectives. This was essentially what happened to the Republican party in 1964 with the selection of Goldwater as its presidential nominee (p. 71).

One point which has to be clarified before we can discuss the main issue this raises is that the conditions of the 'social optimum' are incorrectly stated. Who 'the clients' of a party are in a two-party system is not predetermined but is a function simultaneously of its own position and the position of its opponent. A party would probably minimize the sum of ideological distances between itself and its clients by adopting a very extreme position. If the other party pursued a maximizing strategy by taking up a position close to it but nearer the median voter, this would of course mean that the extreme party had few clients. Having a small number of clients would in itself tend to produce a small sum of distances; and even if we ask (more sensibly) about the average distance, this would be low because the clients would be clustered at the end of the spectrum, while the other party would have all the rest of the voters as its clients. The 'social optimum' that Hirschman wants must be stated rather as a situation in which the average distance from the nearer of the two parties to the electorate as a whole is minimized. And this, where the electorate is spread uniformly along an ideological dimension, requires that the parties be one-quarter and three-quarters of the way along.

Now I have already argued that Hirschman does not provide adequate grounds for calling such a situation a 'social optimum'. My present concern, however, is with the analysis of party competition implied in the passage quoted. Hirschman assumes (a nice example of domination by a model, incidentally) that Goldwater's defeat must have been due to his 'overshooting' the socially optimum position. This would entail that less than a quarter of the voting population with an opinion found Goldwater too far left, in other words that Goldwater was further over to the right than the seventy-fifth percentile. Whether or not he was is an (in principle) empirical question which I shall not attempt to answer here. What I do wish to observe is that the assumption is not required in order to explain Goldwater's electoral defeat. Let us assume that Goldwater was exactly spot on the 'socially optimal' seventy-fifth percentile point and that Johnson occupied the 'middle ground' of the fiftieth percentile point (the position of the median voter). Following the Downsian assumption, which Hirschman does not challenge, that each elector votes for the candidate nearer his own position, this disposition of the candidates would predict victory for Johnson by a margin of 62·5 per cent of the vote to 37·5 per cent, which is not far off the actual result (Johnson, 61·0 per cent; Goldwater, 38·5 per cent).

The more general point underlying this is that a party following Hirschman's rule for a 'social optimum' will always be beaten by one closer to the median voter. Hirschman's reply would presumably be that, provided the extremist voice operates to the same degree in both parties, a stable equilibrium at the first and third quartiles can be maintained. But there are two problems with this. The first is that Hirschman's voice mechanism has no inherent tendency to finish up at the 'optimum' rather than at a more extreme or less extreme position, if we think of it as a process in which there is a tug-of-war between the professionals aiming at a candidate of the centre (so as to win) and the extremists aiming at a candidate of the extreme left or right (so as to have someone they identify with). More serious, however, is that even the most extreme zealot has an incentive to prefer moderate candidates provided he is really interested more in having the *Presidency* in the hands of someone relatively near his own position than merely in having a candidate doomed to defeat near his own position. For the Downsian analysis shows, as we have seen, that whichever candidate is nearer the centre will win. Let us imagine that the 'left' candidate is expected to be at (say) the thirtieth percentile from the left, and let us consider the calculus of an extreme right-wing zealot. (Put him, if you like, at even the hundredth point from the left.) A candidate near his own preferred position will be defeated, giving him a President seventy percentile points away. But a candidate more than thirty percentile points away from him (that is, less than seventy from the left) will be nearer the median than his opponent and will thus win. The choice is thus between a President seventy percentile points away and one only thirty-odd away.

We can, however, add to this that the left-wing zealots have exactly the same incentive towards moderation, if they too are concerned primarily to have a President relatively near themselves rather than a defeated candidate who is close. The equilibrium outcome, therefore, *even in a country where one party was run by extreme right-wingers and the other by extreme left-wingers*, would be exactly the same as Downs predicts on the assumption that politicians are concerned only to maximize votes, namely, that the parties would be next to one another round the position of the median voter.[30]

IX

I stated, at the end of section I, my belief that the existence of a growing core of concepts and associated theories had been on balance of advantage to the discipline of political science in the USA. How should we rate the concepts of exit, voice, and loyalty and the theory associated with them?

In order to answer this, we need to distinguish the leading ideas from the detailed analysis. The leading ideas are two: first, the idea of some sort of inverse relationship between exit and voice; and, second, the idea that under some circumstances exit may operate on those running a collectivity not as an incentive to improve but as a licence to deteriorate. I hope that I have shown these to be ideas of great fertility and synthesizing power.

The detailed analysis in which they are embedded is, as I have also tried to show, not satisfactory as it stands. In particular, although there is no question that a concept of loyalty is needed to account for the presence of voice and the absence of exit in some circumstances, the conceptualization offered by Hirschman is seriously defective. But this is not, of course, to say that he might just as well have stopped after setting out the basic ideas. By creating a theory with a clear logical structure he can be credited with having taken the major step towards a more adequate analysis.

It is a well-established academic custom to conclude an article by putting forward a programme of work for other people to do, so let me suggest that the first priority in developing an analysis is to look more systematically at the ways in which exit and voice can be related and to try to bring all the variables relevant to each kind of relationship into an explicit theoretical structure.

Thus, if we go back to the illustrations that were mentioned in section II, it seems to me that the only one fairly unambiguously exhibiting the kind of relation assumed by Hirschman was the case of

---

[30] For further discussion of this matter, see my *Sociologists, Economists and Democracy*, pp. 149–50.

educated Blacks leaving the southern USA, and thus failing to develop voice on behalf of the Black community. The other cases involved (or may well have involved) different or at least additional mechanisms. In particular we need to pay attention to the effects of exit other than those of removing potentially active carriers of voice.

In some kinds of situation, exit by some leaves those who remain behind better-off. Thus, up to some point (beyond which the community becomes unbalanced or unviable) emigration from an area in which land is in short supply makes the rest better-off by reducing subdivision of holdings or weakening the position of landlords. Voice may be decreased simply because the position improves.[31] In other situations, exit by some leaves those who remain worse off, quite apart from the fact that those who have left are not available as a source of voice. The most obvious example of this is the way in which the uncontrolled growth in the use of the private car makes public transport worse by taking away custom. The excellence of public transport in Venice is indeed due to everyone's being 'locked in', but the connection between the two probably owes at least as much to the fact that this provides plenty of customers for the *vaporetti* as to the fact that even influential Venetians have to use them.

[31] This presupposes that voice is inversely related to well-being. It seems plausible, however, that up to some threshold the struggle for existence is so grim as to leave no energy for voice. Thus, in the nineteenth century the Irish peasantry were politically inert during the terrible years of famine but became much more active when things improved—to a considerable extent as a result of massive emigration.

# 8

## POWER
### An Economic Analysis

I    INTRODUCTION

Although controversy continues to rage about the proper definition and analysis of power, we find no great difficulty in understanding in a general way what is meant by ascriptions of power. The Norwegian government, for example, in a brochure for visitors entitled *Glimpses of Norway*, tells us: 'Today, Norway is a constitutional monarchy, with political power centered in the 150 member parliament (Storting).'[1] Obviously, political scientists might not be entirely happy with this. Stein Rokkan, in his contribution to *Political Oppositions in Western Democracies*[2] speaks of 'numerical democracy and corporate pluralism', suggesting that much of the power of the Storting has been delegated to corporate groups so that in practice the Storting often merely ratifies their deals. But even so the statement that political power is centred in the Storting serves to distinguish Norway from, for example, contemporary Chile, where it would not be true to say that the National Assembly has any political power at all, since it has been dissolved by the military junta. And we know roughly what is meant by saying that in Chile the President and the Assembly both *had* power until a group of generals *seized* power. One crude but practical criterion of power would be to ask: suppose you were an officer of the CIA or some multinational corporation with large funds available for buying favours in terms of public policy, what kind of person would it be rational to spend the money on? And it does seem reasonable to say that you could do worse than buy some members of the Storting (if any were for sale) but would be wasting your money in Chile on anything except a member of the government or perhaps the armed forces.

Robert Dahl's 'intuitive idea of power', in his essay on 'The Concept of Power', was that 'A has power over B to the extent that he

---

[1] *Glimpses of Norway* (Oslo: Royal Ministry of Foreign Affairs, n.d., c. 1971), 3.
[2] R. A. Dahl (ed.), *Political Oppositions in Western Democracies* (New Haven, Conn.: Yale University Press, 1966), 70–115.

can get B to do something that B would not otherwise do'.[3] Power is thus the ability to cause things to happen when the object is actions by other people. Bertrand Russell, in his book *Power*,[4] goes further and in effect identifies power with the ability to cause things to happen. He equates the use of power with the production of intended effects. The ability to cause actions of other people (social power) is then a subclass of power in general. The word 'power' is indeed employed in this general sense, as when we say that a man is 'powerfully built': we mean that he has strong muscles and is thus able to produce more intended effects by his own exertions than most people can. But there is no sense in looking for a general theory of power in this sense. We should simply be asking for a general theory of the ability to cause things to happen. Nor is it much more sensible to look for a general theory of social as against natural power. We should then be asking for a general theory of the ability to get people to do things.

What we have to do is divide up the phenomenon of getting other people to do things so that each method of getting people to do things can be analysed in the terms appropriate to it. And I think that as a first shot at this Talcott Parsons's division of the methods into four categories has much to commend it. He calls these methods 'activation of commitments', 'persuasion', 'inducement', and 'coercion'.[5] I propose to put inducement and coercion together but then add a further category, physical constraint, which has often been included—for example by Hobbes. I now want to explain these four categories and show that each calls for different techniques of analysis.

## II  FOUR VARIETIES OF POWER

Getting somebody to do something by 'activating a commitment' is a matter of cashing in on some norm that he already has to the effect that he *ought* to act in accord with a demand from a certain source. If B accepts a norm giving authority to A, then A has the ability to 'activate commitments' for B. To take a central political example, let us say that someone has a general belief that he ought to obey the law of the country in which he lives. A new law is passed by whatever procedure constitutes the 'rule of recognition' for a valid law in the country, and the person obeys it. Obviously, this process raises questions about the

[3] Dahl, 'The Concept of Power', *Behavioral Science*, 2 (1957), 201–15 repr. in Roderick Bell, David V. Edwards, and R. Harrison Wagner (eds.), *Political Power: A Reader in Theory and Research* (New York: Free Press, 1969), 79–93 at 80.

[4] B. Russell, *Power: A New Social Analysis* (London: George Allen and Unwin, 1938).

[5] Talcott Parsons, 'On the Concept of Political Power', in Bell, *et al.*, *Political Power*, pp. 251–84 at p. 258.

circumstances under which people acquire and retain such norms. The relevant studies are in the sociology of law and more generally of legitimate authority.

The second way of getting somebody to do something is to bring about a change of mind so that he does now want to do it. In principle we can distinguish between on the one hand supplying him with new information (whether true or false, sincerely or insincerely believed by the giver) which leads him to conclude that a different action will be a more effective means of reaching his goals, and on the other hand working on his goals by some method or another so that they become different. But in practice the distinction is often not clear because many goals are valued only (or partially) as means to something further. In any case, it is apparent that the kind of analytic tools necessary to discuss this phenomenon (Parsons's 'persuasion') are those relevant to the psychology and sociology of attitude change, the sociology of knowledge, propaganda analysis, and so on.

The third process involving power that I want to mention is one that Parsons does not. (It is, of course, characteristic that, compared with most discussions, he should include a normative conception that is not usually mentioned and leave out a conception involving the direct use of physical force.) Sir George Cornewall Lewis, in his *Remarks on the Use and Abuse of Some Political Terms*, said that the word 'power' 'appears to signify the possession of the means of influencing the will of another, either by persuasion or threats; or of constraining his person by means of physical force'.[6] This process is embodied in the usage of 'overpowering' someone and also (less explicitly) in that of 'having someone in one's power'. Notice that Lewis carefully sets off this kind of power from others in that it does not act on the will but directly reduces the range of actions open to the person over whom power is being exercised. By holding fast to this distinction we can see that power in this sense of incapacitation need not be embodied in anything as dramatic as chains or prison walls. If someone wants to do something that involves his travelling by car and I immobilize the only car available to him then I have prevented him from doing what he wanted more surely than if I had, say, threatened to burn down his house if he went.

An important case of physical constraint in this extended sense is that of reducing the capability of another to resist the imposition of sanctions, increasing his need to accept offered advantages, reducing

---

[6] Sir G. C. Lewis, *Remarks on the Use and Abuse of Some Political Terms* (Oxford: Clarendon Press, 1898), 92.

his capacity for doing similar things to oneself, or reducing his capacity to impose sanctions on oneself. Thus, in a war one side may improve its relative bargaining position by destroying the other side's anti-missile system so that its cities are more vulnerable, by destroying its stores of food so that the offer of food in return for compliance is more attractive, or (covering the last two categories) by destroying the other side's offensive capabilities. Thus, physical constraint may be used as an instrument for increasing power in the fourth sense, which I now discuss.

The fourth and final method by which one person (A) can get another (B) to do something is for A to change the incentives facing B. A can do this by attaching the promise of something B desires to gain to some action that he would not otherwise propose to do (Parsons's 'inducement'). Or A can do it by attaching the threat of something B desires to avoid to some action which he would otherwise propose to do (Parsons's 'coercion'). It is possible to combine a promise and a threat in respect of the same action.

This method of getting someone to do something he would not otherwise do is different from the 'activation of commitments' in that it appeals purely to self-interest. In effect, A says to B: 'I will make it worth your while to do x'. It differs from the second method—Parsons's 'persuasion'—because it does not alter the attractiveness of the action in question in the eyes of B. In itself, the action demanded by A remains unattractive. What happens is that, if B's behaviour is successfully modified by A, this comes about because B has been convinced that A will provide rewards or sanctions, or refrain from providing them, according to the way B acts; and that the balance struck when he takes account of the direct effect of his own actions or inactions and the consequential actions or inactions of A is such as to make it more advantageous to do what A demands than not to do it. Finally, this fourth process of inducement and coercion differs from the third one in that, although force may be used, it is used in order to affect the will rather than to affect the capabilities. The distinction, which is central to Clausewitz's analysis, is between changing someone's choice among his options from what it would otherwise have been and actually removing some options from him.

For many purposes—ethical, legal, and (as we shall notice later) practical—threats have to be treated as different from promises. But for analytical purposes we can assimilate threats and promises into one theory. This is important because it means we can handle the case where A combines the two and says: 'If you don't comply with my demand I'll do something you don't like but if you do comply then I'll do something you do like.' Alexander George has remarked[7] that foreign policymakers tend to neglect the combined use of sticks and carrots. The Mafia, however, would appear to be well aware of the strategy, if they really go around saying 'I'll make him an offer he can't refuse'.

This fourth variety of power lends itself naturally to theoretical development from within an 'economic' or 'rational choice' framework. It falls within the province of ordinary economic theory, since an exchange in a market is in effect a case in which $A$ promises $B$ that he will do something that $B$ likes (give him money or some commodity) on condition that $B$ does something he would not otherwise do that $A$ wants him to do (give him some commodity or some money). And obviously the whole subject is centrally related to bargaining theory and to the theory of games.

### III   POWER AND POLITICAL EXPLANATION

Since power is the *ability* to get people to do things, we can obviously construct a characterization of power corresponding to each of the four methods of getting people to do things that we have just outlined. Thus, power in the first sense is the ability to activate commitments: the capacity at one's own discretion to get people to do what they would not otherwise do by invoking some standing commitment to obey some source of instructions. Power in relation to the second process is the capacity at one's own discretion to change people's perceptions or goals by some means or other so that they want to do something they would not otherwise do. Power in relation to the third process is the capacity physically to restrain or constrain the actions of others. And, finally, power in the fourth sense is the possession by one actor ($A$) of the means of modifying the conduct of another actor ($B$) by means of an expectation in $B$ that one or more of the alternative actions available to him will (with some probability) result in reward or punishment brought about by $A$. The exercise of power on a given occasion is the threat or promise by $A$ of employing his means of modifying the conduct of $B$ contingently upon $B$'s doing some action (or one of a set of actions) out of the alternatives open to him.

There are two points about this fourth variety of power which are worth clearing up at once. First, if $A$ has the means of modifying the

[7] A. L. George, D. K. Hall, and W. E. Simons, *The Limits of Coercive Diplomacy: Laos, Cuba, Vietnam* (Boston, Mass: Little, Brown, 1971).

behaviour of *B* by making *B* better off or worse off contingently upon what *B* does, it must follow that *A* also has the ability to make *B* better off or worse off unconditionally. Thus, if *A* has power he has the means of making *B* better off or worse off than he would be if *A* did not exert himself. But if *A* in fact chooses to make *B* better off or worse off unconditionally this is not an exercise of power. The converse relationship usually but not invariably holds: if *A* can make *B* better off or worse off unconditionally he can normally also create an expectation in *B* that he will make him better or worse off depending on *B*'s actions. Thus, possession of the means of making someone better off or worse off normally constitutes power, that is to say possession of the means of modifying behaviour. But there are two prerequisites of there being a connection between the two. First, *A* must be able to communicate his threat or offer to *B*. And second, *A* must be able to find out whether *B* has in fact complied or not. Thus, as Schelling has suggested, if the families of kidnapped persons were locked up and kept incommunicado, this would make it impossible for kidnappers to get their demands through to their victims, thus making the kidnap pointless.[8] And the object of the secret ballot is to make people immune to threats and bribes.

Second, following on from this, it should be noted that the communication of threats and promises need not be explicit—all that is needed is that *A* should be able with some reliability to create an expectation in *B* that certain acts will have certain consequences brought about by *A*. This may be done explicitly or implicitly in speech, in writing, or even in gesture; or it may be done (where the situation is of an appropriate kind) purely by a sequence of reactions to moves by *B*. In other words, if every time *B* does something of a certain sort something nasty happens to him, or if every time he does something of another sort something nice happens, he is liable sooner or later to get the message, especially if *A* is visibly behind the nice or nasty things that happen each time.

Power, to repeat, is not an event but a possession. The event that is associated with this possession is the *exercise* of power. Someone *has* power over a period of time and during that time he has the means of modifying the behaviour of more or fewer people to a greater or lesser extent. He *exercises* power at a particular time within that period, in relation to a particular person or persons, and in respect of a particular modification of action. The exercise of power may of course be either

[8] T. C. Schelling, *The Strategy of Conflict* (Cambridge, Mass.: Harvard University Press, 1960), 39, n. 11.

successful in achieving its object or unsuccessful. Dahl remarks in 'The Concept of Power' that 'unfortunately, in the English language power is an awkward word, for unlike "influence" and "control" it has no convenient verb form. . . .'[9] But is this a mere grammatical deficiency in English (as, for example, the fact that there is no infinitive or past tense of 'must'), or does it (like most linguistic phenomena) reflect something about the nature of the concept itself? In the present case the answer is surely the latter. Since 'power', like 'wealth', refers to something possessed, there is no more sense in regretting the absence of a verb form than there is in regretting that there is no expression 'he wealths'. In both cases everything that can be said logically, given the meaning of the word, can be said with auxiliary verbs: he has power (or he has wealth); he exercised his power (or he spent his wealth).

If politics is, as Harold Lasswell said, the study of 'who gets what, when, how',[10] it is easy to see why we should feel that a knowledge of the distribution of power is so basic to the explanation of political events. But a knowledge of the distribution of power is not enough to enable us to predict with complete confidence who will get what. Someone may try to exercise his power but, through lack of skill, fail to alter behaviour in the way he wants. This possibility of slippage is not a defect but is in fact what saves the whole idea from triviality: it means that we have a framework for causal explanation. Weber and Dahl close the logical gap by equating power with the probability of one actor's being able to change the behaviour of someone in the direction desired. To say that A got B to do something that B would not otherwise have done because A had power over B becomes as vacuous as saying that someone became angry on a given occasion because he had an irascible temperament, or that opium makes people sleepy because it has the *virtus dormitiva*.

In any case, a complete explanation of 'who gets what' must take account of the fact that there are ways of getting things other than by the exercise of social power. First, you might get what you want by your own unaided efforts (the exercise of natural power). Second, there is the possibility of getting something without exercising power at all: people may simply give you what you want, either because they like you or feel a sense of duty to provide for your wants. And third, you may be able to benefit from the exercise of power by somebody

[9] Bell *et al.*, *Political Power*, p. 80.
[10] H. D. Lasswell, *Politics: Who Gets What, When, How* (with postscript) (New York: Meridian Books, 1958).

else without having to bestir yourself at all. The first of these does not have a great deal of importance in explaining difference in success between people in getting what they want. As Hobbes pointed out, the distribution of natural power is fairly equal—certainly such inequalities as there are in its distribution are dwarfed by the inequalities that exist in social power. Being lucky in your friends, guardians, or allies is of considerable significance in determining the degree to which different people get what they want. I shall not take it up in this chapter, but it will form a large part of the subject-matter of chapter 9.

IV   THE MEASUREMENT OF COMPLIANCE

Power is the possession by $A$ of the means of modifying the conduct of $B$. To begin with, then, we need some way of talking about how much the conduct of $B$ is modified. In 'The Concept of Power', Dahl throws up his hands over this: there can be nothing except an unsorted list of things that $B$ can be got to do. 'Suppose that I could induce my son to bathe every evening and to brush his teeth before going to bed and that my neighbour could induce his son to serve him breakfast in bed every morning. Are the two responses I can control to be counted as greater than the one response my neighbour can control?'[11] But there is not necessarily any difficulty about this. Surely, if both sons agree that providing breakfast is a bigger chore than bathing and brushing teeth, the neighbour is incontrovertibly obtaining more compliance than is Dahl.

   This example is of course complicated by the fact that we are asked to compare responses of different people. Even here, as I have suggested, it can be done quite simply in some cases, but Dahl does not even suggest a technique for the easy case of comparing the responses of a single actor. Surely there is an obvious criterion: $A$ can be said to secure more compliant behaviour from $B$ the more $B$ doesn't like complying with $A$'s demand. Thus, in any area where $A$ and $B$ have some conflict of goals (i.e. where the preference orderings of $A$ and $B$ for outcomes are not identical) we need to begin by constructing a compliance schedule for $B$. In its most modest form this can consist simply of a listing of all the possible demands that $A$ might make, with at the top the item that $B$ would least mind conceding, and then the other demands in order of increasing reluctance on $B$'s part to accede

[11] Bell *et al.*, *Political Power*, p. 84.

to them. When a negotiation is being undertaken by agents, the principal will normally brief them in precisely these terms.[12]

For the purpose of geometrical representation, let us put $B$'s degree of possible compliance on a horizontal axis, with zero compliance on the left and increasing compliance as we move right. In Figure 8.1, o represents zero compliance—the baseline against which the degree of compliance is to be measured. It is what $B$ would choose to do if his behaviour were entirely unmodified by $A$. Moving right from o, we get to $w$, which is the possible demand of $A$ that $B$ would least mind conceding. Compliance with successive demands as we move right would be increasingly objectionable to $B$. Let us call this horizontal axis $B$'s compliance line, since it is constructed from $B$'s compliance schedule. It is important to notice that compliance is measured entirely in terms of $B$'s reluctance and takes no account of $A$'s satisfaction. Zero compliance by $B$ may in fact be quite satisfactory to $A$ if what $B$ most wants to do suits $A$ well. And there is no suggestion that greater compliance by $B$ is necessarily preferred by $A$.

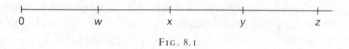

FIG. 8.1

For some purposes an ordinal scale is all that is needed. For other purposes, it is very useful to have a cardinal scale, and the obvious one is to have monetary units. Sometimes, money is actually the subject of $A$'s demand—as in blackmail, kidnapping, protection rackets, and all other forms of demanding money with menaces. In many others, money is not itself the subject of the demand, but it would make sense to ask $B$ how much money he would have to be given to just compensate him for complying with each demand. Thus, we can now space out the four demands on a cardinal scale, as in Figure 8.2.

It is important to notice that 'getting someone to do what he does not want to do' must be understood to include 'inhibiting someone

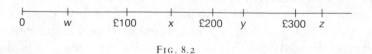

FIG. 8.2

[12] Fred C. Iklé, *How Nations Negotiate* (New York: Harper and Row, 1964).

from doing what he does want to do'. Both are equally an exercise of power. What this means in terms of the compliance line is that the zero point—no compliance by *A* with *B*'s demands—may be a point at which *B* is doing something that *A* does not like. The point at which *B* is *not* doing anything that has any interest for *A* may, by contrast, be a long way along the compliance line.

Figure 8.3 provides an illustration. Suppose that *B* owns the land at the bottom of *A*'s garden and has planning permission to erect four houses on it. *A* would most like the status quo, that is to say open space, but if there is to be any building he would prefer one house to two, two to three, and three to four. *B*'s preferences are the inverse, as shown in Figure 8.3: he would most like to build four houses and would like least the continuation of the status quo. Suppose now that *A* somehow has the means to make it worth *B*'s while to desist from building more than three houses. The outcome is that *B* builds three houses, but he is complying with *A*'s demand to the extent that he does not build the fourth house that he would otherwise have built.

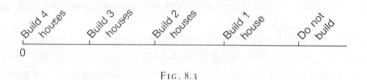

FIG. 8.3

That non-action can constitute compliance as well as can action has an obvious bearing on the 'community power' debate. Inaction where we might have expected action requires just as much explanation as action where we might have expected inaction. In both cases the answer may (though it may not) lie in discovering that the agent is complying with the wishes of someone else. Moreover, it is no refutation of the existence of a 'power élite' to show that some things happen contrary to the wishes of the putative power élite. There may nevertheless be many things that this power élite would intensely dislike that it is able to prevent from happening.

For example, a Labour government in Britain undoubtedly does things that the Confederation of British Industries dislikes. But are there other things that the CBI would dislike much more that the government would like to do and is inhibited from doing because of the sanctions that the members of the CBI could deploy? It seems as if the CBI believes so, since its spokesmen have developed over the years

an elaborate Aesopian terminology for threatening Labour governments that unless 'business confidence' is created businessmen will not
invest and may contract their operations.

The standard 'behaviouralist' objection to counting inaction as
compliance is that we can see compliant action but we cannot see
compliant inaction. This is an absurd piece of (to use a word of which
the behaviouralists are fond) metaphysics. Action and inaction themselves are equally observable. On the other hand, *compliance* is never
observable: to say that a piece of behaviour is compliant is always a
theoretical statement entailing a counterfactual conditional. But this,
again, is the same whether compliance is ascribed to action or to
inaction. In one case we say that an actor is doing something that he
would otherwise not do. In the other case we say that an actor is
refraining from doing something he would otherwise do.

Obviously, this analysis of compliance fits most naturally into the
analysis of our fourth variety of power, the ability to modify
behaviour by the manipulation of rewards and costs. And it is on this
that the rest of the chapter will concentrate. But consider also our first
variety of power: your ability to get someone to do what he would not
otherwise do by appealing to a norm that says he *ought* to obey you.
Surely we wish to be able to say whether his accepting your authority
and obeying your order changes his behaviour a lot or a little. And I do
not see any alternative way of answering that question except by
asking how much he has to give up by obeying—in other words what
it costs him, taking as the baseline what he would have preferred to do
in the absence of the order.

Our other two varieties of power require rather different treatment.
Although both are instances of 'getting someone to do what he would
not otherwise have done', neither is a case of 'securing compliance'. In
the second case you persuade someone to change his preferences so
that his 'zero compliance' position is nearer your own. You do not
move him along his compliance line. And in the third case you reduce
the number of alternatives open to him (in extreme cases to one), so
that what he would originally have chosen to do (his original zero
compliance position) is no longer available. In a different way, this is
also therefore a matter of changing the compliance line rather than
moving someone along it.

The analysis of the second and third varieties of power in terms of
changing the compliance line is especially useful where one of these
methods of changing behaviour is combined with one of the others. It
enables us to think of the methods in relation to one another. Thus, for

example, you might (starting from an initial position of sharply opposed goals) modify someone's behaviour in the desired direction partly by changing his mind so that his zero compliance position is no longer as distasteful to you as it was, and partly by operating on his new compliance schedule by offering rewards or threatening sanctions. Or, again, you might physically limit the alternatives open to someone (by putting a wall around him, for example) but then, within this restricted range of choices, attempt to elicit a choice he would not otherwise make by the exercise of authority or by offering a reward for certain behaviour.

### V GAINS AND LOSSES FROM COMPLIANCE

It is tempting to pursue further the possibility of fitting into a broad framework the special analyses appropriate to each of our four varieties of power. But space limitations demand that if I am to reach some definite conclusions I must follow up only one line of analysis. In the rest of this chapter, therefore, I shall concentrate on the analysis of the fourth, 'economic', variety of power.

Obviously, such an analysis must rest on the relations of gains and losses for the actors. We therefore introduce these on the dimension lying at right angles to the compliance line. The vertical axis then measures various gains and losses for A and B associated with any given level of compliance on the part of B. The curve that can be drawn in most directly is the curve representing B's loss from each level of compliance with A's demands. Where the same units are used on both axes, the curve becomes quite trivial, since it is just a straight line running at 45° to the horizontal downwards to the right from the origin. But the units on the two axes do not, of course, have to be the same. Thus, if compliance is measured in money and loss in cardinal utility, we might suppose the curve to have the shape shown in Figure 8.4. The curve is marked 'B's gross loss from compliance' (the

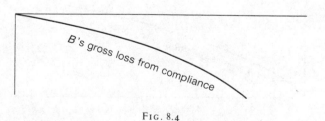

F I G. 8.4

significance of 'gross' will be explained below). The weakest interpretation of the vertical axis is that it measures ordinal utility, in other
words that a greater distance from the origin measures a greater loss
than a smaller distance (and the same for gains), but that any part of the
vertical axis could be arbitrarily stretched or contracted without
changing the information given. All we can say here, of course, is that
the curve for $B$'s gross loss from compliance will slope down strictly
monotonically from the origin. (In other words, it will go down all
the way.) But any assertion about its shape would be meaningless. As I
shall show, quite a lot can be got out of curves constructed on this very
undemanding basis.

Let us now turn to $A$'s gross gain from $B$'s compliance. (The
significance of 'gross' will, again, be explained below.) Everything
that has been said about the units for measuring $B$'s loss applies here,
but the question of the shape is much more interesting. We could say
definitely that the curve for $B$'s gross loss from compliance must slope
strictly monotonically down to the right, because this was guaranteed
by the rules for constructing the horizontal axis: the further right, the
more distasteful the thing in question. There is no such inevitability
about the shape of $A$'s gross gain curve. It is quite possible for it to
slope up to the right strictly monotonically, as in Figure 8.5. Here
there is the maximum conflict of interest: the more $B$ dislikes doing
something, the more $A$ would like him to do it. Situations which are
straight transfers of money or of something else that is valued by both
sides (e.g. territory for states) inevitably have this form. So are
situations in which $B$'s suffering is itself the source of $A$'s satisfaction.

Many other situations, however, are not of this kind. These are
situations with pockets of relative congruence of interest within a
general context of conflict of interest. For example, T. R. Marmor and
D. Thomas have pointed out that in negotiations between doctors and
those responsible for running national health schemes, doctors are

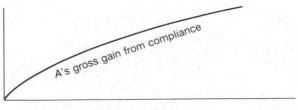

FIG. 8.5

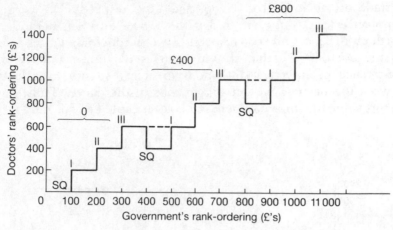

FIG. 8.6

deeply interested both in more money and in getting a method of payment that they like (in fact, normally what they have been used to). Governments, however, are interested almost entirely in keeping down the cost of the settlement, with the result that the deal always includes adoption of the doctors' preferred position on method of payment.[13]

Graphically, the doctor–government position might look something like Figure 8.6. The horizontal axis here represents compliance by the government with the doctors' demands and the curve represents the utility (which need be measured only ordinally) that the doctors get from each level of compliance. If each point on the compliance line represents some combination of total cost and method of payment, the far right end is obviously a very large total cost, plus the government's least relished payment method. Assuming that there is a conflict of goals over payment methods as well as total costs, but that the government cares less about payment methods relative to costs than do the doctors, we get the first trough (from the left) where the government, having begun by conceding on methods of payment, starts giving away more money; the second trough represents the same thing at a higher cost. On the figure it is imagined that there are three possible concessions on methods (I, II, III) and two on pay (£400, £800). If the concessions on methods are thought by the government

[13] T. R. Marmor and D. Thomas, 'Doctors, Politics and Pay Disputes: *Pressure Group Politics Revisited*', *British Journal of Political Science*, 2 (1972), 421–42.

to trade off against £100, £200, and £300 respectively, we get a
compliance line as shown; and if the concessions on methods are
worth £200, £400, and £600 respectively to the doctors, we get a curve
for the doctors like that shown. This is of course a fairly mild
coincidence of interest. If there is greater disparity in valuation
between the parties, we get bigger dips in the curve. Thus, if the
doctors value the three payment methods at £500, £1,000, and £1,500,

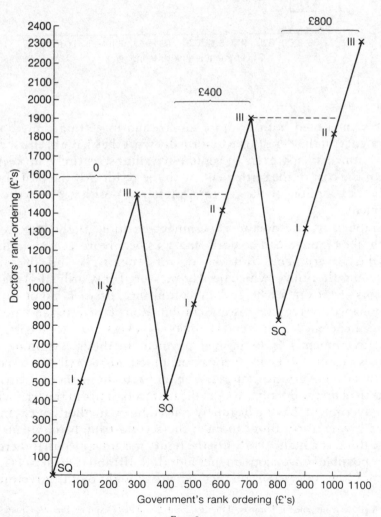

FIG. 8.7

we get Figure 8.7. In both these cases the thing most disliked by the government is still the thing most wanted by the doctors, but this is by no means inevitable. A blackmailer, for example, may be able to drive his victim to suicide but he would sooner stop short of exercising that degree of power at the point where his victim is paying as much as possible. We may thus often get a turning-point on the curve which does not again change direction or which at any rate has no higher peak to the right of it (see Figures 8.8 and 8.9).

The dotted horizontal lines in Figures 8.6–8.9 are there to assist the exposition of a simple theorem: that no point to the right of and below any other point on the gain-from-compliance curve can be an equilibrium position for a settlement. In other words, the sections of curve under a dotted line can be ignored as feasible outcomes. Thus, in Figure 8.8 there is no advantage to $A$ in securing more compliance than $Ox$, since he can gain no more than $px$ and beyond $x$ stands to gain less. And, in Figure 8.9, if the most compliance $A$ can get is a little less than $u$, he cannot do better than get $t$ compliance—as he moves to

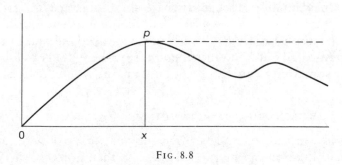

FIG. 8.8

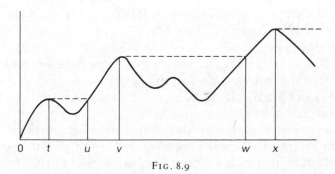

FIG. 8.9

the right from $t$ he actually makes himself worse off. He is also, of course, making $B$ worse off, but we can see from the shape of the curve that that in itself is not what he wants. (If $A$ simply wants $B$ to comply because it makes $B$ suffer, $A$'s curve must inevitably rise strictly monotonically; that is, it cannot have any dips or even flat sections in it.) In the same way, $A$ can get no advantage from enforcing compliance between $v$ and $w$ or beyond $x$.

Naturally, other things being equal, the greater congruence of interest, the smaller the length of the compliance curve that forms a possible location for an equilibrium. Thus, in Figure 8.6, with only a relatively small congruence of interest between the doctors and the government, we can see that of the twelve possible outcomes (including that of no compliance with the doctors' demands by the government) only two are ruled out—£400 and £800 plus no change in payment methods. In Figure 8.7, however, where there is a bigger difference between the preference rankings of the two sides, six of the twelve possibilities are ruled out. In the combinations with £400 and £800 only payment method III stays in the set of equilibrium outcomes. (Incidentally, especially where the things at issue are finely divisible, there may be more than one outcome associated with a given degree of compliance by $B$. In such a case we need only take notice of $A$'s highest-rated outcome at that point, since he would obviously not press for something equally hard to obtain but which he liked less.)

VI   OBTAINING COMPLIANCE BY 'ECONOMIC' MEANS

Having now introduced the basic idea, I shall explain how the analysis of a given situation can be carried out, and then go on to discuss the implications for the study of power.

How does $A$ actually get $B$ to comply with his demands? The process we are analysing is one where $A$ makes it worth $B$'s while to comply. $A$ must in other words make $B$ believe that on balance he will be better off if he complies than if he does not. He must threaten $B$ that, if $B$ does not comply with the demand, $A$ will see to it that he suffers a loss greater than the cost to $B$ of complying. The incentives facing $B$ are therefore rigged so he will be better off if he complies than if he does not comply. If $A$ operates by means of promises, he must promise $B$ that if he does comply he will receive a reward that will more than compensate for the loss represented by complying. Thus, taking the loss and the reward together, and comparing them with the no compliance/no reward alternative, $B$ must find that he will be better off by complying than by not complying. Finally, if *A* employs a mixture of rewards and threats, he must ensure that between them they make the expectation of (compliance + reward + no sanction) preferable to the expectation of (non-compliance + no reward + sanction).

In all three cases, *B* must believe with some degree of confidence that *A* will carry out his promises and threats. He must also believe that *A* will not carry them out otherwise. *A*'s threat must be 'sanction if *and only if* non-compliance'. There is nothing to motivate *B* to comply in a belief that *A* will apply the same sanction even if he does comply. Conversely, the prospect of a reward following compliance will be effective only if *B* does not believe the reward would be forthcoming anyway.

We can see how all this works out diagrammatically by looking at Figure 8.10. Let us suppose that *A* wants to obtain an amount of compliance O*x* from *B*. (We shall ask what determines the level of *A*'s demand later.) This means that *A* is trying to get *B* to incur a loss of *rx*. This is *B*'s gross loss from compliance, and *r* is simply the point on *B*'s gross-loss-from-compliance curve perpendicular to the point *x* on the compliance line. Somehow, *A* has to overcome the degree of reluctance on the part of *B* expressed in the length of the line *rx*. How can he do it? As we have seen, he can use threats or promises, or he can use a combination of the two.

Let us suppose that *A* uses threats exclusively. He then has to make *B* believe that a sanction bigger than *rx* will be applied if he does not comply. If *B* believes this and consults his own short-term advantage,

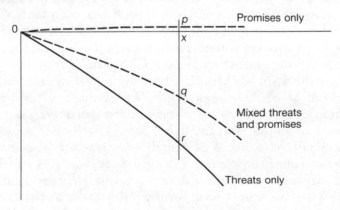

FIG. 8.10

we expect him to comply. The outcome therefore is that $B$ complies (with a loss of $rx$) and $A$ subsequently does nothing. If we define $B$'s *net* loss from compliance as the loss he suffers from compliance adjusted to take account of $A$'s actions in response, the net and gross losses are in this case the same, because there is no action by $A$ in response to $B$'s compliance.

Now suppose that $A$ operates entirely by means of promises. His task is then to convince $B$ that the reward consequent upon compliance will more than outweigh the loss inherent in compliance, so that his gross loss is transformed into a net gain. Thus, in Figure 8.10, $A$ is shown as offering a reward of $pr$ to $B$ in return for compliance. $B$ therefore stands to make a net gain of $px$: his gross loss of $rx$ is more than wiped out by his gain of $pr$.

Finally, suppose that $A$ employs a combination of threats and promises. I have illustrated in Figure 8.10 one possible combination that should provide $B$ with adequate motivation for compliance. $A$ threatens $B$ with a sanction of $qr$ if he does comply. If he left it there, $B$ would be better off not complying and suffering a loss of $qx$ than complying and suffering a loss of $rx$. But $A$ makes up the difference by also offering a reward of $pq$ if $B$ does comply. $B$ therefore faces a net loss of $qr - px$ from compliance. This is less than his gross loss. He is thus better off than when being subjected to only threats but he is, of course, worse off than when $A$ operates entirely by means of rewards.

For ease of exposition, I have carried out the analysis for just one point on the compliance line, namely, $x$. But the same analysis can be applied to every point along the compliance line. The result of joining up the points so obtained is the two curves for $B$'s net loss under conditions of promises only and mixed promises and threats. (The net and gross loss curves under conditions of threat only always coincide.)

Let us now turn to the other side of the relationship and focus on $A$, the actor making the demands on $B$. What, within our model, determines the demand that he makes—or indeed whether he makes any demand at all? To begin with, let us make the simplifying assumption that $A$ has at his disposal means of rewarding and/or punishing $B$ of infinite size, and that it costs $A$ nothing to deploy these resources if he so chooses. We can in this case read off the demand that $A$ will make from a knowledge of $A$'s gross gain curve. $A$ will demand whatever degree of compliance maximizes his own gross gain. Thus, in Figure 8.11, we simply look for the point at which the gross gain curve reaches its greatest height $p$, and drop a perpendicular to the

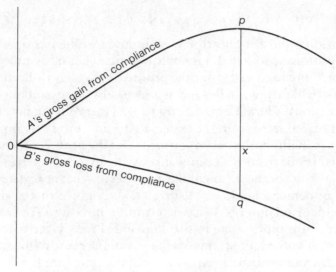

FIG. 8.11

compliance line. The point of intersection $x$ gives the level of compliance $A$ will demand.

Figure 8.11 also shows $B$'s gross loss curve. From our previous discussion we know that if $A$'s demand for the degree of compliance $Ox$ is to be successful, he must lead $B$ to believe that he has a high probability of carrying out threats and/or promises, contingently on $B$'s behaviour, that make it preferable to comply (with the associated loss $qx$) than not to comply. In the present case, we are assuming that $A$ disposes of infinite rewards and/or sanctions at zero cost. If $B$ knows this then any threat or promise made by $A$ will seem extremely plausible, since $B$ knows that it will cost $A$ nothing to carry it out. $A$ simply has to make a threat and/or promise big enough to counterbalance the inherent loss $qx$ involved in doing the thing demanded, and he wins. His gain from the operation is, of course, $px$.

However, the assumption that $A$ has threats and promises of infinite size available for use at zero cost is not realistic. Normally, it costs something, in time, money, effort, personal risk, and so on, to carry out a promise or a threat. And, though there are no doubt exceptions, it is reasonable to suppose that in general the larger the threat or promise to be delivered on, the greater the cost of doing so. How should we work this fact into the model?

### VII   COSTS OF CARRYING OUT PROMISES

The situation is most straightforward in the case where $A$ operates by making promises, so I shall take this one first. Let us assume that $A$ does in fact intend to carry out the promise he makes to $B$, if only to maintain credibility with $B$—and whoever else knows about it—on future occasions. The anticipated cost to $A$ of carrying out his promise may then be deducted from the anticipated gain from $B$'s compliance. The gross gain minus the cost of carrying out the promise gives us $A$'s anticipated profit from $B$'s compliance with any given demand.

Leaving aside for the moment the question of what now determines the level of demand made by $A$, let us take as given that $A$ makes a particular demand upon $B$. What determines the cost to $A$ of carrying out the promise appropriate to that demand? Pretty clearly, there are two factors involved. First, there is the size of the reward (measured in terms of $B$'s values) that $B$ requires to compensate him for doing the thing demanded. The more distasteful the object of $A$'s demand the larger the reward $B$ will require for compliance. The other factor is how much it costs $A$ to generate any given level of reward for $B$. This is, if you like, the transformation function for $A$'s costs into $B$'s rewards.

Thus, the cost to $A$ of producing the reward appropriate to elicit a given degree of compliance from $B$ is given by the size of reward multiplied by the cost to $A$ of producing a reward of that size. Given a certain transformation function, the cost to $A$ of carrying out the appropriate promise will be lower the less onerous to $B$ is the demand. Conversely, given the onerousness of the demand, the cost to $A$ of carrying out the appropriate promise will be lower the less it costs $A$ to provide any given amount of reward for $B$, measured in $B$'s terms.

It obviously follows from what has been said that we can in principle associate with each point along the compliance line a cost to $A$ of carrying out the appropriate promise for securing that degree of compliance from $B$. If we draw $A$'s gross gain curve and at each point deduct from the gross gain the cost associated with obtaining it, we get a second curve under the first, giving $A$'s profit or net gain. The net gain curve will coincide with the gross gain curve at the origin, since zero compliance requires zero promises at zero cost. Thereafter, it will fall increasingly far below the gross gain curve if we accept that bigger promises cost more to carry out. Figure 8.12 illustrates the relation hypothesized between gross and net gain curves.

We are now in a position to return to the question of what

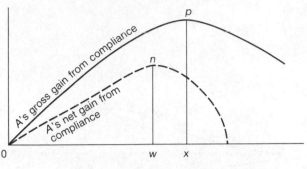

FIG. 8.12

determines *A*'s demands when it costs something to carry out promises. The answer is that the optimum demand for *A* is the one that maximizes his net gain. In Figure 8.12, *A*'s net gain curve reaches its highest point at *n*, which is perpendicular to *w* on the compliance line. *A* therefore demands O*w* degree of compliance from *B*. We can in fact now say looking back that our example with costless promises was a special case where the gross and net gain curves happen to coincide. It too therefore falls under the general rule that *A*'s optimal demand is the one that maximizes his net gain.

There are three implications for *A*'s optimal demand that are worth noticing. First, there will be many cases where *A*'s gross gain from *B*'s compliance would at every point be cancelled out by the cost of securing that compliance. Graphically, these are cases where, although the gross gain curve is (at least at some point along the compliance line) higher than the origin, the net gain curve is at no point higher than the origin. The maximum height of the net gain curve then occurs at the origin—in other words at the zero compliance point. The optimum demand by *A* would therefore be nothing (see Figure 8.13).

Situations of this kind are so ubiquitous that we do not usually even think about them. Almost any human being could find some way of benefiting from the compliance of almost any other human being. But the vast majority of these possibilities are never realized, or even contemplated, because the cost of securing any level of compliance would outweigh the gain. In a market economy there is no limit to the goods and services one can obtain from other people if one is willing and able to pay. But out of the vast gross gains obtainable from the shops we in fact pursue only that tiny fraction that we expect to yield a net gain. In political analysis, too, we do not bother to think about

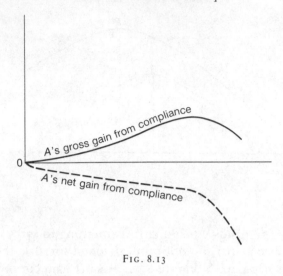

Fig. 8.13

gains, however large, that would obviously cost more than their value to obtain.

For the second point, we need to return to Figure 8.12. It may be seen there that, wherever the highest point on the gross gain curve occurs, the highest point on the net gain curve must fall to the left of it if there are costs of securing compliance and these costs increase strictly monotonically with the degree of compliance secured. What this means is that the existence of costs will always make the optimum demand less than it would be in the absence of costs. And we can add that, for any given gross gain curve, the higher the costs of securing compliance (and the greater the gap between gross and net gain curves) the smaller will be the optimum demand. Our first point, that the optimum demand may be zero, is simply a special case of this general implication of the existence of costs.

The third point is illustrated by Figure 8.14. This is like Figure 8.9 in that horizontal lines have been drawn from the top of each peak to indicate segments of the compliance line that it would not pay A to move B on to. But this time the same exercise has been carried out on both the gross gain curve and the net gain curve. It will be seen that the segments of the compliance line (*tu*, *vw*, and beyond *x*) that were unavailable even with zero cost of carrying out any promise are still unavailable when we allow for a gap between gross and net gain. But the segments that are unavailable when carrying out a promise has

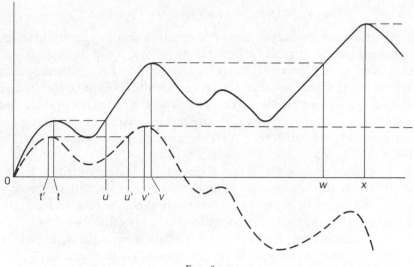

FIG. 8.14

costs may be seen to be greater: $t'u'$ and everything beyond $v'$ are now ruled out. This is a necessary consequence of the assumption that the gap between gross and net gain increases the greater the degree of compliance demanded. We can say generally, then, that the unavailable segments where there are costs must include the segments that would be unavailable if there were no costs and will extend from these at both ends.

We might wish to relax the assumption that it always costs more to carry out a bigger promise. Rewards may be 'lumpy' rather than finely graded, so that the cheapest way for $A$ to offer a reward over some size is to offer a reward that (in $B$'s eyes) is much bigger. All the intermediate degrees of compliance will then cost the same. In other words, costs of securing compliance will go up in steps instead of smoothly. If we have lumpy rewards like this, the truth of the first of our three implications of costs of promising remains intact. The other two, however, have to be withdrawn. It *may* still be that the optimal demand will be to the left of the maximum height of the gross gain curve, but all we can assert categorically is that it will never be to the right. And, similarly, although the available segments of the compliance line cannot exceed those available in a zero-cost situation, they will not necessarily be smaller.

### VIII   COSTS OF CARRYING OUT THREATS

It is my intention to analyse the use of threats using the same apparatus of gross and net gain as for promises. As before, it will be maintained that $A$'s optimum demand upon $B$ for compliance is given by the point at which $A$'s net gain curve reaches its maximum height. But, because of the basic difference between the way in which promises operate and the way in which threats operate, the interpretation of $A$'s 'net gain' must inevitably be different for threats and, unfortunately, rather more complicated.

If $A$ makes a promise to $B$ and $B$ does what is demanded, $A$ has to provide the promised reward to maintain credibility. It is therefore reasonable to deduct the costs to $A$ of providing the reward from the gain he would make from $B$'s compliance, and say that the result is $A$'s net gain from $B$'s compliance. For this simply reflects the nature of the process. But if $A$ threatens $B$ and $B$ does what is demanded, $A$ is committed to *not* doing anything. His total gain therefore is the whole of the gross gain that he derives from $B$'s compliance. It is only if $B$ does not comply that $A$ is committed to acting, and in that event $A$'s final position will be worse than it was before he made the threat, since he gains nothing from $B$ but incurs the cost of carrying out the threat.

How, then, are we to interpret the notion of $A$'s net gain from $B$'s compliance? The answer is that we must understand it as the *expected value* of $A$'s gain from threatening $B$. 'Expected value' has its usual meaning here: the expected value of an action is the value of each of the possible outcomes discounted by the probability of its occurring. Just as we assumed that $A$ will in fact carry out his promise if $B$ complies, so let us simplify things here by assuming that $A$ will in fact carry out his threat if $B$ does not comply. We do not therefore allow for $A$ to bluff in calculating $A$'s expected value of threatening. But we must allow for $A$ to think that there is some probability that $B$ will *believe* that $A$ is bluffing. For suppose that $A$ does not think that $B$ will ever suspect him of bluffing—or, more precisely, suppose that $A$ does not think that $B$ will ever believe that $A$ will fail to carry out his threat (whatever his intentions may have been at the time of making it) if $B$ does not comply with $A$'s demand. On this supposition, it will always pay $B$ to comply so long as $A$'s threatened penalty for non-compliance is greater than the costs to $B$ of compliance. However great the cost to $A$ of carrying out the threat would be, therefore, he will still expect with certainty that $B$ will comply, even if (to borrow Schelling's example) $A$'s threat is that he will blow his brains out over $B$'s new suit unless *B* gives him the last slice of toast.[14] (We assume that *A* is sure that having to get the suit cleaned is worse for *B* than forgoing the toast.)

If we assume, then, that *A* will always in fact carry out his threat, but does not know whether or not *B* will comply, his expected value (or net gain) from threatening *B* is made up of two items. The first is the gross gain (*G*) from compliance discounted by the probability (*p*) of obtaining compliance. The second is the cost of carrying out the threat (*C*) discounted by the probability of having to carry it out. This probability is simply the probability that *B* will not comply, so that, if the probability of *B*'s complying is 0·9, the probability of having to carry out the threat is 0·1. The expected value (or net gain) is the expected gain minus the expected cost: symbolically, we can write it as follows: $pG - (1-p)C$.

Let us consider in more detail the precise mechanism by which threats work. We know already that, to have any hope of succeeding, the sanction threatened must be greater than the cost of compliance. Otherwise it would obviously always pay to accept the sanction —even if one were certain it would be applied—rather than comply. But this sets only the minimum level below which a threat will not be at all effective. If *B* has any doubt about *A*'s willingness (or ability) to apply the threatened sanction for non-compliance, he may not comply even if the sanction is a little greater than the cost of compliance. For any given expectation by *B* that *A* will carry out his threat (and let us suppose for now that this expectation is independent of the level of the threat), we can say that the probability of compliance is greater the more the sanction exceeds the cost of compliance.

Now turn the situation round and look at it from the point of view of *A*. For any given demand (represented by a point on the compliance line) he knows that there is a minimum threat below which *B* certainly will not comply. But beyond that minimum, the more he threatens the better becomes the chance of *B*'s complying. Thus, as the level of threat goes up *pG* increases. At the same time, however, $(1-p)C$ may or may not go up. *C* will definitely go up, if we assume that a greater sanction costs more to carry out. But $(1-p)$ will obviously go down, since *p* has gone up. In effect there is a trade-off between the advantage that *B* is more likely to comply and the disadvantage that if he nevertheless does not comply the cost of carrying out the threat will be greater.

[14] Schelling, *The Strategy of Conflict*, p. 127.

The optimum threat corresponding to any given demand will depend on the precise interaction between the cost of the sanction to A and the probability of compliance that a sanction of that size produces. For our present purpose we need only say that our 'net gain' curve will reflect the optimum choice corresponding to each point along the compliance line. We may note here that, if A can carry out costlessly a threat of infinite size, he will threaten an infinite sanction whatever the degree of compliance he demands. The earlier statement that the gross and net gain curves are identical for costless threats and promises can now be seen to require a slight qualification. The formula for net gain, as we know, is $pG-(1-p)C$. The second item $(1-p)C$ must be 0 because $C$ is 0. But $pG = G$ only if $p = 1$. We should therefore say that gross and net gain are identical only if an infinitely large threat is certain to secure compliance. Provided that the cost of compliance is finite (as it was at the maximum point on the gross gain curve in Figure 8.11) this seems reasonable. But if the cost of compliance is also infinite the outcome is indeterminate: even the most appalling tortures do not always succeed in obtaining compliance.

Now that we have seen how A's choice of threat is determined, we can raise the question of the relation between the gross and net gain curves. In Figure 8.15 we have taken two pairs of points, $q$ and $r$ and $u$ and $v$, fairly close together on the compliance line. How does the gap between gross and net gains change as A moves from $q$ to $r$ and from $u$ to $v$, making the optimal threat at each point? In terms of Figure 8.15, this means that we have to compare the lines $ah$ with $bi$ and $dk$ with $el$.

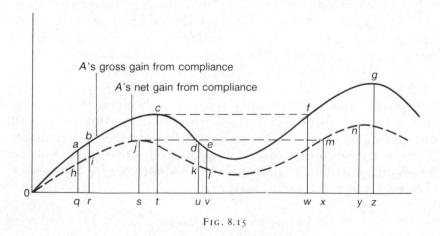

FIG. 8.15

It can be shown that, provided a bigger threat costs more to carry out, the gap necessarily widens as we move along the compliance curve under a gross gain curve that is rising to the right, and that no point at which it is falling is a possible point for a demand by $A$. Let us suppose that $A$ has selected the optimum threat for the demand represented by $q$ on the compliance line. He now wants to find the optimum threat for $r$. Let us consider two possibilities: that he maintains the same threat and that he maintains the same probability of compliance.

If $A$ maintains the same threat, the probability that $B$ will comply must go down because the cost of compliance relative to the sanction is higher. $(1-p)C$ will therefore increase, since the cost of carrying out the threat remains the same but the probability of having to carry it out increases. Whether $pG$ goes up or down or stays the same depends on what happens to $G$ as well as what happens to $p$. $G$ is going up between $q$ and $r$, and the gap between $G$ and $pG$ widens for two reasons. So long as $p<1$, the gap $(G-pG)$ will increase as $G$ increases if $p$ stays the same. But in addition $p$ here declines as $G$ increases, so the difference between $G$ and $pG$ is even greater.

We are looking for the way in which $G-[pG-(1-p)C]$ changes as we move along the compliance line. At points where $G$ is increasing, both of the other expressions change in value to increase the gap: $pG$ at best goes up more slowly than $G$ and $(1-p)C$ increases. Where $G$ is decreasing as we move to the right, $(1-p)C$ will still necessarily continue to increase, but the gap between $G$ and $pG$ need not increase, though $pG$ will of course decline. This is because if $p$ were to stay the same, the gap between $G$ and $pG$ would decrease as $G$ declines. Whether or not the gap widens, however, the important fact is that net gain must decrease because $pG$ is decreasing while $(1-p)C$ is increasing. It remains true therefore that points at which the gross gain curve is declining are not available as possible demands by $A$. Thus, in Figure 8.15 we have shown the gap narrowing between $u$ and $v$. In other words, $dk$ is greater than $el$. But the net gain curve is necessarily falling.

The same conclusions may be derived by supposing that, in moving from $q$ to $r$ or from $u$ to $v$, $A$ is concerned to keep the probability of $B$'s compliance constant. In this case $pG$ must obviously stay the same as a proportion of $G$, while $(1-p)C$ will increase because the only way in which the same probability of compliance can be obtained for a demand further along the compliance line is to threaten a larger sanction, and we are assuming that a larger sanction costs more to carry out. Therefore, as before, the gap between the gross and net gain must increase while the gross gain curve rises, moving right along the compliance line, and when the gross gain curve falls the gap may widen or narrow but the net gain curve must move down.

In any particular case, the optimum move as the demand changes is hardly likely either to constitute keeping the threat exactly the same or to constitute keeping the probability of compliance exactly the same. But, since these two moves have the same general implications, so would the most likely actual optimum: a bigger threat but not sufficiently bigger to prevent the probability of compliance from falling.

What are the general implications? The answer is that all the general findings for promises carry over to threats. First, the net gain curve will always start turning down before the gross gain curve (provided the curve is smooth) because the gap between the two widens all the time the gross gain curve rises. The optimum demand by $A$ will therefore always be less than it would be with costless threats or rewards ($y$ as against $z$). And second, it remains true that all the segments of the compliance line that are ruled out because the gross gain curve is below a peak to its left ($tw$) are also ruled out because the net gain curve has a peak to its left. And, thirdly, more of the compliance line is ruled out on the basis of the net gain curve than the gross gain curve ($sx$ as against $tw$).

### IX   CREDIBILITY AND COST OF THREAT

The analysis set out in the previous section may be strengthened by suggesting a further reason why the net gain curve will tend to fall relative to the gross gain curve as one moves along the compliance line. Until now we have assumed that the probability of $B$'s complying with $A$'s demand is a function of the difference between the cost to $B$ of complying and the cost to $B$ represented by the sanction threatened by $A$. But it is surely reasonable to postulate that $B$ will also try to form an estimate of the likelihood that $A$ will in fact be willing or able to enforce the sanction in the event that $B$ does not comply with $A$'s demand. Other things being equal, the less likely $B$ believes it to be that $A$ will enforce the threat, the less likely $B$ is to comply with $A$'s demand. And, other things being equal, the less likely $B$ is to comply, the lower is $pG$ and the higher is $(1-p)C$.

What determines $B$'s estimate of the likelihood of $A$'s enforcing his threat? No doubt there are many factors entering into the estimate, most of which cannot be accommodated within our simple model.

But I suggest that one factor is the cost to $A$ of carrying out the threat. Other things being equal, the higher the cost to $A$ of carrying out the threat, the less likely $B$ is to believe that it will in fact be carried out if he fails to comply with $A$'s demand.

If this line of argument is acceptable, it means that an increase in $C$ has a direct effect in depressing $p$, therefore lowering $pG$, and in increasing $(1-p)$, therefore raising $(1-p)C$ in two ways at once. Since we have been assuming all along that a bigger threat costs more to carry out, the addition of this new consideration means that it is more likely than we have suggested previously for any attempt by $A$ to step up the level of threat to be self-defeating. So far we have envisaged the possibility that as $A$ moves rightward along the compliance line he may increase the level of threat so as to keep the probability of compliance constant. The drawback so far emphasized has been that because $(1-p)C$ goes up as $C$ goes up and $p$ stays the same, it may not pay $A$ to make a bigger threat, even if the gross gain from success in obtaining more compliance would be greater. Now, however, we have to add that increasing the threat will in itself have an adverse effect on $p$. The increase in threat that would otherwise have been necessary to maintain the level of $p$ has to be augmented yet further to overcome the depressing effect on $p$ of the cost of carrying out that greater threat. So the cost of maintaining the same probability of compliance goes up more than it would otherwise do.

Indeed, the cost may be infinite, as each increase in threat actually makes the goal of compliance recede further. This will be so if each successive dose of possible threat in relation to a given degree of compliance increases the cost to $A$ of carrying it out so much that it more than counteracts in $B$'s mind the greater incentive to compliance contained in the greater excess of the sanction over the cost of compliance.

In other words, there may be no way of maintaining more than some particular probability of compliance at any given level of compliance, however great the cost that the party making the demand would in fact be prepared to bear in order to obtain compliance. This observation was reflected in the line of argument used by critics of the doctrine of 'massive retaliation' enunciated by President Eisenhower's Secretary of State, John Foster Dulles. According to this, any misbehaviour by the Soviet Union anywhere in the world would be met by a large-scale nuclear attack on the Soviet Union itself. The critics argued that there was simply no way in which Soviet leaders could ever be convinced that some minor move in an area not of vital importance to the USA would lead to the American President unleashing such devastation, with incalculable consequences for his own country.

It is true that the abandonment of 'massive retaliation' paved the way for the Vietnam War—a land war fought with conventional weapons in an area of very little strategic significance for US security. But this does not show that the critics were wrong. Rather, what happened was that the same mistake was repeated on a smaller scale. The leaders of North Vietnam and the Vietcong were simply not prepared to believe, however often American Presidents reiterated it, that the United States would indefinitely bear the costs of fighting in Vietnam when the real bearing of Vietnam on the security of the United States was so minimal—one might even say symbolic only. And in the long run they proved to be correct.

Incidentally, it should be borne in mind that among the costs of $A$'s carrying out threats is the repugnance that $A$ may feel about it. This clearly played a part in the US withdrawal from Vietnam, and an even clearer example is provided by the way in which the death penalty for sheep stealing and theft of over £2 proved counterproductive in England in the eighteenth century because juries refused to convict even on clear evidence. At a more domestic level, a parent is more likely to obtain compliance by making a threat sufficiently moderate to make it plausible that he or she would be willing to carry it out than by uttering some blood-curdling threat like 'I'll skin you alive'.

So far we have been assuming that a bigger threat costs more to carry out. But, as with promises, this need not always be so. Threats, like promises, may be 'lumpy': if you want a sanction bigger than a certain size, there may be nothing efficient between it and a much bigger one. That is to say, intermediate-sized sanctions (if available at all) may be even more expensive to carry out than the much bigger one. The cost of making threats will thus go up in steps.

As with promises, once we allow for lumpiness we have to modify our arguments in some respects. It remains true that, if there are costs at all, the net gain curve will be below the gross gain curve at all points; and it will still be true that many cases in which a demand for compliance would be profitable with zero cost will show a net gain curve that is at no point positive once costs are taken into account. Moreover, the conclusions of section VIII remain valid. Whereas with promises lumpiness made it no longer true that the net gain curve would turn down before the gross gain curve, the effect of the size of the 'excess' sanction on the probability of compliance saves the relationship for threats. We are, *ex hypothesi*, dealing with a case where the size of the threatened sanction (and its cost, of course) stays the same along a stretch of the compliance line. This being so, $p$ must decline and $(1-p)C$ increase as the demands become more unacceptable, so the gap between $G$ and $pG-[(1-p)C]$ will increase while $G$ increases and the net value itself $pG-[(1-p)C]$ will start to decline before $G$ does.

All that is lost is the reinforcement for that conclusion provided by the present section, which does depend on the assumption that at each point there is a slightly bigger sanction available at a slightly higher cost.

## X  THE 'MYSTERY OF POWER'

I suggested at the beginning of section III that power in the 'economic' sense should be understood as the possession of the means of securing compliance by the manipulation of rewards or punishments; and I have now set out a model of the process by which rewards and punishments may be used to modify behaviour. It is now time to come back to the concept of power, and look at it in the light of this analysis. What are the problems with which we have to deal?

First, 'getting someone to do what he would not otherwise do' (Dahl's 'intuitive idea' of power) is not necessarily the same as 'getting someone to do what you want him to do'. A may be able to secure massive compliance from B without this enabling him to get B to do anything that he (A) wants him to do. For there may be nothing that A wants B to do. This might incline us to follow Alan Goldman and say that 'the extent of a person's power with respect to an issue is (*ceteris paribus*) inversely related to the degree of desire required for him to obtain a preferred outcome'.[15]

On the other hand, we might regard A as lucky rather than powerful if he can get something he wants a great deal by overcoming only small resistance on the part of B. To push it to an extreme: would we wish to say that A was exercising infinite power if he could get something he wanted very much from B merely by asking for it? If not, should we not concentrate on the amount of resistance A can overcome? We may then be inclined to adopt a definition of power like that of Karlsson,[16] according to which A's power over B is a function of the difference between how *well off* A could make B if he tried and

[15] A. I. Goldman, 'Towards a Theory of Social Power', *Philosophical Studies*, 23 (1972), 221–68, at 253.
[16] Georg Karlsson, 'Some Aspects of Power in Small Groups', in Joan H. Criswell, Herbert Solomon, and Patrick Suppes (eds.), *Mathematical Methods in Small Group Processes* (Stanford, Calif.: Stanford University Press, 1962), 193–202.

how *badly off A* could make *B* if he tried. (See for further discussion chapter 11, below.)

These two approaches would lead us to say widely differing things about power in some situations, for the ability to get what you want and the ability to secure compliance need not be correlated. But both of these conceptions have one feature in common: they deal in terms of *A*'s *gross* gain and *B*'s *gross* loss. This itself seems implausible, however. If we concentrate on what *A* gains, should we not deduct the expected cost of getting it from the gross gain and say that *A* has more power the larger his *net* gain from securing compliance?

Alternatively, if we start from *B*'s end and identify power with compliance, do we really want to ignore the distinction between compliance secured by promises and compliance secured by threats? In other words, should we not look at *B*'s *net* loss (if any)? Perhaps we should not call a case where there is no net loss to *B* a case of 'power' at all: we might say that threats are associated with power and promises with exchange, as Blau does.[17]

Here then we have four quite different conceptions of *A*'s power over *B*: as *A*'s gross gain, *B*'s gross loss, *A*'s net gain and *B*'s net loss. More could be added. For example, we might identify *A*'s power with the smallness of the *difference* between his gross gain and his net gain. Nor is this the worst, for I have deliberately skated round the problematic relation between having power and exercising power. Obviously you can't exercise power that you don't have, but you can have power that you don't exercise. When we talk about power are we talking about what *A could* do or what *A does* do? Or should we perhaps be talking about what it would *pay A* to do?

It is not my intention exactly to *answer* these questions. In the tradition of philosophical analysis developed by Wittgenstein and Austin, I would say rather that my object is to attempt to dissolve the puzzlement that such questions reflect. My method, however, is not the orthodox 'linguistic' one of minute attention to nuances of meaning, but the construction of a model designed to give insight into the processes involved. When we see the way in which the various uses of 'power' reflect a concentration on different aspects of the process, we will be, I hope, relieved of the feeling that it matters to ask what is the meaning of power. What has been called ironically 'the mystery of power'[18] results from the fact that there are a number of

[17] P. M. Blau, *Exchange and Power in Social Life* (New York: Wiley, 1964).
[18] Herbert Kaufman and Victor Jones, 'The Mystery of Power', *Public Administration Review*, 14 (1954), 205–12.

aspects of power, and it is easy to move between them without noticing that they are different. De-mystification requires that we get them clear. Whether, after that, we want to go on using the word 'power' and, if so, how we use it, is of secondary importance.

### XI   A PARADIGM OF POWER

I think that the best way of approaching the analysis of power relationships in terms of the model is to construct a case such that nobody would have any doubts in saying that *A* did have power over *B*. I shall then offer an example. Finally, I shall take each element in turn and see what happens if we vary it.

**I**   **A has the opportunity of exercising power over B.**
(1)   *A* can communicate demands, threats [and offers★] to *B*.
(2)   *A* can monitor *B*'s degree of compliance with his demands.
(3)   *A* can, at low cost to himself, impose severe sanctions on *B* [and/ or provide large rewards to *B*★].

**II**   **A has the motive for exercising power over B.**
(1)   There is at least one demand on *B* that *A* could make, compliance with which by *B* would be (in gross terms) highly advantageous to *A* and highly disadvantageous to *B*.
(2)   There is no alternative demand to that specified above that would be (again in gross terms) at least as advantageous to *A* while being less disadvantageous to *B*.

**III**   **A has an incentive to exercise power over B.**
(1)   There is at least one demand on *B* that *A* could make, compliance with which by *B* would be highly advantageous to *A* in net terms and highly disadvantageous to *B* in gross terms.
(2)   There is no alternative demand to that specified above that would be at least as advantageous to *A* in net terms while being less disadvantageous to *B* in gross terms.

(N.B. If promises are to be included, the sections in brackets marked ★ should be included; if promises are to be excluded, the sections in brackets marked ★ should be excluded.)

Crudely, the logic of this is

   **I** Could *A* probably obtain a lot of compliance cheaply if it paid him to?

**II** Would it pay *A* to attempt to obtain a lot of compliance if he could probably obtain it cheaply?

**III** Putting the two together: will it pay *A* to attempt to gain a lot of compliance, given the cheapness with which he can probably obtain it?

Thus, to give an example from industrial relations, the *opportunity* of a trade union to improve its members' pay by striking increases (i) the less the cost of a given length of strike (e.g. the more the state pays strikers or their families in lieu of wages), and (ii) the greater the cost to the employer of a given length of strike (e.g. the more capital-intensive the process and the more full the firm's order books). The *motive* of the trade union would be greater the more profitable the firm was, since this would mean that there was more in the kitty to share out.

An example that scores high on all the elements listed above may be drawn from Benjamin Barber's book about the history of the Swiss canton of Graubünden. After the Raetian Republic took possession of the fertile Tellina valley (now part of Italy) in 1512, 'the executive and judicial offices which comprised the colonial administration were officially put up for sale to the highest bidder' and 'corruption was limited only by the confines of the officeholders' imagination'. 'One judge . . . passed an arbitrary sentence of death on anyone who appeared before him, for whatever reason. It is a tribute to the catalyzing effect of fear on human generosity that this particular official amassed in fifteen months a fortune surpassing that of his most imaginative colleagues.'[19] Running through the list, it is clear that this provides for communication of threat, monitoring of compliance, and a low-cost means of applying a severe sanction. The Tellina valley was fertile and prosperous, so there were resources of high value to be transferred to the judge's pocket, and money has the characteristic that the more *A* gets the more *B* loses. These factors together meant that the judge was in fact in a position to extort large rewards at low cost.

## XII    ARE PROMISES AN EXERCISE OF POWER?

The first point we ought to take up is one that was left open in the paradigm for '*A* has power over *B*'. This is the question of whether compliance secured by offering a reward is an exercise of power. As I

---

[19] B. R. Barber, *The Death of Communal Liberty: A History of Freedom in a Swiss Mountain Canton* (Princeton, NJ: Princeton University Press, 1974), 152–3.

have already suggested, it matters less how we answer a question like this than that we should see what is at stake in giving different answers.

If we say that promises do constitute an exercise of power, we are saying that A can exercise power over B even if B actually gains in comparison with the *status quo ante*. Thus, we are in effect saying that B need suffer no net loss from compliance. What matters is simply that A should be able to secure B's compliance at an acceptable cost to A.

Why might we wish to take this line? The argument would have to be that compliance is compliance whether it is induced or coerced. A rich man can have servants around him who will do his bidding. Is this not power? And when people (in either a capitalist or a socialist economy) work within some firm at the direction of others in return for pay, are they not subject to power?

The argument on the other side is that power should be contrasted with exchange. To be in someone's power is something we would prefer to avoid: people seek to escape from the power of others. But the possibility of exchange is never something that we would prefer to avoid, because it enlarges our freedom of choice without at the same time ruling out the opportunity of staying as we are if we do not like any of the additional alternatives. Here, too, plausible cases can be cited in support. If I buy a pound of parsnips in the greengrocer's shop, there is an exchange—money for parsnips—but am I exercising power over the shopkeeper by promising him money for complying with my demand for parsnips?

If we are unhappy about either saying that we look only at the degree of compliance (and therefore ignore the question of means) or saying that no case of gaining compliance by promises can ever be a case of exercising power, we must look for some other criterion that will sort out the cases in the way we feel happy with. I think this is the right move, but it is not at all easy to formulate the criterion precisely. There are two false trails that can I think be found in the literature.

One of these misguided suggestions is that we use 'power' only to refer to cases where someone can obtain a large amount of compliance with a high degree of probability, and it is simply a matter of fact that most cases of this sort are cases where the means are coercion rather than inducement. As a matter of usage, I think it is true that if we simply say that someone has power we imply that he has a lot of power. In the same way, though, if we say that someone has money we mean he has a lot of money. This does not entail that we cannot say someone has a little money, and similarly we can say someone has a little power.

The other misguided suggestion is that we use 'power' for relation-ships of which we disapprove, and that as a matter of fact we disapprove of coercive attempts to produce compliance rather than attempts employing the prospect of rewards. Again, usage is against this idea. It makes perfectly good sense to say that one approves of someone's power. Conversely, we may disapprove of attempts to modify behaviour by means of rewards. Bribery (of judges, for example) is almost by definition disapproved of, but it is not coercion.

I am myself inclined to think that the criterion for a power relation is an asymmetry between the parties. The tendency for power to be disapproved of could then be explained as a reflection of our disap-proval of asymmetry in social relations, since there is a close connec-tion, though not a perfect one, between asymmetry and unfairness. By 'asymmetry' I mean simply that one party stands to gain more out of the relationship than the other, because it is in a position to exploit the weakness or necessity or vulnerability of the other. (See for further discussion chapter 13 section II below.) By this criterion we get the result, which I think is in accordance with common usage, that threats are *always* an exercise of power, rewards only sometimes. If *A* is in a position to make a plausible threat against *B*, this must mean that he is able to exploit *B*'s vulnerability; and if he succeeds in obtaining compliance by issuing a plausible threat, then the transaction must be one-sided because it is inevitably one in which *A* gains and *B* loses. But an exchange may take place between parties with sufficiently equal positions to enable us to say that there is no asymmetry in the relationship. In terms of the model, we can indifferently describe an equal exchange as a case where *A* offers *B* a reward in return for compliance or a case where *B* offers *A* a reward in return for compliance. There is no reason in general why in an equal exchange both sides should not share the benefit arising from the transaction roughly equally. However, an exchange may be between unequally placed partners. If *A* is a single buyer or seller, facing an unorganized mass of sellers or buyers, he can set the price so as to get almost the whole surplus from the transaction. Similarly, as Marx correctly argued, the fact that a labourer in nineteenth-century Britain could survive only a short time without a job gave employers a great advantage in the labour market and enabled them to extract almost the whole surplus from the transaction of employment. Obviously, in terms of our model, to say that *A* is in a position to get nearly all the total gain out of the transaction is precisely to say that *A* can obtain a large amount of compliance of high value at low cost, while *B* has to accept, because of his weak position, compensation for the gross loss inherent in compliance that is only just enough to make compliance better on balance than non-compliance.

One final point. I noted before that if *A* makes *B* worse off unconditionally this is not an exercise of power, because it is not associated with any attempt to modify *B*'s behaviour. But suppose that after *A* has made *B* worse off he then comes along and, taking advantage of *B*'s distressed situation, is able to obtain compliance in return for an offer that *B* would have turned down before. Even more, suppose that *A*'s reduction of *B*'s well-being was deliberately designed to bring about a state of dependence. I think that in such a case we would be inclined to say that *A* was exercising power over *B* through offering rewards for compliance, even if we might not say the same if the relative positions of *A* and *B* had come about without the intervention of *A*. This has an obvious bearing on the question of whether the countries of the 'Third World' are subject to the power of the developed (and especially the ex-colonial) countries. Those who argue that they are not will point to the existing pattern of trade relations and say that these relations are mutually beneficial. But if what has just been said is true, the 'dependency' theorists are right to say that we have to ask how these patterns of trade came about in the first place.

## XIII   THREE CONCEPTS OF POWER

Having decided to admit the ability to make promises as a form of power under certain circumstances, we can now return to the other questions that were raised in section X. As I said there, I do not think that there is anything much to be gained from simply picking a definition and saying 'That's the one everybody ought to use'. But I do think that it is useful to see the implications of alternative definitions and to notice the way in which the choice of a definition is affected by what it is that we want to explain.

If we are interested in predicting how people will behave, then we want to know when it will *pay* *A* to try to get *B* to do something. It is no good *A*'s being able to derive enormous potential benefit from some compliant action by *B* if either *A* has no way of getting *B* to do it or if the cost to *A* of getting *B* to do it is so great as to cancel out the benefit. At the same time, it is also no good *A*'s being in a position to make sizeable threats or promises to $B$ at low cost to himself if there is nothing that $B$ has that $A$ wants, or, more generally, if no compliant behaviour of $B$ would produce a worthwhile gross gain for $A$.

In other words, if you are interested in predicting action—attempts by one actor to achieve compliance by another actor—you need both motive and opportunity. And that means that you have to insist on a certain amount of both **I** and **II** in the paradigm, such that between them they satisfy **III**. The resulting definition would be on the following lines: $A$ has power over $B$ if and only if $A$ can profitably get $B$ to do something $A$ wants or, more formally, if and only if there is some level of compliance by $B$ such that $A$'s net gain from it would be positive. The measure of power would be the maximum net gain obtainable by $A$ at any level of compliance by $B$.

Notice that this definition concentrates on $A$'s net advantage from $B$'s compliance. Any given net advantage may arise either from $x$ gross gain and $y$ cost to $A$ (e.g. a huge gross gain and high cost) or from $x-a$ gross gain and $y-a$ cost (e.g. a small gain and a minuscule cost). The present measure of power would produce the same result in both cases, and this is reasonable if what we are interested in is predicting action by $B$. For it is surely plausible, if we accept a general cost-benefit framework of analysis, to predict that the greater the profit to $A$ that can be anticipated from action (in this case making an attempt to obtain compliance from $B$) the more likely $A$ is to undertake that action.

But prediction of actions is not the only thing we may be interested in. I have already mentioned the Lasswellian conception of the *explananda* of politics as 'who gets what, when, how'. This implies a distributive focus to our inquiries: we are interested in the outcomes of social behaviour, in who gains and who loses. The obvious way of defining power from this point of view is in terms of inequality. $A$'s power over $B$ will consist in $A$'s ability to gain at the expense of $B$.

In the simplest case this means that $A$ has the ability to make a profit from gaining $B$'s compliance while $B$ makes a net loss. In other words, $A$'s power consists in his ability profitably to coerce $B$. But, as I argued in section XII, there can also be an asymmetry in net gains. Suppose that both sides make a net gain from the transaction but that one of the parties ($A$) is able to appropriate almost all the profit by manoeuvring the other ($B$) into a position where the choice is between the status quo and a small improvement on it. There is then an unequal distribution of the gains from trade between $A$ and $B$.

The implication of this is that power should be defined in terms of the *difference* between what *A* gets and what *B* gets if *A* pursues the course most profitable to him. It would follow from this that there were two ways in which *A* might have no power over *B*. If it would not pay *A* to attempt to obtain compliance from *B*, the equilibrium position would obviously be one in which no attempt was made, and there would by definition be no gains and no losses to either party, so no power relation. But even if it would pay *A* to obtain compliance from *B* by offering a reward for compliance to *B*, there may still be no power relation because the outcome may be a fair exchange between *A* and *B* in which both make a roughly equal gain over their positions in the status quo ante. (Of course, *A* and *B* might both lose equally from an attempt by *A* to coerce *B* that fails. But it must be recalled that our analysis of net gains and losses is *ex ante* not *ex post*. If *ex ante* the net gain that *A* anticipates is negative, because the product of the probability of *B*'s non-compliance and the cost of carrying out the threat exceeds the product of *B*'s compliance and the gross gain from *B*'s compliance, then *A* has no incentive to attempt to obtain compliance. The case is therefore *ex ante* of the first type.)

Formally, then, the definition of power on this conception would be on the following lines: *A* has power over *B* if and only if the maximum net gain for *A* from compliance by *B* entails either a net loss by *B* or a smaller net gain by *B* than that enjoyed by *A*. And the measure of *A*'s power would be the size of the difference between *A*'s net gain and *B*'s net loss or between *A*'s net gain and *B*'s net gain, measuring these values at the equilibrium level of compliance demanded by *A*, that is to say the point that maximizes *A*'s net gain.

Unlike the first definition, this would enable us to predict changes in the pattern of distribution: if *A* has power over *B*, we predict that *A* will become better off and *B* worse off relative to the status quo. But it does not predict behaviour as well as the first definition does. First, all equal exchanges are simply ignored, so we eliminate a great deal of market behaviour. Second, if the probability of action by *A* is related to prospect of profit by *A*, the second definition, by contaminating *A*'s profit with *B*'s loss, entails that we can no longer move from power to motive so confidently. If what pays *A* most is to try to get *B* to do something he very much doesn't want to do, that must entail on this definition a great deal of power for *A*. Yet the net gain to *A* may be quite tiny, either because the gross gain is small (recall that *B*'s hating to do something does not entail that *A* loves having him do it) or because the cost of getting *B* to do it is so high that it almost outweighs a large gain. This observation of course illustrates the general point that different definitions serve different intellectual (or indeed practical) interests.

Both of the definitions canvassed so far have one thing in common: they both include within them a reference to the prospective gains of $A$ from securing $B$'s compliance with a demand. And clearly to predict either behaviour or distributive outcomes we do need to take $A$'s prospective gains into account. But I think there is a further object we may have in attributing social power to people or groups and that in order to pursue that object we ought to leave $A$'s prospective gains out of the definition of power. I want to argue that, in some sense, we grasp social reality at a deeper level by looking at what $A$ could get at low cost rather than what it actually pays $A$ to get. In other words, I am suggesting that we might conceptualize power purely in terms of opportunity and not at all in terms of motive. $A$'s power would then consist simply of the ability to obtain low-cost compliance. Even if there were currently nothing $B$ could do that $A$ would wish him to do, $A$ would still, on this conception, have the same amount of power as would be attributed to him if there were something $B$ could do that $A$ very much wanted him to do.

What interest would be served by such a definition? My answer is that an interest in *security* will lead us to such a definition, and that we ought to take an interest in security because of its importance for the dignity of individuals and societies and (related to this) their capacity to plan for the future with confidence. If $A$ has power over $B$ in the sense that $A$ can at low cost to himself obtain compliance from $B$, then $A$ has $B$ in his power. $B$ may not be subject to demands from $A$ at the moment but he cannot count on that happy state of affairs continuing. $B$'s freedom depends on $A$'s not choosing to exercise his power. (In our cost-benefit framework this means that it depends on $A$'s net gain from securing compliance being negative, and if the cost of obtaining compliance is low this can come about only if $A$'s net gain is low.) If at any time $B$ happens to get into a position where he does have something that $A$ wants, to more than a negligible degree, he knows that $A$ is in a position to demand it.

Let me give two examples of this kind of power in practice, the first from interpersonal relations, the second from international relations. The first is a little frivolous but illustrates an important point. It occurred to me, while reading an omnibus edition of the Jeeves short stories by P. G. Wodehouse, how often the plot turns around the dependence of one of Bertie Wooster's fellow Drones on an allowance from some aged relative, and on the need to meet (or appear to meet) the more or less cranky demands of this relative in order to keep the allowance. Even Bertie, in one of his more reflective moments, remarks that 'It's a curious thing how many of my pals seem to have aunts or uncles who are their main source of supply.'[20]

It may be noted that this constitutes a case where *A* (the aunt or uncle) operates on *B* (the Drone) by rewards rather than sanctions. The Drone would prefer a situation in which he has the option of complying with the whims of his aged relative and getting an allowance to a situation in which this option is withdrawn. (Of course, he would like even better to get the money without having to placate the aged relative, but this opportunity is not available, at any rate until the decease of the relative.) If we reflect on this, we can see that the relationship may not be one of power in the sense of an unequal exchange. It may be that the relative receives less benefit from the Drone's compliance than the Drone does from the allowance. But the point is that the Drone *is* dependent—his behaviour is open to control by the aunt or uncle—and the truth of this is not affected by the fact that he prefers dependence to independence on the only terms on which independence is available.

At the other extreme, many grave illustrations may be drawn from relations between states. If we define a weak state as one which at least one other state could, if it chose, occupy and control at fairly low cost, it must follow that the independence of a weak state at any time depends on its not having anything that makes it worth the while of a state that could occupy and control it to do so. Woe betide it if in an industrial era valuable raw materials are discovered on its territory or if economic and technical developments mean that its land and perhaps its inhabitants could be used profitably to grow some valuable cash crop like cotton, rubber, tea, or coffee. Woe betide it if, because of its location, it suddenly becomes strategically or commercially significant, as a coaling station or the site for a canal, for example. What has protected the independence of mountainous areas like Montenegro, Switzerland, or Ethiopia over the centuries? Partly the relative difficulty of conquering such mountainous territories but more, I suggest, the fact that their poverty has made them unattractive acquisitions. The possession of a mass of gold was the undoing of the Incas, and the Transvaal would no doubt have remained an independent state of poor farmers but for the discovery of diamonds in extraordinary quantity on the Rand. Again, Egypt lost its

[20] P. G. Wodehouse, *The World of Jeeves* (New York: Manor Books, 1973), 180.

independence to Britain and France largely to protect the Suez Canal, and the state of Panama was carved out by the United States to create a buffer for the Panama Canal.

The argument in favour of the conception of power as the ability to secure compliance at relatively low cost is that it focuses on the realities of dependence. Even if a state is independent, it is surely a relevant fact about it that its independence is contingent on the apathy of those states with power, and that its independence will be in jeopardy should it ever happen to become interesting to such a state.

## XIV   TECHNICAL LIMITATIONS OF THE ANALYSIS

I shall not expand any further on the limited scope of the 'economic' approach to the analysis of power. Instead I want to end this chapter by asking what are the limitations on the analysis that I have developed earlier *within* the general area where it applies. I shall consider three kinds of limitation: technical limitations, limitations on applicability (in the sense of operationalizability), and limitations on applicability in the sense of limitations on the usefulness of threats and promises themselves.

The model that has been presented here is extremely simple and primitive. Three technical limitations in it are, I think, especially serious. First, we were always considering cases where $A$ is trying to get $B$ to change his behaviour, but never cases where $B$ is also trying to get $A$ to change *his* behaviour. Of course, we can say that $B$ is trying to change $A$'s behaviour if $B$ refuses to comply until $A$ offers a larger reward for compliance. And indeed the 'pure reward' case can often be equally well presented with either party as the active one trying to change the behaviour of the other. (For example, in an ordinary economic exchange we could make either party $A$ or $B$.) But where each party has threats at its disposal and each is trying to move the other to a position worse than that of non-compliance, we do have to extend the model.

Second, we need to be able to allow for the fact that $B$ may respond to a demand of $A$ backed by a threat not merely by refusing to comply and then leaving $A$ to decide whether it is worth the cost inherent in carrying out the threat: $B$ may in addition attempt to reduce the probability of $A$'s carrying out the threat by making a conditional threat in turn to the effect that if $A$ carries out his threat then $B$ will do something to $A$ that $A$ will not like. ($A$ may of course counter with a conditional threat against $B$ to the effect that if $B$ retaliates $A$ will do something else.) The threat of retaliation differs from the case of mutual threats that I mentioned first in that *B*'s move here is defensive in nature: *B* is content to be left alone by *A* and simply to deter *A* from carrying out his threat, but *B* is not using his threat-capacity to attempt to get *A* to comply with a demand from *B* for a change in his behaviour.[21]

Third, there is a rather worrying tendency to slither between subjective and objective values in the model. Ideally, we want one set of curves to represent *A*'s actual benefits from any degree of compliance by *B* and the actual costs to *A* of carrying out any given threat or promise; and another set for *A*'s estimate of what a given degree of compliance would cost *B* and his estimate of what a given threat or promise would be worth to *B* if carried out. And the same *mutatis mutandis* for *B*.

I shall not discuss these three extensions any further here, since any attempt to incorporate them formally into the analysis would result in turning what is already a very long chapter into a treatise. I have, however, done enough work on the formalization of these extensions to have convinced myself that they can be accommodated within the general framework of 'economic' analysis put forward here. I have to warn, though, that the complexity of the analysis increases very rapidly as one adds refinements.

## XV   LIMITATIONS ON OPERATIONALIZABILITY

The next question that I want to raise concerns the possibility of getting actual measurements for the variables used in the analysis. Can this be done, and if not how serious a problem is this? I have three comments to make.

The first is that there is at the very least scope for experimental tests. Much work on threats and promises has already been done (as one can see by consulting *The Journal of Conflict Resolution*), but a good deal of this research has been carried out by social psychologists with a poor grasp of the relevant theory. The paucity of clear results is a reflection, I believe, of poor theory. It does not mean that experiments cannot yield clear results.

Second, I do not despair of the possibility of obtaining estimates even in real-life situations. It might be possible to get the actors in a

---

[21] I should perhaps mention, though, that in the US/Soviet example discussed in section IX I implicitly treated the Soviet response to an American nuclear attack as a cost to the USA of carrying out the policy of 'massive retaliation'.

real-life (but not life-and-death) negotiation to set down their own estimates of the quantities in advance, if necessary in a sealed envelope. One could then deduce from the theory the expected equilibrium outcome and compare it with the actual one. Of course, it is to be explicitly allowed that skill is an intervening factor between the model's predicted outcomes and actual outcomes. But over a number of cases it would become pretty clear whether skill was at all plausible as a gap-filler or whether there was something wrong with the theory's predictions in a more fundamental way.

Finally, my fall-back position is that a theory may throw light on real problems even if it cannot be operationalized. We may be better off with a formal model in our heads, even if we cannot make direct estimates of the variables. (It should be borne in mind that almost all of economics is like this. Nobody even tried to estimate a demand curve until the 1920s.) I may illustrate this by pointing out that what I have offered here could be looked at as a formalization of the purely verbal discussion of 'coercive diplomacy' and the alternatives in the book to which I referred at the beginning of this chapter, *The Limits of Coercive Diplomacy* (see note 7). As it happens, I did not read this book until I had gone through a number of drafts of this chapter, so the analysis contained in it is in no sense designed as a formalization of the implicit theory of the first chapter of *The Limits of Coercive Diplomacy*. It would, however, be an interesting exercise to have someone read that book and then this chapter and see if it helped in making clear the logic. I hope and believe that it would.

## XVI   LIMITATIONS ON THE USEFULNESS OF THREATS AND PROMISES

The question with which I shall conclude is the following: how useful are threats and promises, compared with other methods, in eliciting desired behaviour from other people? There is an obvious answer, namely, that what you can get is in any given case limited by the size of the threats and rewards you have at your disposal and your willingness to use them. This is primarily the sense in which 'coercive diplomacy' is deemed to have limits in the book to which I have just referred. Although there is not much theoretical interest here, it is of great practical importance. Thus, the protraction of the Vietnam war was caused, as the authors of that book argue, by the failure of American leaders to appreciate the size of the demand they were making on the leaders of North Vietnam in calling for them to give up the unification of the country. George Canning identified the phenomenon when he wrote a dispatch in rhyme to the British government to the effect that 'In matters of commerce / The fault of the Dutch / Is giving too little / And asking too much'.

Suppose, however, that someone were to say that the account just given of Pentagon policy, as based on a miscalculation, while perhaps true for the period up to the mid-60s, thereafter seems less and less applicable and that after that time collective psychopathology increasingly takes over as the right explanation. This would raise a new and more interesting issue about the usefulness of threats and promises. For we can see that, if threats and promises are to be of any use, both parties to the transaction must be minimally rational. The initiating party must be able to deliver what it threatens or promises, and also to withhold it. And there is no point in even trying to use threats or promises on someone who is too stupid to understand them or too lacking in self-control to act on them. We do not rely on deterrence with young children, for example: we put bars around the fire or across the windows. In other words we rely on what I called physical constraints.

The biggest questions along these lines about applicability arise when the actors are not individuals but collectivities (e.g. states). Obviously, all the difficulties that individuals experience in putting together coherent behaviour (in which information is processed, calculations made, and decisions reached and then implemented) are greatly magnified when a number of different people are involved in each stage. For this reason Graham Allison in his book *Essence of Decision*[22] cast doubt on the applicability of what he called a 'rational actor' model to international politics. I think that it is important to recognize limitations on the rationality of organizations, and in the case of relations among the superpowers this ought to entail very great caution in making use of strategies that rely on a quick and precisely calculated reaction by another.[23] But even so I think that Allison overstates the case for pensioning off the 'rational actor' model. For his other two models—that involving the examination of the standard operating procedure of an organization and that involving the analysis of in-fighting among top-level decisionmakers—can in my view be made sense of only in relation to the 'rational actor' model.

The bureaucratic machine, although it of course develops a life of its

[22] G. T. Allison, *Essence of Decision: Explaining the Cuban Missile Crisis* (Boston, Mass.: Little, Brown, 1971).

[23] J. P. Cornford, 'Review Article: The Illusion of Decision', *British Journal of Political Science*, 4 (1974), 231–43, at 233.

own, is after all set up with the object that it should serve the interests of the collectivity (say, the United States) rather than the individual interests of its members; and its 'standard operating procedures' are designed with the object of producing appropriate responses in the organization, 'appropriateness' again being conceived of in terms of serving some overall collective goal. Moreover, if a state (or any other organization) is to survive in a challenging environment, we can predict that constant efforts will have to be made to correct tendencies towards the pursuit of personal self-interest at the expense of organizational goals and tendencies for standard operating procedures to degenerate into rituals which play no useful role. We can only understand the notion of *correcting* tendencies in relation to some norm, and this norm is provided, I suggest, by the 'rational actor' model.

As far as political infighting is concerned, it is no doubt true that cabinet ministers fight for their departments. But this is built into the whole procedure for allocation, and may be regarded (analogously to 'multiple advocacy' in a trial) as contributing to rational decisionmaking. We should also not get too carried away by the idea that 'where you stand depends upon where you sit'. Allison's own analysis of the Cuban Missile Crisis does not, on the whole, suggest actors moved by a desire to aggrandize their own services or departments. The military were cautious, and Robert Kennedy, who played a key part, was hardly acting to build up the office of Attorney General.

A different though related question is that of the relative effectiveness of promises and threats as against alternative ways of getting people to do what you want. It may be possible to combine them so that their relative efficacy does not matter: for example in a smoothly running state the demands of the criminal law are backed both by normative acceptance—'mobilization of commitments'—and by sanctions. Here the existence of the sanctions does not detract from the authority of the law because the sanctions themselves are regarded as legitimate. But in other cases it seems likely that the introduction of promises and threats into a situation shifts people on to a self-interested way of looking at the matter, thus undermining the possibility of a normative appeal. This is the argument put forward by Richard Titmuss in his book *The Gift Relationship*,[24] where he suggests that the introduction of payment for blood has the effect of drying up the supply from voluntary unpaid donation of blood. The two kinds

[24] R. M. Titmuss, *The Gift Relationship: From Human Blood to Social Policy* (London: George Allen and Unwin, 1970).

of motive—in this case social responsibility and commercial self-interest—cannot, the argument goes, coexist in the same society in respect of the same category of transaction. Again, the attempt to mix punishment and rehabilitation in prisons may founder on the inflexibility of prison personnel, but it may also be affected by the problem of one method of eliciting desired behaviour cutting across another.

Finally, there is a point mentioned only in passing by George in *The Limits of Coercive Diplomacy* but which has big implications for the applicability of the 'economic' approach in both senses of 'applicability' that I have distinguished. George points out that an almost invariable effect of actually carrying out a threat—i.e. imposing sanctions—is to harden the attitude of the person subjected to the sanction to the original demand. In our terms, a given concession (expressed in descriptive terms) becomes greater in terms of the loss it would be felt to represent. To the extent that this is so we can say two things. The first is that recurrent demands backed by successively greater threats—even if the demand stays the same—may well actually fall further and further short of being sufficient to overcome resistance. The cost represented by the demand may, in other words, increase faster than the sanction for non-compliance. The other is that if we want to analyse a series of threats we may need to allow for a shift in curves between stages. We can of course carry out the analysis of each stage on the basis of a new set of curves giving us a comparative statics of bargaining with an equilibrium outcome corresponding to each set of curves. But how do we get from one set of curves to the next? That seems to take us outside the 'economic' approach. It requires some propositions in individual psychology (e.g. the frustration–aggression hypothesis) and, where groups are concerned, some notions about the way group solidarity intensifies as a result of common experience of deprivation.

# 9

# IS IT BETTER TO BE POWERFUL OR LUCKY?

I

There are two ways of getting outcomes that you want. One is to bring them about yourself by exercising power. The other is to have them occur (often as the result of the exercise of power by others) without exercising any power yourself. Someone who is commonly in a position to obtain wanted outcomes by exercising power is powerful; someone who commonly obtains wanted outcomes without exercising any power is lucky. This chapter is devoted to an examination in depth of the relation between power and luck. That the relation is not straightforward should already have become apparent to anyone who has noticed that 'power' is defined as a capability whereas 'luck' is defined as a tendency or probability. I shall, in fact, argue that the concept parallel to luck is decisiveness. 'Power' can then be defined as the capacity for decisiveness.

My strategy in this chapter will be as follows. In section II I shall expound the two most well-known power indexes, that proposed by Lloyd Shapley and Martin Shubik and that proposed by John Banzhaf. Then in section III I shall offer a critique of both indexes. Section IV begins the constructive half of the chapter. Here I put forward a rigorous analysis of the relations between luck, decisiveness, and success, and on the basis of this analysis show how the so-called paradoxes of power generated by the standard power indexes can be dissolved. Section V applies the analysis to one historical example of great significance: the American Constitutional Convention of 1787 that created the present US constitution. This will, I hope, show the utility and plausibility of the analysis. Finally, in section VI, I offer a definition of power in terms of the conditions under which an actor can be decisive. I conclude by suggesting an answer to the question posed in the title of the chapter: power is more important to an actor, in relation to luck, the more uncertain that actor is of the likely alignment of forces within the relevant period of time.

Among the problems which I shall seek to illuminate by means of this analysis are the following. Is an increase in one's power always to be welcomed? Is it better to be powerful oneself or to have powerful friends? Must the power of a group be conceptualized as the sum of the power of each of the individual members of the group, or could a group be powerful while each of its members is individually power-less? I shall also seek to throw light on the so-called pluralist-élitist debate, arguing that each side's conclusions follow from its concep-tion of the nature of power.

Let us begin by asking why anybody should ever want to have power. One answer would be that the possession and/or the exercise of power are intrinsically gratifying. It can hardly be doubted that the phenomenon exists. We can all think, for example, of academics who go around collecting committees in the way that Indian braves of an earlier day collected scalps. Some people, no doubt, get their kicks simply from taking part in decisionmaking, even if they are quite indifferent to the outcomes. But this enjoyment of power is parasitic upon the activities of those who do care about the outcomes and are prepared to work for the outcomes they want. A committee made up entirely of people who had no interest in pursuing some particular outcome but were fascinated by the process as such would be as frustrating as a brothel all of whose customers were voyeurs.

I think that the importance of the desire for power as an end in itself is often overestimated as a motive force in politics because of a tendency to conflate two phenomena that are analytically quite dis-tinct. If a civil servant relishes power because this gives him a chance to further some policy to which he is attached—road pricing, free school meals, or whatever—this is a case where power is sought not for its own sake but in order to increase the chance that the favoured policy will be put into effect. The tendency to lump together the pursuit of power for some relatively disinterested public purpose and the pursuit of power as an end in itself comes about, I think, as a result of an implicit assumption that power must be sought either for some self-interested end or as an end in itself. If we take care to avoid this kind of cheap and fashionable cynicism we shall, I believe, conclude that in the great majority of cases people value power because of the chance it gives them to bring about states of affairs that they desire, and not primarily for any intrinsic gratification that they derive from power itself.

At any rate, for the purpose of this chapter I shall disregard the pleasures of power inasfar as they are detached from any notion of enabling one to bring about preferred outcomes. The view of the value of power to be adopted, then, is an instrumental one: power is desired because it gives its possessor the opportunity to change outcomes from what they would otherwise have been, in the direction that the possessor wishes. However, once we say that power is not going to be treated as an end in itself but only as a means to an end, we must define that end. Clearly, the end assumed in what I have just said is that of getting the outcomes you want. The question to which this chapter is addressed can then be put as follows: what is the relation between having power and getting the outcomes you want?

It should be apparent that there is no simple connection between the two. If an individual's power is defined as his ability to change outcomes from what they would otherwise have been in the direction he desires, the likelihood that outcomes will correspond to his desires does not depend solely on his power. It also depends on what the outcome would have been in the absence of his intervention. This is what I shall call luck. Someone with a little power (or no power) but a lot of luck may thus consistently obtain more of the outcomes he wants than someone who has a lot of power but only a little luck.

With enough power you can get everything you want without any luck. With enough luck you can get everything you want without any power. In between these two extremes, things get more complicated, and we need some more formal apparatus in order to keep clear heads. I shall provide that formalization in section IV. But before that let us see what can be learned from the most popular of the existing power indexes.

## II

Although I have not so far made the limitation explicit, I am concerned in this chapter not with power in general but with political power. I shall take political power to be the ability of an individual or of a group to change the outcomes of some decisionmaking process from what they would otherwise have been in the direction desired by the person or group, where the decisions made are binding on some collectivity. For many purposes of analysis, it is convenient to consider a special case, namely the case of a body that reaches decisions binding on some collectivity by fixed rules that have the effect of aggregating the preferences expressed according to some specified means by the members of that body. Call such a body a committee and call the means for expressing preferences and the rules for aggregating them a voting procedure.

There are two standard 'power indexes' which purport to measure the relative power of the members of such a committee under alternative decisionmaking rules (weighted voting, chairman's casting vote, and so on). The older-established of the two is the Shapley–Shubik index, which was first put forward by Lloyd Shapley and Martin Shubik in 1954.[1] The other, the Banzhaf index, was introduced in 1965 by John F. Banzhaf III, and has been used by the New York State Court of Appeals.[2]

Briefly, they work as follows. To construct the Shapley–Shubik index for the power of each member of a committee under given voting rules, we consider every possible order in which all the members of the committee might vote in favour of the measure to be decided upon. Then, for each possible order, we identify the member of the committee whose vote pushes the measure over the line so that it wins. We call that voter 'pivotal' within that particular sequence. The power of any member of the committee is then simply the proportion of all the possible voting-orders in which that member is pivotal.

Thus, take the simple case of a committee operating under a majority-rule procedure with three members who have a vote each. The possible orderings are $A(B)C$, $A(C)B$, $B(A)C$, $B(C)A$, $C(A)B$, $C(B)A$. In each ordering, the bracketed member of the commitee is the pivotal one, since the second positive vote makes the measure pass or the second negative vote makes it fail. Out of the six possible permutations, each member of the committee is pivotal in two cases, so each has (unsurprisingly) a score of $\frac{1}{3}$ on the Shapley–Shubik index.

Whereas the Shapley–Shubik index is permutational, the Banzhaf index depends on counting coalitions. To establish the scores of committee members according to the Banzhaf index, we have to consider every possible minimum winning coalition, that is to say every set of committee members sufficient to carry a measure that would become insufficient if any member of the set were to withdraw. Thus, in the example given above, there are three minimum winning coalitions, that of $A$ and $B$, $A$ and $C$, and $B$ and $C$. To get the score on the Banzhaf index we count the number of ways in which each actor

---

[1] L. S. Shapley and M. Shubik, 'A Method of Evaluating the Distribution of Power in a Committee System', *American Political Science Review*, 48 (1954), 787–92 (repr. in Roderick Bell, David V. Edwards, and R. Harrison Wagner (eds.), *Political Power* (New York: Free Press, 1969), 209–13). Page refs. are given to this reprint.

[2] J. F. Banzhaf III, 'Weighted Voting Doesn't Work: A Mathematical Analysis', *Rutgers Law Review*, 19 (1965), 317–43; and 'Multimember Electoral Districts: Do They Violate the "One Man, One Vote" Principle?', *Yale Law Journal*, 75 (1966), 1309–88.

could make a winning coalition into a non-winning one by withdrawing from it. (Each here could bring down two.) Then, in order to
make the scores sum to unity, we simply divide each of them by the
total. So, in the present case, the total is six, each committee member
has a raw score of two, and the Banzhaf index, again not surprisingly,
ascribes a final score of $\frac{1}{3}$ to each member.

Although the Shapley–Shubik and Banzhaf indexes are computed
differently, and in any complex voting scheme usually produce
different numerical results, it is generally the case that a change in
voting rules that increases an actor's power on the Shapley–Shubik
index also increases it on the Banzhaf index, and vice versa. In the
example that was worked through above, the two indexes produced
the same answers, but in such a simple case they could scarcely have
failed to. If we constrain the answer so that the amount of power
within the committee must sum to unity and must somehow be
totally allocated among the individuals who make up the committee,
we must expect that any completely symmetrical voting scheme will
attribute equal power to each. This must be true simply because there
is no basis on which to distinguish the members.

Note that the equality thus ascribed to the committee members in
no way depends on the details of the actual scheme, so long as it treats
all alike. Consider, for example, a rule requiring unanimous agreement. This would make the last voter pivotal in each of the six
Shapley–Shubik permutations. We can see that each committee mem-
ber is going to be last twice, giving each a score of $\frac{1}{3}$. On the Banzhaf
measure there is only one minimum winning coalition (made up of *A*,
*B* and *C*). Each committee member is thus in the single winning
minimum coalition. The total score is therefore three, so we divide
each individual's score by three, giving each $\frac{1}{3}$.

The point is, however, that we do not really need to carry out the
calculations, because we can deduce directly from the symmetry of the
voting rule that the power of the committee members is going to be
equal. We may, of course, observe when we realize this that any
measure of the distribution of power that is unable to distinguish
between majority voting and a *liberum veto* is hardly telling us
anything we would like to know. But that result is unavoidable right
from the start once the commitment is made to treat power as
something that must always be allocated to individuals in such a way
that the individual scores sum to unity.

III

Both indexes are designed to try to capture the idea of an individual voter's chance of making a difference to the outcome. But both fail because they substitute something else. One counts the proportion of times an individual voter is pivotal out of all pivots, the other the proportion of defections from a minimal winning coalition an individual can engage in out of all such defections. But there is no reason for supposing that what we count is related in any direct way to what we want to know about.

The irrelevance of the measure advocated by Shapley and Shubik is patent. In their article they make the following claim: 'Our definition of the power of an individual member depends on [i.e. makes it depend on—B.B.] the chance he has of being critical to the success of a winning coalition.'[3] But their definition of a pivot does not in the least capture the notion of being critical to the success (or failure) of something. We can see this by thinking about the following case. Let us imagine that a million pounds has to be raised in a given time for some purpose—for example to prevent the export of a picture. And suppose that, as the deadline approaches, contributions to the appeal are coming in at the rate of a thousand pounds a day but that there is still a shortfall of a hundred thousand pounds. If some donor gives that amount, his contribution might well be said to have been critical to the success of the fundraising effort, because it is likely that in its absence the target would not have been reached. Now suppose instead that funds flow in at a rate of a thousand pounds per day and the target is reached with several days to spare. There was still some contribution that pushed the total over the line. But in this case it would be an abuse of language to call the donation critical, because if it had not been sent the target would still easily have been reached. Similarly, if a bridge has been weakened over the years by traffic, it would be unreasonable to say that its being crossed by the particular car that caused it to collapse was critical if there is every reason to suppose that the next car in line would have done the same thing. If, however, it was being crossed by a tank that made the bridge collapse, we might reasonably say that that was critical because with normal traffic the bridge would probably otherwise have lasted for many more years.

Thus, when we say that some event is critical for something's coming about, we are necessarily involved in a counterfactual

---

[3] Bell *et al.*, *Political Power*, p. 209.

assertion that, with everything else remaining the same, in the absence
of the event in question the thing would not have happened. (There is
an implicit qualification here: we mean that it would not have
happened roughly at the same place or at the same time or in the same
form. What constitutes sufficient closeness to count depends on the
context.) In particular, an event is not critical if it could be foreseen
with confidence that in its absence another event with the same effects
would have occurred in its place.

Now recall how the Shapley–Shubik concept of a pivot is derived.

Let us consider the following scheme: There is a group of individuals all
willing to vote for some bill. They vote in order. As soon as a majority has
voted for it, it is declared passed, and the member who voted last is given
credit for having passed it. Let us choose the voting order of the members
randomly. Then we may compute the frequency with which an individual
belongs to the group whose votes are used and, of more importance, we may
compute how often he is *pivotal*. This latter number serves to give us our
index. It measures the number of times that the action of the individual
actually changes the state of affairs.[4]

I hope that it is not necessary to belabour the point that the pivot, so
understood, does not in the relevant sense change the state of affairs.
Since we have a group of individuals 'all willing to vote for some bill',
it makes no difference who happens to provide the vote that gives the
measure the winning margin, since, *ex hypothesi*, if any of the
remaining members of the body had replaced that person in the
sequence, he would have voted for the measure instead.

In other expositions, the pivot is said to be 'decisive', and this is the
term that I propose to use later in developing a more satisfactory
conception of power in a committee. But again it should be clear that
the pivot in the Shapley–Shubik scheme is not decisive. Thus, Steven
Brams writes:

For all the different ways in which the buildup of the grand coalition can
occur through a sequence of additions of one player, there will be one player
in each sequence who will be decisive to a coalition's becoming winning. We
call this player, who makes the difference between a coalition's being
winning or losing, the *pivot*. . . .[5]

But obviously, if what we have is 'the buildup of the grand coalition',
the place of any member of the committee in the voting sequence is

---

    [4] Ibid. 210, italics in original.
    [5] Steven J. Brams, *Game Theory and Politics* (New York: Free Press, 1975), 162, italics in
original.

neither here nor there. If a simple majority is all that is required and everybody is going to vote 'aye' anyway, then nobody is decisive because nobody individually makes a difference to the outcome.

To say, however, that no individual member of the committee has any power violates one of the postulates upon which the Shapley–Shubik index is constructed, namely that the power of the members of a committee must always sum to unity. The deeper point here is that the whole approach embodied in the Shapley–Shubik index is inappropriate. The index arises out of, and is indeed simply a special case of, Lloyd Shapley's work on the problem of the value of a game, and we need briefly to backtrack to look at that.

The question that Shapley set himself is a good one, and one of central importance to much political analysis. Indeed, one of my objects in this chapter is to provide a framework within which it can be answered (see sections V and VI below). The question is: how can we estimate a priori the value to someone of playing a certain game? It is evident that this is central to questions of accession and secession. The voters in the various American states had to estimate, for example, the value of the game constituted by the proposed Federal constitution. More recently, the British electorate had to estimate the value of the game constituted by the enlarged EEC. When the value of the game played within a state falls below some level we may expect that secession will begin to appeal. And so on.[6]

As Shapley wrote: 'In attempting to apply the theory [of games] to any field, one would normally expect to be permitted to include, in the class of "prospects", the prospect of having to play a game. The possibility of evaluating games is, therefore, of critical importance.'[7] Thus, we know that for zero–sum games there is a plausible case for assigning to each player his minimax value and calling that the value of the game to him: it is what, on the basis of sound theoretical arguments, he can expect to get. The problem is how to extend the assignment of the value of a game to other kinds of game. The Shapley value of a game to each player is derived by considering all subsets of

[6] See Ronald Rogowski, *Rational Legitimacy: A Theory of Political Support* (Princeton, N.J.: Princeton University Press, 1974) for an original analysis of legitimacy in terms of expectations about the course of decision making. Rogowski relates the acceptability of a regime to an actor to that actor's probability of 'uniquely determining' outcomes. This measure is a cousin of the Shapley–Shubik index: the total power of all actors sums to unity and each actor's score is supposed to reflect his individual responsibility for producing outcomes. Therefore the criticisms made here of the Shapley–Shubik index apply to Rogowski's treatment as well.

[7] L. S. Shapley, 'A Value for *n*-person Games', in H. W. Kuhn and A. W. Tucker (eds.), *Contributions to the Theory of Games II*, Annals of Mathematical Studies, 28 (Princeton, N.J.: Princeton University Press, 1953), 307–17, at 307.

one or more players that can be formed out of the set of players and treating each subset as equally probable. Some of these coalitions will have no value, others will (in the general case) have different values depending on their composition. The value of the game for each player is based on the increment that that player brings to each coalition. In other words, for each possible coalition (subset of players) we take its value and then subtract from that its value without the player for whom we are carrying out the calculation. (Obviously, if the player is not in a coalition, the difference must be zero.) That player is then credited with the whole of the increase in the value of the coalition that his presence brings to it.

The procedure can be stated in a way that brings out clearly the parentage of the Shapley–Shubik index: we can imagine

the random formation of a coalition of all the players, starting with a single member and adding one player at a time. Each player is then assigned the advantage accruing to the coalition at the time of his admission. In this process of computing the expected value for an individual player all coalition formations are considered as equally likely.[8]

The Shapley–Shubik index may be seen as the Shapley value for the special case where coalitions do not have a variety of values but are either winning (value 1) or losing (value 0). Adding members to a coalition thus does not increase its value until the threshold of winning is reached; then, once the 'winning' point has been reached, adding more again does not increase the value further. The pivot—the member of the committee whose addition to a coalition changes it from losing to winning—thus gets credit for the whole value of a winning coalition.

The trouble is that the basic model is inappropriate to the typical phenomena of politics. It belongs to the branch of game theory that presupposes perfectly divisible and transferable utility—something like money only even better. When we spoke above about the 'value' of any given coalition we were talking about a sub-stance—utility—that could be divided in any way among the members of the coalition in such a way that it remained the same size. This assumption violates the first principle of political analysis, which is that a public policy is a public good (or bad). If the death penalty is reintroduced, that pleases those who favour it and displeases those

---

[8] Kuhn and Tucker, *Contributions to the Theory of Games II*, p. 303. Cited in R. D. Luce and H. Raiffa, *Games and Decisions* (New York: Wiley, 1957), 250. See, generally, pp. 245–50 for a discussion of the Shapley value.

who do not. Similarly, a tax break is good or bad for people according to their situation. The gains are not confined to those who voted on the winning side nor are the losses confined to those who were on the losing side. The measure creates its own gainers and losers by its content: if you are advantaged or disadvantaged by it that will be so whether you voted in favour or against, or did not vote at all.

There are, of course, some cases in which people get paid off according to the way in which they vote. American presidential nominating conventions are the textbook example. Delegations are usually concerned with the symbolic/ideological characteristics of the candidates, and they also have a natural preference (at least *ceteris paribus*) for a candidate who has a good chance of winning the election. But, in addition, there is some advantage in having backed the candidate who actually gets the nomination—and to have backed him before it was clear that he was going to get it. The analysis of such a case in terms of transferable utility is at any rate partially appropriate in that we can think of a fixed amount of 'patronage' to be divided up among supporters. But it is, I suggest, a basic error to take a presidential nominating convention as a paradigm of political decisionmaking.

In saying this, I am not committed to a particularly high-minded view of politics. We can, if we wish, follow Lasswell's formulation and say that politics is 'who gets what, when, how'. The crucial question is precisely in virtue of what it is that they get whatever it is they get. What I am saying is that the standard way in which people get what they get is through the contents of public policies. Private pay-offs related to the way in which they vote are a by-product.

What about cases where a majority of legislators get together and cook up some scheme for providing geographically specific benefits for their own constituents? This presents no problem for the present analysis. That it is often thought of as a counter-example illustrates just how difficult it is to keep things clear. It is still true in such a case that the outcome is a public policy that distributes benefits and costs in a certain way. The benefits derive from the adoption of the policy, not from having voted for it. Naturally, we would expect the prospective beneficiaries (or their representatives) to be the ones to vote in favour and the prospective losers (or their representatives) to vote against. But the point is that there is no advantage in 'being a member of the winning coalition' if all we mean by this is voting for the measure. If one legislator whose constituents stand to benefit votes against, and one whose constituents stand to lose votes in favour, the measure is still passed and has exactly the same distributive effects. It is remarkable how much of the application of game theory to politics falls foul of this simple and elementary observation: the whole of William Riker's *The Theory of Political Coalitions*[9] is invalidated by it, and so is almost every analysis of power in decisionmaking bodies. They operate as if the pay-offs arising from a vote could be allocated according to the way people vote. They do not take account of the fact that a public policy is a public good.

On its own premisses, the Shapley–Shubik index is quite correct in identifying the value to an actor of taking part in a certain decision-making process with his power. If the utility arising from any play of the game (any vote of the committee) is divisible and transferable and it all goes to whoever makes the coalition win (the pivot), then indeed power and value are directly related to one another. But the whole point about a public good is that there is no way in which the person who provides it can appropriate all the value arising from it. There can thus be 'free riders', who gain the benefits without having done anything to bring the public good into existence. Hence the distinction on which I am insisting between power and luck as alternative ways of getting outcomes that you want. You may get them by exercising power and thus making them come about when they would not otherwise have done. But if you are lucky you will be able to take a 'free ride' on the efforts of others. Provided your policy preferences are like those of people who have power, you will finish up with no less than they get, even though you have done nothing to bring about the outcomes that are mutually desired. This shows plainly that if we are to talk sensibly about the anticipated value to an actor of a political process—a state, a federation, a common market or whatever, operating by known decisionmaking rules—we must break away from the approach embodied in the Shapley–Shubik index.

I have so far said nothing specifically in criticism of the Banzhaf index, but much less needs to be said. The Shapley–Shubik index is perfectly consistent, given its premisses (which happen to be inappli-

---

[9] William Riker, *The Theory of Political Coalitions* (New Haven: Yale University Press, 1962). Riker's notion that 'winning' is a universal value in politics depends on precisely the equivocation identified in the text, and his 'proof' of the minimum size principle depends upon the assumption of divisible, transferable utility. Riker's theory would work if politics were nothing but a matter of allocating spoils, in other words if it had no connection with policies that are public goods or bads. For a discussion of these two aspects of politics and of the problem of integrating them in a single analysis, see my 'Review Article: "Crisis, Choice, and Change", Part II, Games Theorists Play', *British Journal of Political Science*, 7 (1977), 217–53.

cable), and it has a certain theoretical elegance.[10] The Banzhaf index, by contrast, is a mere gimmick, with no coherent theoretical underpinnings. It has all the drawbacks of the Shapley–Shubik index in that it too assumes that the power in a committee sums to unity and can be exhaustively allocated among the members. But in addition it incorporates equiprobability in a very queer way by in effect assuming that each coalition should be weighted in the computation according to the number of different ways in which it can be brought down by the withdrawal of a member. Thus, in a committee with weighted voting it may be that a certain coalition is vulnerable to the defection of only one particular member, while another is vulnerable to defection by any of three members. (An example will be given a little later.) Then the Banzhaf index counts the first coalition towards one member's score, whereas the second coalition counts separately in the scores of three members. Yet, if one were going to depart from equiprobability, it would seem more plausible to go in exactly the opposite direction and assume that, the more different ways there are in which a coalition is open to being brought down by defection, the less likely it is to form.

Up to this point I have treated the Shapley–Shubik and Banzhaf indexes as a priori indexes, which in practice means that I have followed their authors in assuming that all orderings or defections from a minimum winning coalition are equally probable. But in real life we know very well that in any actual committee it would be very extraordinary for the votes of different members not to be related in some systematic way. Any adequate treatment of power in a committee must be able to deal with departures from equiprobability, and I shall show in the next section how that can be done within the framework of analysis I propose. The attempts that have been made to modify the application of the Shapley–Shubik and Banzhaf indexes, however, produce such absurdities that they underline the fundamental inadequacy of these indexes.

The method of analysis used is pretty crude. What is done is to postulate that some committee members always vote on the same side or always vote on different sides, and then see what this does to the power index for all the members of the committee. It is hardly surprising that the Shapley–Shubik index goes haywire when the attempt is made to move away from the equal probability of every ordering. The index is constructed, as we saw, by assuming that all the

[10] Luce and Raiffa, in *Games and Decisions*, pp. 245–50 and 253–5, provide a clear exposition of this point.

members of the committee vote in favour of a measure and by counting pivots. The introduction of the idea that some committee members vote one way and others vote the other way on the same measure therefore violates the assumption upon which the index is founded. What is done to fudge it is to assume that those who vote *before* the pivot must still all vote the same way, but that those who vote *after* the pivot can be allowed to vote either way. The Banzhaf index might appear less vulnerable, since we can always simply strike out some minimum winning coalitions on the basis of a stipulation that they will never form. But in practice both indexes give rise to exactly the same kinds of absurd conclusion.

The most dramatic illustration of this point is the so-called paradox of quarrelling members, described in the following terms by Steven Brams.

We may suppose, for example, that two players are involved in a quarrel and refuse to join together to help form a winning coalition. Although one might suspect that they could only succeed in hurting each other, it is a curious fact that the quarrel between two players may actually redound to *their* benefit by increasing both their individual and combined voting power. We call this phenomenon the *paradox of quarreling members.*[11]

Consider an example in which there are three committee members, with weights of 3, 2, and 2 votes, and where 5 votes out of a total of 7 are needed for a committee decision. Call the player with 3 votes $A$ and the other two $B$ and $C$. Under normal circumstances the Shapley–Shubik values are $\frac{2}{3}$ for $A$ and $\frac{1}{6}$ apiece for $B$ and $C$, and the Banzhaf values are $\frac{3}{5}$ for $A$ and $\frac{1}{5}$ apiece for $B$ and $C$; but if for some reason $B$ and $C$ never agree the figures become $\frac{1}{2}, \frac{1}{4}, \frac{1}{4}$ on both indexes. Both indexes thus have the implication that $B$ and $C$ gain power by quarrelling.

On the Banzhaf criterion this is a result of the fact that when $B$ and $C$ quarrel only two minimum winning coalitions, that of $A$ and $B$ and that of $A$ and $C$, are possible. Thus, $A$ can bring down two coalitions (i.e. make them less than winning) while $B$ and $C$ can bring down one each. Thus, there are four possible ways of bringing down a coalition, two involving $A$ and one each $B$ and $C$. Hence the scores are: $A = \frac{1}{2}$, $B = \frac{1}{4}$, $C = \frac{1}{4}$. If the coalition of $A$, $B$, and $C$ can form, however, we have an extra way in which a coalition can be brought down: by $A$'s withdrawal from this 'grand coalition'. (Neither $B$ nor $C$ can bring it down by withdrawing from it since it would still have 5 votes. Thus, the coalition of $A$, $B$, and $C$ is minimal with respect to $A$ but not to $B$

[11] Brams, *Game Theory and Politics*, pp. 180–1, italics in original.

or C—an awkward notion but one integral to Banzhaf's way of doing the calculations.) Therefore, if all combinations are possible, there are 5 ways in which a coalition can be brought down, in 3 of which A figures, leaving one apiece for B and C. This produces the scores of $\frac{3}{5}$ for A and $\frac{1}{5}$ each for B and C.

On the Shapley–Shubik index it is a matter of the number of orderings in which each member is pivotal (i.e. makes up the required majority of 5 votes). $A(B)C$, $A(C)B$, $B(A)C$, and $C(A)B$ are all the available permutations where B and C disagree, making A pivotal in 2 out of 4 and B and C pivotal in one each, producing scores of $\frac{1}{2}$, $\frac{1}{4}$, $\frac{1}{4}$. But if B and C do not necessarily disagree, there are also available $BC(A)$ and $CB(A)$, which add two more permutations where A is pivotal. (A is pivotal because B and C together do not make up the required 5 votes.) Thus, A would be pivotal in 4 cases out of 6 ($\frac{2}{3}$) and B and C in one each out of six ($\frac{1}{6}$). Yet the conclusion, that the power of B and C has increased, and that 'there is an incentive for them to quarrel and increase their share of the voting power'[12] is manifestly absurd. When B and C are always on opposite sides, this has the consequence that A, by casting his 3 votes, is always able to ensure 5 votes for the side he favours, since there will be 2 votes in favour of each side automatically.

Another so-called paradox, which either reduces to the paradox of quarrelling members or makes no sense, is one that says it is better (in the sense of producing more power) to split up than vote as a bloc. Thus, consider the same committee as before, with simple majority voting. The members might as well have one vote each, since no one and any two constitute a majority. The Shapley–Shubik and Banzhaf indexes therefore assign each member a score of $\frac{1}{3}$. 'Now assume that the 3-vote player breaks up into constituent 1-vote members.'[13] But *what* exactly are we to assume here? If the three members with one vote all vote the same way, nothing has changed. But if they vote differently (in accordance with the equiprobability assumptions of the two indexes), we have a change from (in effect) agreement between three voters to random association. The idea that a bloc whose members agree would split up and start voting against one another simply in order to increase their 'power' is bizarre, though not, it must be said, too bizarre to have inspired empirical research presented with a straight face.[14] In any case, if they do, the three members with a vote

[12] Ibid. 181.    [13] Ibid. 177.
[14] G. A. Schubert, 'The Study of Judicial Decision-Making as an Aspect of Political Behavior', *American Political Science Review*, 52 (1958), 1022–4; W. Riker, 'A Test of the

each increase their aggregate power from $\frac{1}{3}$ to $\frac{3}{7}$ on the Banzhaf index and $\frac{2}{5}$ on the Shapley–Shubik index.[15] But obviously it is better to have two allies on a committee than not, so this is an absurd conclusion. (For those who distrust their intuitions on this point, a demonstration is offered in the next section.)

Brams says of 'paradoxes' like these that 'this term is not meant to imply that they in any way invalidate the power indexes. Quite the contrary: They illustrate their usefulness in showing up aspects of voting power whose existence would have been difficult to demonstrate convincingly in the absence of precise quantitative concepts.'[16] I hope it is clear that these are not paradoxes in even the loosest sense of that much-abused term. Their only use is to drive home to anyone who is not persuaded by more abstract considerations the utter inadequacy of the indexes. Brams is like someone who owns a broken thermometer and says that the fact that it does not register a higher temperature when it is put in a flame shows us something new and interesting (albeit counter-intuitive) about the nature of heat.


IV

The approach that I shall take in developing an alternative to the measures of power considered and rejected is quite simple in principle. For the sake of ease of exposition, let us assume that any member of a committee has to choose only between acting and not acting in respect of any given proposal, and that each proposal admits only of a 'yes' or 'no' vote. It is an advantage of the analytic scheme to be put forward that it admits both of these restrictive assumptions to be relaxed, permitting us to consider different degrees of effort (for example, lobbying as well as voting) and also to consider cases where several alternatives are proposed. But let us for now follow the other indexes in taking the simplest kind of situation.

Suppose that the member of a committee does nothing in order to further the passage of a certain measure which he favours. (He may, for example, be ill and unable to attend the meeting at which it is voted on.) The outcome may nevertheless be the one he wants. We can estimate how often the outcome will correspond with the one he

Adequacy of the Power Index', *Behavioral Science*, 4 (1959), 276–90. I am not, of course, denying that those who are pivotal in a body whose members can be arrayed on one dimension get the outcomes they want. What I deny is that it makes sense for somebody to vote against what he is in favour of simply in order to be pivotal.

[15] Brams, *Game Theory and Politics*, pp. 177–8.          [16] Ibid. 181–2.

desires if he never does anything. Call the proportion of adventitious successes that this member of the committee has his *luck*. There is also some proportion of the time that the outcomes will correspond to his preferences if he does act. Call this his *success*: it represents how frequently he gets what he wants if he tries. Now take the difference between his success and his luck. This is his *decisiveness*: it represents the difference that acting makes to his success. The formula is then:

$$\text{success} = \text{luck} + \text{decisiveness}.$$

For any given individual each of these three measures will take a value between 0 and 1, but the scores of all the committee members do not have to sum to 1, and generally will not.

In order to apply this method of analysis to a committee we need to feed in some information about the degree of association between the votes of the different members of the committee. If we want to establish a priori values, we should assume that there is no association: that, from knowing how *A* voted, we are no better placed for guessing how *B* voted than if we knew nothing. Let us take the simple case of a three-member committee that decides by majority voting and where each member has one vote. Consider the situation from the point of view of *A*. We have to establish his luck and his success and we can then obtain his decisiveness by subtracting the first from the second.

To estimate his luck we need to know how often he will get the outcome he wants even if he does nothing. Suppose that he is in favour of a proposal. There is a fifty-fifty chance that *B* supports it and a fifty-fifty chance that *C* supports it. Since these probabilities are independent of one another, the probability that when *A* favours an outcome *B* and *C* will also do so is $\frac{1}{4}$. The probability that *B* and *C* will agree with each other but disagree with *A* is also $\frac{1}{4}$. The probability that *B* and *C* will be split is $\frac{1}{2}$. It may help to think of coin tosses. If you toss two coins, there is a one in four chance of getting two heads, a one in four chance of getting two tails and a one in two chance of getting a head and a tail.

Thus, if *A* does not act (i.e. abstains from voting), the measure that *A* favours will be carried one quarter of the time, will lose one quarter of the time, and will be tied half the time. If ties are resolved randomly, *A* may expect that half the ties will go in his favour and half against him. Thus, his expectation overall is that he will get what he wants half the time: this is his luck score.

Although I have worked it through here, this was not in fact necessary. For it must be the case that any actor whose preferences are randomly associated with a set of outcomes will on the average get the outcome he wants half the time. Think again of tossing coins. If you always pick your side on an issue by tossing a coin, you will inevitably like half the outcomes in the long run, *whatever* they are, just so long as the outcome in each case is independent of the result of your coin-toss. Even if all measures pass or all measures fail, you will still get half of the outcomes you want, provided that your preferences are randomly associated with these outcomes.

Now we have to ask what happens when $A$ takes part in the proceedings. We know that a quarter of the time the measure he favours already has the votes of $B$ and $C$, so it will pass without his help. And we also know that a quarter of the time $B$ and $C$ will agree in being against the measure, so it will still lose even with $A$ voting in favour. In the remaining half of the cases, however, $B$ and $C$ are split and $A$ is able to turn a tie into a win for the side he supports. All ties are now resolved in the direction he prefers, rather than only half of them. His success is therefore $\frac{3}{4}$. Since his luck is $\frac{1}{2}$, his decisiveness is $\frac{1}{4}$.

To extend the analysis, let us reconsider Brams's example of the 'paradox of quarrelling members'. This example will enable us to see how the method of analysis put forward deals with departures from equiprobability. It may be recalled that the example had another special feature, namely that a majority of five out of seven votes was needed for the passage of a measure. This requires us to treat 'yes' and 'no' votes separately, because the probabilities will be different. To take an extreme case, a committee every member of which had a veto would give each member the certainty of getting a 'no' outcome when he was against a measure, but only a low a priori probability of getting a 'yes' outcome when he favoured one. The question then arises of how to aggregate the probability of getting a desired 'yes' outcome and the probability of getting a desired 'no' outcome. I shall take the obvious step, in the absence of any reason for doing anything else, of averaging them. But for some purposes one may wish to consider them separately, and it is an advantage of the measure proposed that it enables us to do so.

The results can be presented in summary form as follows. We concentrate first on $A$'s scores. Table 9.1 is drawn up on the assumption that there is in each case a random association between $A$'s preferences and those of $B$ and $C$, but that $B$ and $C$ may always disagree (I), have randomly associated preferences (II), or always agree (III). In all three conditions $B$ and $C$ cannot pass anything by themselves since they command only four votes between them and it

TABLE 9.1

| Conditions | A's success (1) | A's luck (2) | A's decisiveness (3)=(1)-(2) |
|---|---|---|---|
| I. *B* and *C* always disagree | 1 | 1/2 | 1/2 |
| II. *B* and *C* have random association | 7/8 | 1/2 | 3/8 |
| III. *B* and *C* always agree | 3/4 | 1/2 | 1/4 |

is stipulated that five votes are required. Therefore, if *A* does not take part, nothing is passed, which we assume suits *A* half the time on average. His luck is therefore $\frac{1}{2}$ in each of the three conditions defined by differing associations between the preferences of *B* and *C*.

If *A* votes, we get different results for each condition. We know that he can always have a 'no' outcome without taking part. But in condition I, *B* and *C* are always deadlocked 2–2, so whenever *A* is in favour of a measure he can make it win 5–2 by voting for it. *A* therefore has a success score of 1 (which must be correct since he always gets the outcome he wants) and a decisiveness score of $\frac{1}{2}$ (which we get by deducting his luck score of $\frac{1}{2}$, based on the assumption that he is against half of all measures).

In case II, where the preferences of *B* and *C* are associated at random with each other (and also with *A*'s preferences), *A* will get a 'yes' outcome by voting for a measure so long as *B* and *C* do not unite against it. Thus, *A* loses, in spite of using his vote when he is for something, when *B* is against it and when *C* is also against it. Since these are three independent probabilities of $\frac{1}{2}$, we multiply them together to get the probability of their joint occurrence and find that *A* loses $\frac{1}{8}$ of the time. The rest of the time when *A* favours something, either *B* is in favour and *C* against, or *B* is against and *C* in favour, or both are in favour. All three cases make *A* decisive, since they provide the margin of victory. Each has a probability of $\frac{1}{8}$, so *A* is decisive $\frac{3}{8}$ of the time, lucky $\frac{1}{2}$ of the time, and successful $\frac{7}{8}$ of the time.

Finally, in case III where *B* and *C* always agree, *A* loses in spite of voting whenever he is in favour of something and *B* and *C* are against it. Since, *ex hypothesi*, they always vote together in this case, we have only two independent probabilities to multiply together: the probability that *A* wants a 'yes' outcome and the probability that *B* and *C* want a 'no' outcome. Since these probabilities are independent, we multiply them together and get the answer that *A* loses $\frac{1}{4}$ of the time. He is decisive $\frac{1}{4}$ of the time (when he is in favour of something and *B*

TABLE 9.2

| Conditions | B's success (1) | B's luck (2) | B's decisiveness (3)=(1)−(2) |
|---|---|---|---|
| I. B and C always disagree | 1/2 | 1/4 | 1/4 |
| II. B and C have random association | 5/8 | 1/2 | 1/8 |
| III. B and C always agree | 3/4 | 3/4 | 0 |

and $C$ are too) and lucky $\frac{1}{2}$ of the time (whenever he is against something), so he is successful $\frac{3}{4}$ of the time.

It may be recalled that the supposed paradox arose from the way in which the scores of $B$ and $C$ rose on the Shapley–Shubik and Banzhaf indexes when they quarrelled. It is therefore interesting to see how things appear from the point of view of $B$ (who is of course isomorphic with $C$). The results are presented in Table 9.2. The underlying calculations can best be presented in tree form, as in Figures 9.1, 9.2, and 9.3. The trees show all the logically possible combinations of preferences that $A$, $B$, and $C$ could have on some issue. The figures are probabilities. Thus, following down the leftmost line of Figure 9.1, the probability that $A$ will be in favour (i.e. 'yes') on an issue is $\frac{1}{2}$; the probability that $B$ will also be in favour is $\frac{1}{4}$, since there is no association between $A$'s and $B$'s preferences; but the probability that $C$ will also be in favour is 0, since (in case I) $B$ and $C$ always disagree. The final row gives the result of each contingency from the point of view of $B$. Table 9.2 is derived by adding up the figures in this last row.

If we look at the two tables, Table 9.1 for $A$ and Table 9.2 for $B$, we can see how this mode of analysis illuminates what is really going on in the example. Table 9.1 shows, as we should expect, that $A$'s success is least when $B$ and $C$ agree with each other, is intermediate when there is a random association between their preferences, and is at a maximum when they disagree. Since there is a random association between the preferences of $A$ and those of $B$ and $C$, his luck is constant and all the difference is made up by increased decisiveness. Thus, the analysis confirms the time-honoured view that it is better to face a divided opposition than a united one (*divide et impera*) and that the most advantageous position in a triad arises when the other members quarrel (*tertius gaudens*).[17]

---

[17] 'Literally, "the third who enjoys", that is, the third party which in some fashion or another draws advantage from the quarrel of two others.' Kurt H. Wolff (ed.), *The Sociology of Georg Simmel* (New York: The Free Press, 1950), 154n. The whole of Simmel's subtle discussion of the *Tertius Gaudens* and the principle of *Divide et impera* (pp. 154–62 and 162–9 respectively) is well worth reading.

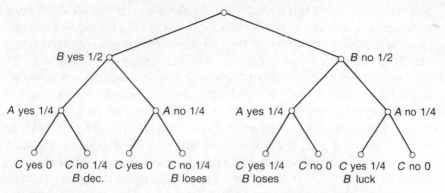

FIG. 9.1   Outcomes for *B* under condition I

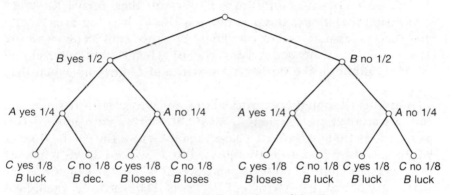

FIG. 9.2   Outcomes for *B* under condition II

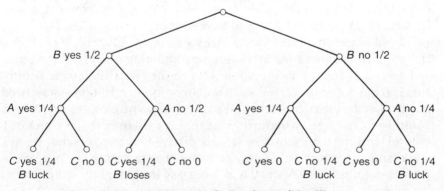

FIG. 9.3   Outcomes for *B* under condition III

Table 9.2 is more intriguing because it shows why, with a defective measure, the 'paradox' arose. We see here that $B$ gets what he wants most often when he agrees with $C$ all the time, loses most often when he disagrees with $C$ all the time, and gets what he wants with an intermediate frequency when there is a random association between his and $C$'s preferences. This is all as we should expect, and shows that it is better to agree with others than to disagree with them.

However, when we look at the final column in Table 9.2, we see that decisiveness goes in the opposite direction to success, to the point where $B$ has no decisiveness at all when he and $C$ always agree. We can now see easily enough how the 'paradox' comes about: if we take decisiveness as something valued for its own sake, and compress the scores of the actors so that they sum to unity, we are bound to get the answer that $A$'s 'power' (i.e. decisiveness) goes down and that of $B$ and $C$ goes up when they quarrel. We can then derive the crazy conclusion that it pays them to quarrel. But by keeping decisiveness and success separate and not making the scores sum to unity we are able to see (1) that $A$'s decisiveness goes up when $B$ and $C$ quarrel; and (2) that, although the decisiveness of $B$ and $C$ goes up when they quarrel, their success rate goes down.

A moment's thought is sufficient to show why $B$ is more successful but not at all decisive when $C$ invariably agrees with him. If $B$ is against something, $C$ is (*ex hypothesi*) against it too. But, in the absence of any effort by $B$, a measure opposed by $C$ will go down whatever $A$'s views about it. Therefore, whenever $B$ is 'no' (half the time), he gets a 'no' outcome in virtue of $C$'s efforts. Half the time, then, he is lucky. When $B$ is 'yes' (the other half of the time), $C$ is also (*ex hypothesi*) 'yes'. If $A$ is also 'yes' (which he will be in half of these cases), the measure will carry without needing $B$'s vote; but if $A$ is 'no' (which will occur in the other half), the measure goes down anyway because no measure can pass unless $A$ supports it. So, when $B$ is 'yes', he has an equal chance of being lucky or losing. Overall, he is lucky three-quarters of the time and loses the remaining quarter of the time.

There is nothing strange about this result. What it says is simply that if $B$ can count on $C$ to vote in the direction that he favours he need not bother to exert himself. To make the point clearer, consider a committee that acts by majority vote (e.g. a parliament) and contains a bloc of committee members (e.g. a disciplined party) who always agree and constitute substantially more than a majority. No single member of this bloc has any decisiveness: so long as all the others vote, his absence will never make any difference to the outcome. Yet he always gets the outcomes he wants. Thus, his success is 1 while his decisiveness is 0.

This implies, of course, that there may be situations in which a group of people collectively bring about an outcome but none is individually decisive. There is nothing wrong in this conclusion: on the contrary, it is one of the defects of the Shapley–Shubik and Banzhaf indexes that they rule it out by insisting that 'power' must always sum to unity. But we must beware of deriving absurd conclusions by ignoring the relevance of levels of analysis. If six people shoot at somebody and any single shot would have been fatal, none of them was individually decisive (or critical) in causing the death. Yet they were certainly collectively responsible in that the victim would not have died if none of them had fired. We may therefore say—and must say—that a *party* was decisive even though no individual member of it was decisive. In other words, we must be prepared to carry on our analysis at the level of groups as well as individuals.

This has considerable relevance for the inconclusive pluralist–élitist debate about power. Both sides are probably right, given their level of analysis. This is why one has the impression of people talking past one another. The 'pluralists', who are really individualists, look at a situation and point out that no single actor—no single banker or industrialist, say—could have made much difference to what happened. They conclude from this observation—in most cases a perfectly reasonable one—that 'nobody has power'. The 'élitists' on the other hand insist that, if the whole group of bankers or industrialists wanted something different to happen they could make it happen, and tend to move from this to saying that individual members of the élite have power. Karl Marx showed a better grasp of the concept of power than either of these recent antagonists when he maintained both that the capitalist class has power and that individual capitalists are powerless.

As a coda to this section, I shall mention briefly that the second alleged paradox that I discussed in section III can be quite easily disposed of. It may be recalled that this involves a three-member committee with weighted voting as before (*A* with three votes, *B* and *C* with two votes each), but with a majority decision rule. For ease of exposition (and without affecting the analysis) let us think of *A* as a bloc of three members who always vote together, and *B* and *C* as blocs of two members who always vote together. The claim is, then, that if bloc *A* splits up and its members vote independently, they will in

aggregate have more power than they did when they constituted bloc
*A*. Before the split the situation is the same as it would be if each bloc
had one vote, since no one and any two blocs constitutes a winning
coalition. The figures in Table 9.1 therefore apply here. Now consider
one of the members of bloc *A* after it has split up. (Call this member
$A_1$.) His scores are given below those for *A* in Table 9.3. Thus, we get
the reasonable answer that $A_1$ has the same luck as *A* (since their
preferences are randomly associated with those of the others and this
always provides a luck score of $\frac{1}{2}$), but *A* is more decisive than $A_1$ and
therefore more successful by that margin. To ask whether the three
successors of *A* (obviously $A_2$ and $A_3$ are isomorphic to $A_1$) are more
decisive *together* is a senseless question, like asking if one bright person
has more total intelligence than three dullards. Everything we need to
know is contained in the table: a bloc with three votes is more
successful than any of its constituents would be separately—and
because public policies are public goods success is not a lump to be
shared around. The idea that it would pay the members of the bloc to
split up and start voting against each other can be seen to be absurd.

TABLE 9.3

|  | Success | Luck | Decisiveness |
|---|---|---|---|
| *A* (3 votes) | 3/4 | 1/2 | 1/4 |
| $A_1$ (1 vote) | 5/8 | 1/2 | 1/8 |

V

One of the central problems of politics, I suggested earlier, is that of
the expected utility of a regime. How can a country or a group,
deciding whether or not to accede to a large political entity or secede
from an existing one, form a sensible judgement without estimating
the expected utility to be derived from the alternatives? But how is this
to be done? The answer that flows from what has been said above is
that the thing to concentrate on is the probability of getting desired
outcomes, and not the probability of being decisive.

   To illustrate this theme, I shall devote this section to a single case:
the Constitution of the United States of America. The problem for the
delegates to the constitutional convention was to come up with a
proposed Constitution that could be ratified. The delegates of the
smaller states maintained that they were afraid of their states' votes

being swamped by those of the larger states in the new Congress. The delegates of the larger states tried to reassure them that they had nothing to fear, but in the end the smaller states prevailed and obtained the still existing system, according to which each state regardless of size, has two seats in the Senate.

James Madison, representing Virginia, the largest state, made a long speech (one of the very few that he records himself as making) in favour of the proposal to have both houses of the Congress elected on a basis that would tie representation to population. His speech was an extraordinarily acute attempt to argue that, if the small states paid attention to the probabilities of coinciding preferences, they need not fear that a coalition of the largest states would dominate the new federation.

TABLE 9.4

| | | | | |
|---|---|---|---|---|
| Va. | 10 | } | Va., Mass., Penn. | 26 |
| Mass., Penn., | 8 | | | |
| NY., Md. | 6 | | | |
| Conn., NC, SC | 5 | | | |
| NJ | 4 | } | Others | 39 |
| NH, Ga. | 3 | | | |
| RI, Del. | 1 | | | |
| | | | Total | 65 |

The numbers of seats allocated to the states in the House of Representatives had already been agreed on, and are as given in Table 9.4.[18] Thus, Virginia, Massachusetts, and Pennsylvania were between them only seven votes short of a majority. This was the context of Madison's speech, which, in part, ran as follows.

That it is not necessary to secure the small States ag$^{st}$ the large ones he conceived to be equally obvious: Was a combination of the largest ones dreaded? this must arise either from some interest common to V$^a$ Mas$^{ts}$ & P$^a$ distinguishing them from the other States or from the mere circumstance of similarity of size. Did any such common interest exist? In point of situation they could not have been more effectually separated from each other by the most jealous citizen of the most jealous State. In point of manners, Religion, and the other circumstances which sometimes beget affection between different communities, they were not more assimilated than the other

[18] James Madison, *Notes on Debates in the Federal Convention of 1787*, ed. with intro. by Adrienne Koch (Athens, Ohio: Ohio University Press, 1966), 617.

states—In point of the staple productions they were as dissimilar as any three other States in the Union. The Staple of Mas$^{ts}$ was *fish*, of P$^a$ *flower*, of V$^a$ *Tob$^o$*. Was a combination to be apprehended from the mere circumstance of equality of size? Experience suggested no such danger. The journals of Cong$^s$ did not present any peculiar association of these States in the votes recorded. It had never been seen that different Counties in the same State, conformable in extent, but disagreeing in other circumstances, betrayed a propensity to such combinations. Experience rather taught a contrary lesson. Among individuals of superior eminence & weight in Society, rivalships were much more frequent than coalitions. Among independent nations, pre-eminent over their neighbours, the same remark was verified. Carthage & Rome tore one another to pieces instead of uniting their forces to devour the weaker nations of the Earth. The Houses of Austria & France were hostile as long as they remained the greatest powers of Europe. England & France have succeeded to the pre-eminence & to the enmity. To this principle we owe perhaps our liberty. A coalition between those powers would have been fatal to us. Among the principal members of antient & Modern confederacies, we find the same effect from the same cause. The contentions, not the Coalitions of Sparta, Athens & Thebes, proved fatal to the smaller members of the Amphyctionic Confederacy. The contentions, not the combinations of Prussia & Austria, have distracted & oppressed the Germanic empire.[19]

It is interesting to apply the apparatus developed so far to the numbers in Table 9.4. First of all, we might ask: how reasonable were the fears of the small states that the 'big three' would dominate the Congress if both houses were filled on a basis proportional to population and the 'big three' voted together as a bloc? Obviously, before we can make any estimate of this we must postulate some probability of each other state's representatives voting the same way as the 'big three'. Let us make the 'neutral' assumption that when the 'big three' vote together any other state's representatives have a 0·5 probability of voting the same way. Further, let us assume that between the representatives of any two states outside the 'big three' there is a 0·5 probability of being on the same side of an issue where the 'big three' vote together. The last proviso is important. Suppose that each of the other states voted on the same side as the 'big three' half the time, but that they always voted the same way as one another. The 'other' states would then constitute a majority bloc which would always get what it wanted. The 'big three' would get what they wanted half the time, but only in virtue of wanting the same thing as the 'others' half the time. The 'big three' would never be decisive.

[19] Madison, *Notes on Debates*, pp. 205–6.

Take, then, the case where the 'big three' are united and the other states fragmented—as likely to agree with one another and with the 'big three' as not. What is the probability that the outcome will be 'yes' when the 'big three' vote 'yes', and that it will be 'no' when the 'big three' vote 'no'? The answer is 0·973. In other words, the 'big three' would be defeated only three times in a hundred votes. What about the expectations of the 'other states'? A state which had no vote or, because of the peculiarities of the distribution of votes, could never change the outcome from what it would be on the basis of the votes of the remaining states, would have a 0·5 chance of getting an outcome it would like. (This follows from the random association between the preferences of 'other states' and outcomes.) To the extent that a state has the possibility of altering an outcome by the direction of its vote, its probability of getting the outcomes it favours rises from 0·5. However, the range of increases is not very great. For New York or Maryland, the largest of the 'other states', the probability of getting a 'yes' outcome when the state's representatives vote 'yes' and a 'no' outcome when they vote 'no' is 0·525. For Rhode Island or Delaware, the smallest of the 'other states', the comparable figure is 0·506.

No doubt if we concentrate on the increase we can say that the difference is considerable. Rhode Island can raise its chance of getting an outcome it wants by 0·006 over the 0·5 it would have if it had no vote at all, whereas New York can raise it by 0·025—over four times as much. (It may be recalled that New York has six votes to Rhode Island's one.) But the point to emphasize is that even 0·025 is a tiny amount. It would be swamped by a relatively small downward adjustment in the estimate made of the probability of agreeing with the 'big three'. For example, it would obviously be preferable from the standpoint of 'rational legitimacy' to be Rhode Island, with its small addition to the basic probability of coinciding with the 'big three' but with a basic probability of 0·5 of agreeing with them, than to be New York with its larger addition to the basic probability of coinciding with the 'big three' if that basic probability were lowered to, say, 0·45. Rhode Island's probability of getting a desired outcome would be 0·506, while New York's would be 0·479.

This consideration should head off any recrudescence of the idea that decisiveness (in the sense of probability of changing the outcome) should be the basis of rational legitimacy. The significance of variations in decisiveness is liable to be smaller than even minor variations in probability of agreeing with other actors. Even worse, decisiveness may increase as the probability of getting an outcome one wants decreases. Thus, suppose that all the states except the 'big three' always voted together. Each member would then always get the outcome it wanted, however the 'big three' were to vote—even if the 'big three' were always on the other side. But since the majority over the 'big three' would be 39–26—a margin of thirteen votes—no single member of the 'other states' could make a difference to the outcome by casting its vote differently. Even if New York or Maryland were to change sides, the result would be a 33–32 vote in favour of the remaining 'others'. Thus, no single state would have any decisiveness, because the outcome would be the same however it voted. Yet it is surely plain that under the conditions stipulated the Union would be extremely attractive to the smaller states.

Madison's argument was that the relationships of interest or policy preference between states are more relevant to someone trying to decide if the new Constitution offers his state a good deal than are the relations of power between them. And the analysis I have offered supports that view. Luck is far more important than decisiveness within the range of votes allocated to the states, in that a quite large increase in votes is wiped out, in terms of any increased probability of success, by a quite small decline in luck. This seems no more than common sense. If no state has as much as a sixth of the votes, it is obvious that the most important determinant of success for a state is going to be how often other states agree with it. (Accession to the European Economic Community, which I mentioned above as another example, illustrates the same point.) But what do you do if you have no idea whether others will agree with you or not? Then you have to fall back on power. But what is power?

VI

I have so far defined luck, decisiveness, and success. But I have not defined power. It is tempting to identify power with decisiveness, and that is what the Shapley–Shubik and Banzhaf indexes would do if they worked. But the temptation must be resisted. Power is undoubtedly related to decisiveness but it is conceptually distinct. To put it in a slogan, decisiveness is a probability but power is a capability. An actor's power is his ability to overcome resistance—not his probability of overcoming resistance. For the probability of overcoming resistance depends on the probability of encountering resistance, and not just any resistance but resistance of the right amount. You can only overcome resistance if you meet some and if it is not too great for you to be able to overcome it.

The contrast between decisiveness and power can be seen more concretely if we consider the way in which the concepts of a dummy and a dictator should be defined within our scheme. Any satisfactory analysis should produce the result that a dummy—somebody who can never under any circumstances alter an outcome by his efforts from what it would otherwise be—has no power. At the other extreme, any satisfactory analysis should enable us to say that a dictator—that is, someone who can under all circumstances get the outcomes he wants—is all-powerful. Decisiveness will not give us the answers that we want. A dummy, it is true, is not at all decisive, but his being a dummy cannot be identified with his not being at all decisive. For a dictator may also not be at all decisive in some situations. If he is a very lucky dictator, all the outcomes he wants will occur even if he does nothing. Suppose, for example, that there is a National Council whose decisions the dictator can overrule whenever he wishes to. If it always does what he wants, the occasion never arises for him to overrule it. In this situation he is totally non-decisive: he never has occasion to change an outcome from what it would otherwise have been. But he is no less a dictator for that.

Clearly, what is missing is the counterfactual force of 'dummy' and 'dictator'—a counterfactual force which shows that they belong to the same logical family as 'power', which is also an inherently counter-factual notion. A dummy is someone who, however precisely matched the opposing sides might be, would still not be able to make the outcome shift in his preferred direction. A dictator is someone who, even if every other actor in the system had the opposite preferences to his own, could still bring about the outcome he wanted. Thus, if power is the ability to overcome resistance, a dummy has no power because he cannot affect outcomes even in the most favourable conditions, and a dictator is all-powerful because he can get the outcomes he wants even in the most unfavourable conditions.

It may be helpful to think of a physical analogy. Imagine a beam-balance from which weights of various sizes can be hung. If the aggregate weight on one side just matches the aggregate weight on the other, even a tiny weight will be sufficient to bring down the beam on the side to which it is added. Conversely, take the case where one weight can more than counterbalance all the other weights put together. Then we can say that, whenever that weight is placed on the balance, the beam will go down on its side regardless of the way in which the other weights are disposed. Power is the weight (metaphorically speaking) that an actor brings to the side he supports. To estimate an actor's power we need to find out how much of a disparity between the weight of the supporters and the weight of the opponents he can reverse by taking part in the decision on a measure. (It is worth noting that the metaphor of weight is in common use: Madison used it in the quotation given above.)

To put it non-metaphorically, we can describe an actor's power by cataloguing the kinds of situation in which he can change a prospective loss for the side he supports to a win for it. Consider, for example, a majority system in which there are three blocs, any two of which constitute a majority, and examine the situation from the point of view of one, bloc *A*. If the other two blocs disagree most of the time with each other and one of them agrees most of the time with bloc *A*, it both gets what it wants most of the time and gets it by being decisive most of the time. If the other two blocs agree with one another and disagree with *A* most of the time, *A* seldom gets what it wants and is seldom decisive. If the other two blocs agree with one another most of the time and also agree with *A*, then *A* gets what it wants most of the time but is seldom decisive. Thus, decisiveness and also success in getting desired outcomes vary according to the patterns of agreement and disagreement. Yet power—the ability to overcome resistance—is the same in all these cases. In each case, *A* can overcome the resistance of one bloc by forming an alliance with the other, but it cannot overcome the resistance of both the other blocs. There is no way of reducing that statement to any other.

Power is not an essentially contested concept but it is an essentially messy concept. There is no neat way of packaging together in a single index the ways in which actors can overcome some opposition with some allies to get a desired decision, block other unwanted decisions (perhaps with fewer allies or—in a *liberum veto* system—with no allies at all), and so on. But we can nevertheless say that some people have more power than others or that one person's power has increased over a period of time, so long as we recognize that this is a way of aggregating a lot of things without any precise rule for doing so. Not surprisingly, there is room for disagreement, but that does not mean that anything goes. (One might think in this context of the problems that arise in comparing the standard of living in different countries.)

One particular temptation that must be avoided is a return to the notion that the 'amount of power' in a system must add up to some fixed amount. Again, I think that we can illuminate the pluralist–élitist debate by seeing how the two sides arrive at their conclusions quite automatically, given their concepts.

Consider again the case of a dictator. If we say that a dictator has all the power, it might seem reasonable to conclude that nobody else has any power. But this is fallacious: it follows only if we are entitled to assume that the amount of power in the system adds up to 1, so that if a certain actor has 1 everybody else must have 0. Suppose $A$ can overcome the opposition of $B$ and $C$ (the only other actors in the system). Then he has all the power in the sense that he can get whatever he wants against the opposition of the other two. But suppose that, whenever $A$ does not care about the outcome on some issue and takes no part in the decision, $B$ can always overcome the opposition of $C$. Then surely $B$ has some power. There are some situations in which he can make a difference to an outcome. In terms of our physical analogy, if $A$ outweighs $B$ and $C$ but $B$ is heavier than $C$, $B$ can tip the balance in its direction whenever $A$ is not on the scales.[20]

This bears on the pluralist–élitist debate in the following way. The 'élitists' say that such-and-such people *could* get the outcomes they wanted if they tried and that they therefore have all the power. The 'pluralists' counter by saying that if you look at the day-to-day decisionmaking process you see that on most issues these people who are alleged to have all the power do not stir themselves and there are real struggles in which some actors win and some lose. They conclude from this observation that power is widely distributed. The answer that follows from my analysis is that both may be true at once, and it is a conceptual mistake to suppose that they are incompatible. The existence of a small group of people who could squelch any serious threat to their common interests does not entail that there is not real power exercised within the many policy areas where none of the proposed outcomes threatens those interests. But, conversely, the claim that there is an élite capable of overcoming the opposition of all other actors in the system is in no way disproved by showing that there are real stakes in the issues that are actually contended.

Let me try to draw all this together and then answer the question that I left dangling at the end of the previous section: how can you take rational decisions in the absence of estimates of the probability that

[20] It follows from this that a true case of a dummy on a committee with weighted voting is going to be very rare, since most so-called dummies could be decisive if some of the members of the committee did not vote. Indeed, in any committee with no minimum number of votes required for passage of a measure, no actor with a vote can be a dummy, since it is possible for all the others to abstain from voting.

others will agree or disagree with you on matters of public policy? To summarize: I assume that the thing to be valued in a political association is getting the outcomes you want. I call the probability of getting the outcomes you want success and I define success so that it is the sum of luck and decisiveness. Luck is the probability of getting what you want without trying and decisiveness is the increase in the probability of getting what you want that occurs if you try. Power cannot be defined directly in terms of any of these because it is a capability rather than a probability. An actor has more power the greater the range of unfavourable distributions of preferences within which he is decisive, in other words the more opposition he can overcome.

Given any specified amount of luck, it is better to be more powerful than less, because the more powerful you are the better your chance of being decisive; and, since success is the sum of luck and decisiveness, the more decisive you are the more successful you are, holding the amount of luck constant. Even if the particular constellation of preferences in which you find yourself is such that an increase in your power does not make you more decisive, it cannot make you less decisive, so at the worst your success rate remains the same—always assuming of course that your luck is unchanged.

On the other hand, if you could be equally successful with more or less power, it is by no means apparent that you should prefer to have more power. If you can get the same results either by engaging in political action or not, why not let others do the work? If power is not an end in itself, it would seem that it is better to have powerful friends than to be powerful yourself—provided, of course, that you have some way of being sure that they will remain your friends.

But that brings me to the question I left hanging: what happens if you cannot estimate future alignments? In that case you can only fall back on power. Thus, I would predict on the basis of this analysis that we will find a greater concern with the distribution of power the longer an association is to run (hence the concern for the distribution of power in constitutions), and a greater concern with the pattern of interests the shorter the period in which the decisionmaking body is to operate. For it is surely true that it becomes more and more difficult to predict the pattern of interests the further we look into the future.

It is important, however, to recognize how little surety about getting the outcomes one wants can be derived from any contemplation of the distribution of power if one insists on total agnosticism about the pattern of interests. (Random association of preferences is not, of course, agnosticism but a quite specific assumption.) It has often been remarked that those ordinary people who say in response to the surveys asked by political scientists that they personally could do something to change a national or even a local political decision of which they disapprove are not so much fine unalienated examples of the democratic citizen as—if they really mean it—sufferers from delusions of grandeur on a massive scale. I do not think that there is anything in this peculiar to liberal democratic regimes as they are in fact now organized. Even the most utopian set-up, if it gives equal power to everyone, is going to mean that (even in a society of a few thousands, let alone one of millions) the capacity of a single individual to overcome the resistance of others is going to be confined to those cases where the strength of his allies is very closely matched with the strength of his opponents. No individual can conceivably have the confidence that his power will be such as to change an outcome from one that he dislikes to one he likes where the balance of forces is significantly stronger (in the absence of his intervention) on the other side.[21]

The judgement about power must therefore be made about social groups, and any individual who is so agnostic about the future as to refuse to estimate with which groups his interests will lie must, I think, exclude himself from trying to make *any* rational estimate of his prospects within any polity. Even currently powerful individuals would presumably be unwise to count on remaining powerful in the future.

Looking at the future from the point of view of a social group rather than an individual, it would still be uncomfortable to have to rely on power as the sole basis on which to judge prospects of success. Unless one expects that the social group with which one's lot is bound up is always going to have all the power (in the sense in which I defined it), there must necessarily be some combinations of the other actors that can beat it. So in principle it could be on the losing side on every single

---

[21] This is a point that seems to be clearer to ordinary people than to social scientists. In the course of the research for her book *Beyond Adversary Democracy* (New York: Basic Books, 1980), Jane J. Mansbridge interviewed a number of the inhabitants of Selby, a small New England town. In her comments on an earlier draft of this chapter she recounted the following experience: 'When I was planning my Selby study, I originally included a set of questions from Almond and Verba's *The Civic Culture* [(Princeton, N.J.: Princeton University Press, 1963), p. 528]. Q. 22: "Suppose a regulation were being considered by the town of Selby that you considered very unjust or harmful. What do you think you could do? Anything else?" Q. 23: "If you made an effort to change this regulation, how likely is it that you would succeed?" In my pretest in a neighbouring town, several people answered the second question with some annoyance and surprise at my stupidity, "Why, it depends on how many people agreed with me, of course." I dropped the second question when I did my interviews in Selby.'

issue that comes up. It therefore seems that *some* estimate must be made of the likelihood that those combinations will in fact form. Otherwise, the whole notion of giving a value to a prospective association collapses.

# 10

# THE OBSCURITIES OF POWER

The conceptual core of Steven Lukes's *Power: A Radical View*[1] is the contrast between three 'views' of power, which are called the one-dimensional, the two-dimensional, and the three-dimensional view. (The terms, it need hardly be said, are not neutral. Who would willingly accept a one-dimensional or two-dimensional view of something if a three-dimensional view were also available?) The author sets them out economically and I can do no better than to quote his description of each.

The 'first, one-dimensional view of power involves a focus on *behaviour* in the making of *decisions* on *issues* over which there is an observable *conflict* of (subjective) *interests*, seen as express policy preferences, revealed by political participation' (p. 15, italics in original). This is the 'pluralist' or 'decisionmaking' approach identified especially with Dahl, Polsby, and Wolfinger and articulated most fully in Polsby's *Community Power and Political Theory*.[2]

Lukes says that 'the two-dimensional view of power involves a *qualified critique* of the *behavioural focus* of the first view (I say qualified because it is still assumed that nondecision-making is a form of decision-making), and it allows for consideration of the ways in which *decisions* are prevented from being taken on *potential issues* over which there is an observable *conflict* of (subjective) *interests*, seen as embodied in express policy preferences and sub-political grievances' (p. 20, italics in original). This view (and the notion of two dimensions versus one) is drawn from Bachrach and Baratz, especially the version of 'Two Faces of Power' they published in *Power and Poverty*.[3]

The 'three-dimensional view of power involves a *throughgoing critique* of the *behavioural focus* of the first two views as too individualistic and allows for consideration of the many ways in which *potential issues* are kept out of politics, whether through the operation of social forces and institutional practices or through individuals' decisions.

---

[1] Steven Lukes, *Power: A Radical View* (London: Macmillan, 1974).

[2] Nelson W. Polsby, *Community Power and Political Theory* (New Haven: Yale University Press, 2nd edn., 1980).

[3] Peter Bachrach and Morton S. Baratz, *Power and Poverty* (New York: Oxford University Press, 1970), 3–16.

This, moreover, can occur in the absence of actual, observable conflict, which may have been successfully averted—though there remains here an implicit reference to potential conflict . . . [or] *latent conflict*, which consists in a contradiction between the interests of those exercising power and the *real interests* of those they exclude' (pp. 24–5, italics in original). This, as may be inferred, is Lukes's own preferred conception. It is obviously a descendant of the Marxist notion of 'false consciousness', especially as developed by Gramsci. It figured in a shadowy way in the original version of 'Two Faces of Power', before Bachrach and Baratz retreated in the face of hostile methodological criticism from the 'behavioural' camp, to produce an emasculated version in *Power and Poverty*. Lukes also finds an element of this 'three-dimensional' view in Matthew Crenson's book *The Un-politics of Air Pollution*,[4] in that Crenson takes it as axiomatic that human beings would prefer not to suffer the health and amenity costs of gross air pollution and therefore regards lack of any attempt to curb it as a phenomenon prima facie in need of explanation.

The point of the book is not simply to say that there are these three conceptions of power but to argue a thesis about them. This thesis seems to me both obscurantist and—even worse—obscure. The obscurity is partly a result of the fact that in a book of about twenty thousand words most of which is given over to exposition there is no space for the proper articulation of arguments. To give one example, the crucial thesis that every conception of power incorporates a distinctive concept of interest, and that 'the notion of "interest" is an irreducibly evaluative notion' (p. 34) is contained in a chapter of three hundred words! (Chapter 6). Lukes begins his argument for this: 'Extremely crudely, one might say. . . .' But should one say things 'extremely crudely', since there is presumably nothing (except possibly the prospect for Macmillans to make a quick killing—scarcely a cause which I would expect a self-styled radical like the author to look upon with favour) to prevent one from saying them in a way more in accordance with the normal canons of scholarly discourse?

But, even leaving aside the problems of horseback scholarship, there is still I suspect a deep obscurity at the heart of the author's own thought. For it appears that he wants to hold two positions simultaneously. The first is that the concept of power is 'essentially contested' (pp. 9, 26). Power is 'one of those concepts which is ineradicably value-dependent', so each of the three views of power

---

[4] Matthew Crenson, *The Un-Politics of Air Pollution: A Study of Non-Decisionmaking in the Cities* (Baltimore: Johns Hopkins University Press, 1971).

'arises out of and operates within a particular moral and political perspective' (p. 26). The second position is that the third ('three-dimensional') conception is *superior* to the others, where this apparently does not simply mean that it happens to fit in with Lukes's own values or moral and political perspective. He devotes a number of pages (especially chapter 7, 'The Three Views Compared') to trying to show that the other two views of power are inadequate, rather than simply distasteful to anyone who happens to share the author's own brand of radical politics.

He says, for example, that the one-dimensional view is 'blind to the ways in which [the] political agenda is controlled' (p. 57) and that the two-dimensional view 'remains superficial precisely because it confines itself to studying individual decisions made to avert potentially threatening demands from becoming politically dangerous' (pp. 37–8). By contrast, the three-dimensional view offers 'the prospect of a serious sociological and not merely personalised explanation of how political systems prevent demands from becoming political issues or even from being made' (p. 38). (So sociology really does equal socialism, just as those American Congressmen whom we laughed at believed all along!)

I do not see how, if the first proposition (irreducible value-conflict) is true, there can be any room for rational arguments of the second kind. Conversely, if it makes sense to assert, with the appearance of claiming the assent of anyone prepared to consider an argument, that one conception is 'blind' and another 'superficial' then I do not see how it can be true that our values and political outlooks automatically lock us into one or other conception of power. Presumably anybody who was convinced that his views were 'blind' or 'superficial' would be obliged, on pain of forfeiting his own self-respect and the regard of the scholarly community, to abandon them. But does that mean that he must become a convert to socialism?

Something has got to give. My own solution, for what it is worth, is that the superiority of the two-dimensional over the one-dimensional view is patent in that ability to control the agenda is obviously power. I would also say that one aspect of the three-dimensional view is also patently superior to either. It is simply obvious that a power relation may be exhibited (and in an extreme form) when the inferior does not raise an issue that he would like to, either because he knows it is hopeless and does not want to waste effort or because he fears that he will suffer a sanction even for raising it. Moreover, it need not be difficult to prove that somebody would like to raise an issue but does not do so for either of these reasons. We can simply ask him. (There is the risk that we may be putting the idea in his head for the first time but this can be got round by a suitably non-directive interviewing technique.) Up to this point it does not seem to me that there is any proper place for values or political outlooks. Anyone who denies what I have just said is either silly (and a lot of 'behavioural' fanatics were that) or is dishonestly trying to prevent awkward but clearly valid questions from being asked (and I am afraid some American political scientists in the late 1950s and early 1960s may have done that too).

On the other hand, when it comes to imputing 'real interests' to people and saying that they must be victims of power because they are not pursuing these 'real interests' (even if the reason is simply that they are not aware of these 'real interests'), we do have something that—at least on some interpretations—*is* a value dispute, in that it may turn on a non-empirical conception of human nature and its needs.

Suppose that two social scientists observed a society within which one group had a subordinate position, that this group was not being coerced into accepting its position, and that it was not subject to overt attempts at manipulation (e.g. by propaganda) by the superior group. And suppose that one social scientist concluded from these agreed facts that the subordinate group was not subject to power while the other concluded that it *must* be (even if there was nothing to observe) because it was contrary to human nature for a group authentically to accept a subordinate position. That would, I think, be a value dispute.

Notice, incidentally, that both these observers might agree in predicting that the subordinate group would be led to demand an end to their subordinate position if its members were subjected to a sufficiently intensive campaign from outside. But they would describe and explain it differently. One would say that their attitudes had been changed as a result of exposure to a propaganda campaign, and that this merely shows the plasticity (within certain limits) of attitudes. The other would say that they had been exposed to 'consciousness raising', that as a result their previous 'false consciousness' had been replaced by authentic consciousness, and that this shows how unnatural subordination is.

# 11

# THE USES OF 'POWER'

Why are we interested in power? In an ambitious and admirable study, *Power: A Philosophical Analysis*,[1] Peter Morriss takes this question as his starting-point. There are, he suggests, three quite different contexts within which questions are asked about power. One is practical: we sometimes want to know who has power because we want to get something done or prevent something from happening. We therefore need to know who has to be mobilized or stopped. Sometimes a way of focusing this kind of inquiry is to ask: who is worth bribing?

The second context in which we want to know about power is 'the moral one of blaming, excusing and allocating responsibility' (p. 38). Here, Morriss rightly scotches the claim, made especially by William Connolly, that ascribing power is also ascribing responsibility. As Morriss points out, people are held responsible for what they do actually do (or fail to do), not for what they could do: 'we are blamed for our acts (and omissions), not for having power' (p. 39). The question of power arises here only because powerlessness in some matter necessarily negates responsibility for the outcome, while power to have prevented an outcome entails responsibility for it.

The third context Morriss calls 'evaluative'. Here what we are interested in is assessing the goodness or badness of a set of social arrangements. Morriss rejects the so-called 'radical' conception of power promoted by Steven Lukes and William Connolly, which entails that a set of social arrangements can be criticized only if we can lay responsibility on somebody for its existence. For, as he points out, we can perfectly well condemn a distribution of power without having to find culprits.

The work done by 'power' will differ in these three contexts, since the questions we shall be seeking to answer with its aid will be different. This has the implication 'that some arguments ostensibly about power (or about "power") are really arguments between competing perspectives. The CIA analyst [concerned with practice] and the democrat [concerned with evaluation] do not disagree about

---

[1] Peter Morriss, *Power: A Philosophical Analysis* (Manchester: Manchester University Press, 1988). Page references in the text are to this book.

the distribution of power: they have such different perspectives that they never reach the point of disagreement' (p. 205).

Despite the variety of contexts within which 'power' is deployed, it has, Morriss contends, a fixed core of meaning. All power, he says, is 'a sort of ability: the basic idea is that your powers are capacities to do things when you choose' (p. 49). This entails the rejection of the claim made by (among others) Dahl and Polsby to the effect that there is something epistemologically suspect in talking about anything except actual events. As Morriss says, we may in suitable circumstances have perfectly good evidence for the existence of a capacity, and this evidence need not consist of the actualization of that very capacity. 'When I go to a zoo, I can see that a lion is powerful enough to eat me up by observing its jaws, teeth and muscles, and combining these observations with my general knowledge of animals' masticatory performance. If I am still in doubt, I can observe what the lion does to a hunk of meat, and induce. Not even the most dogmatic positivist would declare that he couldn't know if the lion could eat him up until it had actually done so' (p. 16).

This is all well said, but what Morriss fails to make explicit is that, whereas all power is ability, not all ability is power. Notwithstanding Napoleon's palindromic lament 'Able was I ere I saw Elba', 'power' and 'ability' are not interchangeable. A case in point is Morriss's claim that, while both rich and poor have the physical ability to feed off caviar and champagne, in another sense of 'ability' the poor are unable to do so and must rest content with beer and pickles (p. 81). How does this translate into talk about power? We do unquestionably speak of natural strength as power. Hence we could quite accurately speak of the lion in the zoo as powerful. But we do not I believe regard the legally sanctioned ability of the rich to eat extravagantly as in itself a manifestation of power. They do indeed have means to the acquisition of power denied to the rest of us: they can, for example, hire people to do their bidding, or they can donate money to political causes and hence acquire political power in a very painless way. But they may not choose to employ their money in ways such as these. Then we may if we like say that they have the possibility of acquiring power in ways not open to the rest of us, but we cannot properly say that they actually have power. We must, then, insist that there is more to (social) power than being able to do what you choose to do. Your having power entails that you have the ability to overcome resistance or opposition and by this means achieve an outcome different from the one that would have occurred in the absence of your intervention.

In equating power with the capacity to do things, Morriss is reacting against what he sees as a misguided tendency in the academic literature to treat '*A* has power over *B*' as the paradigmatic use of the word 'power'. He argues (pp. 32–5) that this skews the whole analysis and that '*A* has power to do *x*' should instead be taken as the basic expression to be defined. For every use of 'power over' can be paraphased in terms of 'power to', whereas the reverse is not true.

In this context, Morriss notes that, although Robert Dahl's formal definition of power gives us a meaning for 'power over', 'in his empirical work he equates a person's power with their success on matters of key importance' (p. 35). It may perhaps help to make the point here more clear to consider the case of a voting bloc in a committee or legislature. Let us suppose that it achieves the outcome it wants by exercising its power. How might this come about? One way is that it might exercise power over other committee members or legislators, causing them to change their votes by blackmailing them (as it is said the Americans and Russians achieved power over Kurt Waldheim at the United Nations by threatening to expose his deception about his war record) or less colourfully by calling in some political debt for favours rendered in the past. But a bloc need not do any of this to exercise power, and in fact the standard way in which a bloc exercises power is simply to use the power inherent in its votes. By this means it may be able to swing the result of the vote from what it would have been if only the other blocs had participated to the outcome that it supports. This is 'power to' without 'power over'. But in taking 'power to' as the expression in terms of which others are to be defined, we should always bear in mind that power is not just a matter of getting what you want but of overcoming resistance or (net) opposition.

Having identified the common element in all uses of 'power', Morriss next draws an important distinction between power in a generic sense (what you *could* do under various conditions) and power in a particular sense (what you *can* do under the conditions that actually obtain). The first kind of power Morriss calls power as ability while for the second kind of power he revives the word 'ableness'. When we look at your power as ability we take your resources (the number of votes controlled by your bloc, or the sticks and carrots you can deploy) as given, but we allow the configuration of the other forces to vary. Thus, if your bloc has thirty votes in a hundred-seat legislature we ask what thirty seats are worth in enabling the bloc to bring about desired outcomes, abstracting from the possible ways in which the other seats might be divided among blocs and also from the extent to which those blocs might agree with one another or with your bloc. It would obviously be hopelessly cumbersome to list all the contingencies under which thirty votes would produce the desired outcome, so summary measures of power as ability (the typical a priori power indexes) are developed.

In interpersonal relations, power as ability is what you could achieve by overcoming resistance, if resistance were offered. But we must recognize that, as soon as we move away from the context of a decisionmaking body with precisely-defined criteria for winning, there is little hope of constructing a summary measure. A good deal of the difficulty in making empirical assessments of power lies precisely in the impossibility of stating in a concise form all the things that might be brought about by deploying a certain quantity of resources against varying degrees of resistance.

It would be highly convenient if 'power' could be made to work in the same way as 'income' does in economics, and much analysis has proceeded as if this were feasible. Economists would not have got very far if the only thing they could do was describe all the alternative baskets of goods that somebody could buy. The existence of a common set of prices enables them to avoid such catalogues and talk about income. But when we study power we do not have any similar way of rendering commensurable all the outcomes that people could get by overcoming resistance.

All we can say in general, then, is that power as ability is what you could achieve in various contingencies, where the contingencies are defined by the preferences of the other actors (including, in cases of committees or legislatures, their formation into voting blocs). If you could overcome a lot of resistance, or prevail over the combined force of all the committee members who do not belong to your bloc, then we can say that you have a lot of power as ability. If you could overcome only weak resistance, or prevail only over a divided opposition, then we can say that you have less power as ability. In contrast to power as ability, power as ableness is, Morriss suggests, 'measured by your set of compossible outcomes [i.e. outcomes that are obtainable together], and now the fewer obstacles in your path the better, if that allows you strength (or other resources) to achieve more. The less of your resources you have to expend, the more you have left over for doing other things, and therefore the more powerful you are' (p. 88). This should, let me point out, be read with the caveat already introduced, that not all ability is power. The ability to get something if there is nobody stopping you from getting it is not a form of (social) power. We are thus still concerned here with your ability to change outcomes from what they would otherwise have been. But we are now interested not in your ability to overcome *possible* resistance or opposition but in your ability to overcome *actual* resistance or opposition. This is your ableness, in Morriss's terminology.

We can illustrate ableness by going back over the two cases considered in the context of power as ability: power in interpersonal relations and power in a committee or legislature. I have power as ableness, then, in relation to you if I can overcome your actual resistance to what I want you to do. It is immaterial how slight this resistance is. What matters is that I should have the power (in the sense of ableness) to bring about the desired result by overcoming the resistance that exists. Thus, it could be that I have rather little power as ability in relation to you, in that I could not overcome very strong resistance on your part. But if you never resist very strongly anything I want, I have a full measure of power as ableness because I can always get the outcome I want over your resistance. Conversely, I may have quite a lot of power as ability, but if you are almost always violently against what I want, the result will be that I have little power as ableness.

How does power as ableness work when applied to a committee or legislature? Let us return to the case of a legislature in which your bloc, which we shall call bloc C, has 30 votes. Now let us add that there are two other blocs—bloc A with 40 votes, and bloc B which has 30 votes. The power of bloc C depends on the way in which the preferences of bloc A and bloc B are similar to one another and how similar the preferences of each of them are to those of bloc C.

Suppose, for example, that blocs A and B always voted together. Then bloc C would have no power as ableness because it would never be able to overcome the united forces of the other two blocs. But now imagine, conversely, that on every issue bloc A voted on the opposite side to bloc B. Then (so long as we assume that every issue has only two sides), bloc C would have total power as ableness, since it would always be in a position to obtain the outcome that it wanted by adding its votes to one or other bloc to make a majority.

There are two peculiarities about power as ableness. These make it a very tricky concept to work with and contribute a good deal to the confusion rampant in the literature on power. (Even Morriss is not entirely immune, as we shall see.) The first point about ableness is that it seems a bit strange to say that, while my power as ability remains unchanged, my power in some other sense waxes and wanes according to the preferences of others. Thus, suppose I have a certain amount of power as ability in relation to you: I can overcome a certain degree of resistance on your part. And suppose that I want you to do something that you do not want to do, but that my limited amount of power as ability is insufficient to overcome your reluctance to do it. Then my power as ableness is zero in this situation. But now let us imagine that for some reason your reluctance to do the thing in question decreases to an extent such that my power as ability becomes adequate to overcome your remaining resistance. Then I have suddenly acquired power as ableness while my power as ability has remained unchanged. Surely, however, the more natural way of describing the phenomenon is to say that my power, while remaining unchanged in amount, was insufficient to produce results initially but later became sufficient as a result of a change in the strength of your resistance. Obviously, the relevant sense of 'power' here is power as ability.

There is, nevertheless, an argument for keeping power as ableness in the vocabulary, while recognizing that it will sometimes lead us to say things that seem counter-intuitive. This is that in the context of committees and legislatures it does seem quite natural to talk of power in a way that is clearly power as ableness, even though such power has exactly the same disconcerting tendency to come and go as the environment changes. Thus, if we look at the US Supreme Court, it is manifest that, knowing only the voting rule for decisions of the Court, we must say that each Justice has an equal amount of power. This is power as ability: each Justice has an a priori equal chance of being able by his vote to bring about the outcome he favours. But now suppose that there are two blocs of four Justices which take opposite sides on every question that comes before the Court. We shall, I suspect, feel little reluctance in saying that the remaining Justice, who sometimes votes with one bloc and sometimes with the other, has more power than his brethren. We may, indeed, say that he has all the power since he is always in a position to ensure by his vote that the outcome will be the one that he favours. Clearly, this is power as ableness, since it depends on the distribution of preferences among the Justices.

Manifestly, the power of this Justice who occupies the pivotal position is fragile. All that is required is for one Justice to leave the bloc to which he belongs and join the other, or for one Justice to be replaced by an adherent of the opposite bloc's ideas, and the power of the erstwhile all-powerful Justice vanishes completely. In the new situation, there is a five-man bloc which can always get its way. We must now therefore say that the members of this bloc have all the power between them, and the previously pivotal Justice has none.

Although we recognize how evanescent is the power of the pivotal Justice, this does not inhibit us from being inclined to say that he truly is all-powerful so long as his good fortune lasts. This being so, we should perhaps reconcile ourselves to the idea that in interpersonal relations you have a lot of power if you are able to overcome the actual resistance you encounter, even if this power arises from your good fortune in not meeting much resistance.

The second peculiarity of power as ableness, which is again not crippling but requires careful handling, is that it is not always applicable. Consider an interpersonal case in which there is no resistance to overcome because the person whom you want to do something would do it anyway, or a legislative case in which the outcome your bloc wants would occur anyway because there is a majority for it without the votes of your bloc. We have no difficulty in ascribing power as ability to you in such a case because to say you have power in this sense is to say that you *could* overcome resistance if necessary, or that you *could* prevail over a certain balance of opposing votes if necessary. But we cannot intelligibly say that you have power as ableness in such a case. For it makes no sense to say that you can bring about over resistance or opposition an outcome that, given the actual preferences of the parties involved, will happen anyway. If power as ableness is the ability to overcome the actual resistance or opposition, it simply has no application when there is no resistance or opposition.

This is not an insuperable objection to power as ableness. Once we understand how the concept works, we should be prepared to recognize that it will not always have application to single-shot cases. Moreover, we can still apply the concept of power as ableness to a sequence of cases by simply leaving out of account the cases where it does not apply. Thus, we can say that I have complete power as ableness in relation to you so long as, whenever you do resist, I can overcome your resistance. Similarly, we can say that my bloc has complete power as ableness if it can change the outcome in the desired direction whenever it would otherwise be adverse.

An alternative way of formulating power as ableness over a sequence of cases would be to say that your power as ableness is the proportion of all cases in which (*a*) there is resistance or opposition, and (*b*) you can overcome it. This would entail that the power as ableness of bloc *C* in our example would be only one half if the outcome without its intervention (i.e. a win by bloc *A* with 40 votes over bloc *B* with 30 votes) were to be in line with its desires half the time and even less if its preferences were more congruent with those of bloc *A*. Such a measure would correspond to what I have called decisiveness: the proportion of all outcomes that are brought into line with your wishes by your intervention (see chapter 9 above). However, if we wish to use the language of power, I think that we shall reasonably wish to say that if you are in a pivotal position you have all the power, and we can achieve this by dropping from the denominator cases where you are successful without any need for intervention. The rationale is that, although the pivotal actor does not always win by using power, he always *can* win by using power. As far as I can see, Morriss wishes to operate with the concept of power as ableness in the way I have described (see p. 247 n. 5).

Power as ableness is the ability to bring about desired outcomes by deploying some resource to overcome resistance or opposition. But, as Morriss points out, for some purposes we may be interested in the ability (more precisely tendency or disposition) to finish up with desired outcomes, whether this occurs by the exercise of power as ableness or not. From some points of view, what matters most is the prospects of success, not the means by which success comes about. Thus, from ableness we can move to a different but related concept, which Morriss calls in the context of a committee or legislature the 'expected probability of winning' (EPW).[2]

This is all straightforward enough, but what makes it controversial is that Morriss wishes to describe success not arising from ableness as another kind of power, passive rather than active. Thus, he writes: 'when we investigate people's power to obtain some given end we sometimes find three sorts of people: those who have the power to obtain it; those who do not have the power to obtain it; and those who do not have the power to obtain it but obtain it anyway. . . . Sometimes we want to lump together people in the first and third groups; when we do, we can say that those in the third group have passive power' (p. 102). And again: 'we frequently don't want to

---

[2] Unfortunately, having made it clear that the EPW index includes success that falls outside the scope of ableness (pp. 171–2), Morriss goes on to call it an index of ableness (p. 179), and indeed entitles the chapter in which the EPW index is developed 'Measuring Ableness'. I shall assume, however, that the meaning of 'ableness' should be restricted to include what Morriss calls 'active power' (see below).

differentiate between people who do get something and people who *can* get it, but we want to distinguish these people from those who *cannot* get it. A concept of power that includes passive power does the job' (p. 100). No doubt it does—if we start with the assumption that all success should be attributed to some form or another of power. But why should we make that assumption?

Morriss distinguishes two kinds of passive power. One is getting things without intervening, where you could prevent the outcome you want by intervening against it. The other is getting things without intervening, where you could not prevent the outcome you want even if you intervened against it (see p. 102). Although Morriss makes much of the second case, and indeed some of the time seems to identify it with passive power (see pp. 99–100 and 172), I can see no reason for attaching any significance to the question of whether or not you could overturn a favourable outcome achievable without intervention if you were perverse enough to intervene in an attempt to stop it. A more important distinction, which may be at the back of Morriss's mind here, is the following. In some cases you can get what you want without exercising power as ableness because there is no resistance or opposition, but you have power as ability because you could overcome resistance or opposition if it existed. In other cases you can get what you want without exercising power as ableness, but you have no power as ability, so that if there were resistance or opposition you would lack the ableness to get the desired outcome.

Especially if we concentrate on the second kind of case, we must surely ask how it can contribute to clarification to make powerlessness a subclass of power. Morriss concedes that it is 'apparently bizarre' (p. 100), and I think that appearances here are veridical. We may agree that for some purposes it is convenient to group together all instances of being able to get what you want. But we still need an argument for calling them all instances of *power*, and this it seems to me Morriss does not supply.

There are, I believe, very good reasons for resisting the proposal that 'power' should be extended so as to include cases where desired outcomes occur with no intervention. For we surely want, in looking at people who do well under some set of arrangements, to distinguish between those who do well by exercising power and those who are the passive beneficiaries of the activities of others—the powerless members of a powerful class or clan, for example.

Thus, to move to the most significant issue that is implicated, when we find a pattern of privilege in a society we should surely wish to treat it as an empirical question how far this state of affairs arises as the result of the exercise of power by the beneficiaries. But if we equate power and success, the empirical gap is closed and it becomes a logical truth that the beneficiaries are powerful.

Here, I think, Nelson Polsby has the best of Morriss. Morriss quotes him as writing the following: 'Even if we can show that a given status quo benefits some people disproportionately (as I think we can for any real world status quo), such a demonstration falls short of showing that these beneficiaries created the status quo, act in any meaningful way to maintain it, or could, in the future, act effectively to deter changes in it' (p. 106).[3] Morriss's response runs as follows: 'Polsby is here quite right; but he is aiming at the wrong target. There is no need to claim that because someone benefits she must *cause* her good fortune, nor that she can control it. All one need do is note that a status quo that systematically benefits certain people (as Polsby agrees it does) is relevant in itself. One can deplore—or praise—such a situation without wishing to suggest that the beneficiaries cause it or (*pace* Lukes and Connolly) are somehow to blame for it' (p. 106, italics in original). Of course we can, and of course we may well be interested in inequality as such. But the context of the quotation from Polsby is his insistence that we should not move from the existence of inequality to the existence of power relations unless we *are* prepared to make assertions of the kind that he describes. Morriss, by extending the notion of power to include all cases of getting what you want, opens the way to just that move.

Ironically, Morriss is here engaging in a practice that he criticizes in others, namely, the use of tendentious definitions to score rhetorical victories. He thus criticizes William Connolly's idea that by redefining 'racism' so as to include 'institutional racism' (i.e. actual disadvantage, however caused) you have thereby shifted the terms of debate because people who do not want to think of themselves as racists in the old-fashioned sense now feel obliged to be against institutional racism as well. Obviously, any clear-headed anti-racist in the old-fashioned sense will be unmoved by the redefinition. It can therefore be effective only to the extent that it is a successful subterfuge.

As Morriss says, 'such tricks have absolutely nothing to do with philosophy and absolutely nothing to do with sorting out concepts. There is no doubt that institutional and old-fashioned racism are different concepts; that Connolly's "militant black activists" do not

---

[3] Nelson W. Polsby, *Community Power and Political Theory* (New Haven: Yale University Press, 2nd edn., 1980), 208.

like either; and that they can save themselves the trouble of showing exactly what is wrong with "institutional racism" if they can label it so that it looks like another sort of old-fashioned racism. This is a move that only a dishonest philosopher should applaud. If there *is* something wrong with institutional racism (and I agree with Connolly that there is), then it can be shown by reasoned argument, rather than by linguistic sleight-of-hand' (p. 204, italics in original).

Exactly the same analysis can be applied to Morriss's proposed extension of the concept of power, though I do not wish to accuse him of wilful obfuscation. We may suppose that many people would regard inequalities brought about by the exercise of power as more objectionable than the same inequalities *per se*. If so, then redefining 'power' so that all inequalities necessarily arise from the exercise of power saves the trouble of showing that they arise from the exercise of power in the ordinary sense. The move is exactly parallel to that from old-fashioned racism (active discrimination) to institutional racism (the bare existence of unequal outcomes between races). And the same objection can be made to both moves.

Leaving on one side the propriety of calling them all 'power', there can, however, be no doubt that we do need the concepts of power as ability and power as ableness, and also the broad concept of prospects of success, which includes in its scope what Morriss calls passive power. Let me conclude this review by giving examples of the ways in which we have to make use of these different concepts to deal with different problems.

I shall begin by considering the problems faced by a constitutional convention. Now, in drawing up a complex constitution, for example one that gives power to sub-units such as states and provinces in the national government, there are two possible approaches that may be followed. One is to rule out as irrelevant any speculation about the way in which these sub-units may be expected to form alliances on the basis of shared interests, ideologies, or membership of ethnic or racial groups. What we then want is to implement some distribution of a priori power, and this means that we shall be concerned with the power of sub-units in the sense of power as ability.

Alternatively, however, we may be concerned that what looks like a perfectly just a priori distribution of power will in fact result in a persistent pattern of alliances such that some groups in the society find themselves almost always on the winning side and others almost always on the losing side. To deal with this, we obviously need to think about power as ableness. Or perhaps we should think in terms of prospects of success, since it seems that we are more interested in the tendency of groups to win or lose than in their ableness, that is to say their ability to get the result they want by exercising power rather than being the passive beneficiaries of power exercised by others.

Another use of power as ability, which Morriss goes into at some length (pp. 183–97), is to deal with the problem of weighted voting. Where constituencies are of unequal size, representatives may be given unequal numbers of votes in a committee or assembly. But if their proportion of the votes is made equal to the proportion of the electors they represent, it can come about that some representatives have no power (they can never make a difference), while representatives of large constituencies will tend to have more than their 'fair share' of power. 'Power' here is invariably reckoned by taking the measure of the a priori probability of being decisive or forming part of a winning coalition. In these computations no account is taken of possible alliances between different representatives, so that a party's under-representation (in terms of a power index) in one constituency might be compensated for by its overrepresentation in another. The relevant notion is therefore one of power as ability.

In a pregnant sentence which is unfortunately not followed up, Morriss notes that 'the comparable problem with ableness is how to detect and eliminate gerrymandering' (p. 184). It is at any rate clear that power as ability is not relevant, since we can describe a partisan gerrymander only if we know the party preferences of voters in each area. A partisan gerrymander occurs where, in a system of single-member districts, boundaries are drawn so as to enable one party to maximize its number of seats. (Typically this is done by concentrating opposing voters in a few constituencies leaving the rest to be won by one's own side with modest majorities.)

Quite extreme gerrymandering is consistent with equal constituency sizes, and as far as power as ability is concerned equal constituencies give each voter the same a priori power. It is only by introducing the notion that if $x$ per cent of the voters are Republicans they should get $x$ per cent of the seats (or some more sophisticated variant) that we can talk about the unequal voting power of different voters depending on their party. (Typically this is expressed by objections that 'It takes $x$ voters to elect a Democrat but $y$—some larger number—to elect a Republican'.)

Especially interesting in this context are the so-called benign gerrymanders designed to give racial or ethnic groups power by ensuring that they have a majority, or at any rate a strong presence, in a certain proportion of constituencies. The jurisprudence that has grown up around this in the USA is quite mind-boggling and could, I think, be used to illustrate the great difficulties that lie in the path of those who seek to deploy the concept of power as ableness. They would also, I think, lead us again to wonder if it is ableness or prospects of success that is relevant.

Although orientated to practice, these applications of the concepts of power (and the concept of prospects of success) should I take it be regarded as falling in Morriss's evaluative category. A more direct evaluative problem is the assessment of the distribution of power in a society. Suppose that there is a middle class facing a divided working class. It might be said that the middle class is not all-powerful because it could be defeated by a united working class (power as ability). It might also be said that, since the working class is in fact divided, the middle class is indeed all-powerful (power as ableness). And finally, it might be said that the middle class does in fact get the outcomes it wants—which is simply to report success. This is of course a very crude illustration, but it does, I think, illustrate that all three concepts have a use.

If we switch our attention to the practical use of 'power', we can immediately see that it is only worth bribing actors with power. But whether it is ability or ableness that is relevant depends on the context. Thus, if you did not know what the configuration of preferences was going to be but wanted to bribe someone to vote the way you directed, you would want an index of a priori power to tell you what each member of a complex decisionmaking body would be worth to have in your pocket. And Morriss argues ingeniously (pp. 162–5 and Appendix 4) that the Shapley–Shubik index can be made sense of as a measure of the worth of each actor to a potential briber. If, however, you knew what outcome you wanted and how everyone was disposed to vote, you would obviously be asking which combinations of people on the opposing side you would need to bribe in order to change the result from what it would otherwise be to the desired outcome. This would clearly involve some assessment of ableness: the ability of a member of a committee to change the outcome given the votes of the others.

A different action-orientated question is this: suppose that in a parliamentary system you, as monarch or president, are charged with the duty after a general election of inviting the leader of a political party to try to form a government. If one party has a majority of seats, the problem solves itself, but where no party has a majority the question arises of the criteria to be used in choosing a party leader to ask first. There are, as far as I know, only two criteria in use. One is that the leader of the largest party should get the first chance to form a government. This is obviously an application of power as ability since, a priori, the largest party has either more power than any other or at any rate no less than any other. The other criterion is that the job should be entrusted to the leader with the best prospects of attaining a parliamentary majority for a government containing his party. This is clearly not a question of power as ability, since it calls for attention to preferences: a small party of the centre would rate very low on any a priori power index but might be reckoned as an essential partner in any viable coalition, and hence the one whose leader should be asked first.

What is the relevant measure here? This question is discussed extensively by Morriss (pp. 169–81) and he quite rightly points out that ableness is not quite what is wanted since it is not relevant how far the party whose prospects we are assessing plays a role itself in producing a parliamentary majority. It is quite conceivable that in the case of a small party its own votes would much of the time be redundant, but this should certainly not be taken as a drawback to its prospects of having majority support. What we need is, as Morriss says, an index of the expected probability of winning or EPW (p. 172), which is a measure of prospects of success.

Morriss has the idea that a commission of experts could compile an EPW index for each party after an election had produced a hung parliament, and thus resolve the problem of choosing a Prime Minister designate. However, I think he misconstrues the job to be done. He imagines an attempt being made to estimate how often parties are likely to vote on the same side, and hence how often each is likely to find itself with a majorty on its side. This requires, though, that we conceive of a universe of policy issues that is somehow given, and votes cast purely on the basis of policy preferences. In practice, the policy issues that come up largely depend on the government's choice, and how parties vote depends on strategic considerations as well as policy preferences. Thus, the probability of a minority Labour government surviving with Liberal support in 1974 would not have been well estimated by looking at the degree of congruence between the parties' policy preferences across all issues. Rather, we would have to take into account that Labour would not introduce legislation known to be obnoxious to the Liberals and that the Liberals might vote for policies that were some way from their own most preferred outcomes because they feared the electoral consequences of precipitating an election.

It is a truism that, if the relevant criterion is the ability to form a government with majority support, the relevant index is one of expected probability of winning. But expected probability of winning cannot be analysed in terms simply of policy distances between parties and the outcomes of votes sincerely expressing their policy preferences. There could still, of course, be a commission of experts to give advice about the party leader to be called, even if we give up on the kind of calculations envisaged by Morriss. But we would then have to recognize that all they would be doing would be asking which party leader, all things considered, has the best chance of forming a government.

It may well appear from what has been said that power as ableness tends to get squeezed between power as ability and prospects of success. I think that this is indeed generally so. There is, however, a clear exception. Of the three uses of 'power' identified by Morriss, I have now discussed the evaluative use (judgement of the distribution of power in a system) and the practical use (estimation of who is in a position to do what). This leaves the moral use, which is concerned with the attribution of responsibility to actors by virtue of their relation to outcomes. Here I think it is clear that power as ableness comes into its own. If we ask whether somebody should be held responsible for failing to prevent some disaster, what we want to know is whether or not in the actual situation he could have done something to avert it. Power as ability does not enter in here: for the strictly limited purpose of assigning responsibility we are not interested in knowing what he could have done under other conditions. We are concerned with what he could have done in the actual conditions.

It is, I suggest, easy to see why 'power' gives so much trouble. The word is employed, as Morriss shows, in the context of three different kinds of inquiry. It is also apparent that 'power' is used both in the sense of power as ability and power as ableness. And although I do not believe that it is used self-consciously to include what Morriss calls passive power, it is very easy to slide from power as ableness to power as prospects of success, and there can be little doubt that this contributes to confusion. Although I have argued that Morriss's book is not without flaws, its publication without doubt marks a real step forward in our understanding of the uses of 'power'.

# INDEX

abortion 20
accommodation, political 100–3
Acton, H. B. 40 n.
Acton, Lord (John E. E. Dalberg-Acton):
  on economists 61
  on Sir Henry Maine 98 n.
  on the national principle 165, 167, 177
  as a Roman Catholic 180
Africa 34–5, 173
  *see also* South Africa
agreement and difference, methods of
    (Mill) 71–2
Allende Gossens, Salvador 33–4
Allison, Graham T. 128 n., 190, 267–8
Almond, Gabriel 104, 129, 141
Alt, James E. 74 n., 77 n.
'Americanization' 182–3
Arrow, Kenneth J. 15, 21, 38–9, 63, 73 n.,
    198
Asher, Robert E. 162 n.
Australia 50, 86, 88
Austria:
  as 'consociational democracy' 53–4, 78,
    105, 116–30, 148–9
  politics in Hallein 127
  Vienna 157–8


Bachrach, Peter 303, 304
Banfield, Edward 14, 201
Banzhaf, John F. III 273
Banzhaf power index 273–4, 281–3
Baratz, Morton S. 303, 304
Barber, Benjamin R. 108, 110 n., 256
Barry, Brian:
  on Almond *et al.* 129 n., 280 n.
  'On Analogy' 62 n.
  basic outlook 11
  on James Buchanan 63 n., 99 n.
  on Jon Elster 72 n.
  *Ethics* editorial 18, 22–3
  at Harvard University 13–14
  *Political Argument*, 16, 18, 21, 29–30
  *Sociologists, Economists and Democracy*
    194–5, 205 n.
  undergraduate experience 12–13
Baumol, W. J. 16
Bay, Christian 41
Beer, Samuel H. 138
Belgium:
  Brussels 181

as 'consociational democracy' 110, 115,
    116, 130–1, 151
as a divided society 50
electoral cycle in 87
ethnic conflict in 34, 133–5, 141, 151,
    175, 181
post-materialist attitudes in 69
sport in 114
Bendix, Reinhard 171–2, 193–4
Bentham, Jeremy 159–60, 175
Bilandic, Michael 166 n.
Black, Duncan 15, 16, 32 n.
Blau, Peter M. 254
Bluhm, William T. 116–17, 119–21, 126–7,
    149, 174 n.
Blumenthal, Michael 75–6
boundaries, state:
  Dahl on 164–5, 166
  Locke on 35, 161–3
  Sidgwick on 162 n., 175–6
  *see also* national principle for state
    boundaries
Braithwaite, Richard B. 15
Brams, Steven J. 276, 282–4, 286
Breton, Albert 74 n.
Britain, *see* United Kingdom
Brittan, Samuel 58 n., 61–2 n.
Brussels 181
Buchanan, James M.:
  as constitutional engineer 22, 99
  on inflation 65, 74, 75
  and social contract theory 63 n.
  'Virginia school' 61
Burke, Edmund 183

Cairncross, Sir Alex 62 n.
Cairns, Alan C. 144
Calhoun, John 138
Canada:
  and 'consociational democracy' 139–44,
    154
  electoral cycle in 88
  electoral system in 141–2, 144
  ethnic conflict in 34, 131
  as a nation state 172
  Quebec 34, 139–41
Canning, George 266–7
Capone, Al 41
Carroll, Lewis 136, 151
Catholicism, Roman 131–2, 143–53, 180
Chile 33–4, 70, 222